e of tennis,

THE
DIVINE
MISS MARBLE

THE DIVINE MISS MARBLE

A LIFE OF TENNIS, FAME, AND MYSTERY

ROBERT WEINTRAUB

DUTTON

□

DUTTON

An imprint of Penguin Random House LLC
penguinrandomhouse.com

LIBRARY OF CONGRESS CATALOGING-IN-PUBLICATION DATA

Names: Weintraub, Robert, author.
Title: The divine Miss Marble : a life of tennis, fame, and
mystery / Robert Weintraub.
Identifiers: LCCN 2019058506 | ISBN 9781524745363 (hardback) |
ISBN 9781524745387 (ebook)
Subjects: LCSH: Marble, Alice, 1913–1990. | Tennis players—United
States—Biography. | Women tennis players—United States—Biography.
Classification: LCC GV994.M3 W45 2020 | DDC 796.342092 [B]—dc23
LC record available at https://lccn.loc.gov/2019058506

Printed in the United States of America
1   3   5   7   9   10   8   6   4   2

BOOK DESIGN BY ELKE SIGAL

While the author has made every effort to provide accurate telephone numbers, internet
addresses, and other contact information at the time of publication, neither the publisher nor the author assumes any responsibility for errors or for changes that occur
after publication. Further, the publisher does not have any control over and does not
assume any responsibility for author or third-party websites or their content.

For Chris Carragher and Mitzi Morgan,
with my thanks and appreciation for the port in a storm

As we acquire more knowledge, things do not become more comprehensible, but more mysterious.

—ALBERT SCHWEITZER

CONTENTS

PART THREE

PART FOUR

THE
DIVINE
MISS MARBLE

Preface

....

The Swiss Alps dominated the landscape. The mountains didn't know it was 1945, or that the world was at war. Those snow-capped heights were likewise disinterested in the drama playing out far below.

On a winding mountain road, a sports car skidded around tight switchbacks, the driver, whose story this is, fighting to keep the vehicle from plunging into the distant valley below. Not far behind, another car, in hot pursuit and gaining.

The driver of the first car was an international icon, a tennis great who had won the sport's most important title, the Wimbledon championship, six years before, the last time the tournament was played before World War II interfered. She was also a four-time US National champion and had accumulated every accolade worth having in the prewar era of sports. She was renowned for her oratory, her singing voice, her appearance, her style, her closeness with the elite of Hollywood and Wall Street, and her optimistic, winning personality. She had become especially famous after coming back from two years away from the sport, stricken down by disease in what had seemed the prime of her career, only to fight her way back to the top.

She was just about the last person anyone would expect to be driving for her life down a European mountain, protecting evidence of Nazi war crimes on the seat beside her, squinting into the inky blackness, afraid to slow down even if it meant a fiery death.

Soon the other car forced her to stop. There was a confrontation. The precious evidence she had stolen a short time earlier, the reason she claimed to have come to the mountains in the first place, was taken from her by force. Alice turned and ran, her breath ragged in the high elevation.

A shot rang out. A blow to the back, a burning sensation, and then, nothing.

What in the world was she doing there?

For that matter, was she really there at all?

. . .

Alice Marble was the foremost female tennis player in the years before World War II. As the Wimbledon Lawn Tennis Museum wrote about her in its *Pocket History of Champions*, "Women's tennis can be put into two eras—before Alice Marble and after. She created the women's game in its aggressive, modern style." Hardly a contemporary match report or profile was written about Alice that failed to note that she "played like a man"—that is, her ferocious serve-and-volley style and powerhouse élan were so overwhelming that only her occasional lack of control could stop her. Using her next-level athleticism and an unreturnable serve, Alice swept to eighteen victories in what today would be called "Grand Slam" events, the US Nationals and Wimbledon (she never played the big tournaments in France or Australia, for monetary reasons). That number includes multiple women's and mixed doubles titles, all but one in the five-year window between 1936 and 1940. Then the war forced Alice into quite different activities.

She was an outsize figure during this time, "Alice Marvel," the "Garbo of Tennis Courts," the "blonde bombshell of her day." She caused a stir by playing in shorts, rather than the skirts then in favor. The press was quick to remind their readers that "her legs are like two columns of polished mahogany, bare to the knees, her figure perfect," as one dazzled reporter wrote. "Miss Marble looks lovely even when she has just come off the court," thought the well-known English writer Charles Graves, in a typical description that focused on Alice's physical presence. "Few girls can do that. On the court itself you see how beautifully built she is. She walks like a prizefighter."

But Alice was just as famous for the times when she was looking and feeling far from her best. A series of illnesses led to a collapse on the historic red clay of Roland-Garros stadium in Paris, which culminated in a diagnosis of tuberculosis that seemed to swerve her budding career into an abutment. Sidelined and committed to a sanitorium, she was forgotten for nearly two years, until a dramatic comeback lifted her to the very top. Her revival to capture victory at the 1936 US National Championships lifted Alice to new heights of popularity, at one stage receiving roughly five hundred fan letters a day from admirers who asked her for health tips, relationship advice, or her hand in marriage.

Her combination of on-court excellence and off-court style had her greatly in demand and opened up many doors. She was a regular on radio programs, as an interviewee, as a guest host, and as a singer, where her contralto voice won enough plaudits that she was asked to sing at posh nightclubs in New York and London. Her writing ability was outstanding, especially for someone who gave up a college education for the courts. She contributed pieces to newspapers and magazines with great frequency, and even was part of the original writing staff for the *Wonder Woman* comic book. She developed a speech based on her "will to win" and relentlessly toured the country to deliver it. Her eye for fashion and love of sporting it led to a side career as a designer of athletic outfits as well as clothes made for everyday use.

A natural athlete such as women's tennis had never seen, Alice had risen from humble beginnings in San Francisco to conquer the sport of royalty. Her father passed away when she was still a child, and the family lived on the edge of poverty thereafter.

She found solace in sport. As a teen, Alice was known throughout the city for her baseball ability, as well as her regular gig shagging fly balls as an unofficial mascot of the San Francisco Seals, the best local nine in the time before the major leagues moved west. Upon discovering tennis, Alice found a home among the municipal players at the courts in Golden Gate Park. Years later, a London *Times* writer surveying Alice's career would note that the "rough-and-ready apprenticeship stood her in good stead when she came to meet more artificially trained players." Tennis was a sport for the idle rich, the country club set, the people who could compete without the bother of earning a living at the game, for it was strictly amateur in that era. Alice didn't fit that description in any way, but her hardscrabble beginnings served her well when she started moving up in the rankings.

She was the top-rated player in California before she turned seventeen and was competing for the US National title (the forerunner to today's US Open) on her eighteenth birthday. She traveled east in 1931 for the first time to play the swells of the sport at its highest level. She fared poorly but came away convinced a top coach would help her reach the pinnacle.

She found that coach in Eleanor "Teach" Tennant, one of the most colorful and successful, if overlooked, figures in tennis history. She, too, had willed her way out of the anonymity of the poor San Francisco streets, becoming the foremost teacher of the game in Southern California, with a clientele stuffed with famous film actors and actresses, the top names of the day—Gable, Flynn, Dietrich, Lombard. It was that last one, Carole Lombard, the "Queen of the Screwball Comedy," who hung Eleanor's nickname on her. Lombard was a serious player, though when Tennant instructed her to attack the ball higher or get in better position, she would respond with a sarcastically sweet, "Yes, Teacher dear." After enough of those, Lombard shortened it to "Teach," and the nickname stuck. Eleanor was "Teach" Tennant after that.

Alice and Eleanor got together and formed one of the most successful coach-student relationships ever seen in individual sports. Their closeness went beyond the typical athlete-coach model—far beyond it. Eleanor essentially adopted Alice and took over her life for more than a decade. The pair lived together, dined together, traveled together. Eleanor took over Alice's finances, fashioned her diet and training regimen, controlled her social life. In that time Alice captured the very highest honors tennis had to offer.

Through Eleanor, Alice was introduced to worlds closed to ordinary tennis players. She hobnobbed with Tennant's acting pals, counting Lombard and her husband, Clark Gable, among her close friends. She was a regular guest at the American Xanadu known as San Simeon, William Randolph Hearst's Palace on the Pacific. Despite her humble roots, Alice was a favorite of wealthy families on either coast and was especially close with Will du Pont, heir to the Delaware chemical and munitions firm.

Alice had a long and enigmatic relationship with Du Pont, not unlike her one with Tennant. Because of her success, Alice gave herself freely to Eleanor's vision. Alice called her "my adopted mother" in the London *Daily Mail*, just as Eleanor called Alice her "foster daughter." Another writer referred to Eleanor as Alice's "psychiatrist," noting "she is particularly frank with her criticism of Miss Marble."

For as long as they were inseparable, the pair were dogged with rumors of a romantic relationship. Neither ever confirmed such an affair, hardly surprising given the times they lived in. Homosexuality, after a brief flash of acceptance in the 1920s, was driven firmly underground by an ensuing backlash. Being openly gay or bisexual, or even "straight with a wink," à la Cole Porter, for example, would have surely damaged Alice's budding and then flourishing career, rife as it was with opportunities off the court.

Even with the passing of the years, and the acknowledgment of affairs and crushes on other women, Alice insisted that she and Eleanor were not lovers—in the physical sense, anyway. They were certainly in love in a more spiritual manner, and when their relationship ended along with Alice's career, blunted at the height of her power by WWII, the breakup was shocking, given how intertwined the two women had been for over a decade.

But the specifics of Alice's relationships with Tennant and Du Pont pale in comparison with other, even more dramatic (some would say "cinematic") liaisons she claimed to have. Alice maintained she got married during the war, to an army air force officer whose death would lead Alice to agree to take on a wartime espionage mission to search out another of her lovers, a man whom she never publicly named and who was in cahoots, or worse, with the Nazis. It was that relationship, and the revenge she sought for her dead husband, that supposedly put Alice on that mountain road, in a car chase that ended with her taking a bullet in the back.

Alice revealed these adventures only in her second memoir, *Courting Danger*, published a year after her death in 1990. She was mostly taken at her word, though attempts to independently confirm her story have always led to dead ends, and challenges to the truth of her story showed up in book reviews and other projects left uncompleted.

I am merely the latest in a long line of Alice Marble admirers. It was always easy to appreciate her at an inch-deep level, but as I learned more about her, going further and further down the rabbit hole (how appropriate my subject's name was "Alice"), the mysteries of her life only deepened. In writing this book I have crisscrossed the United States and scoured international archives in an attempt to chip away at the mystery of Alice's contradictions, how such a public life could remain so shrouded in shadow. I have visited the touchstone sites of her childhood and career. I have followed every trail, every lead—some of which, more than I hoped, ended in further question marks. There are new stories here and old ones with new twists. I've examined faded correspondence and pieces of paper Alice herself touched, recordings she made, articles she wrote, and records she likely never expected would be looked for. And I made contact with the few remaining people who knew her, hoping they could provide some insight into the Marble Mystery.

At the end of the detective work remained a unique, pioneering, fascinating woman, which I suppose I knew was the case even before I went digging around into her life. Alice Marble may be mysterious, but she doesn't disappoint.

PART ONE

Chapter One

....

HIGH SIERRA

Alice Marble began her life far from the Swiss Alps, in the shadow of different mountains, ones that, for a brief, sparkling period, were the center of the world.

The Sierra Nevada range forms the border between Nevada and northeastern California. While the range may not soar toward the heavens quite as spectacularly as the Alps, or stretch quite as far, they are every bit as beautiful. The area is replete with vistas and valleys and astonishing sights, like the Half Dome or El Capitan in what is now Yosemite National Park, or Lake Tahoe, the largest of the multitude of high-altitude bodies of water in the region, or the sequoia trees that tower in timeless majesty over the slopes.

In the mid-nineteenth century, however, the thousands upon thousands of people who swarmed the area cast their gaze downward. For it was the gravel in the foothills and beneath trickling streams that caught the eye. There, ribbons of gold shimmered amid the gray rock. And the whole world, or so it seemed, had flocked to the Sierra to pry it from the earth.

In January 1848, a man named James Marshall, a carpenter originally from New Jersey, was building a sawmill owned by John Sutter when he spotted flakes of gold in the shallows of the American River, where he was working. It was a major strike, and days later, the treaty ending the Mexican-American War officially handed the territory of California to America. In an instant, a bull's-eye was painted on the Sierra range. By June, three-quarters of the men in San Francisco had left the city for the mountains, seeking their fortune. The following year, 1849, saw a massive invasion of the area by gold hunters from around the country (and the world). By the end of the year the non-native population of California had grown from around eight hundred in March of 1848 to an incredible one hundred thousand. And the influx of newcomers never stopped.

Two of them were Alice's grandparents.

Alice's paternal grandfather, Solomon Marble, was born in a small town in central Maine called Shirley. He married another Pine Tree Stater, Sarah Frances Hewins, nearly two years older, who was from a venerable, tiny village near Bangor called Old Town. According to Alice's first memoir, *The Road to Wimbledon*, published in 1946, Solomon left Maine as a teenage boy, sailing on a trading ship through the Panama Canal before taking a "jolting stagecoach to the coast" and then another ship to San Francisco. He then made his way northeast, in the direction of Sutter's Mill. It isn't known for sure if Hewins was with him for every leg, or exactly where they got hitched—some sources have them marrying in Maine in November 1858, others say the nuptials took place in California.

Mines were being sunk all over the area, and Solomon did his best to find a fortune-making vein. He and Sarah bounced around the Sierra Valley, seeking gold in several camps and settlements, including the propitiously named Gold Run. The lucky strike never did come for Solomon. But in all that moving he couldn't help noticing how fertile the valley was for farming and grazing. So he turned to life on the land, setting up a sheep farm in a small settlement called Holland Flat (since renamed Dutch Flat), just west of the huge wilderness now preserved as Tahoe National Forest. Here, the Marbles raised their family.

Alice's father, Harry Briggs Marble, was born on May 4, 1866, in Holland Flat, having been preceded by two older brothers, Heckton and Melvin (a third brother, Eugene, was born three years later). After the children had grown a bit, the Marbles left the farm at Holland Flat for a mining camp called Long Bar along the Yuba River, where they were living when visited by the local census taker in 1880. Exactly why Solomon gave up the first farm is not known, but his son would have a similar hot and cold relationship with the farmer's life.

Indeed, the adult Harry at first was desperate for more adventure than the staid life of planting and shearing. He did the expected thing, seeking the color, moving around the watersheds of the Yuba and Bear Rivers and, especially, the Feather River. But he wasn't any luckier in mining for gold than his father had been, so he soon turned his attention to logging.

Beginning with the gold rush, the Sierra Valley became a "logging epicenter," to the point that today there is virtually no virgin timberland remaining. Wood was desperately needed for housing all the gold rushers and for building transport to and from and especially down into the mines. Clearing the old-growth forests of towering sequoias and coast Douglas firs and ponderosa pines became a major industry virtually overnight.

Harry rushed to join in and wound up in a particularly important and difficult job, that of the high climber (often referred to as the "high rigger"). Spending weeks at a time under the immense emerald canopy, he would don spiked climbing shoes and a heavy climbing belt and, using nothing but strength, balance, and somewhat insane courage, scale the trees. The lumber from smaller trees was considered less desirable by local builders, so the loggers targeted the biggest trees that blanketed the southern slopes. Harry's daily work site was up to two hundred feet in the air. Once atop the green beast, Harry would lean back against the belt, attach ropes to the tree, and begin to saw away at the branches and the thick trunks.

"As it begins to sway and crack," Alice wrote in *The Road to Wimbledon*, "he calls a warning to the logging crew at the base of the tree.

With a surging sound like the sea, the treetop falls, crashing its way to earth. The high-climber sways with the lashing, vibrating shaft, keeping his balance by a sixth sense and the grace of God."

The casualty rate among loggers was absurdly high. Danger came from above, as crashing trees wiped out entire work crews, and below, with mudslides and hidden ravines causing equipment- and lumber-laden men to plummet to their deaths. Transporting the immense logs via ox-pulled wagons was also a treacherous process. Men were killed or lost limbs to out-of-control timber or beasts at regular intervals.

Harry had made good money in the forests, much more than he ever made looking for gold, but in the 1890s he quit the timber business for, surprisingly enough, the same farming life his father had struggled with. Unlike his father, Harry raised cattle instead of sheep.

He started in a place called Sierraville, then spent some time prior to the century's turn in a small settlement in Plumas County called Kettle, named for the family that founded the camp, in the spot they happened to hop off the stagecoach and put a shovel into the ground.

Harry was a tall, strong man, a classic "husky pioneer," in Alice's description, with broad shoulders and brown hair that climbed farther up his forehead with the passing years. But even out of the tall trees, Harry discovered life in the Sierra was unforgiving. Once, a horse he was shoeing kicked him and nearly cleaved off his kneecap, and in 1898 he caught a fever severe enough to lay him up for most of the spring. While healthy he helped erect barns and build roads, and occasionally he headed back into the forest to hew timber from the giants that grew along the local slopes, all of which kept him out of debt when the beef market was slow. When times were good, he made the rail journey to San Francisco to sell his stock.

As a rancher Harry was dependent on good grazing conditions and plentiful water, and the climate in Kettle turned against him (forcing the settlement to be abandoned), so he picked out a spot about six miles northwest, a speck on the map called Beckwith (now known as Beck-wourth), roughly fifty miles from his birthplace of Holland Flat. In the summer of 1904 he "report[ed] business in that part of the county to be reasonably lively," so it made sense to get closer to the action.

He cleared a spot in the old growth, near a hot spring that reeked of sulfur, and began building a house, one that was far too large for just one man. The local paper, the *Feather River Bulletin*, took notice. "Harry Marble of Kettle, is building a comfortable dwelling house for himself. Looks very suspicious, Harry!"

Indeed, it was a house built for a family. Not long before, Harry had journeyed to San Francisco to sell some of his cattle, as well as to get his troublesome asthma checked. He went to a renowned throat doctor named George Gere. Alas, the doctor was out for lunch, he was informed by the nurse, but perhaps he would like to wait?

He sure would, for Harry was quite taken with the nurse. Her name was Jessie Birdsal Wood, and it turned out she was Dr. Gere's sister-in-law (he was married to Jessie's sister Josephine). Jessie was born in Oakland in 1877, but her family moved across the bay to San Francisco in time for grammar school. She was a graduate of the Hearst School, blessed with a lovely singing voice to go with a large oval face and wide, deep eyes so blue they were nearly cobalt.

Harry hung around the office for several hours making nervous conversation and, after getting his exam, stayed in the city for far longer than he had planned. He learned that Jessie was a thwarted singer, limited to the church choir as her family didn't think much of their daughter hanging around clubs late at night to sing. She had a beau, a younger man who had a good business in the city. She lived with her sister Jo and the doctor in Haight-Ashbury, and for the next few weeks Jessie juggled her two suitors, at length finding herself falling for the tall timber from the northeast.

Harry proposed immediately, and Jessie said yes. They married in San Francisco on December 22, 1905, at Jo and Dr. Gere's place. "The bride was in white satin," reported the *San Francisco Call*, and "two little flower girls completed the bridal train." Harry told the paper he was taking his new bride back to Plumas County, "where he owns a pretty home on his large stock ranch." They were considerably older than the typical be-trothal age of the time—he was thirty-nine; she was twenty-eight.

It was a leap for Jessie to leave the city she had known all her life to follow her man into the wilderness. Unlike the Bay Area, the Sierra Valley had true winter, with heavy blizzards and deep snowdrifts that often cut the farm off from the outside world. While Jessie had to look up at the soaring peaks of the mountain range that dominated the horizon, she was certainly no longer at sea level—Beckwith sat at nearly five thousand feet, a mile high where the air is thin and breathing difficult for the unacclimated.

Of course, the area had its charms, dazzlingly beautiful in a different way than San Francisco's steep allure. Harry had planted apple orchards on his acreage, which towered over the verdant grass meadows that dappled in the summer sun and blew with the breezes year-round. From the farmhouse, a "rambling white house with a wide veranda around all four sides," according to Alice, the Marbles could look out on an incredible view, the landscape either emerald green or brilliant white, depending on the season, dotted with animals and trees, the sunlight reflected by the nearby Big Grizzly Creek and the Middle Fork of the Feather River.

It was also a lot quieter than the big city—a lot quieter than many small ones, for that matter. Their nearest neighbor was four miles down the road. The town of Beckwith was a single thoroughfare with a hand-ful of shops. The nearest "large" town, Quincy, a mining community of several hundred people that was the Plumas County seat, was nearly forty miles away, a long, uncomfortable journey at the best of times. When Jessie made it to Quincy, it was noted in the *Feather River Bulletin*—on the front page!

The farm, called Hathaway Ranch, was on Sattley Road, little more than a lumber trail that branched off from a larger one called Loyalton Road. Both were roads that Harry helped build, which accounted for his knowledge of the area. The work, for Beckwith Road District con-struction crews, earned him two separate payments of around a hundred dollars. The Marbles were rather progressive for the period; Jessie was one of just sixteen women in Beckwith Precinct to register to vote in the 1912 elections, while Harry lent his name to many social causes, including the establishment of a unified school district that would encompass Plumas and Sierra Counties.

In the meantime, a family burgeoned. Jessie gave birth to a pair of sons, Dan in 1907 and George a year later. The family added its first girl, named Hazel for her eyes, in March 1910.

Alice Irene Marble was the fourth child to come along, born six years after Dan and three post-Hazel, on September 28, 1913. "I must have been a healthy, well-cared for scrap of humanity," Alice wrote in *The Road to Wimbledon*, "but not a spoiled baby."

On December 1, 1916, the family would add one more child, Harry Jr., whom everyone immediately and thereafter called Tim, who would look up to Alice his entire life. His birth was noted in local newspapers like the *Plumas Independent*, though they only mentioned gender, not Tim's name. "The home of Mr. and Mrs. Harry Marble of this valley is brightened by a new boy, born December 1st," read the *Feather River Bulletin*.

Unlike many elements of her life, Alice's birth went unrecorded by the press.

·   ·   ·

A golden voice trilled across the ranch house. Jessie Marble worked hard, preparing meals for her family and the half dozen farmhands who worked on the land. She also kept house and made clothes on a "rickety sewing machine [that] clattered and banged and jammed and stuck," in Alice's memory. All through the day, Jessie would sing as she toiled, hymns and religious songs in the main. She would pass along her industrious energy to her daughter, along with her lovely singing voice.

A photo taken of Alice at age two displays a startlingly prescient glimpse of the adult to come—wide, alert eyes, relaxed before the camera, an inviting smile on her face. There is no trace of baby fat or features that altered with time. One glimpse at the photo and the future Alice Marble, internationally known as she was, is clearly visible.

"My earliest memory is of when father let me milk a cow," she remembered much later. Alice was four, so it was excusable that her initial go was a farce. She grabbed the udder on the wrong side of "Bossy" and soon was flat on her back, "covered with milk and humiliation." Any milk Alice managed to capture in a bucket was churned into cream, which the family mixed with vanilla and fresh snow to make a kind of farm ice cream.

Alice immediately idolized her older brothers, Dan and George, who pitched in with chores around the farm and were endlessly active. Hazel, on the other hand, with her silver-rimmed glasses and pushover demeanor, Alice had no time for. Even in her dotage, Alice wouldn't much care for Hazel, writing in 1986 to a friend that she "is bossy and sneaky and sometimes I don't like her at all." Another family member, Harry's older brother Melvin, "Uncle Mel," also came to live on the farm after an unsuccessful attempt at politics. He more closely resembled the "Yosemite Sam" stereotype of the Northern California gold rusher, sporting a bushy handlebar mustache and spitting his unpleasantly fragrant chewing tobacco juice into every nook and cranny of the ranch.

Alice recalled an idyllic, if hard-won, lifestyle on the farm. The work began before dawn and didn't end until past dinnertime. Harry was a master handyman, forever sawing, stitching, hammering. The sulfur springs on his land were thought to be curative, so Harry built cabins to rent to arthritis and rheumatism sufferers. Word spread that even if the springs didn't take away the pain completely, the beautiful setting and friendly Marble family were worth the few dollars a week. By 1916 the "Marble Hot Springs" were better known than the Marble stock ranch.

For the young Marble children, the regular influx of new people was a godsend, alleviating the feeling of being cut off in the mountains. They made friends with whoever turned up, though Alice and the other Marbles felt uneasy in their homemade hand-me-down clothes. People arrived "in wagons piled high with bedding and pots and pans, for families often accompanied the invalid, bringing their own equipment." Once a large group of eighteen Spanish gypsies came and put down roots, staying for years.

World War I came and went "without appreciably touching our

lives," Alice recalled. But shortly thereafter, in early 1919, Jessie's nephews, Ray and Harry, Dr. Gere's sons, came home from Europe and to the Sierra for a visit. Remarkably, though Jessie had gone to San Francisco on occasion, it was the first of her family to visit them in the mountains since she moved there over a decade earlier. The little boys she had known in Haight-Ashbury were now men, war veterans, and Jessie wept for the life and family she had missed by following her husband into the wild.

Not long after the visit, Harry disappeared to the city for a week, and when he returned, he had a major announcement—they were selling the farm and moving to San Francisco. Jessie ran up to him and threw her arms around her husband. Alice could never recall her mother being so hands-on, or so happy.

Had the Marbles stayed in the mountains, Alice's life might have remained idyllic, if forgotten. But her descent to sea level led to an extraordinary career climb, one as dramatic as it was unlikely.

Chapter Two

City Lights

San Francisco in the 1920s would be scarcely recognizable to anyone traveling back in time from the modern jewel by the bay.

For starters, the Golden Gate Bridge had yet to span the icy waters between the city and Marin County. Railroad tracks ran right up to the docks, servicing the countless ferries that hauled goods the mile and change across the bay, landing at the Ferry Building or the Hyde Street Pier. Materiel for San Franciscans was loaded right onto the cars "at any hour of the twenty-four" by an army of stevedores and thence spread to merchants throughout town. High, sheer cliffs fringed the waterfront, the harbor protected by enormous naval guns that were in place to intimidate any enemy who dared to challenge America's might.

Commuters without bridges and mostly without automobiles relied on cable cars, electric streetcars, and those ferries, their foghorns piercing the thick morning fog, the same route often bathed by sun that afternoon on the return trip.

The first radio station, KPO, wouldn't start up programming until 1922, and San Francisco was very much a newspaper town, with no fewer than six broadsheets vying for readers—William Hearst's *Ex-*

aminer, its archrival the *Chronicle*, plus the *Bulletin*, *Daily News*, *Post*, and *Call*. They informed the public about local attractions, such as Neptune Beach in Alameda, the "Coney Island of the West," where dancers and stunt performers vying for daily prizes were on display. Miniature golf was a new sensation, and young and old alike flocked to the Agua Caliente course at Eighth and Market.

To the south the Santa Clara Valley, better known today as Silicon Valley, was mostly undeveloped farmland, covered with harvested fruit drying in the inland sun.

Despite all the modern advances and as many drawbacks, one thing has stayed constant through the decades—the hypnotic spell San Francisco casts on visitors and locals alike. As a writer named Robert Welles Ritchie put it in 1929, San Francisco was even then a "City of romance and portal to adventure, City of padre and Argonaut, City of sunshine and fog, City of light and shadow, City of fascination and allure."

· · ·

A surrey trip to Oroville, a train ride to Sausalito, a ferry across the bay, and the Marble family arrived in the "Paris of the West." They settled in the northwest portion of the city, an alluring neighborhood called the Inner Sunset district, at 1619 Twelfth Avenue. Their new home was a white house high on an archetypically steep San Francisco hill, requiring a lung-busting, thigh-burning walk up several blocks from the flat land at Irving Street, where the streetcar tracks connected the area to other parts of the city. The neighborhood was near the northwestern edge of the Peninsula, along the straight shoreline of Ocean Beach, before the land takes a right turn and the Pacific meets the Golden Gate.

Half a million people lived in San Francisco in 1919, but the terrain served to box residents into neighborhoods that felt much smaller, which helped the Marbles acclimatize to their new home. In their case, the Inner Sunset was hemmed in by Golden Gate Heights, which Alice scaled every day to get to the house (the incline continues up for another thousand feet or so, culminating in Forest Hill, which offers a commanding, if often fogbound, view of the Golden Gate, the ocean, and much of the city), and to the east by the green-backed lumps of Forest

Knolls. To clear the hills and escape, the Marbles had to tromp down the street for many blocks, long-striding and uncertain along the precipitous drop, and then head east or west, or farther north into Golden Gate Park, which would soon become Alice's second home.

Her first home was change enough for now. The house is still there, set back from the road, a long flight of stairs—sixty in total—leading up to the front door, one last heartbreak hill after the long slog up the road. The reward for reaching the front porch was a remarkable view of the bay and the city. There were gardens on both sides and a sandy backyard. Next door lived the Butler family, Mom and Dad and all eleven children under a single roof.

Unlike the house back in Beckwith, this much smaller place required shared quarters for all—the boys in one room, Harry and Jessie in another. At least they had bedrooms—Alice and Hazel shared the rust-colored sofa in the living room. In another change from the ranch, there was indoor plumbing, so no more plowing through snowdrifts when nature called. And another surprise awaited in the hall: the first telephone the Marbles had ever owned.

Harry's occupation in the 1919 city phone directory was listed as "carpenter," though Harry's new gig with a lumber company was less refined, requiring as much hauling as fine craftsmanship. At age fifty-three, he was a bit old for the physical labor required, but he was still strong as an ox. There is no exact record of Harry's pay, but he wasn't making much, given the financial struggles to come.

The city was new and different for Jessie, too, a far cry from the place where she had grown up. "Imagine electric streetcars and automobiles," she said, anticipating the move back to her rapidly changing hometown.

Both newfangled contraptions would affect Alice's life before long.

· · ·

The spanking new Model T Ford screeched to a halt in front of 1619 Twelfth Avenue. At the wheel was a smiling Uncle Mel Marble. Harry's brother had come down south after tying up multiple affairs in the Sierra Valley, using his proceeds from the ranch sale to buy the fancy new car. The Marbles ran outside and piled in the Model T for their first-ever automobile journey, "up and down San Francisco's high hills." The family would joyride in that Tin Lizzie throughout the first half of the year.

But the fun came to an end in the late summer of 1919. Mel and Harry were in the car when it crashed, and Harry in particular was severely injured. His shoulder was broken and his back "crushed," in Alice's words. Carefully he was brought back to the house, where he lay for long nights in the bedroom, unseen by anyone except Jessie. At length, a doctor came and pronounced his life out of danger and recovery in progress. Jessie was so happy she gave Alice thirty-five cents to run and buy a chocolate cake to celebrate.

The celebration was premature. The girls went to school at Columbus Elementary, just down Twelfth Avenue. One morning, even as Harry lay prostrate and broken in bed, Alice was called to the principal's office. Hazel sat there, a ghastly facial color offsetting her striking eyes. She was diagnosed with pneumonia and was "dangerously ill," in the doctor's words. Now there were two critical patients in the Marble house.

At some point in late 1919, Harry also contracted a form of pneumonia known as bronchopneumonia—rather than the lungs filling with liquid, the tissue gets inflamed, constricting the airways and making breathing increasingly difficult. He was already weak from the after-effects of the automobiling (as driving was referred to at the time) wreck, and it is quite probable the ultimate culprit was the Spanish influenza pandemic that scythed across the globe, killing between fifty and one hundred million worldwide between 1918 and 1920. As the National Institute of Allergy and Infectious Diseases reported in 2008, "The majority of deaths . . . were not caused by the influenza virus acting alone. Instead, most victims succumbed to bacterial pneumonia following influenza virus infection. The pneumonia was caused when bacteria that normally inhabit the nose and throat invaded the lungs along a pathway created when the virus destroyed the cells that line the bronchial tubes and lungs."

San Francisco had become the "City of Masks" in 1918, when nearly thirty thousand cases of influenza were reported and many thousands of deaths ("Obey the laws and wear the gauze!" went a popular rhyme amid the misery). This "next wave" of Spanish flu in 1919 was less severe, but newcomers to the city, like immigrants and a certain family used to the mountain air, were particularly vulnerable.

His body mangled, his once-strong physique racked by a lifetime of hard work, Harry Marble was even more susceptible than his children. And not long after his lungs began to tighten, his fight gave out. Dr. Ralph Rabinowitz of the University of California Hospital treated him at home, beginning on December 29 and for the next three days, but there was nothing he could do. Harry was just short of fifty-three years and eight months when he passed.

In *Courting Danger*, Alice wrote that her father died on Christmas Eve and that "the holiday ever after held bad memories for me." Decades earlier, she wrote the same thing, and that the "only reason I knew that something terrible had happened was that there were no presents, no tree and no Christmas carols."

That may have been the case, that the family hadn't celebrated due to Harry's illness. I found Harry's death certificate, however, and a notice in the *San Francisco Chronicle* that showed he actually held on for another week, passing away in the third hour of the new decade, on New Year's Day, 1920. His daughter Alice was just six years old.

• • •

There was a funeral on the third at Gray's funeral home on Geary Boulevard at Divisadero, and Harry was cremated and interred at Cypress Lawn in South San Francisco. For a man of the mountains and the forests, it was a very urban death.

All the boys in the family got sick, too, as well as Uncle Mel, though everyone managed to pull through. Mel returned to the Sierra Valley, where he spent several weeks convalescing at the ranch of friends. "Recently arrived here from the lower country," reported the *Feather River Bulletin*, "[Marble] finds his health much improved since returning to the valley." Only Alice and Jessie remained healthy through that holiday season.

In February Jessie wrote a friend back in Beckwith, Mrs. A. J. Long, a letter saying that the family was "recovered from their illness," referring to Hazel, and it was true—the girl was out of danger, sparing the Marbles any further mourning. But there was no recovering from Harry's absence. There was little money left, as Harry had no insurance and the move had mostly wiped out profits from the sale of the ranch.

The family settled into what one account referred to as a "genteel poverty." Alice wrote that the house was only "partially paid for" when Harry died, indicating ownership, though records I found at city hall listed the property as a rental. Either way, it was a struggle to keep the family sheltered. Jessie took a cleaning job that had her out of the house well before dawn, in order to return in time to get the kids ready for school.

Jessie's family helped as it could. Her brother-in-law, Dr. Gere, had died two years earlier, and her sister Jo contributed when possible but wasn't in a position to do much more. Of greater help was Jessie's older brother, Arthur Wood. "Uncle Woodie," as he insisted the Marble children call him, was a tall bachelor with a large nose, and he held an iconic job—brakeman on one of the city's most enduring symbols, the cable car that hauls tourists and residents up and down the steep, scenic avenue of California Street. Woodie's assistance was monetary, though he wasn't a rich man, but, even more important, corporeal. He moved into the house on Twelfth Avenue and became a surrogate father to the kids, teaching them baseball, doling out change for chores, and even enlisting Alice to help him handicap horses. She didn't much help his losing ways, though one time she picked out a horse that returned sixty-seven dollars on a two-dollar bet, which kept the family in groceries for a fortnight.

He also got Alice a pair of roller skates, and along with her new neighborhood friend, a boy named Billy, she skated everywhere, even up and down the steep slopes of Twelfth Avenue.

One summer evening in 1920, Alice relates in *Courting Danger*, the two pals were skating near streetcar tracks before heading home. Alice skipped over the tracks; Billy tripped. Suddenly, he was under the front fender of a speeding streetcar. "Looking back, I saw Billy stumble on the tracks and fall screaming under the trolley wheels. It is a memory I will take to the grave."

For the second time in less than a year, she wrote, six-year-old Alice was forced to go to a funeral. She would never go to another.

Trolley fatalities were once so common as to be taken for granted in big cities, and the new scourge of automobiling only made the streets more dangerous, so it isn't altogether surprising that this particular accident doesn't seem to have been mentioned in the San Francisco press. Other streetcar-meets-child incidents in 1920 were, however—I found several reports of such deaths. In March, a four-year-old boy named William "Billy" Marshall was killed by a streetcar in the Mission District in similar fashion—dashing in front of a trolley before the startled brakeman could stop. Another boy of the same age went down in May. A sixteen-year-old boy was killed the day after Thanksgiving, nearly cut in two on Market and Eighth. And so on.

Alice doesn't mention this supposedly traumatizing accident in *The Road to Wimbledon*, though it was written much closer to the event. Reasons for this abound, surely. Of course, the fact that a different boy named Billy was killed under similar circumstances shortly before Alice's friend also brings questions as to whether she absorbed someone else's story to augment her own.

Like the fog that rolled in off the bay, the mists of truth and deception were beginning to swirl around Alice and her account of her life.

Chapter Three

....

The Natural

The Marble kids ran amok, exploring the endless enjoyment of the urban jungle and the genuine wild side the city offered them. Today, the area retains a quirky element, with a riot of colors marking the row houses and funkily shaped semidetached homes, though I noted sadly that even the smallest and most ramshackle of them are million-dollar listings. But the beach itself remains unchanged from when the Marbles would light bonfires and fly kites, the powerful wind whipping sand across the open space between the crashing surf and shifting dunes, much as it has for centuries on end. When Alice walked west past Twentieth Avenue, all traces of the city vanished, leaving a seaside paradise that was mostly left for the entertainment of neighborhood kids (recreational swimming and sunbathing weren't anything close to their modern popularity, and the water here was as icy and rough as it remains today). Alice and her friends played French Foreign Legion, pretending the sand dunes were a desert battlefield, or hunted for the myriad treasures that washed ashore with the current from frequent wrecks out over the horizon (like the wreck of the *King Philip*, which slammed ashore and broke up on

Ocean Beach in 1878 and reveals itself to beachcombers at Noriega Street on occasional low tides to this day).

Being a young child in the mountains had been special, but Alice's formative years were spent in this more dynamic environment. Just going about her daily existence in such an unusual and gorgeous place was exhilarating. Always there was the "constant surprise of panoramas laid in cunning traps to jolt [one] out of a growing feeling of familiarity," as a contemporary travel writer put it. "The prospect may be a commonplace vista of wooden-bay windowed houses but turn a corner and presto!—beyond a low wall that guards you from tumbling thirty feet onto somebody's roof is spread a fifty-mile sweep of bay, mountains, forests, cities, two thirds round the compass dial!" Alice got such a view every day, and yet it never grew old.

One favorite activity was the Sunday family hike. The older boys, Dan and George, had to drop out of school to take jobs laying floor to help support the family. The gig required a hard physique but also a certain craftsmanship. With Uncle Woodie working nights, often until 1 A.M. (if the kids could get out of the house without waking him for a week, he would slip them a nickel), Sunday was the lone free day for the entire family.

Alice would rise at five to help cook a monster breakfast for everyone on "our big black coal stove." Fortified, the Marbles would set off down the hill. A streetcar would get them to the Ferry Building, where they would catch a boat across the bay. On the other side they boarded a train for the short ride to what was then a small-town stop called Mill Valley (now, like all of Marin County, a packed, wealthy enclave).

From Mill Valley they set off on foot for the shore, nearly eight miles over the hilly, rolling terrain below Mount Tamalpais. If they took a slightly more southern route, they would tromp through the soaring redwood trees in what is now the Muir Woods National Monument. They would arrive at last at Stinson Beach, where they put on swimming costumes and plunged into the frigid Pacific waters. Afterward there was beach baseball and a picnic lunch. At about four o'clock, they would head back, singing songs and sometimes stopping for chicken and apple pie at the home of one of Dan's friends in Mill Valley. Alice would in-evitably doze off on the long journey home, and that last leg of the mar-athon, up the hill from the streetcar to the house, must have been torture for exhausted bodies, but Alice would remember those Sundays with great fondness.

Jessie was well-known in the neighborhood for being the "fun mom," always with a treat for the kids and their friends and forever going outside to play kick the can, tag, and baseball with the children. Life for the widow Marble was very difficult—a deferred dream, single motherhood, low wages, and the backbreaking work to keep the household running—but she remained enthusiastic and loving, at least around her kids.

For all the outdoor fun the city provided, it was organized sports that captured the fancy of the young Alice Marble. She was immediately good at a wide variety of them: a natural shooter in basketball, swift and strong enough to take over football games, and, more than anything, a stalwart at baseball. Uncle Woodie had taught her the fundamentals, and Dan and George coached her up, to the point she could honestly say she was "as good as the boys."

She played most often with her younger brother, Tim, the two forming a family battery, with Alice pitching and Tim catching. She broke her thumb "a thousand times," which she said would affect her backhand the rest of her life. They played mostly in Golden Gate Park, on its tightly packed fields, of which *Sports Illustrated* would note, "Playing shortstop in one field, you always had the left fielder from an-other ball game nearby for conversation."

Much of that conversation would be about San Francisco's favorite team, one that would soon take Alice as one of their own.

• • •

On July 11, 1927, Lou Gehrig of the New York Yankees walloped his twenty-ninth home run of the season in Detroit, pulling into a tie for the league lead with his teammate and fellow assassin on Murderers' Row, the "Sultan of Swat," Babe Ruth. It was a home run race that would cap-tivate the country, culminating in the Bambino setting his fabled record of sixty dingers come September.

A couple of thousand miles west, major league baseball was still three decades away. But the sport still ruled the California consciousness. And on July 11, 1927, San Francisco baseball fans were introduced to thirteen-year-old Alice Marble, the "Little Queen of Swat."

Prior to the Giants and Dodgers leaving New York for California, the biggest thing going out west was the Pacific Coast League, a top minor league where they claimed to play a brand of ball every bit as good as the major leaguers back east.

In Northern California the San Francisco Seals were the local hard-ball stars. They played games at Recreation Park, more widely known as "the Rec," or "Big Rec," in the Mission District at Fifteenth and Valencia, about three miles east of Alice's house. It held 16,500 at capacity and wasn't a particularly comfortable place to take in a game, even by the standards of the time. The bleachers consisted of warped lumber, and chicken wire surrounded the field. But unlike future baseball parks built on San Francisco Bay, the Rec at least had the advantage of being warm and relatively windless.

It could be a rough place to watch a game. Baseball drew a rowdy crowd in the twenties, especially in a working-class, immigrant-heavy place like San Francisco. Although the Mission was at the time heavily Irish, Italian fans often were in the majority in the park, first attracted by the dead-ball-era star Francesco Stephano Pezzolo, aka Ping Bodie, who was honored with a special day in August 1927. Women were sparse, allowed in but put off by the drunken barbarism that permeated the crowd. The eight rows that wrapped around home plate and up the baselines were pews extremely close to the field. Before Prohibition became the law of the land, this section was known as the "Booze Cage," as the seventy-five-cent ticket included a shot of whiskey or two bottles of beer. Alice's move to the city coincided with dry laws enacted nationwide, but as in so many places, Prohibition was roundly ignored at Rec Park. Fans were given whiskey in soda bottles or simply brought their own bootleg spirits past uncaring ushers. The Booze Cage was an unruly place, with sloshed fans insulting the players and squirting beverages at them through the chicken wire. Usually, but hardly always, their targets were opposing players.

The upper grandstand over first base was reserved for gambling, and fans there wagered on virtually every pitch. Legendary Bay Area gamblers of the period, including "Tomato Face" Harry Cook and Joe Bernstein, the "silver fox of Turk Street," considered this section their summer office. High above, fans unable to get tickets beat the system by watching from rooftops and balconies up and down Valencia and Fourteenth Streets.

For all the vice on hand, Rec Park was a kid's paradise. A quarter got them inside (in 1927 it was $1.25 for adults), except on Fridays, when admission was free. Local schools regularly reported dips in attendance on Fridays as a result. Kids had an open invitation to shag flies during batting practice, and as a result almost all remembered to bring their gloves to the park. The right-field porch was seemingly right on top of home plate, just 235 feet down the line, a dimension directly attributable to the way the field was jammed into the city block. To reduce the number of easy homers, there was a fifty-foot-high screen towering above the right-field wall. A clot of excited kids always gathered there and vied for balls that rebounded off the screen. In center field, an enormous cutout of a bull sat next to the clubhouse. Any player hitting it would receive fifty dollars from the Bull Durham tobacco company. Close by there was a hole in the field where a gas meter was buried. Any ball that rolled into the hole was ruled a home run.

By age thirteen Alice had become quite the sandlot legend. She pitched against much older boys in the "abalone league," the local moniker for neighborhood games, and held her own at the plate. Her favorite catcher was still her younger brother Tim, a good player in his own right who would go on to have a brief minor league career.

"We had a special routine," Alice remembered. "First I practiced my fastballs and curves while Tim caught, then in Tim's turn we stood twenty feet apart while I bunted balls for Tim in fielding because he wanted to become a shortstop."

One time, her fastballs got the best of her little bro. Tim was expecting a curve but got Alice's heater instead—right in the face, in fact. So hard was Alice's throw that the cheap chicken-wire mask Tim wore was smashed and twisted, bent around his face to the point the siblings had to go to a nearby hardware store so a clerk could file it off.

Like most local kids, Alice was a great fan of the Seals. Woodie had taken her to a game that whet her interest, and soon she and Tim were regulars in the bleachers, playing catch with one another before first pitch. She said she earned the money for transport and tickets by stocking shelves for the local grocer, a gig that paid up to "a dollar a day."

On this fateful July afternoon, she and Tim were tossing the ball as usual when a shout came from the field. "Say, boy, how'd you like to climb down and play with us?" Alice realized with a start that it was a Seal inviting her down. The fence was hiding her skirt, and her hair was shorn short, so the gender mistake was understandable, though she claimed to be "indignant." But not too peeved that she didn't race right on down and toss the ball with the pros.

Soon, Frank "Lefty" O'Doul, the Seals' star outfielder and in time a legendary Bay Area figure thanks to his outgoing personality and popular restaurant, joined the fun. He asked Alice to shag some flies with him, and her natural ability and grace in the field raised his brow. He presented her with some balls to toss to her pals in the stands and brought her over to the dugout to meet the team. "Hey, fellas," he yelled, "meet Alice Marble, a girl who's got a better arm than most of you jokers!"

The Seals' manager, Nick Williams, had seen Alice's deft glove and powered throws and was likewise impressed. He invited her to warm up with the team when the Seals were at home on the weekends. In time, she became the team mascot, known across the city as the hard-throwing, slick-fielding girl lucky enough to get close to the ballplayers.

As it happened, someone else was watching the Seals embrace the young girl, a reporter from the *San Francisco Examiner* with a moniker perfect for horsehide—Curley Grieve. He tracked Alice to her house on Twelfth Avenue and came by for an interview. After asking a bunch of questions, he prevailed upon Alice to come downtown the following day for some pictures.

She wore a "middy blouse" and a long skirt to the Hearst Building on Third and Market Streets, and Grieve took her up to the roof for a photo session. Sure enough, a pair of prints ran in the sports pages the following day, July 27, 1927. One photo depicted Alice in action, lunging like a first baseman to snag a high throw.

The copy read, in part,

PRESENTING ALICE MARBLE, 13-year-old diamond star who works out at Recreation Park with the Coast League baseballers. . . . Then a long fly comes whizzing toward the bleacher fence. Now Alice Marble enters upon the scene. Here she comes with graceful strides, her back to the ball. A few feet from the fence Alice wheels about, her judgment has been perfect, and "thunk" the ball is imbedded in her mitt. Then a lusty heave toward home, truly remarkable for a girl of 13, and Alice stands aside while her out fielding compatriot, who gets paid for his efforts, takes in the next fly. . . . With the field all set for action, Alice strides over to the sidelines, dons her sweater, climbs over the fence (there is a gate nearby), takes a seat in the bleachers and becomes just one of the great family of American fans.

The article went on to praise her pitching prowess on local diamonds. "'She's got a fast one and a mean curve,' say some of the young swatsmiths who have faced her when she was on the mound at Golden Gate Park. . . . In her little heart [Alice] probably believes that she could go out there on the mound at Recreation Park and bend a few over the outside corner that some of the Coast Leaguers couldn't hit with an armful of shovels."

For all the plaudits, the piece ended on a sour note. "Miss Alice wears a 'Frank O'Doul Club' button on her sweater, but she says that Snead Jolley [sic—his name was Smead] is her favorite player. Unfaithful woman!"

"I carried the clipping in my pocket until it was barely legible," Alice recalled with a smile.

Alice was a lifelong baseball fan and became a massive Yankees supporter, which makes sense given the number of future pin-striped greats from San Francisco who got their start playing for the Seals—Frank Crosetti, Tony Lazzeri, and of course the great Joe DiMaggio among them. DiMag, fourteen months younger than Alice, ironically was too busy playing tennis to be much into baseball as a youth, but years later he told writer Ralph Hickok, author of *A Who's Who of Sports Champions*, that he remembered Alice patrolling the Seals outfield, saying, "She had a pretty good arm."

Along with the rest of America, Alice idolized Babe Ruth. As the author of a book about the Babe and his first championship in New York, I was particularly enthralled by a story she told later in life, in her second memoir. Alice wrote in *Courting Danger* that when the man himself came to Rec Park to judge a pregame baseball-throwing contest, one of the roughly twenty female participants didn't show up, so the Seals' favorite mascot herself was plucked from the stands to hurl the pill for distance. As she warmed up in center field, the immortal Babe strolled over. "Kid," he growled, "throw it higher."

This went against what Uncle Woodie had taught her. Outfield throws were designed to come in on a hop so they could be fielded and a tag applied in one swoop. But who was she to quibble with the Sultan of Swat?

So Alice threw it high, and her heave carried it all the way into the stands behind home plate, winning the contest.

This amazing event, and the Bambino's role in it, wasn't mentioned in Alice's 1946 memoir, *The Road to Wimbledon*, which was published while Ruth was still alive. As it turns out, it doesn't seem to have happened at all. Alice stated in her 1991 memoir that the Babe was in San Francisco on "his way to the Orient." Presumably she is referring to Ruth's participation in a major league tour of Japan, a well-known saga that actually didn't happen until 1934, by which time Alice was in Southern California and a full-timer at tennis. Also, Ruth and the other major leaguers did not stop in California en route to Japan, instead leaving from Vancouver (one of the other players on the tour was Moe Berg, whose story mixing sports and unprovable espionage mirrors that of Alice). Ruth did indeed barnstorm in California in 1927, but after the baseball season, naturally, as he was rather busy that summer swatting sixty homers and leading the Yankees to a World Series sweep of the Pirates. There is no mention in any of the very detailed reportage covering the Babe's appearances in the Bay Area in October 1927 (he played games against a team starring his Yankee teammate and frenemy, Lou Gehrig) about any baseball-throwing contests, or of Alice Marble.

Not content with a single immortal "Babe," Alice said there were two on the field that day. In *Courting Danger* she relates that a quarter century after her mighty heave would have happened, she encountered the great female athlete Babe Didrikson Zaharias while on a train to Chicago from New York (presumably the fabled 20th Century Limited). While snowbound and waiting for the tracks to be cleared, she wrote, the "other Babe" told Alice that she had been one of the women defeated by her mighty throw that day. "Boy, we felt like fools," she said Babe admitted. "Beaten by a 13-year-old!"

"Then Babe pulled a harmonica from her handbag and entertained our fellow passengers until well after midnight," Alice continued. "Everyone loved Babe, and she could do anything." In a letter to a friend she burbled about Didrikson's versatility—"she could cook, make drapes, play the harmonica, etc."

True enough, but one thing she didn't do was lose to Alice in a throwing contest in San Francisco. There was indeed a distaff baseball-throwing contest at Rec Park on August 7, 1927, and the *Examiner* reported on it. Vivian Hartwick, national champion and soon-to-be Olympian in the bygone field event of the baseball throw, showed her stuff by unleashing a throw of some 247 feet, a mortar shell that, if true, was nearly 20 feet farther than her throw at the first-ever Olympic qualifying meet in Newark the following summer, a toss that caused the AP to marvel, "Babe Ruth himself never lined a keener throw from the outfield to catch a runner tearing home."

Alice *was* in this contest. "Alice Marble competed against [Hartwick]," reported the *San Francisco Examiner*, confirming that as such a known quantity in San Francisco already, especially around Rec Park, there is little chance a contest she won thanks to Babe Ruth would not have been major news. Babe Didrikson, it should be noted, was but sixteen herself in 1927 and still in high school in Port Arthur, Texas.

An amazing story, one containing elements of truth along with other ingredients that don't go down so easily. It is an admixture that Alice, in adulthood an accomplished mixologist, would concoct often, as I came to discover in pursuing the details of her extraordinary life.

Chapter Four

....

Local Hero

A dusty baseball diamond in the spring of 1931. The pitcher for the home team wears a red-and-black uniform with PARROTS emblazoned across the chest. The pitcher stares in at the hitter, goes into a windup, and blows a fastball past the poor devil in the batter's box.

Strike three.

A group of boys surround the pitcher in the dugout, offering back-slaps and lightly punching the player's arm. Anyone in attendance at the diamond at Golden Gate Park would assume the pitcher was just one of the boys.

Actually, it was Alice Marble, star pitcher and team captain of the Polytechnic High School baseball team. And the only female player on the field.

Every morning Alice walked the nearly three miles down the hill (and, later, the same distance back up) to Polytechnic High (known as Poly), which abutted Golden Gate Park and sat across Frederick Street from the newly opened Kezar Stadium. Poly closed its doors back in 1973, but I could still retrace the walk Alice would have taken to get to school, one that took me about forty-five minutes, though I wasn't

35

rushing to get to homeroom. Alice was a much bigger girl than the sprite who chased fly balls around with the Seals. She had sprouted to five foot seven and packed the scales at 150 pounds and was one of the top athletes in the school, of either gender. Eventually she would play multiple sports for Poly, including "basketball and several track events," according to an interview she gave about her days at Poly. She was also the school's representative in the Girls' Athletic Association, which was busily helping fund prep girls' sports teams for schools across the city. Alice would go to occasional meetings and give her opinion on the state of girls' athletics.

Alice would also win "dubious fame by jumping from a three-story building onto a sand pile on a bet," according to a profile published years later in *The New York Times Magazine*.

But athletic success didn't give a huge boost to her self-esteem. "I wasn't much to look at," she wrote later, despite her piercing blue eyes. Her hair was unflatteringly cut, she was pudgy, and like so many teens she had a raging case of acne. Matters were made worse by a speech impediment. She lisped and refused to read aloud. Other than on the athletic fields, the only time Alice opened her mouth was to sing in the brand-new music hall in Poly's basement. "I remember the new . . . music building because mother was musical and we all sang in church," Alice recalled in her Poly oral history. Her favorite songs included "Yes! We Have No Bananas," "Alice Blue Gown," "Margie," "Always," and "Peggy O'Neil."

One teacher, Betty Coyne, was special to Alice. She worked with her after school, enabling her to lose the lisp and be a more confident public speaker. Her attention had a galvanizing effect on Alice, who would call Coyne her "first love" in a letter to her friend, the writer Rita Mae Brown, some sixty years later. "Just a word from her would set me up for days," she wrote.

Coyne had an effect on Alice's future athletic career as well. The girl walked pigeon-toed. Coyne had an unusual prescription to straighten her feet: Irish clog dancing. Alice took it up and became far more agile.

The ability to be light on her feet certainly helped in her new passion.

As Alice became famous in the 1930s, her tennis origin story became of great interest to the American public. The oft-told tale, which Alice wrote about in her memoirs and elsewhere, went like this: While Alice was starring in sports for Poly at age fifteen, her oldest brother, Dan, another exceptional athlete who was the best handball player in the area and ranked nationally, surprised her one day with a tennis racket.

"Allie, you've got to stop being a tomboy," Dan said. "Here's a racket I bought you. Go out and play tennis. It's a game you can enjoy for the rest of your life." He went on to forbid her from playing baseball and basketball and even going to Seals games, or at least from continuing as the team mascot and pregame sideshow. Dan was Alice's "idol" and the de facto head of the household, so defying him wasn't an option. He also possessed a violent temper that manifested itself in fist-size holes in the woodwork at home or on the handball court, so Alice was taking no chances.

But she was disconsolate at losing her special gig with the Seals. "I was heartbroken," she wrote. "I went home and cried in bed all night." She also hated the idea of playing that "sissy game," meaning tennis. She was even more indignant the following day, when she brought the offending racket to school, and because she forgot her locker key the boys all got to see the implement of her new sport and teased her mercilessly. "Marble's playing ten-nis, Marble's playing ten-nis!" they mocked. "Word got around the school and all morning I was pointed to and laughed at," she writes in *The Road to Wimbledon*.

However, she found a pal named Mary who was also a beginner about to start playing, and the duo went together into the park. From there, Alice fell in love with the sport, and though she took her lumps in her first forays into competition, the rest was history.

Teenagers being teenagers, it is possible Alice was teased at some point for enjoying tennis, perhaps in the manner of the locker room, where little is off-limits but even less is meant seriously. More dubious is the notion that Dan Marble would ban her from playing baseball or other sports (which, given that Alice played them for Poly High, clearly wasn't the case). Alice's telling also leaves out a truth that speaks with power: She was an impressive athlete at her age, across sports and gender. She may have been shy and awkward in some ways but not when it came to athletics. The notion that she would have been shamed about any sporting endeavor is hard to fathom.

More to the point, the plain fact is that Alice was playing in tennis tournaments at Golden Gate Park as early as October 1926, just past her thirteenth birthday and nearly a year before her tenure as the Seals' mascot began, well before Dan supposedly ripped away her dreams of becoming the first girl major leaguer and forced the "sissy" game of tennis upon her.

The *Examiner* listed Alice Marble taking on a girl named Helen Wilson in the first round of the Golden Gate Park Junior Girls tournament that began October 22, 1926. Alice was a handicap player, "plus 15" in the parlance, meaning she only had to win three points to her opponent's four in each game unless they were of similar or higher handicaps (which Wilson was). By the time she was ready to move on to much bigger things, Alice's handicap was "owe 30"—she began each game down love–30, needing four points to her opponent's two.

On April 9, 1927, even as the Seals season was just getting underway, Alice played in the San Francisco girls' championship, a tournament that "will probably be won by a player from Berkeley," according to the *Examiner*. Alice was one of the sixty-four entrants, taking on another Helen, this time Helen Lynch, in the first round. Presumably she lost in both opening rounds, for she doesn't appear in any further coverage of the events, and she always mentioned her early futility in tournaments, so that part of the legend appears to be true.

Her brother Dan's foisting the sport of tennis upon Alice, if it happened (and it probably did in some form, given contemporary accounts), took place at this tender age. More than likely, as a multisport athlete and regular at Golden Gate Park, she had already wandered over to the courts and began playing on her own. She does reference starting out with a borrowed racket in a much later article, so Dan's "gift" may have conflated with a brotherly demand in her mind.

Alice also mentioned in her Poly oral history that a classmate named

"Suzy Dorsey . . . taught me how to [keep] score on a court in Golden Gate Park. She also helped me with math lessons."

Another truth: Alice quickly became a regular in the park, spending nearly every daylight hour there when not inside a Poly classroom or on one of its fields.

Golden Gate Park was the city's playground on the west side since it was built atop a former desert of sand dunes starting in 1868. Over one thousand acres of gently rolling terrain and particularly lush green space, the park was one of the city's top attractions long before the eponymous bridge opened directly to the north. It was a uniquely beautiful place with bounteous flora sprung loose by the fact the park was for many years irrigated by raw sewage.

The fertilizer turned the park into an Eden, as a *Sports Illustrated* writer detailed. "Whole hillsides are covered with hydrangeas in spring, and dahlias grow peach-colored and white, apricot, lavender and yellow, some of them a foot in diameter. Fuchsia flushes in dappled sunlight under serene cypresses, and elsewhere are stalwart redwoods, which are among the oldest living things in the world. With the late spring acacia trees around the horseshoe-pitching courts bloom yellow, peacocks rustle out of the punga tree ferns, and across the street kids suck the sugar from the nasturtiums that grow in orange clouds on the trimmed walkways."

Alice had mainly spent time on the baseball diamonds, but there were plenty of other places to have fun. Aside from the miles of walking trails that wound through the glens, there were fields for football, courts for basketball, walls for handball, greens for bowling, pits for horseshoes, and countless places for kids to simply run and play tag or hide-and-seek. The older set played golf and polo behind a "chlorophyll curtain." After Charles Lindbergh made his famous solo flight across the Atlantic in 1927, model airplanes became a craze, and the park was home to a daily air show of homebuilt craft. There was a midway with amusement games—Alice wrote that she was so proficient at knocking bottles over that the "owner of the concession put out a 'closed' sign when he saw me coming."

Water sports were conducted on Spreckels Lake, land sports in the various meadows (one of which was renamed for the actor Robin Williams after his untimely death). There was also a concert band shell, a famous science center, stables for horse riders, and a petting zoo. In fact, animals were spread all over the park. Over by the tennis courts where Alice would wind up playing was a "smelly buffalo," as she described it, that was available for rides, two kids at a time for just a nickel. Actually, there was a small herd of bison on hand, and they often broke free from their confines and roamed the city. Animal attractions were everywhere, from the tame donkeys in the children's playground to a bear who lived in a pit and snarled up at passersby. There was even a pair of elephants at one time. The Steinhart Aquarium opened its doors to add the life aquatic to the scene in 1923. Over the years there were kangaroos, moose, seals and sea lions, and an aviary that housed several hundred birds.

The Golden Gate Park courts had already sent multiple players to the top echelons of tennis. The great "Little" Bill Johnston and the "California Comet," Maurice McLoughlin, got their start on the park asphalt. So, too, did two of the foremost women stars of the day, Helen Wills and Helen Jacobs. These public court stars tended to be the exception; far more of the game's early elite came from backgrounds with access to private clubs and lessons.

Playing at the municipal courts gave Alice's game a hard edge. These were hardly country club conditions. The courts, surfaced with asphalt and concrete, were cracked from weather and usage, and bordered by the same chicken-wire fencing used to hold back fans at Rec Park. The morning dew was heavy and the fog and rain off the ocean unrelenting, leaving the courts thick with water. Players spent hours dragging old blankets across the surface in those pre-squeegee days. "More often than not," Alice said, "it would rain again, and we sat in the little clubhouse or under the heavy trees anxiously waiting for the weather to clear." The courts, four lower and four upper, were laid out with no room between them, so Alice had to constantly watch her footing lest she step on a ball from another court. People walked back and forth on the margins, and watched and kibitzed loudly, with little heed for tennis etiquette. The gray surface of the courts quickly wore off and drained the white tennis balls of their visibility (yellow tennis balls didn't come around until the 1960s and weren't used in professional matches until 1972). As with chess masters who ply their trade on the streets, or basketball greats who come up from city playgrounds, the atmosphere hardened Alice for later travails.

In another similarity to pickup basketball, the courts had a "winners stay" mandate. Applicants for court time were put on a waiting list; if a player lost the first set, he or she went to the bottom of the list and often waited up to two hours before his or her name came to the top of the list again. Players who won remained on the court and played the next person on the list. Alice and other dedicated players were thus incentivized to go all out at all times for fear of sitting and watching.

One aspect of the courts that served Alice well was the outsize Asian population that used them. "There were dozens of Chinese, Japanese, and Filipinos with whom I played," she said. "Several years later when I went out to dinner parties, I found many of these same boys working as butlers and houseboys. And I shocked my hosts and hostesses by carrying on lengthy conversations on tennis with the boys as they served the dinner." An allergy to racist thinking would be a hallmark of Alice's future.

Alice loved the competitive and fitness aspects of the game. She thrashed more experienced players based mainly on her superior athletic ability. Sometimes that caused short-term hard feelings. She had a crush on a local, older boy she calls "Rudy" in her memoir, a football star and class president at Poly, until she walloped him at tennis. He never spoke to her again. "It taught me that romance and tennis don't mix," she wrote in *The Road to Wimbledon*, and that "men hate to be beaten by women at anything." (Though Alice never gives his surname, "Rudy" is quite likely Rudy Rintala, a future four-sport superstar athlete at Stanford and a Poly alum.)

Alice started to spend nearly every free moment at the courts. She would augment her natural skill by watching better players for hours, picking up methods and nuances in their games. Her ground strokes at first were unpolished, so she picked up the habit of rushing the net for volleys whenever possible. It was a trait that she would take with her all the way to Centre Court at Wimbledon.

Alice received seventy-five cents per week in allowance, but it didn't go very far. "Tennis, I found, was an expensive game," she said later, and to buy balls at thirty-five cents a pop, not to mention shoes, dresses, and other accoutrements, required a steady income stream. She made money any way she could, with babysitting, that time-honored teenage fund-raiser, being her main gig. But she also worked in the high school cafeteria and toiled away at night at the local candy store, working the soda fountain. And when in dire need she remained a master at pitching pennies, the classic game where the player tossing a penny closest to a wall keeps the pennies of all who compete.

The park organized tennis tournaments according to class, with fourth being the lowest and first the highest. In 1928, Alice won her first-ever title, the fourth-class tournament, winning a trophy that was all of two and a half inches tall. It didn't make it home in one piece—Alice managed to break the handles off racing up the hill to show it off. Dan put it among his handball trophies regardless.

When Alice began moving up in class, Dan, seeing the makings of another champion athlete as he had become, dipped into his hard-earned income to enroll his sister at California Tennis Club, a swankier set of courts to the north in Pacific Heights near the Presidio. It cost forty-five dollars to join, but Alice hardly got her money's worth. The club was, unsurprisingly perhaps, a cliquish place, and members didn't enjoy playing with rough-hewn, raw kids like Alice. The haughty elite turned up their noses at her—she could scarcely get up a match. After a month she started leaving early, hopping a streetcar back to the park, where her friends were put out by her absence.

Accounts differ as to whether or not she gave up her membership or stayed on to play occasionally once her standing improved. Either way, there was no doubt that she was the product of public courts. But one man at the California Tennis Club took notice of Alice's glaring athletic skill. By the time Alice was a top-ranked player, the idea of her being completely self-taught from the beginning took hold, likely encouraged by her future coach, Eleanor Tennant, who liked to whitewash away anyone else who might have influenced Alice. But even during these early days, a San Francisco native and former Davis Cup player named Howard Kinsey, by then a teaching pro at the club, gave her informal coaching and hit with her when Alice couldn't find a female partner.

By September 1928, Alice was good enough to play in the junior girls section of the California State Championships, held at the CTC. She lost in the semifinals to yet another girl named Helen, this one Marlowe, but had clearly made an impressively rapid rise, even if she had started at thirteen and not fifteen as stated in her legend. That December, scarcely two months past her fifteenth birthday, she was already ranked eighth among all girls under eighteen in the state, and fourth under sixteen. And her excellence in net play and booming serve, made strong from her practice at pitching in baseball, made her a precocious (and much in demand) doubles player.

It was then that her Eden turned to darkness.

Chapter Five

....

Darkest Hour

In her memoir *Courting Danger*, written at the end of her life, Alice reveals the sexual assault that she suffered at the hands of a stranger in Golden Gate Park one evening upon leaving the tennis courts. She doesn't give a date but writes she was fifteen, and it happened "after school," so it likely happened in late 1928 or in the first half of 1929.

Alice writes that she was about to leave the park by the Stanyan Street entrance when a predator, cloaked in shadow and hiding in the considerable flora that grew in the area, grabbed Alice and pulled her into the gloom. He stuffed a handkerchief in Alice's mouth and slapped her in the face several times, making her nose bleed. He tore her blouse, grabbed her throat, and yanked her skirt over her head.

She writes, "I was scared as I'd never been before. . . . I could barely breathe. I was groggy, on the edge of consciousness." The pain was excruciating. Mercifully, perhaps, she passed out. When she came to, she was alone in the woods. When she sat up, she says, she vomited from pain and shock.

After pulling herself together in the gloaming, Alice took stock. Her aunt "Jo," Josephine Wood Gere, Jessie's sister, still lived nearby, in the house where Alice's parents were married. Her husband, the doctor in whose office Harry Marble had met Jessie, was dead, but Jo had been a nurse and was able to provide a modicum of care. She also called over a doctor friend to examine Alice, who asked if she could identify her attacker, which of course she could not. "It's almost over now," he said.

She also called her sister, Alice's mother, and told her Alice had the "flu" and needed to stay where she was for a few days.

Three days later, Alice was back in school, explaining away the bruises with tales of a fall, her family none the wiser. The physical pain abated, but the psychological trauma had only just begun. As she wrote, "I was fifteen, and I had been raped. . . . I knew that virginity was something special, something you saved for the person you fell in love with. Mine had been stolen, and it made me angry, deeply angry. . . . I was also ashamed. . . . I walked the halls at school, certain that 'it' showed, that people somehow knew. . . . Were they all snickering about me, and telling my girlfriends I was a tramp? I was mortified, and repulsed by the very idea of sex."

Counseling for rape victims wasn't readily available in the late 1920s—the profession was geared more toward professional advice, not personal, according to a history of the subject by R. F. Aubry. It also goes without saying that no perpetrator was ever arrested or suspect questioned for the crime, since it was unreported. The FBI would not even be authorized to create a database of criminal statistics until 1929, its tracking efforts starting the following year.

After decades of women's rights movements making a tangible difference, including winning the right to universal female suffrage, the 1920s and 1930s began a half century of backlash to feminist progress. In particular, rape and sexual assault crimes were reclassified. According to Estelle Freedman, a historian specializing in the study of the history of sex crimes, Alice's assault took place in a period when victim blaming rose to the fore. Women—including girls—were sexualized, deemed "responsible for rape." *The American Journal of Urology and Sexology* ran articles warning lawyers of "the great danger that men are often in from false accusations by female children and women."

The incident isn't mentioned in Alice's original memoir from 1946, *The Road to Wimbledon*, nor does she appear to have spoken about it publicly or in any personal correspondence I have seen, encompassing some six decades. Her posthumous memoir from 1991 is the lone mention of it ever happening. And given the horror of her experience, and the loneliness and lack of support she might have felt due to the ignorance of the culture around her, perhaps it shouldn't be a surprise that she did not describe these details until her final memoir.

I tried to locate similar assaults in the contemporary public record, as a typical researcher's way to learn more about what Alice says she experienced, but nothing that would indicate a series of crimes fitting the assault on Alice was found. And it wouldn't have been—that was the major lesson I took away from researching this aspect of Alice's life: that so much history of a person's journey is held inside, often by choice and often because of the unwillingness of the greater culture to hear their stories. This is the kind of tragedy that went unrecorded, ignored by a supposedly civil and law-abiding society that preferred not to engage with it. Thankfully, Alice decided to at least reveal the assault in her memoir, as it is a piece of her we absolutely need to know.

· · ·

It made me tough," Alice wrote in *Courting Danger*, finding a silver lining amid the pain, "and made me turn all the more to tennis to counteract my low self-esteem. . . . Later, tennis became a substitute for sex (though a poor one), the physical activity giving a measure of release."

Chapter Six

....

North by Northwest

By 1929, as the nation blissfully enjoyed the fruits of a still booming economy, Alice was playing in big tournaments in both U-16 and U-18 classes. There wasn't an appreciable difference for Alice. She won her first tournament beyond the confines of Golden Gate Park in June 1929 at the Pacific Coast Championships held in Berkeley. Alice crushed all comers in the U-16s, and the *Examiner* took notice. "Alice Marble, Polytechnic High School girl and product of the Golden Gate Park courts, romped off with the junior girl's under 16 title defeating Betty Wheatly, 7-5, 6-1 in the final round, and displayed a well rounded game and plenty of future promise in her convincing victory." She and Ida Cross, another public court "outsider," teamed to "humble" the top seeds in doubles, too, to make it a brace of titles.

That September, now sixteen, Alice returned to the state tournament, held this time at the Berkeley Tennis Club in the East Bay. She was top seeded in the U-16s (called "girls") and third seeded in the U-18s (called "juniors").

The Berkeley Tennis Club has a swanky-sounding name, and today it is far nicer than in its hardscrabble beginnings, but it was far closer in spirit to the Golden Gate Park courts than the California Tennis Club across the bay. Opened in 1906, the BTC was a magnet for players in the Bay Area, even though it consisted of a single building and a handful of weather-beaten courts, penned in by chicken wire, just yards away from railroad tracks that were inevitably in use by freight trains at critical moments in match play.

In the finals of the U-16s, or "girls," Alice faced May Doeg, a member of California tennis aristocracy. Doeg's aunt and namesake, May Sutton Bundy, in 1905 became the first American (of either sex) to win at Wimbledon, and her brother John Doeg was the top-ranked men's player in the state and would go on to win the US Nationals in 1930. Her sister, Violet, was also a top-ranked junior player and May's doubles partner.

Doeg cruised to a first set win, and Alice evened affairs in the second. In the rubber set, Doeg hit a perfect lob to the backcourt. "In my tomboy fashion I tried to climb the fence after it," Alice recalled, but managed only to slice up her wrist in the chicken wire. She got taped up but mentally was unfixable, and Doeg rolled to the title. "I knew that I might have won despite the little handicap, but self-pity was stronger than the will to overcome it."

Alice had roared to prominence on the local tennis scene without much chance for introspection, but when she began to lose in larger tournaments beyond the bosom of Golden Gate Park, her "little excuses" were always at hand. "I would tell myself I only had eleven hours sleep instead of twelve," she once said. "I would think of excuses and forget to win." After Alice told Dan about the loss to Doeg, he tongue-lashed her. "You should be ashamed of yourself for letting such a bad player beat you. You have no guts." Even accounting for the retrograde times and Dan's immaturity after being forced to become the head of the house after his father's premature death, Alice's memory of their sibling relations was that they left much to be desired.

Alice stormed out and threw a temper tantrum worthy of her brother, heaving all of her tennis equipment at Dan and threatening to quit. Both parties calmed, and Dan prevailed upon his sister to continue playing, as her talent was too great.

He wasn't the only one to see it. Later that month Alice played for the Golden Gate Park U-16 title, and the only other competitor at her level refused to play her, so intimidating was the Marble game by now. Alice won by default.

. . .

One day in the spring of 1930, there was a knock on the door of the house on the hill. Alice opened the door to the one and only "Little" Bill Johnston, archrival of the legendary "Big" Bill Tilden and one of the all-time greats to come out of the Golden State. When Alice picked her jaw up from the floor, Johnston extended her an invitation: to journey to the Pacific Northwest as the representative of the Northern California Tennis Association in several tournaments. She would be given the princely sum of seventy-five dollars for expenses. "I'd never even seen seventy-five dollars!" Alice wrote in *The Road to Wimbledon*.

Dan said no.

Despite Alice's excitement, Dan realized that seventy-five bucks wasn't enough to properly equip, dress, and transport a burgeoning young champion for ten full weeks. Fortunately, Johnston held the door ajar should minds change, and Alice went on a fundraising offensive. She sold her baseball gear, worked at a grocery store on the weekends, and babysat at night, and in the end she scraped up twenty dollars.

Dan still said no.

Just when matters seemed settled, a mysterious plain white envelope arrived in the mail. Inside were three crisp twenty-dollar bills. Alice assumed Dan had come through as the doting big bro, but he expressed his bafflement. "To this day I don't know" who sent the anonymous money, Alice wrote in 1946, and at the end of her life she still had not discovered the source of the largesse.

"Alice, the Lord is good to you," the devout Jessie said.

After buying brand-new clothes and shoes, plus carrying two new rackets courtesy of Spalding in an early sponsorship, Alice set off for the great Northwest with just under one hundred dollars in her "little wallet." She was picked up in a big Buick sedan by her chaperones from the Northern California Tennis Association, including a young woman named Dorothea, who would spend most of her time on the tour hunting for men, while Alice made excuses to stay in and retire by ten every night. Two days' drive through picturesque, timber-laden country brought them to Seattle, where they took a ferry to Vancouver. For the princely sum of seventy-five cents, Alice and Dorothea stayed in Alice's first-ever hotel room, a "tiny and stuffy" place up three flights of stairs.

The tour began tragically, according to Alice's first memoir. At a pretournament get-together at the Vancouver Club, an elder member took Alice by the arm to introduce her around, only to drop dead of a heart attack by her side. But as she had so often already in her young life when faced with death, Alice pressed ahead.

On the courts she cleaned up, regularly besting adult women. Her first stop in British Columbia was at the western clay-court championships in Vancouver. Rain delayed play for several days, meaning Alice wound up playing several matches per day as she advanced in both the ladies' and the junior competitions. She was used to the asphalt at Golden Gate Park, and the slippery clay surface immediately resulted in a rash of blisters on her heels. Not given a chance to heal, they became infected, and the tournament doctor advised Alice further playing was "unsafe."

Alice had a better idea. She cut the heels off the shoes, leaving just sock and sole between her blistered feet and the court, secured them with rubber bands, and went back out to play. It was painful, but at least there was no new blistering.

In the ladies' semifinals, she lost to a woman named Charlotte Miller, but Alice's play was the talk of the town. Only a few minutes after losing in "three torrid sets," 4–6, 6–4, 6–8, Alice had to go right back out for the junior singles final. "Badly tired," a local paper wrote, "she managed to pull out a hard fought victory after a heart-breaking battle" in three sets. It was her first title on "foreign" soil.

Alice got vengeance on Miller at the next stop, the Western Canadian championships, held in a different area of Vancouver. She displayed a remarkable ability to adapt her strategy to her opponents, changing from her usual hard-charging game that came up short the prior week. As *The Vancouver Sun* put it, "Miss Miller has beautiful drives . . . but Miss Marble cut off many of these with neat short drop shots on which she puts lots of stop."

The "young California marvel" put on an amazing display when she came back south across the border to Washington in August.

At the Pacific Northwest championships, she won no fewer than four titles, including the ladies', the doubles, the mixed doubles, and the junior singles. In the doubles she teamed with the aptly named (given the oceanic setting) Margaret Sturgeon. "Sturgeon's brilliant serving and Miss Marble's net work baffled [the opposing] strong Berkeley combination in the final two sets."

A couple of tournaments later, Alice returned to San Francisco in triumph and under budget—she returned her excess $6.37 to the NCTA. She had proven that she was not only good enough on the court to compete with a wider array of competition but mature enough to handle the accompanying duties of the touring tennis player.

Chapter Seven

....

Eastern Promises

In the spring of 1931 Alice's primary objective was to improve her grades in order to be admitted to the University of California, Berkeley, the crown jewel of the UC system and also the alma mater of her two tennis idols, Helen Wills and Helen Jacobs. The Golden Bears tennis coach was a legendary figure named William "Pop" Fuller, and Alice set her sights on playing under Pop's fatherly tutelage across the bay.

Despite the time she spent playing tennis rather than learning her lessons or writing book reports, Alice was accepted into Berkeley. She was helped by what she maintained for her entire life was a photographic memory, an instant recall that she apparently always possessed, though it manifested itself in varying ways, especially while she was young. Generally speaking, if she wrote something down, she said, she'd be able to remember it, regardless of how detailed or how much time passed.

A few months shy of eighteen, Alice had grown still further. She remained graceful and speedy on the courts, and the extra bulk she carried translated to enormous power in her serve-and-volley game. It wasn't the way women played tennis in that era; all the greats, from

Helen Wills to Suzanne Lenglen to Helen Jacobs, won from the baseline, trading ground strokes and wearing down the opponent. "That a woman could win at the net was almost unthinkable in those days," remembered one English writer. But Alice didn't know any other method.

As aggressive as Alice was on the court, she was reserved when it came to the men who began to circle her in hopes of romance. When Alice was thirteen, her sister, Hazel, the lone unathletic Marble child, stunned the family by eloping at the tender age of sixteen. "Her husband was, unfortunately, a bad choice," Alice said. So when Alice turned sixteen, and when potential boyfriends came to call, her family turned them away with alacrity.

The Marbles were especially disturbed by the most significant of these "beaux," as she called them, a man named Harold Dickenson. Harold was a minor figure in Southern California competitive tennis, better known as a teacher, promoter, and purveyor of Wilson sporting goods than for his play. He often came to San Francisco and played with his friend Howard Kinsey at the California Tennis Club (some accounts say he was a member there, but it appears he was just a guest of Kinsey's). One day Harold was introduced to Alice and the two played doubles together. Afterward, Dickenson became her biggest champion and, according to Alice, her most ardent suitor.

He was pushing thirty, and as Alice indicated in her memoir, she was still traumatized from her assault in the park at that point and uninterested in sex. But his overwhelming interest in her, and his talk of promoting her at the highest levels of tennis, was nevertheless dizzying. The family, Dan and Jessie in particular, thought it wrong for Alice to be squired by an older man at that point; "Because of my family's disapproval, he never came to the house," she wrote.

In *The Road to Wimbledon* Alice describes the afternoon Harold proposed to her in Solari's Grill, a popular eatery in the Cannery district at 354 Geary Street. "I was tired and very hungry and began to eat my steak with the normal healthy appetite of a seventeen-year-old. Harold chose that very moment to ask me to marry him. I was furious and very frightened, and told him he might have picked a more appropriate place and time than a booth at Solaris [*sic*] restaurant. I walked out and went home alone, and I cried and cried because I realized that I wanted very much to marry him."

This seems a good spot to mention that in 1946, Dickenson seemed crucial to Alice's story and important in her memory, but when she wrote *Courting Danger* nearly forty-five years later, she doesn't mention him at all, in any context, nuptial or tennis. That doesn't mean he wasn't, indeed, smitten with Alice or that the proposal didn't take place. If in her first memoir Alice was overstating her actual interest, the idea of an older "sponsor with benefits" would become a recurring theme throughout her days.

And Dickenson did have an important role in Alice's life, as on March 9, 1931, he introduced her to a friend from Los Angeles, a fellow teacher and one-time top player and the "person that would change my whole life," in Alice's words—Eleanor Tennant.

The future coach/student tandem that would come to dominate the sport of tennis met for the first time in the O'Connor Moffatt department store in Union Square at 101 Stockton Street (in 1945 the store would be acquired by a large concern from the east and thereafter renamed for its new owners—Macy's). Eleanor was thirty-five years old, "with prematurely gray hair and a broad smile," Alice recalled. They chatted for a spell, while Harold gushed over his pride and joy (Eleanor would say years later that she thought "Harold was in love with Alice"), and the trio ferried north across the bay to Dominican College at San Rafael, where Tennant was giving one of her patented mass clinics.

"If only I had a teacher like that!" Alice wrote of her memory of that day, and indeed, Tennant's lessons were easy to digest and immediately effective. The coach had to return to Los Angeles the following day, but the seed had been sown in Alice's mind that this was a woman who might take her game to another level.

Meanwhile she continued to do just fine against her local competition. San Francisco summer arrived, and with it cold, foggy mornings and bitter, windswept nights. Alice, however, was hot as an East Bay afternoon. In June she put on a display that showed why coaches like

Tennant and Fuller were eager to work with her. Alice swept to the California state title, beating Dorothy Weisel of Sacramento, the third-ranked player in the nation, at the Berkeley courts. Weisel had soundly beaten Alice in their previous encounters, but this time it was Marble turning the tables in a thrilling match, 8–6, 4–6, 6–4. "Alice had her slams working to perfection. . . . The winner drove [Miss Weisel] to the back court throughout the tilt and forced the play," reported the *Examiner*. "She plays a smashing type of game," added the *Calexico Chronicle*.

After the match Little Bill was back in Alice's ear. This time he passed along the opportunity for an even greater adventure than the trip to Canada. The Northern California Tennis Association chose Alice to represent the region in the coming junior national championships, to be held that September in Philadelphia. To acclimate her to eastern conditions, she would also play in some of the tournaments that comprised the "eastern circuit," events that led up to the US Nationals at the tennis palace in Forest Hills, Queens—the West Side Tennis Club. The circuit took players to swish places like Brookline and Marlborough, Massachusetts; East Hampton and Rye, New York; and Sea Bright, New Jersey. To cap it all she would compete at Forest Hills itself, in the biggest and most prestigious tournament the country had to offer.

Alice was an obvious choice, given her on-court resume, but it wasn't an invitation that she could automatically accept.

Being a tennis player of national level in 1931 meant, of course, that there was no prize money in the tournaments. That went without saying, the amateurism being a central tenet of the sport, much as in the Olympics. The various tennis associations, such as the NCTA and, if one were good enough, the United States Lawn Tennis Association (USLTA), would front the player expense money for travel, food, and shelter, a strict accounting of which was to be kept, with any excess being returned to the coffers (as Alice had done after her sojourn in the Pacific Northwest).

But for women, there was an added financial stress. Whereas men could get away with a handful of interchangeable pants, collared shirts, and a jacket, the female players required an array of skirts, blouses, and accessories to be deemed "properly attired" at the country clubs that staged most events. Further, she was expected to travel with several evening gowns, hats, and fancy shoes for the postmatch and nighttime affairs that were as much part of the scene as the overhead smash.

For someone like Alice, without much financial security or backing, this was a far more difficult hurdle than overcoming her opponents across the nets. "The player is really on a shoestring," she noted, and that was at the best of times. It was difficult enough for adults to handle the constant accounting of available funds and how best to use them. For a teenage girl to be asked to travel across the country and spend several weeks competing up and down the eastern seaboard, surrounded by friendly but at heart self-interested competitors and administrators, was quite a burden.

Stepping in to ease that burden was Alice's big brother. Dan Marble had encouraged his sister to take up tennis; now he ensured she wouldn't be stymied due to money. He tangibly proved his belief in his sister's ability by funding her with enough clothing and equipment to make the trip.

The entire Marble clan took the eighteen-minute ferry ride across the bay to Oakland, docking at the bustling point where the water met the continent—the Oakland Mole. A huge wood-framed train terminal was here, just steps from where the ferries tied up to the wharf. Nearly two dozen tracks ran right up to the wedge-shaped pier, with still more, designated for freight cars, just north at the Long Wharf. Every day thousands and thousands of passengers passed under the enormous clock that was the hallmark of the Oakland Mole, some connecting to a boat that would take them farther west to San Francisco, others, like Alice, catching a train to points east. Alice was to board the Southern Pacific night train. "Harold and I had said our goodbyes earlier in the day," she wrote. Perhaps the more telling lines come next. "I had told him how much I would miss him and that I couldn't bear to be separated from him, but I was much too excited really to mean what I had said."

Traveler's checks secured, and fortified with Jessie's reminder to drink plenty of milk, Alice settled in as the train pulled away from the station and made its way through the wild country east of the coast. The train chugged its way across the mountains not far from where she had been born. Her old isolated farm life in the Sierra must have seemed a universe distant.

Alice, gregarious by nature and friendly to strangers her entire life, made an unlikely pal on the train, a "lovely-looking old lady with white hair" named Mrs. Trask. The two gabbed their way east and by journey's end were close enough that Alice would make the trip to Beacon Street to visit Mrs. Trask whenever she came to Boston for many years afterward.

After about eighty hours in transit, she arrived in the big city, New York, for the first time. There was no fanfare, or any friends or chaperones in sight. She made her way via the Lexington Avenue tunnel to the Roosevelt Hotel, where she immediately broke out her iron and turned on the hot bath in order to steam away the wrinkles and dirt that had accumulated on the black-and-white dress that she had worn for the entirety of her journey.

"Half an hour later," she remembered, "the entire side wall was covered with a combination of black dye and a four-day collection of dirt from the non-aircooled train." A desperate wiping of the wall only made matters worse. "In the meantime I had forgotten to turn off the electric iron, and it broke the sheet of glass on top of the table."

Perhaps it was an omen for Alice's initial foray into eastern tennis.

After marking her room at the Roosevelt, Alice moved out to Queens, staying at the Forest Hills Inn in order to spend several days practicing at the West Side Tennis Club before her first eastern tournament. The inn was a classy spot at 1 Station Square, with ballroom dancing, bridge and supper clubs, and a lovely outdoor tea garden, described by *The Forest Hills Bulletin* in 1924 as "a veritable fairyland when lighted with Japanese lanterns, with the trickling fountain heard in the background and a new moon shining over head. There is no more delightful place in Greater New York for one to spend the dinner hour." But Alice never mentioned any social whirl during her stay, preferring to simply hit the ball and retire early.

The eastern press was eager to see this California prodigy. Alice had, after all, "swept through the tournaments out in the golden west like a cyclone." A prenationals feature called her a "coming champion" and a "girl of Junoesque stature" who would "be one to watch." The *Brooklyn Daily Eagle* called her "the girl who threatened to achieve mighty feats in the East on her first trip thitherwards from California."

Howard Kinsey told writers he expected Alice to be the successor to the great Helen Wills Moody (her name after marrying in 1929), that she was "a young cyclone" (apparently a popular descriptive word at the time) who would exceed all other players from the west. "It is my prediction that this young lady will be one of the leading contenders for the national title within two years," Kinsey said. "She is capable of dynamiting her shots in a manner not to be duplicated by any woman in the world. Likewise, she is fleet of foot, something that is not in evidence in the game as Mrs. Moody plays it."

But from the first, Alice had issues. "I felt lost in the big [West Side] club," she said, "and the atmosphere was not warm, nor were the members friendly." The club sat in an idyllic, tree-fringed section of Forest Hills, a mostly residential neighborhood in the center of the quiet borough of Queens. It was a less distinctive outer borough than its western neighbor Brooklyn, possessor of a baseball team and the navy yard and a defiant insularity, or the Bronx, with its rural trappings giving way to rapid development, thanks to the still-new Yankee Stadium, opened eight years earlier in 1923, its gravitational pull drawing sports-loving New Yorkers inexorably north.

Queens then was airy, hushed, swampy. The din of frogs cascaded through the nighttime air, and local children caught snakes and salamanders steps from their homes. Many Manhattanites were migrating there, seeking a less hectic pace off the Avenue. Forest Hills, in particular the exclusive enclave of Forest Hills Gardens (designed by Frederick Law Olmsted, with no Jews or nonwhites allowed), provided a more suburban setting while still only a short subway ride from "the city." Stately Forest Park was the public playground, with meandering paths and hordes of families roasting hot dogs in the summer. In winter, one longtime resident recalled to *The New York Times*, "Tolerant fathers in families with cars towed boys and girls on sleds through streets that, if memory serves, had little traffic regulation."

Then, as now, Queens Boulevard was busy and traffic clogged. Alice would have seen trolleys, with stoves inside to warm their riders from October to April, fighting for space with sleek cars with running boards and turret tops, double-decker buses run by the Fifth Avenue Coach Company, belching trucks delivering locally made Breyers ice cream, bicycles tracking mud from their wheels, and knots of pushcarts peddling melons and cloth and Bibles. Underneath, the tunneling to create the Independent Subway System (IND) was well underway. Off the boulevard, row houses, rather than apartment buildings, lined the streets, many of which remained unpaved.

Amid it all, the tony West Side Tennis Club, home once a year to the biggest tournament in the country, the US Nationals. "Like a small town that becomes a lodestone with its annual county fair," Richard Shepard wrote in "Memories of My Queens," "Forest Hills became world-famous once a year." The parking lot filled with automobiles sporting license plates from Maine to California. The entire borough would get swept up by the excitement of the world coming to Forest Hills, even Jewish kids who were not allowed membership in the club or even to be hired to sell the cushions that softened the seats of tennis fans.

The club got its name from its ancestral beginnings on the Upper West Side of Manhattan, moving to a ten-acre plot in Forest Hills Gardens in 1913. A year later the Tudor-style clubhouse was erected, matching the construction palate of the nearby homes, and membership expanded from its original 13 to over 500 (currently there are roughly 850 members). The sport's governing body, the USLTA, moved its headquarters from Newport, Rhode Island, to the club, and in 1923, even as the far larger Yankee Stadium was erected in the Bronx, a 13,500-seat stadium ("The realization of an ideal!" according to promotional material offering the chance to reserve the right to purchase ten years of "choice seats" for the low price of 110 dollars) was built at Forest Hills, three-quarters enclosed to leave room for further expansion. It was purpose-built for the national championship, which the club had hosted since 1915, in style.

Inside the club, elitism suffused the air. There was a lavish dining room and an exclusive pro shop, and portraits of the original members lined the halls. "In every detail this was an American Wimbledon, a citadel of the gentlemanly ideal," wrote Jeffrey Hart, a former junior player. "The manners required of all players were casual but strict. Polite, understated, broadly Protestant. Tennis clothes had to be white. Only a touch of quality might suggest self-expression. In every respect, the game was more important than a player's personality." The grass courts were every bit as lavish as those at the All England Club, the sine qua non of the gentlemanly standard. The gin and tonics were every bit as biting, the whites worn by the players every bit as crisp, the flower beds as colorful.

Players from outside of the upper class, like Alice, were expected to "level up," act as though they were actually men and women of means and class, even if they came from nothing. The game was what was important, not individual personalities. Alice, possessor of an electrifying talent and a joyful persona that sometimes mixed with a volatile temperament, would oft struggle to conform to this standard.

Her manners weren't the issue in that first trip east, however; she was simply overwhelmed. In her first match ever in the east, at the Seabright club, she was pummeled in the first round by Agnes Lamme, a thoroughly nondescript player. Similar beatings took place in East Hampton and at Rye, where she suffered humiliating defeats in doubles as well as singles.

Her problems went beyond merely facing stiffer competition than she had before. Eastern surfaces were almost uniformly grass, with occasional clay. Alice was used to the high bounce and consistent inflexibility of the Golden Gate Park asphalt. Her strokes didn't help. Alice held her racket with the so-called Western grip, which had the fingers faced upward on the top of the handle and the thumb over them. That grip created a ton of topspin on the ball, resulting in a high, fast bounce, and allowed the user to hit the ball well out in front. It was a grip tailor-made for Alice's hard-charging style and one copied directly from watching Little Bill Johnston at the public courts. Her strokes were, as a result, looping and unsuited for the much deader grass courts—as she put it afterward, "The balls didn't bounce high enough for my odd California strokes." She also tired easily in the humid conditions, such a far cry from the crisp oceanic climate she was used to.

So far her initial trip east was merely disappointing. It became far-cical upon release of the draw sheet for the nationals in mid-August. Alice, along with everyone playing in the tourney in Rye, craned to look at a bracket held by a reporter, and she was stunned to realize that her name was not on it! The USLTA said her entry form had not been received. On an emergency call to Bill Johnston, it was discovered that he had receipts—a dated copy and cable to show he had submitted Alice's entry before the deadline.

According to J. P. Allen, syndicated sports columnist, tournament officials were about to swap Alice in for a player named Gladys Hawk, who "was ready to make a sacrifice of herself" (her husband was president of the West Side Tennis Club). It only required the okay of Hawk's/Marble's first-round opponent, a young woman named Virginia Rice. "At this juncture Mrs. Rice, mother of Miss Virginia, stepped forcibly to the fore stating in no small voice that she would not" sign off on the change. After a sit-down in the proverbial smoke-filled room, an unprec-edented solution was reached—a complete redraw, a do-over in play-ground parlance. "The fathers of tennis foregathered for another solemn drawing occasion," in the words of the *Brooklyn Daily Eagle*. It would be one that was certain to include Alice. "It's one of the worst national tournament messes in many years," Allen concluded.

Most agreed with this assessment. The redraw left Helen Wills Moody, the six-time national champ looking to get her hands back on the winner's trophy after missing the 1930 tournament due to injury, with a much more difficult field to wade through on the way to the final (it wasn't too much of a hindrance, as Moody won the championship). As Alice put it, "Many of the players were resentful, because they had drawn easy opponents in the first draw; others were my best friends, because they came out better in the second."

All the publicity led the tournament organizers to capitalize on the headlines and place Alice on one of the stadium courts for her first match, at 3 P.M. against a solid veteran from Kansas City named Mary Greef. "From the moment I walked down the four steps of the marquee onto the grass court I was frozen with fright," she wrote. "I felt every eye peering at me. A dozen photographers snapped pictures of us . . . [and] in less than half an hour I was beaten."

The 6–2, 6–2 beatdown by the ninth-ranked player in the country had many onlookers feeling deflated. As Allen wrote in the New York *Sun*, "The little matter of a lost letter between California and New York caused more trouble for the USLTA than all the other sixty-three entries put together, and after watching Miss Alice Marble, husky player from San Francisco, lose to Mary Greef (Harris), this writer feels that the trouble caused by Alice Marble was for naught. We hear about so many 'coming champions' from California that we are beginning to cry 'Wolf, Wolf.'"

Allen rubbed it in the next day. "There is the sad, sad mistake of heralding unwisely a young player of mediocrity. . . . In the past, to this writer's knowledge, players have come forth from California possessed of far greater possibilities than this girl who is actually the victim of too much trumpeting. . . . She has no defensive game to speak of and is apt to be uncertain on her ground strokes."

After the mauling, Alice buried her head in her hands in the club-house, weeping in shame. After a while she managed to pull herself to-gether and head out to watch some of the other matches. "A pleasant, dark-haired woman walked in and sat beside me" in the stands, Alice recalled, and gave her a crucial pep talk, noting Alice's ability and great promise and mentioning that she had lost in the first round three straight years at Forest Hills. "Watch all the tennis you can," she advised. Also, Alice should find herself a teacher.

Alice liked this friendly fan of her game but had no earthly idea who she was. Later, she pointed the woman out to another player and was told, to her astonishment, that it was Mary K. Browne, whom Alice would call "Brownie," three-time national champion in the 1910s.

It was the beginning of another key relationship, one that would last nearly to the end of Alice's life.

In another beneficial turn of events, Alice had an easier assignment ahead, the junior championships in Philly, the reason for her eastern crusade in the first place. At the Philadelphia Cricket Club she learned she was top seed, a boost for her confidence. Unlike virtually every player, Alice wasn't escorted by family or chaperone or boyfriend, so she spent most of her time writing letters home or staring at other players in hopes of gleaning some tips on improving her own game.

Something clicked, for she made the finals before losing on a "hot and damp Saturday" to the "tall and slender" Ruby Bishop. Bishop was from Pasadena and was headed for UCLA after the summer. She "used soft lobs and chops to defeat her rival, and gave the gallery an exhibition of spectacular tennis" in the straight sets win.

"I ran off the court and into the dressing room and cried," Alice remembered. "How could I ever face people again?" When given the silver medal for second place, she hurled it across the room. "I don't want the damn thing!" she screamed.

Still steaming, Alice went out to play in the doubles final shortly afterward. "I was in a white heat," and she just walloped every ball that came to her without regard for tactics. Her partner, Bonnie Miller, was frustrated as her partner played without caring to win. Given a stern talking-to by tournament officials after dropping the first set, Alice belatedly realized it wasn't Miller's fault Alice had lost in singles, and from then on she played under control, leading to a comeback victory. "I almost forgot I had lost in singles less than two hours before," she said.

But there was one thing she wouldn't forget about the loss to Ruby Bishop. She ruminated on it on her long trip back to California. Bishop had an excellent teacher to help develop her game. Alice decided she needed help, and would get it from that same source.

Eleanor Tennant.

Chapter Eight

....

THE FIGHTER

"My whole life changed the moment she walked into our house," Alice wrote of Eleanor, the woman responsible for turning her into a champion.

Of all the people in Alice's life, from her bygone father to her domineering brother to her songbird mother, none would have the instant impact and lifelong influence of Eleanor Tennant, her coach/teacher/manager/Svengali and likely, for at least a brief time, lover. She would drive Alice to greater heights than she could have achieved on her own and nurse her back from depths that would have entombed others for good. She would move mountains for her protégé, go far further to ensure her well-being than she would for any of her many other students; and in the end, her closeness with the woman she molded into greatness would undo their relationship.

That they came together in the first place was testament to Eleanor's incredible will.

• • •

Eleanor, like Alice, was a child of the Bay; her San Franciscan childhood was peripatetic for a while, the Tennant family moving around a few times before settling on Broderick Street near the Presidio, several blocks north of Marble's future home in the Sunset District. Born in 1895 to John Henry Tennant, an Englishman, and his American wife, Eliza Cosgrove, Eleanor was the seventh child of eight. As with Alice, Tennant's family moved to the city upon hard times. John Henry, a proper gent with a large nose, white mustache, and usually seen wearing a top hat, had made a small fortune during the gold rush (unlike the Marble men), and invested his money in the Gilroy Hotel, which went belly-up. He was a political animal and self-funded multiple unsuccessful runs for local office, including mayor. He was leveraged to the hilt, thanks to mortgaging everything he owned and not doing much to bring in income. "There were many years my father didn't work," Eleanor would remember.

In response, her mother, Eliza, didn't speak to Eleanor's father for many years, right up until his death in 1910, when Eleanor was fifteen. "[Mother] never reprimanded him or carried any torch about it," Eleanor said, and given her strict religious fervor, divorce was out of the question. Should there be an issue that required contact with her husband, Eliza would relay a message through one of her children, and the child would be expected to wait for a reply.

The household was further divided along religious lines, with the first four children raised Protestant, the next quartet (including Eleanor) Catholic, after Eliza converted.

As a child Eleanor would run to church every day to pray to Saint Anthony, but around the time of her father's death she questioned her faith. She would cast about for a higher power for many years, studying the finer aspects of other Christian denominations, Judaism, Christian Science, even an esoteric sect called Theosophy that gained brief sway in the early years of the twentieth century. But Eleanor never was satisfied with their "paths to understanding" and "gave them all back to the Indians" (i.e., gave them up); she reluctantly returned to the flock late in life.

The house on Broderick Street was a fun place to grow up, a sprawling pile with a large basement that was a child's dream house, as well as a yard and stately garden. But it was hardly a loving environment, made even more contentious by Eliza's austere nature. She was a tyrant about cleanliness; the house was expected to be swept spotless before the kids left for school, and Saturdays were given over to a stem-to-stern tidying that was to be completed by noon, "No ifs and buts about that," Eleanor said. "Our reward would be to take a walk, which was usually six or eight miles, and go up into the hills and pick wild flowers. That was a big treat for us."

Illness was simply not permitted at the Tennant place. Eliza never gave in to being sick, never complained, and insisted her children follow suit. Bellyaching, even about a legitimate ailment, was strictly verboten. If a child got so ill that bed rest was unavoidable, Eliza refused to give the stricken kid any food—just a glass of water. John, "who was very chicken-hearted," according to Eleanor, would smuggle bread and other morsels past his despotic wife in order to ease the stomach rumblings.

Eleanor responded to the Dickensian household not with expected resentment but gratitude. "If I hadn't had to work I'd have been a first class loafer," she often claimed, and she fairly idolized her mother—the sterner she got, the more Eleanor dug it. Even the harsh bedside manner got a thumbs-up. "Illness can be treated too softly," she mused years later. Her main ambition from an early age was to be an earner, to help out the strapped family, especially after John passed away.

Eleanor's main household chore was to keep the family woodpile— ensure that there were always logs to burn, which meant a lot of cutting in the local glens (even urban San Francisco was heavily wooded at the time) and taking a strop to the cutting tools, keeping the axes and saws sharp. Meanwhile, she was forever running errands for neighbors at a quarter a pop, or dashing to pick up men's hats that had blown from passing streetcars, a retrieval service that was worth a dime per lid. When the great earthquake of 1906 leveled much of the city (the Tennant house was spared, fortunately), Eleanor gamed the relief effort by wearing roller skates to food lines, thus appearing older and entitling her to a larger handout of free goods.

Ironically, given the financial straits of the family, and the fact her older brothers were off working rather than in school, the de facto response in the Tennant home was to knock Eleanor's hustle. They called her "money-grubber" and jealously said that she "always had a dollar."

She was so much like Alice in so many ways, right down to her early stammer and a speech impediment, one that left her unable to pronounce her r's properly. Combined with a slight British accent courtesy of her old man, Eleanor was the subject of playground cruelty. She was teased endlessly. "Their laughter was very cruel," she told her biographer, Nancy Spain, with a wince. At times she would be sent to the grocer for food, only to return empty-handed, as the clerks couldn't make out her order, so bad was the stuttering. Sheer will and fast fists got her through the day. "I was quite the scrapper," Eleanor said, and she left a steady string of busted noses and bleeding mouths in her wake.

She soon added larceny to her rap sheet. With much of the city reeling after the earthquake, the Tennants regularly took in boarders, who ate at the table along with friends the children had brought home for supper, so Tennant family dinners could be crowded affairs. "I often wondered where we got the money for them," Eleanor mused later in life. One passer-through was a woman named Myers, who showed up with a tennis racket she had saved from her burning house. Eleanor had never seen the device before and promptly stole it. Mystified and heartbroken, Miss Myers turned the house upside down looking for it, but Eleanor had hidden the racket in her woodpile, and "no one ever went near my woodpile."

Now sporting a boosted racket, Eleanor went looking for a use for it. One morning en route to school she spotted a woman carrying a racket with a waterproof cover embarking a streetcar to Golden Gate Park. Roused by curiosity, Eleanor ran alongside the streetcar all the way to its sylvan destination. Once in the park she followed the woman to the court and hid in the bushes, studying the game she was playing.

Fortunately for Eleanor, she had miraculously tailed and reconnoitered not some weekend hacker but a top player from the dawn of women's tennis, Golda Meyer (later to compete under her married name, Gross). Her smooth play and the overall vibe at the park appealed to Eleanor, just as it would to Alice roughly two decades hence. Soon she became absorbed in the game, skipping school almost every day to head to the "Chicken Coop," the outermost court with the worst, roughest surface and the least experienced players. Completely self-taught, Eleanor relied on the scrappiness she picked up battling schoolyard tormentors to overcome her lack of polish. "It was the serve that bothered me chiefly," she remembered. "Took me ages to figure out it was the same movement as the way one throws a baseball."

Word got out that a new player was cleaning up the Chicken Coop, and soon she was invited to join the Girls' Tennis Club. She was rated a four on a scale of one to four, with one the best, but she walloped all but the top players. She couldn't get past the experienced girls, who toyed with her. It would be a lesson that would inform her coaching days. She believed thereafter in "keeping your player back a bit, have them play against tougher opponents, so that they're working and learning something, so that they profit from their losses."

John's death at age seventy-nine in late February 1911 sapped Eleanor's already wavering attachment to higher education. Inevitably, her school wearied of the abandonment and sent word to the Tennants that Eleanor had essentially dropped out. At age sixteen, she made it official when her older brother Lytton paid for her to attend business college, which left evenings for tennis.

By 1915 she was among the best players in the Bay Area and a regular competitor at larger competitions like the Pacific Coast Championships, though she was not yet a threat to crack the national or international scene. She was particularly adept at doubles, while also winning the Shreve trophy, given to the winner of the ladies' handicap singles title at Golden Gate Park each year, three times (Eleanor was "owe 15"—she started down a point in every game).

While Eleanor's game improved, she took on a steady stream of jobs to repay her brother and help her mother. She became a secretary for a local businessman even though she couldn't spell. Fortunately, neither could the man. "Maybe we'll both learn," he said cheerfully. Instead, Eleanor moved on, to gigs in real estate, at a grocer, and then selling newspaper subscriptions, hawking the *Examiner* and the *Chronicle* door-to-door.

She proved a gifted saleswoman, despite her stammer, refusing to take no for an answer. One customer was impressed enough to recommend Eleanor for a different job, as the first female commercial traveler for Standard Oil. The gig was selling oil and petroleum distillate to motorists and service stations, and it required lots of hard travel on California's primitive roads (yes, the "Freeway State" once was anathema to automobiles). The cars provided for her by Standard often blew out engine parts on the road, leaving Eleanor to dip into her sales stash in order to make it to the next garage.

It was a rough job, and as a woman, she faced no shortage of harassment and harsh treatment. But she was good at it, amassing enough commission after just a few weeks to take a vacation to Los Angeles in the early winter of 1913.

Chapter Nine

....

La La Land

"I've never been shy about going after what I want," Eleanor once said to Alice. What she wanted in this critical journey south down Highway 101 was to meet Maurice McLoughlin, aka the "California Comet," the top tennis player in the country at the time. Somehow she determined where the Comet lived and boldly rolled up to his front door. Remarkably, not only did McLoughlin not have her arrested, but he allowed himself to be talked into doubling with Eleanor in a match he was about to play at the Beverly Hills Hotel.

Save perhaps her theft of Miss Myers's racket, it was the sparking incident of Eleanor's life. Awaiting the newly formed partnership at the hotel were their opponents: William Churchill de Mille, film director and writer and the older brother of the more famous Cecil B. DeMille (William used the family's original spelling), and Rear Admiral Cameron Winslow, a naval hero in the Spanish-American War and commander in chief of the Pacific Fleet. More important, he was married to Theodora Havemeyer, heiress to a sugar fortune and the uncreatively named daughter of Theodore Havemeyer, who cofounded the Newport Country Club and was the first president of the US Golf Association. Most important, he was an ardent tennis player.

"They were real Newport blue bloods," Eleanor recalled, and the Winslows, including their six children and nanny, had taken over the entire top floor of the hotel. She could scarcely countenance the surreal scene. Here she was, a girl scant months removed from her teenage years, from a poor background and sporting a good but hardly precocious tennis game, playing doubles with a film impresario, a top naval officer from a superrich family, and the best male player around. Unsurprisingly, she floundered about for two sets, though their opponents took mercy on them. Then she "came up for air" in the third set, and miraculously they pulled out a victory, which "sort of saved my bacon." The quartet continued to play regularly over the next two weeks, playing for "five dollars a set." Fortunately for Eleanor, she wasn't expected to come up with the cash herself, and she played well enough to keep the ledger close enough to level.

The *Los Angeles Times* even took note of a couple of matches, ones that had Winslow partnering with Florence Sutton—a highly accomplished player who lost the 1911 US Nationals in three thrilling sets—against Eleanor and McLoughlin. The *Times* reported that the naval officer's play was "remarkable for one who gets as little practice as he does, and who has sixty-two summers to his credit, a fact which would never be believed on the tennis court."

Admiral Winslow invited Eleanor to dinner after that first match, and though heads spun and tongues wagged at the sight of a poorly dressed commoner supping with the "blue bloods," the family, especially the half dozen children, ranging in age from three to eighteen, was quite taken with her. She anointed herself camp director for the fortnight, playing endless games of Ping-Pong and splashing about in the hotel pool with them, relieving the Winslows of chasing after their brood.

At trip's end she took McLoughlin aside. "Maurice," she confessed, "I'm sorry but I have to go home now, and I don't know what I'm going to do, because I am not going to be happy living in San Francisco and being a saleswoman for Standard Oil. This opportunity I've had has awakened me to another world. And I want to get into it."

Fate intervened. As it happened, the assistant manager of the Beverly Hills Hotel, Stanley Anderson, had just asked McLoughlin about Tennant—specifically, whether or not she would be interested in hiring on as tennis instructor.

And just like that, she became the first tennis pro at the Beverly Hills Hotel. She was all of twenty years old.

• • •

The girl who seemingly moments before had been hustling after wind-blown hats for spare dimes was now at the center of the poshest scene in the burgeoning Los Angeles area. The director of the Beverly Hills Hotel was a woman named Margaret Anderson. She had moved west in the 1870s at age fifteen from Iowa and promptly married a Danish immigrant and had a pair of children, including her oldest, the aforementioned Stanley. A contentious divorce left Margaret with almost nothing, save a small home in what would become downtown LA, at a time when most of the city was still farmland. She turned the home into a boarding house, and due to its location it became the spot for out-of-town moneymen to bed down and get a good meal, cooked by Margaret herself. In due course she parlayed the business into owning and operating the Hollywood Hotel.

A couple of her satisfied customers had heavy investments in bringing water to the Southern California desert, and they were particularly interested in the Beverly Hills area, "halfway to the sea" from downtown, as a place for further development. They asked Margaret and her partner, Martha Stewart (no, not that one), if they wanted to run a hotel in Beverly Hills. She did, of course, and her backers spent half a million dollars (nearly $15 million today) to construct a T-shaped structure designed by eminent architect Elmer Grey in Benedict Canyon. Grey based the design on a Franciscan mission, with a long, winding driveway, several outlying bungalows, and enormous gardens, where future guests could grow and pick their own flowers. BEVERLY HOTEL TO BE

WONDER OF SOUTHLAND, bugled the *Los Angeles Times* in May 1911, when plans were announced. It opened a year later, on May 12, 1912, a month after the *Titanic* went to her watery grave.

At the time, Beverly Hills was hardly the ultra-swank playground for the rich it would become. Thirty dusty miles from Los Angeles, there was hardly anything there beyond horse trails and leafy canyons, though the streetcar system extended through the small downtown, so the commute to and from LA wasn't as difficult as it might have been.

The hotel was a key turning point for the area; another was when Stanley Anderson, on his mother's behalf, managed to convince Douglas Fairbanks Jr. and Mary Pickford, the biggest stars of the silent film era, to move there. They established the "Pickfair" ranch, and suddenly the Hills were the in spot for Hollywood's elite. Another megastar, Marion Davies, moved just above the hotel, and the star power drew in wealthy oil and water magnates as well.

The hotel tennis courts were just in front of the sloping lawn that led to the street, and large crowds often gathered with picnic lunches to watch silent stars like Tony Moreno and Edith Storey hit with Eleanor. One of her first pupils was Harry Aken, a studio executive who sent plenty of people in the industry to learn from the pro at the hotel. A young ingenue named Joan Crawford was very enthusiastic, to the point she overdeveloped her right arm. Eleanor had her play lefty for weeks to even out her physique.

Of course, Eleanor was hardly Suzanne Lenglen. Though she was good enough to be considered among the best twenty or so players in the state, and was named to play in the Pacific Coast Championships during her first week on the job, she was still learning the game and, more important, how to improve other people's games. Aken would turn up every day at 7 A.M. for his lesson, so Eleanor would arrive well before that and take forty-eight balls onto the court, hitting and dissecting her own abilities. "I learnt I was critical and analytical and discerning. And I loved people, I loved tennis. So teaching was duck soup." Her chipper attitude belied the fact that she wasn't actually living at the hotel. She bunked with some friends who lived six miles away, and she walked to and fro each day, meaning she often arose well before dawn to get to the hotel in time.

She had the run of the facilities when she got there, though, and soon tennis instruction became just one of her duties. As she had been with the Winslow children, she became something of a camp counselor, organizing bowling games, Ping-Pong matches, and, to win over what she called the "rocking-chair crowd"—that is, the older guests—bridge foursomes.

She also began leading early morning horse tours into the beautiful, largely undeveloped hills behind the hotel. The kitchen would send a car stuffed with the makings of a hearty breakfast to a sylvan glen, and Eleanor would take a half dozen guests to meet it. A chef would cook over an open fire, and elegantly dressed waiters would serve the fixin's out in the wilderness. Occasionally a bear would smell the repast and investigate, leading the group to clank the pots and pans together or seek shelter in the car.

Tongues wagged, and soon magazine writers were turning up, hoping to enjoy some of the California sunshine, especially while the rest of the country froze. Eleanor became a de facto public relations agent, arranging rides down to Santa Monica and the ocean, where guests (and travel reporters) could splash into the sea, on or off their mounts.

Amid the fun, Eleanor took the time to improve other life skills. She hired a tutor from the hotel to give her the high school education she had missed, learning spelling, history, science, and math. She became well-known in the area. "Miss Tennant is a crack tennis player from San Francisco, who came here recently and has been playing a game which has attracted much attention to her since her arrival," cooed the *Los Angeles Times*. She was considered a "breezy westerner" who embodied the California openness guests from the East and Midwest lapped up. She was also notable for her chain-smoking, even while giving her tennis lessons or leading a trail ride (presumably she took a break for dips in the pool).

Later, Alice would note that "Eleanor loved being the center of attention. . . . This was true whether she was with movie stars or millionaires or servants. Everybody loved [her]. She could tell stories—clean or raunchy, depending on the company—for as long as she had an audience."

That charisma was on full display at the Beverly Hills Hotel. Guests followed her lead on everything, all over the hotel, even to the ballroom, where she was an enthusiastic, if hardly graceful, dancer. She was even photographed for the *Los Angeles Times*—which was quite taken with her—having "high tea" with Sutton at the hotel. Europe was in flames, losing the cream of a generation to the mindless meat grinder of World War I, but at the Beverly Hills Hotel, all was gay. Fridays there was dancing late into the night. Sundays were for singing, with the legendary singer-songwriter Carrie Jacobs Bond in residency. It was a glorious life for a young woman from little to no means.

In October 1917, Tennant was involved in a bizarre incident that would presage many automotive difficulties for both her and Alice. On a visit back home to San Francisco, she motored off for a relaxing day on horseback with a friend, Mrs. Samuel Shumons of Atlanta. The women returned to San Francisco only to be caught up in a pitched battle between striking streetcar employees and strikebreaking thugs sent to rough them up. They crashed the car (Mrs. Shumons was driving) at Twelfth and Mission and narrowly avoided being hit by flying bullets fired by the rioters, according to a report in the *Oakland Tribune*. "I am thinking of driving an ambulance at the front as a change," quipped Mrs. Shumons.

Eleanor was indeed living a rich and interesting life. But she wasn't making much money to show for her hard work, at least at first. She was loath to present bills or complain about overwork or extra duty like the guided tours, and since many guests didn't settle up until checkout, which might not come for weeks or even months, Eleanor had to stretch her small income. She continued to commute by foot and ate her meals at her flop spot, not in the sumptuous dining room (though sympathetic staff slipped her food). At least cigarettes were cheap, and Eleanor sucked down several packs a day.

Eleanor's monetary fortune started to turn when her notoriety as a teacher and good companion grew to the point where she was asked to head east during the summer of 1918. Some guests from Ohio enjoyed her company so much they staked her travel for a couple of months as pro at the Cleveland Yachting Club. "So I ceased to be just a California sunflower," she remembered. Indeed, it was her first trip out of state. It was a good deal—Eleanor lived for free at the club and was paid 500 dollars a month on top of it. She sent 150 dollars of that home to Eliza. Other swells fell hard for her, too, and paid for Eleanor to come to New York for more lessons. They then provided a car and driver to ferry her to other teaching gigs in Washington and Atlantic City. "I became a well-traveled young woman," she said, and all due to her incisiveness at analyzing the tennis games of strangers.

The gravy train ended abruptly, however. Upon her return to Beverly Hills, the grande dame herself, Margaret Anderson, strolled out to the courts. She at last offered Eleanor an actual staff job at the hotel, which would focus more on PR than tennis, at 150 dollars a month. Eleanor naively blurted that she was making considerably more than that from tennis, and Margaret, who ran the operation with a ruthless eye on costs, fired her.

As the writer Elizabeth Wilson put it in her tennis history, *Love Game*, "A pattern of highs and lows was to develop in [Eleanor's] life. Each employer liked and valued her to begin with, but eventually there was usually a falling-out."

Worse than losing her job was the loss of her amateur status. While teaching at the hotel, Eleanor had played in tournaments around the Southland, always keeping one eye on her ranking. She didn't push as hard as she could for the top, perhaps, because she was devoting so much time to the hotel. Now, however, the United States Lawn Tennis Association, the arbiter of all things tennis in that era, decided that because she had made money for playing, even if it was just teaching and some well-publicized bets, she was a "professional," and thus no longer welcome in their strict amateur world.

Eleanor, as was her wont, did not take the decision lying down. She appealed to anyone and everyone to lobby the USLTA to change its mind, and after many months of lost play, in the fall of 1919 she was at last allowed back on the hallowed amateur circuit. "Local tennis fans are delighted," reported the *Times*. "She plays with an easy grace, no effort being wasted." Sure enough, she won the very first tournament she entered, the LA City Championships in September 1919.

In the meantime, Eleanor exploited her foothold into society. She was often in the company of Rosamond Runyon, the daughter of an eastern coal baron who moved west and became active in social circles, especially horse-related activity (Runyon Canyon Park, at the east end of the Santa Monica Mountains, is named for him). The Bay Area papers also noted Eleanor's vacations to the golf resort at Wawona in Yosemite Valley with Valerie Timken, wealthy heiress to the Timken Roller Bearing Company of Canton, Ohio. Gossip flew about the closeness these ladies shared, with men and marriage apparently not particularly important to them. Ignoring it all, Eleanor moved into Valerie's home in Beverly Hills.

But before the rumor mill got completely cranked up, Eleanor was on a train east. In the spring of 1920, Eleanor challenged the top ladies in the nation at tournaments up and down the Atlantic seaboard. She took them on while wearing the getup of the day—a long pleated skirt that fell to just above her ankle, a collared blouse with a thin belt, and a black necktie. Her dark hair was cut short and parted severely in the middle. During colder tournaments she wore a thin sweater and a thicker tie. She grabbed the national clay-court title and made the doubles final at the US Nationals, losing with partner Helen Baker. She finished the season ranked number three in the country. Her 1921 season wasn't as successful, though she got a lot of practice time in with a "young girl in pigtails" named Helen Wills, who soon would be much more prominent.

Though she was a top-five player by any ranking, Tennant mysteriously pulled out of the '21 US Nationals, to be played in Forest Hills. While the great Suzanne Lenglen was dramatically collapsing due to a "renewal of her attack of bronchitis" and defaulted in the early going of the tourney, Eleanor was on a train back west, missing a chance to play against a less accomplished group of opponents.

And then, suddenly—shockingly—she was married.

The first anyone knew of the nuptials was from reports in the press a couple of days later, with the lede in the *San Francisco Chronicle* reading, "Coming as a surprise to even their closest friends . . ." and the *Los Angeles Times* running an illustration of Eleanor and writing, inevitably, that she had made it "love-all in marriage game."

Eleanor had indeed married, alongside her "intimate friend" and housemate Valerie Timken, in a double wedding in Hollywood on August 30, 1921. So out of left field was the ceremony that the only witnesses were Valerie's grandparents. Eleanor married a friend of her older brother Lytton, Lyman Potter, a stolid, bluff man with a perpetual frown, then a stockbroker in San Francisco. Five years her elder, Lyman was friendly with Eleanor back when both were young, but hardly great pals. There was no mention of Lyman in Eleanor's very public doings over the previous few years, but according to Valerie, they had reconnected in the past year after not seeing one another since the old days. "Mrs. Potter will make her home in Burlingame [a suburb of San Francisco], where they expect to build," Valerie told the papers. Eleanor was not quoted about any of it.

Valerie likewise married a broker, George Sturgis, a Texan who had come out to Pasadena in order to squander some of his fortune. There was a small affair at the Beverly Hills Hotel bungalow where Valerie's mother lived, but that was the extent of the celebration of Eleanor and Lyman's "love."

"We are mailing out announcements now," Valerie told reporters who caught wind of the snap wedding. "This is the first inkling of the wedding to our friends."

For the next couple of years, Eleanor made a go of being Mrs. Potter, San Franciscan housewife. She gave up competitive tennis, playing only occasionally in exhibitions. She took up golf, and got so skilled she won some citywide tournaments. Lyman was recruited to become president of the Castoline Lubricating Oil company on Mission Street, an ironic turn in his career given his wife's former role hawking motor oil in the early days of automobiling.

But it all went downhill in the second year of the marriage. In September of '23, Eleanor sued for divorce. Her attorney, Algernon Crofton, told the court that Lyman "almost from the time of their wedding has refused to provide her with amusement or entertainment." He was "sullen, morose, and even insolent" and had caused "great mental anguish." He said in July that he was "through with her," and in August, on their second anniversary, he presented her with a check for seventy-five dollars, then "snatched it from her, tore it up, cursed her and then laughed at her."

Worst of all, Eleanor claimed Lyman "seized her by the throat and shook her violently." Eleanor said she was forced to live in Lyman's mother's house, a few blocks from her girlhood home, compounding her humiliation.

She asked for 250 dollars a month in alimony, a large sum for the time, and she filed and won a restraining order for her property. Potter fought back angrily. At one point in the proceedings his lawyers introduced testimony that Eleanor had racked up an 800-dollar clothing bill, including "shoes, gowns, $15 stockings, and hats" since she had brought suit. He argued that she was not in need of any new clothing, given how well he had provided for her in marriage.

It was hard to argue that particular point when Eleanor set down her alimony terms. Judge Clinton Morgan asked Eleanor, "What's the least amount you could live on?"

"I couldn't possibly do with less than $80 a month," she replied. "My golf lessons alone cost me $40."

Judge Morgan considered the request sagely before intoning, "If lodge and club dues help to keep alimony down there seems no good reason why golf should not send it up. These are the days of equal rights. The alimony is allowed."

San Francisco—enlightened even in 1923.

She won her divorce as a matter of course, and they parted, with Eleanor allowed to return to using her maiden name in addition to winning 200 dollars a month in alimony and 14,000 dollars in "securities." In early January of 1925 she was forced to sue Potter again, this

time for an outstanding 299 dollars she was owed from the divorce settlement. She won, and he paid up, but the continuing "tish-tush," as she
described the airing of her dirty laundry in public, was causing her more
mental stress than the marriage itself had. According to Alice's memoir,
the true reason behind it all was that Lyman had run off "with a well-
known lesbian" named "Madame Helene," for a brief but torrid affair.
What is known for sure is that in short order Lyman had found someone
else—he eloped with Lydia Franzina, a "prominent member of the
younger set," according to the *San Francisco Examiner*, and they revealed
their marriage in the spring of 1925.

Meanwhile, for the next few years Eleanor continued to play in West
Coast tourneys, as well as an annual one in Mexico City that she would
capture several times. While she never ventured east, she did have an
impact there—the French-style watchman's cap she wore on court
sparked a brief craze in 1926. "Here it is, girls—the latest in tennis head-
pieces!" screamed papers across the nation. Eleanor's crooked smile and
poor teeth were displayed in the photo accompanying the wire service
story.

Beyond fashion, she harbored dreams of returning to the pinnacle
of the sport, because, as she put it in her inimitable argot, "tennisly
speaking I had loads of aptitude and coordination and ball-sense in car-
load lots." But her day had passed. Helen Wills was now the "Queen of
ice and snow and all the rest of it" (more Tennantese). She turned pro
instead (or, if you count her days at the Beverly Hills Hotel as professional, "re-turned" pro). But there wasn't much demand for her services
anymore outside of Golden Gate Park, where it all began for her, and
those were small-time paydays.

She also claimed to have been "knocked for such a loop" that she
was on the verge of a nervous breakdown, though she continued with
her regular appearances in tennis and golf events. In another presaging
of future events, she was even diagnosed as tubercular, though that
proved to be false.

She took a job as a desk woman at a small hotel, the Del Monte Inn, part of the larger development in Monterey that included the luxury Hotel Del Monte and the Pebble Beach Golf Links. It became a cooler, foggier version of Eleanor's time at the Beverly Hills Hotel, complete with autodidacticism—she read Plato and the Greek philosophers during the day to "give herself a mental lift." She hobnobbed with celebrities, including the likes of Douglas Fairbanks, whom she introduced to badminton. The star returned to Hollywood and made the game a brief fad among the film community. She lived on her alimony and her small paycheck ("My salary was really an Irishman's promotion compared to what I had before," as she put it). And she had occasional dalliances with women who came to stay at the hotel.

It was an interesting, if hardly lucrative, life, one that Eleanor might have kept with had she not stumbled upon an offer to head south to La Jolla and teach tennis to a pair of wealthy brothers for a week. She dropped her last 125 dollars on a Model T Ford with tires that were so worn "they could only last 125 miles before a blowout." The stint at the Casa de Mañana was a success, and the quiet San Diego suburb was rich with potential clientele, so she stuck around and put out her tennis-coaching shingle.

Needing a place to practice regularly, she found a couple of courts that were in perfect condition but hardly touched by human feet. They belonged to the Bishop's School, a private Episcopalian institution a few blocks from the Pacific. She didn't bother asking permission—she just rolled up and began her clinics. Soon she was teaching several dozen people a day. Occasionally she taught mass clinics of one hundred kids at a time.

Teaching the multitudes instilled a certain mentality in Eleanor. She was not capable of nuance, of adapting her methods to her individual students. She took on a "my way or the highway" approach, one that only hardened as she got more popular as a teacher, her success reinforcing her ways.

Belatedly, someone at the school confronted her usage of the courts, but instead of giving Eleanor the boot, the school hired her to run the tennis team. In return, Eleanor stayed there as a part-timer for over a decade. She also began to take on students from farther afield, including a wiry young girl from Pasadena, Ruby Bishop.

Ruby improved mightily under Tennant's tutelage, but it wasn't enough for Eleanor. Her oft-stated dream was to find a municipal player, one who hit from love and hunger rather than wealth and societal expectation, and turn him or her into a champion. She was still fostering that fantasy when Alice Marble began charging the net at the Golden Gate Park courts.

It was too perfect—another poor girl who had found her way to the same courts where Eleanor had gotten her start with a stolen racket and a dream. Soon Eleanor would help make both their dreams come true.

Chapter Ten

CANNONBALL RUN

Alice had a spot waiting for her when classes began at UC Berkeley in the fall of 1931, but "things looked different to me now," as she put it. She had taken her lumps in her initial eastern jaunt but also felt she belonged, and with so many people touting her blooming talents, Alice decided to forgo college for the time being. She took a job at a neighborhood book-shop to help raise cash for another eastern swing in 1932, and stepped up her practicing, mostly by playing with her favorite unofficial coaches, Kinsey and Fuller.

Harold Dickenson, still supposedly the love of her life at this point, was called "one of Kinsey's assistants" in an *Examiner* report on Alice's training, but any talk of marriage or ardor had apparently cooled, certainly on Alice's side of the love net, if it had ever really existed.

In the summer of 1932, Alice showed off her improved game, winning the California state title once again, this time not dropping a set in five matches. That earned her another train ride east, where she determined to concentrate mainly on the US Nationals at Forest Hills (save one warm-up tourney at Rye). Remembering the entry-form debacle of the previous year, "this time Alice put in five entries," wrote sportswriter George Currie, "not with the idea of being entitled to five eliminations, but with the notion of making sure that the draw committee would stumble across one of them."

She spent two full weeks in Queens practicing on the grass courts, stoically not taking the opportunity to take the train to Brooklyn to see her favorite, Lefty O'Doul, now with the Dodgers, patrol the Ebbets Field outfield. Such dedication paid off, for this time, she won a match.

Her opening opponent was the seventh-ranked player in the country, "little black-eyed Sarah Palfrey," according to the United Press, just a year older than Alice but far more experienced in big-time eastern play. Alice was her usual mix of breathtaking skill and wince-inducing butchery. She "played like Ellsworth Vines [the defending men's champ]," wrote one reporter. "Easy shots she flubbed and tough ones she tucked away." She put in enough tough ones to come back to win in three sets after dropping a tough opener 8–6.

In the second round Alice lost in three sets to Englishwoman Joan Ridley, appearing to give credence to Ridley's claim that "American girls eat too much. . . . They eat an hour before play a lunch enough for three of us. No wonder they get tired in a three-set match." Ridley's gamesmanship, rather than Alice's appetite, played the crucial role in this match. The "taffy-blond, green-eyed young miss from San Francisco" was a mere five points from victory when she hit an apparent ace that caught the chalk line.

Ridley, channeling her inner Depression-era John McEnroe, vociferously argued the call. "The ball was good beyond all doubt," reported Currie, but Ridley was insistent. "The linemen's view was blocked, the ball was out," she argued, and refused to budge. At length, the ball was ruled good, and "tension between Washington and No. 10 Downing Street was relieved," but Alice knew a crucial moment had passed. "My concentration was gone." Ridley stormed back to win in three sets, despite hitting but two "earned points," the period term for winners, to Alice's twenty-five over the last two sets, thanks mainly to Alice's lost focus and unimaginable eighty-two unforced errors. "Miss Marble probably broke all existing records when she committed 24 errors in five consecutive games of the second set," reported the Associated Press (AP) in recounting Alice's epic failure of control and nerve.

Despite the loss, Alice's booming serve from her "American twist" stance and sensational smashing and volleying made a great impression. One writer called her "Cannonball Alice." "It is high time," wrote another columnist, "that the 47 other states which have been seeking for so long to end California's domination of women's tennis, got wise to themselves, gave up, and turned to producing a rope climbing, hoop rolling, or jockstraps champion. For in women's tennis they aren't going to get to first base for many years to come. . . . Reason No. 1 is Miss Alice Marble of San Francisco."

Longtime tennis observer Henry McLemore opined, "Miss Marble's service . . . [i]s far and away the most severe in the business. When that first ball of hers smacks home, nine out of ten women players can't hit it with a butterfly net. This booming delivery works in beautifully with her ability at the net, affording her as it does an opportunity to storm the webbing for a sharply-angled volley or an outright kill."

These attributes were on display in the doubles competition, where Alice teamed with "a tall, likable girl from Boston," Marjorie "Midge" Morrill. They reached the semifinals, only to tangle there with Joan Ridley and her British compatriot, Elsie Pittman. For two and a half hours they played, well into the outer borough gloaming, the huge crowd "caught up in the fury of our match," as Alice put it, the players "straining to see balls in the lengthening shadows."

Fred Hawthorne of the *New York Herald Tribune* captured the excitement of the match:

> The most stirring play of the tournament was seen late last night when the sun had set behind the top rim of the lofty stadium bowl. . . . Consummate masters of the doubles game, the English pair were regarded as pretty sure to come through the match. But largely through the sheer speed and crushing power of the blonde and stalwart California girl, Alice Marble, well backed by Miss Morrill, the English pair were turned back. The

Californian's service was a deadly weapon of attack and many times Miss Ridley was not even able to get her racket on the ball. At times in the manner in which she leaped clear off the ground to bring down a high lob, Miss Marble brought back to mind that famous master of the smash, Maurice McLoughlin.

Indeed, Alice's game was regularly called "masculine" and compared to legendary male players such as McLoughlin. This form of backhanded compliment would become a common descriptor when analyzing her play in the years to come. But while her power tennis blew away opponents, she was still struggling with stroke play, especially on that deadening eastern grass. Tactics and court generalship were completely foreign to her—it was nothing but heavy artillery. And, as the match against Ridley had shown, she was still quite prone to maddening bouts of error-laden play. The tendency showed up more often in singles, without a partner to talk her down from the ledge.

The magnificent Marble/Morrill duo lost in the finals, but a national runner-up trophy was a heckuva pelt to bring back west. Alice seized the momentum, taking the train back to San Francisco for a week of intensive training with Kinsey, then raced down to Los Angeles, where she played in the Pacific Southwest tournament for the first time.

"It was difficult to keep my mind on tennis," she remembered, "for the boxes were filled with so many famous movie players."

The Pacific Southwest had been around for several years, but starting in 1930 it captured the attention of Hollywood, coinciding with the colony's rabid devotion to the sport. Half of the major studio talent, it seemed, were watching the action at the Los Angeles Tennis Club, just off Melrose Avenue in south Hollywood. Errol Flynn, Myrna Loy, Charlie Chaplin, Marlene Dietrich, Bette Davis, Claudette Colbert—the stars were in the sun! As *Sports Illustrated* later put it, "The big star who didn't occupy a front-row box at the Pacific Southwest tennis tournament sometime during the autumn week was pretty well obliged to turn in his sunglasses and unlisted phone number and find another occupation."

Alice was a massive fan of the "moving pictures," having been a regular in the cinema since childhood. Her idea of fun on Friday nights was to hit the movies with her family, and at around thirty-five cents per ticket, the price was right. In the near future she would be chiding Tennant for not recognizing many of the stars she encountered in her travels. Alice played very well despite her eyes wandering over to the gallery between every point. She made the finals and walked onto center court, which she recalled was "surrounded with the flags of every nation." Actor Robert Montgomery, the recent star of *Private Lives* with Norma Shearer, introduced the players "with a charming speech." "God, he was handsome," Alice gushed in *Courting Danger*.

Perhaps distracted, Alice beat herself in a loss to Anna Harper. After a tight 10–8 first set, Harper watched as her callow opponent sprayed balls all over the court, few of them within the lines, and took the title. Nevertheless, Harper had been a finalist at Forest Hills in 1930, so giving her a good battle was proof of the distance Alice had covered in just a year. And she proved to be a quick study once again, gaining revenge on Harper the following week back in San Francisco, winning the Pacific Coast title over the veteran to close out her season.

She would finish 1932 ranked first in Northern California and, amazingly, seventh in the country, a meteoric rise for someone so inexperienced. But she wasn't satisfied. There were still gaping holes in her game, and to make the leap to the next level she needed a coach like the woman who had been watching her from the stands at the LA Tennis Club.

·   ·   ·

Her upbringing in moody, chilly, Euro-flavored San Francisco had been forgotten. Eleanor Tennant was now fully a Southern Californian, a lady of the oranges, the golden sunsets, and the newly sprouted and instantly iconic palm trees (in 1931, as part of a work relief program, roughly four hundred men planted some forty thousand of the non-native trees along LA boulevards). The city was filling in around Beverly Hills and the surrounding communities between downtown and the ocean—horseback riding in the canyons was still a part of local life, but motorized transport had unequivocally taken over. Even then, cars and buses and trucks choked the streets, all utilizing the unique and ubiquitous service stations that suddenly popped up, like the umbrella-shaped station that sold General Petroleum on South La Brea or Howe's Complete Motor Service on Melrose Avenue ("Stop at the Sign of the Indian!"). Eleanor retained her passion for automobiling that was stoked by her early job with Standard Oil, and was only too happy to drive up and down the coast as her lessons demanded. But she was also a fashionista, and loved the "Dollar Day" sales at local department stores that were an LA tradition, where she could dress well on a budget.

She was hardly well-off, but by the standards of the day, she was in better shape than most, for the Depression was starting to bite California hard. "Look pleasant! Chin up! . . . Faith still does the impossible," exhorted the *Los Angeles Times* in an editorial on Christmas Day 1931, but far too many Angelenos were jumping off bridges to keep their chins aloft. The lack of tall buildings in the city meant the financially ruined used bridges to end it all, with the Arroyo Seco bridge in Pasadena being so popular for that macabre use that it earned the nickname "Suicide Bridge" and the city had to erect a high barbed-wire fence to stop the jumpers.

In August the Summer Olympics were held in LA, with Babe Didrikson the American star of the games. But they scarcely made a ripple in the city, with an unusually low number of athletes competing and fans attending, due to the worldwide downturn.

Eleanor, however, "sailed through the Depression without a hitch," as Alice marveled. Her skills as a teacher won her client after client. As one satisfied student wrote her, "I have found your suggestions most helpful. There are many who can criticize but there are so few who are constructive in their criticism and, while I have played with many good players and professionals, you are the only one that could show me in an understandable way how to proceed to overcome my faults." She was working hard but steadily; by this point Eleanor would winter in La Jolla but spend her summer and many weekends in Los Angeles, teaching at her old stomping grounds at the Beverly Hills Hotel and many other spots. Her skills as a teacher and renown as a formerly top-ranked player brought plenty of business her way, especially bold-faced names from the film colony to the east.

Tennis fever had gripped Hollywood. Loy, Flynn, Jean Harlow, Joan Crawford, Clifton Webb—there were few A-list movie stars who didn't line up and smack a forehand under Eleanor's watchful eye. She was well-known in the area and got many referrals, and it didn't hurt that she had visibly turned Ruby Bishop from a nonentity into a top-ten player. Many of her (famous) satisfied customers sent her signed notes of thanks, which she treasured. Peter Lorre wrote her one such note, reading, "My love for you is as great as my respect (that's enough, aint [sic] it?). All the best mama, always Peter." Barbara Stanwyck did, too: "Jeepers what a 'Teach' you are. Thank you for all your kindness and patience. Your most ardent fan, Barbara."

Marlene Dietrich, the German-born femme fatale, was another regular student. Her exotic looks and provocative style made her a film legend, both in silent film and the talkies, but off-screen she was far less flamboyant, even reserved. She was also quite athletic. While still in Berlin she was one of the rare female students of boxing, training in the gym of Turkish fighter Sabri Mahir. The actress brought her fitness to the tennis court, where she was more eager than refined, a lesser, Teutonic version of Alice Marble.

"Marlene wore a deeply tragic air," Eleanor said, "but every now and then would peel off and catch that ball such a sock I would say to myself, 'Oh baby there's nothing wrong with you.'"

Dietrich was famously bisexual, which would slot her in comfortably with many of her tennis-playing friends, including Eleanor, though by this point the coach had given up on men, even for appearances' sake. The scandalous end to her marriage had seen to that. She was "long on memory and short on forgiveness," as Alice wrote.

Dietrich had recently made the film *Morocco*, during which she kissed another woman on-screen, a daring, even shocking move for the time. Dietrich filled the moment with such allure that she became a lesbian icon thereafter. She had a string of love affairs that encompassed a wide range of talented artists of both sexes. She would later angrily denounce her homeland when the Nazis rose to power, and spent a large chunk of World War II entertaining troops across Europe, often getting uncomfortably close to the action.

But for Tennant, Dietrich's career might have been crippled, even ended. Both attended a party thrown by Carole Lombard held at a San Diego amusement park. The most popular sideshow was called the "Barrel of Fun," a revolving wooden drum that flung people around by centrifugal force. At one point Eleanor spotted Marlene about to be clobbered by a flingee and dove in between him and the actress. Eleanor got dragged around for her effort, but Marlene took only a glancing blow, thanks to Eleanor's quick action. La Dietrich ensured her irreplaceable legs were okay, then closed her eyes and muttered, "I must be taken from here."

Her thanks to Eleanor came in the form of paying for expensive private tennis lessons.

Eleanor had caught some of Alice in action in LA, but Harold Dickenson continuously encouraged her to travel north and watch his favorite young player more closely. So she arrived at the Golden Gate Park courts, a triumphal homecoming for the Park-bred Tennant that went unremarked upon, and took stock of the Marble oeuvre. Initially, Eleanor wasn't overly impressed by the seventh-ranked player in the USA.

There was "little to commend her game but bad temper," Tennant told a reporter some years later. She was "fat and heavy," with eccentric strokes and zero control over her anger. "When she didn't get the play she thought she would get, she would sock the ball—and I'm not kidding—it would go almost to the Chicken Coop a block from where we were playing."

And yet. "Something happened in my solar plexus," Eleanor confessed to her biographer. "This thing came to me which said she could be a world's champion."

That alchemy or second sight or magical ability to see beneath the outer layer to the champion waiting underneath was akin to the sculptor who sees the finished product within the marble slab. Alice was Eleanor's dream protégé, a wildly talented lump of clay that required industrial molding, a player with the innate ability and coordination to become a champion but one who desperately needed a complete mechanical overhaul, like the ones provided at LA service stations.

And when Eleanor was finished, and Alice was a champion, she would ensure that no one could ever doubt who it was that had made the difference.

PART TWO

Chapter Eleven

······································

Training Day

The ball appeared in front of Alice, waist high, a perfect position for a sock down the line. Winding up and taking an almost underhanded swing, like a baseball player going after a pitch in the dirt, she walloped it over the net, savoring the connection between racket and ball. She did it again and again. She was finding the sweet spot, hurtling the ball just over the net and on a flat line to the corners of the opposite court. It felt great.

After about ten of these a male voice yelled, "That's enough!"

Confused and angered, Alice stared at the man who had shouted.

"It'll never do," he continued, "and that's all there is to it."

. . .

Alice had wanted to ask to train with Eleanor, thanks to her admiration of the work the coach had done with Ruby Bishop. Eleanor came to her first. She offered Alice the opportunity to come to La Jolla and train at the Bishop's School (no relation to Ruby, who attended the prestigious Westridge School for Girls in Pasadena). The idea at first was to spend a month at a time down south during the winter months, to get Alice ready for the following summer.

The Marbles still were close to the poverty line, and work was ever more hard to come by. But Eleanor fixed this—Eleanor always could. She had ties at Wilson Sporting Goods, in addition to Harold Dickenson, and used her contacts to swing Alice a gig as a typist and file clerk that paid forty dollars a month. That would raise the money necessary to travel and pay Eleanor's fees and also begin an association with the equipment manufacturer that would last Alice the next quarter century.

Eleanor made a good impression on the two people who counted in the Marble clan—Dan and Jessie—though she almost blew it by taking Alice to Berkeley to hear some live music and keeping her out past Jessie's iron curfew of ten o'clock. Mother Marble was "curt and angry" but Dan talked her into approving, and after a month, Alice took the train south, into her future.

.   .   .

At first, Eleanor was regretting her decision. Upon arrival in La Jolla, Alice displayed a "truly shocking temper" and was "desperately untidy." When she first arrived, she "dropped her coat on a chair and her hat in some place else and her bag some place else," according to Tennant, who had grown up learning that untidiness was a waste of energy and insisted she keep everything clean and orderly.

Every day became a battle of wills, as Eleanor tried to break down her young charge completely, in order to rebuild her, while Alice struggled to retain her individuality. She wasn't a complete neophyte, after all—she had gone from a novice on a public court to the national championships. She resisted her new mentor's instruction at every turn.

Alice was confused by her new teacher's attitude and perhaps by her private life. Shortly after Alice arrived, someone had mentioned to her that Eleanor couldn't be her coach, as she was a lesbian. "What difference does that make?" Alice replied, not wanting to admit that she didn't actually know what the term meant, according to *Courting Danger*. She said she went straight to the dictionary: "Women from the island of Lesbos," it read. Could that be her nationality? Alice wondered.

"Finally an old friend enlightened me," she wrote.

At the moment, Alice was more concerned about Tennant's methods than her sexuality. "Tennis is a game of control and discipline," Eleanor told her. The accent seemed to be on the discipline. She demanded complete obedience from Alice, and the pupil's inner teenager rebelled. Her famous temper tantrums erupted daily, almost hourly. "She socked the ball all over the place," Eleanor said, "and acted like a spoiled brat and made it difficult for her opponent by hitting the ball in the bottom of the net or in the next court and other sort of insulting actions."

Early on, coach and student realized that Alice's strokes had to be revamped. Eleanor was at wit's end, but this allowed her to make an end run around the impasse they were at. One morning, Eleanor told Alice to get in her car, and they made the drive up the coast to Montecito, just east of Santa Barbara. They were going to meet someone, Eleanor said, who would help with coaching. After all, as she often said, "No one knows everything, least of all 'Teach.'"

They arrived at a tennis club in Montecito, and Alice was introduced to a "stern, tall fellow" whose gray eyes were "piercing" and whose bald head dripped with sweat. "His smile revealed tiny white teeth, which gave him a slightly carnivorous look," Alice wrote, but his manner was friendly. This was Harwood "Beese" White, a well-known, if eccentric, coach who specialized in working with women players, including Helen Jacobs, the current national champion.

He watched Alice hit for just a short time before ending the session, telling her in no uncertain terms that her entire approach to her ground strokes was wrong.

White immediately switched Alice from her Western, underhand grip to the Eastern grip, more commonplace today, which involves "shaking hands" with the racket and loosening the death grip of the Western style. Alice had noticed that when White played, he generated enormous pace without much arm movement. Alice, by contrast, was taking a giant baseball-style swing at every ball. In her mind, that was the "fun" way to play, one that incorporated more lively body movement.

Her initial foray with the new grip was tragicomic—balls sprayed everywhere, and she tripped over herself. "I thought I was about to lose my mind—I couldn't seem to *do* anything!" For a natural athlete like

Alice, it was torture. Finally she threw one of her patented tantrums and left the premises.

Eleanor managed to talk her down, and Alice agreed to give White one more hour. They drove up to his large home high up in the Santa Ynez Mountains overlooking the Pacific, a manse "isolated by citrus groves and woods." White was the scion of a wealthy furniture family from Michigan and had taken up tennis after a severe injury ended his gymnastics days. His lovely home included a sumptuous view and, more important, a tennis court.

White took Alice through the steps of what would become her new swing. Stepping into the ball. Meeting the ball where it was played, not whacking it mindlessly. "This is not a game of strength," he told her. Soon Alice came to realize that Beese knew what he was talking about, and she appreciated his patience. "If it had been me I would have told Teach to take her brat elsewhere," she admitted.

After some initial clumsiness Alice was all in on the new approach. She savored the sweet feeling of the ball going where she wanted it to with a minimum of effort. She could feel her command growing with every ball she hit.

Beese had her rally with male players, the only ones available who could hit at her level. Tennant insisted on playing five-set practice matches, instead of three, for similar toughening reasons—she felt five practice sets were the equivalent of three sets under match conditions. Alice built up her physical stamina while also learning to become far more mentally tough. At heart, Alice possessed little of the predatory nature so intrinsic to championship athletes. As Eleanor said, she was "basically not a fighter. She did not have in her ten cents worth of fight. Not a killer at all. Alice does not like me saying this." That killer instinct had to be beaten into her by Tennant. "You have to be mean to be a champion," she would say. "How can you lick someone if you feel friendly toward them?"

Beese insisted Alice read instructional pamphlets by the greats— Lenglen, Lacoste, Wills Moody. She said her photographic memory helped her digest the pages, but she disagreed with the lessons. It was all too technical, she found. They made the game too complex, more like an anatomy lesson or a ballroom dance than a sport. As it happened, White agreed with her take. He encouraged his students to figure out things independently, rather than take it all in via the drill sergeant method, as Tennant preferred.

The two coaches complemented one another. Tennant was keenly aware of the strengths and weaknesses of opponents, of the vagaries of different courts and the elements, and could design specific game plans for each. She also played a large role in changing the women's game of tennis from a defensive baseline game to an all-out attack with aggressive serves, overheads, and volleys. The style matched Eleanor's personality; it also played perfectly into Alice's existing strengths, the way she had played since she first picked up a racket. As such, Alice wasn't necessarily inclined to give Eleanor all the credit in this regard. "Miss Tennant was inclined to resent a pupil's assuming credit that she believed was due to the teacher," Alice wrote in *The Road to Wimbledon*.

White, by contrast, encouraged Alice to vary her tactics, to gain a keener sense of when to "storm the webbing" and when to set up her opponent with ground strokes. He valued the cognitive, almost mystical, approach, as much guru as athletic mentor. White was patient and intellectual; Tennant was tyrannical but highly motivating. It was like having both the bookish "Zen Master" Phil Jackson and Vince "Winning isn't everything; it's the only thing" Lombardi as coaches.

For the next decade Alice would return every winter for several weeks of training with White, staying in his guesthouse and enjoying the Edenic environment. It would prove a welcome respite from Tennant's full-on and unrelenting approach to coaching.

Chapter Twelve

···

DUEL IN THE SUN

As Alice prepared to travel east for play in the summer of 1933, she had traveled far from the chubby, slovenly, talented but raw player who had come south that winter. "She was in the family of Pygmalion," Eleanor said of her protégé, and it showed. Alice began a Spartan training program, at least by the standards of the time, that she would maintain the rest of her playing days. "She went to bed every night of her life at 10 pm," marveled Tennant. "She had the same breakfast every morning [lemon juice, half a grapefruit, egg, one piece of toast, and a cup of coffee] and after that she took a walk around the block and jumped rope for half an hour."

Of course, there were limits, as ordained by the strictures of the times. Alice began copying her coach and took up smoking, not to the same chain-puffing extent but enough to contribute to the lung problems that would plague Alice her entire life. She greatly enjoyed bartending, and wasn't averse to the odd drink or three. Red meat was a crucial part of her "athletic" diet, taken very rare, her hamburger mixed with scallions and parsley and cooked in butter. Alice dropped some twenty pounds and looked far leaner and more muscular than ever before.

Her appearance tightened to match her newly svelte physique.

"Alice always looked like a bandbox on the court," Tennant said. "She would never sit in her shorts before a match. She always cleaned her own tennis shoes. She packed her bag very meticulously. She was always on time." Soon Alice became so "orderly and meticulous I must say that at times I wondered if I was as orderly and meticulous as she was. . . . Once you told her something she did it."

Others were noticing. Little Bill Johnston assessed Alice at age nineteen. "Right now I would say she is a better prospect than Miss Moody was at her age . . . with seeming greater natural ability. With experience and hard work, she should be ripe to take Helen's place."

Alice cruised to the title in the minor Ojai Valley tournament in April, notable only in that the win earned Alice her first of what would become a multitude of mentions in *The New York Times*. Her first chance to truly test out her new game and look came at the Los Angeles Tennis Club in the Southern California championships in May. Here she displayed a sartorial change that would also have far-reaching effects. She exchanged the long skirts that were commonplace in the women's game at the time ("I just could abide skirts no longer," she said) for a pair of shorts. It is hard to imagine the shock that caused at first from today's perspective, where the idea of wearing anything but shorts for competitive tennis is asinine. And they weren't merely cut short but were tight and revealing, too, akin to what would later be called "hot pants."

She made the semifinals, where Alice fell in an epic three-hour-and-fifteen-minute match to old rival Helen Marlowe (now sporting the married name Dimitrijevic), 8–6, 10–12, 7–5. "It was 'pick up the marbles, the game's over for Alice Marble'" read the lede in the *Los Angeles Times*. Alice had match point and hit a seemingly unstoppable volley, but Marlowe "somehow scrambled over and got the shot, which she lobbed over her opponent's head. The ball just barely went over Miss Marble's racket, and landed right square on the baseline."

From there Alice "fell back on her old style, without the confidence that had carried those inferior skills," and lost the last five games and the match.

Despite the loss, Alice wowed the crowds with her play and style.

WELL, SHE LOST, read one headline after the defeat—everyone knew who "she" was. She whipped Anna Harper again in early July for another California State title, despite wearing a skirt for the home folks for unexplained reasons (it would be the last time she made that sartorial choice). From there, Alice boarded the train for points east, an ambitious schedule ahead. The *Examiner* thought "this summer will mark her third and most strenuous campaign," and she confessed, "I was still very unsure of myself," to the point she practiced her forehand in the train aisles. "People thought I was crazy," she said.

Alice proved up for the challenge. At the Longwood Cricket Club in Brookline, Massachusetts, Alice won her first eastern title, "showing no respect for the seedings or the national rankings" by taking care of top-seeded Carolin Babcock in straight sets. The following weekend she bested Babcock again over in Manchester-by-the-Sea, as the Massachusetts town is known, for her second silver cup. *The New York Times* was gaga. "A week ago at Longwood the San Francisco girl astounded the Eastern tennis public by overwhelming her higher-ranked California rival in straight sets. Few thought she was capable of repeating the feat," but Alice was, thanks in part to "a vicious kill that upset Miss Babcock into double-faulting" and tilted the match to Alice.

She stumbled on the Jersey Shore, falling in the third round at Seabright, owing to what she described as a stiff neck from little sleep. "I sat up last night looking at a misty sea," she told reporters while "wrapped in a huge blue-and-white striped muffler and an even huger white polo coat." Regardless, she figured to rebound the next weekend up the coast at the Maidstone Club in East Hampton.

Her play was "smooth, confident and decisive" (*Boston Globe*); "overpowering" (AP); "revealed speed beyond the hopes of most players today" (*The Californian*); "exceptionally effective" (*Oakland Tribune*). The stretch of excellence was surely enough for Alice to cinch a spot on the Wightman Cup team, in the opinion of all onlookers. Well, all but one, and he was the one who mattered.

The Wightman Cup was the women's equivalent of the Davis Cup, though its international competition only pitted the US against Great

Britain, not other countries. Held annually since 1923, the matches alternated between Forest Hills and Wimbledon. The USLTA chose the seven-woman squad based on results, presumably, but also on things like box-office power and back-channel politicking.

The USLTA consisted of multiple associations, but power was consolidated into the office of one man, the onetime president of the association turned untitled tyrant, Julian Myrick. Myrick was a life insurance salesman and tennis enthusiast from North Carolina who became instrumental in the construction of Forest Hills Stadium while serving as president of the West Side Tennis Club, a role he held in conjunction with the presidency of the USLTA. He helped popularize the sport in the media (delivering the first known speech about the sport ever broadcast on radio, on WJZ in New York in 1922). But he was also a court czar who ruled with an iron decree, even as he built a highly successful career in selling life insurance.

Myrick was not possessed of an imposing physique, nor commanding voice, nor hearty joie de vivre. How he came to foist his will upon the national tennis scene so thoroughly is a bit puzzling, though some of it was due to his capabilities as a paper pusher—his thorough knowledge of the personalities and eccentricities of the various state and local tennis organizing bodies allowed Myrick to arrange matters to his liking before they came up for debate at the national level.

Myrick's autocracy was, inevitably, controversial among the players. As early as 1927 star pro Vincent Richards called him a "dictator" who organized the various regional associations and fiefdoms "into a perfect political machine, which he controls. His policies have been the source of perpetual friction between the players and his associates; and it has almost come to the point where the former are ready to tear him from his throne and shout: 'Sic semper tyrannis!'"

Myrick commanded the Wightman Cup roster, and in that position he demanded Alice play both singles and doubles at East Hampton, a trial considering the tourney was to last just three days. He told Alice he was doing this because Helen Wills Moody had requested Alice as a doubles partner. This was, of course, a high honor, in particular because

Moody was, as one writer put it, "at home playing singles and at sea playing doubles." Choosing Alice as a partner was like being given an audience with the queen.

Alice offered to pass up on the singles, saving herself for the Cup matches, which would begin the following week. But Myrick dismissed the idea.

"You will have to prove your worth by making a good showing in that event," Myrick answered.

Alice countered by noting she had won two tournaments recently, and that neither Carolin Babcock nor Sarah Palfrey, two women Alice had beaten repeatedly of late, were required to "prove their worth" at the Maidstone Club on the island. Myrick, angry at his authority being challenged, yelled, "We will be the judge of who is to play—not you!" and stormed away.

It is important to note here that Eleanor was still in California, swanning around the courts with Carole Lombard and Marlene Dietrich and Errol Flynn. Had she been there to go toe-to-toe with Myrick, history may have been altered. But Alice was, as she put it, "nineteen, ambitious and stubborn." She would show Myrick what was what by winning by his rules.

A heat wave had settled over New York, with temperatures in the nineties for the first two days of competition. Alice played through it with gusto, advancing to the final day in both disciplines. Perhaps she would have been better served to throw a match, because her schedule for Monday, July 31, was insane.

Her journey began with the singles semifinal at 10 A.M. on a "dewy morn" that became a furnace as the sun rose in the sky. Marble beat Midge Van Ryn in three tough sets, 6–3, 6–8, 6–1. "Mrs. Van Ryn . . . gave the top-ranked player from California a rugged battle under a broiling sun," wrote the AP, and the pace slowed mightily as temperatures soared near one hundred degrees. Alice's visor, which she disliked as a fashion choice but admitted it helped "keep her hair back and was more comfortable than a bandanna," did little to ease the harsh glare of the midday sun. Sweat poured off her body, and the high humidity sapped even more moisture. "The pounding in my temples reverberated through my body," Alice remembered, "echoing painfully in my joints and turning my stomach into a queasy knot."

The doubles semis were next. She had but ten minutes of recovery time, as "Miss Moody is ready to play," a nervous official reminded Alice. Royalty doesn't wait for the commoners, after all. Moody's back was stiff, and she commanded her partner to chase down and hit all lobs and smash all overheads, which Marble dutifully did.

Alice appreciated Moody's greatness ("She whacked the hell out of the ball," she once exclaimed) but wasn't a fan of her haughty demeanor. Other players called her "Poker Face" or "Garbo" for her unapproachable mien. At age eighteen Alice had attended a luncheon held in Moody's honor, overseen by Pop Fuller, the great Helen of Berkeley's coach. Fuller had brought the two players together by somewhat naively asking Moody, now that she had won "everything in sight," if she wouldn't like to help Alice do the same.

Moody looked at the old coach like he had three eyes. "No, I wouldn't."

You couldn't blame Moody for not wanting to groom her replacement, but Alice resented her nonetheless. On this day, though, she hustled all over the Hamptons chasing down shots for her queen, and the duo won their way into the finals, 6–2, 9–7.

"How do New Yorkers stand this heat?" wondered the California girl. According to Alice, "the locker room scale showed I had lost five pounds. Every move was becoming an effort. My feet were on fire, my knees and elbows ached." She had less than an hour before she had to walk back out onto the scalding court for the singles final. She choked down a piece of toast and some tea with sugar and went back out for more.

Her nominal opponent was "Bounding" Betty Nuthall, but Alice's real enemy was the heat, which had climbed to 104 degrees, the mercury threatening to rocket through the top of the courtside thermometer. Alice gritted out a 7–5 first set but had nothing left after that, losing the next two sets, 6–3, 6–0. "I was completely exhausted," she wrote afterward. "My whole world had become the searing sun and the blur of a speeding tennis ball; sometimes I couldn't separate the two." Even Nuthall was concerned, asking the ashen Alice, "Are you all right?"

And yet, there was still another match to play: the doubles final. This was bordering on cruel and unusual punishment, but neither Moody nor Myrick let Alice off the hook. She could have—should have—simply defaulted, and few would have blamed her. But Alice refused to give in. She changed into her fourth outfit of the day, so exhausted she said she could barely button her blouse, and walked—more of a shuffle, really— onto the court again.

"Neither my muscles nor my brain cared to function," she said. Somehow the Marble/Moody pair took the match to three sets, which under the circumstances was hardly a consolation. They lost, and when Alice got to the dressing room, she was startled to see how loosely her clothes hung off her wrung-out frame. Out of morbid curiosity, she stepped on the scale once more and discovered she had lost a further seven pounds, down twelve pounds from when she trotted out to play her first match of the day.

She essentially had run an ultramarathon in dangerous conditions. She totaled 108 games across the four matches and nearly nine hours under the merciless sun. Her "yeoman work" was applauded heartily. "Hardened writers forgot their apathy for the moment and dramatized her exploit," wrote syndicated columnist Davis Walsh. "Spectators audibly marveled at her stamina and courage."

Another report waxed, "She met one opponent after the other, broke them down, swept them out of her pathway—and played on and on. She fought until the last ounce of energy had gone from her splendid body, and when still more was demanded of her, she played with all that was left—fierce determination, flawless courage.

"At the end she collapsed."

While her valor was undeniable, the effort took a toll on Alice that would reverberate for years.

Myrick and the USLTA came under heavy fire for forcing Alice to play so much merely to gain a spot on the Wightman team, which rightfully was hers all along. U.S.L.T.A. MAKES ANOTHER BLUNDER, read a typical headline. ALICE MARBLE LATEST VICTIM OF "OVERTENNIS EVIL," read another. Seven people died from the brutal heat that day in New York City, but "East Hampton was a little cooler than New York, so I guess [Myrick] thought it was all right," Walsh fumed. The fact that a girl "barely out of high school" would have to press on in such oppressive conditions merely to appease Moody and the crowds made Walsh wonder, "Is it sport?"

Alice was staying as a guest at a local home near the shore. Eleanor telephoned once she heard about the way her pupil had been treated. "If she'd had immediate salt injections she would have been right on her feet and ready for Nationals," she later fumed. "But instead of that they just threw some water on her." Too exhausted to eat dinner, Alice fainted. Tennant would later say she fell down the stairs as a result, but Alice said it was onto a couch. Either way, she was diagnosed with sunstroke and mild anemia stemming from the exertion in the heat.

But there was some good news, at least—Myrick, when he wasn't howling in protest at his rough treatment in the press, magnanimously announced that Alice had made the Wightman Cup roster.

Two days later, a doctor forbade Alice from playing singles, saying she hadn't recovered enough.

Her incredible effort wasn't completely for naught. The US side won four of the first six matches to clinch retention of the Cup, so with the seventh match a dead rubber (today they wouldn't have played the match at all), Alice took the court to play doubles with Midge Van Ryn. On the other side was Bounding Betty and her partner, Freda James. The Forest Hills courts "were in terrible condition. Patches of brown, dead grass mingled with stretches of green to give them the appearance of a crazy quilt. When the ball hit one of those patches it bounced like a drunken lunatic." That wasn't the reason Alice and Van Ryn lost in straight sets, however—Alice's "strength gave out."

She felt somewhat better the following week on the same courts at the nationals. She blew out three straight opponents to reach the quarterfinals, losing just four games total in the process. There she met—who else?—Bounding Betty Nuthall, on the western court of the three in the stadium.

It was another brutally hot day in New York. The great sportswriter Paul Gallico noted that both Nuthall and Alice wore shorts (Helen Jacobs had taken Alice's advice and also donned the culottes) "with the navy blue stripe down the side. It looks like a cool, sensible tennis costume. Eventually the men will come to it and why they haven't is a mystery."

While the gentlemen played in slacks despite the ferocious heat, the two bare-legged ladies put on an epic show for the packed gallery. Alice pulled out a tight first set, 8–6, but then the heat got ahold of her, and she was bageled in the second, 6–0. The ten-minute recess restored some of her ability to "come up to the net in a masculine way to zowie the ball for the kill," as the New York Daily News put it. Alice was on the brink of the semis at 5–1, 40–15—then it all fell apart.

Nuthall, the "fightenest girl ever to pull on a pair of tennis shorts," fought back to win that game, then reeled off five more on the trot to shock Alice and the eight thousand fans who were "screaming with every shot." At match point Alice was passed, and she tossed her racket in the air in frustration. "Letting patriotism slip aside," reported the London Times, "the crowd cheered the ever-popular English girl to the echo." Alice then retired to the clubhouse and fainted once again.

Amazingly, her summer grew worse. The 1933 US Nationals were notorious for Moody's default while trailing Helen Jacobs, who had tilted at this particular windmill for years with little success, 3–0 in the third set. Poker Face bluntly told Jacobs and the umpire that her "leg was hurting," then proceeded to march off the court, out of the club, and two blocks back to her room at the Forest Hills Inn. There were screams of poor sportsmanship, that Moody smelled defeat and preferred shame. Moody was clearly hurting, however. "I felt that I was on the verge of collapse on the court," she told reporters.

Alice had stuck around to catch the end of the tournament, which she came to regret. Moody had reached the doubles finals with Elizabeth Ryan but, of course, withdrew; not wanting to cheat the large gallery again, officials prevailed on Alice to fill in for an exhibition match. Playing her bêtes noires from Britain, Nuthall and James, Alice came to the net. Nuthall smacked a forehand off Alice's eye. Still perhaps a touch slow from her anemia, Alice collapsed and had to be helped into the clubhouse.

The eye was okay, though she sported remnants of a shiner upon detraining in California at the Oakland Mole. Tennant was there to greet her and was shocked at what she saw. "When Alice came back she looked like death warmed over for my money," she remembered.

A couple of weeks' rest and a family reunion did wonders for Alice's constitution. Dan had recently joined the San Francisco Police Department, and he watched proudly in blue as Alice rebounded to win the Pacific Coast title, besting Dorothy Round, who had beaten her in the finals of the Pacific Southwest in LA the week before.

During the tournaments she turned twenty and celebrated her birthday by going to the movies with Dan and turning in at ten o'clock. She happily described her life as "boring" and completely devoted to tennis. The only excitement came from watching the nascent construction of the new bridge that was to span the Golden Gate from the city across to Marin County, known around town as "The Bridge That Couldn't Be Built" due to the difficult conditions—fog, wind, and tide. But thanks to the brilliance of engineer Joseph Strauss, it was, indeed, being built. Every day Alice watched as dozens of workmen, carrying the newest thing in safety headgear, what the workers called "hard hats," tromped through the park on their way home from another day spent high over the roiling bay. She could look from the net on the Golden Gate Park tennis court to a similar, if far larger, net that stretched the length of the works beneath the bridge. Strauss had insisted on its use, despite the huge price tag ($130,000, nearly $2.5 million today), as another safety precaution. The netting wound up catching nineteen workers who fell from the bridge. The survivors called themselves the "Half Way to Hell Club."

The action back east had taken Alice more than halfway to hell, and she was still feeling the effects of her difficult summer when she got a call from Eleanor. They had been invited to see an architectural and aesthetic wonder that would put even the Golden Gate Bridge to shame.

Chapter Thirteen

Castle in the Sky

The Pacific Ocean at twilight. The sun dipped below the horizon, leaving the final traces of its brilliant hue imprinted upon the waves. But Alice had her back to nature's wonder. She was, instead, transfixed by another dizzying admixture of water and light. Alabaster lamps threw shades of gold onto the surface of an enormous pool, 104 feet long, filled with 345,000 gallons of spring water, a body of water seemingly as large as the sea below. The color cast "ethereal reflections on the Greco-Roman statuary, colonnades, and temple," Alice wrote. The scene was so sublime and otherworldly that "I felt as if I had left my seat in the theater and stepped right into the silver screen."

It was called the Neptune Pool, and anywhere else it would be the single most incredible structure on the property that held it. But this was San Simeon, the "Enchanted Hill" where there were similar amazements to be found around every corner, every trail, every corridor. The pool was just another wonder across forty thousand acres of them.

Alice was fortunate enough to explore it all, at the height of its grandeur.

. . .

They called George Hearst "the boy that earth talks to," for his supposedly uncanny ability to mine "the color," gold and silver, in the west. In reality he failed more often than he succeeded, but when he discovered the Comstock Lode, the richest vein of silver ever found in America, his fortune was made. In 1865, he bought a stretch of land in Monterey County along San Simeon Bay, a former whaling village two hundred miles down the coast from San Francisco. He and his family would go there and camp out, enjoying the distance from the city and the heavenly beauty of the area, including a high hill above the Pacific fog that rolled in almost daily, a summit called La Cuesta Encantada—the Enchanted Hill.

George's son, William Randolph Hearst, would become even more famous and wealthy than his father. William took his inherited family fortune and built a media empire. Beginning with the *San Francisco Examiner*, Hearst snapped up over two dozen papers and multiple periodicals, servicing every large American city. Over time he added a film studio, Cosmopolitan Productions, and multiple radio outlets to the mix, commanding markets in an arms race with his great media rival, Joseph Pulitzer. He was to modern communications what Carnegie was to steel, or Rockefeller to oil.

He spent most of his time in New York but grew increasingly homesick for California and would invent reasons to travel west. While rambling around the Golden State, Hearst revisited his boyhood home and was thunderstruck with nostalgic longing. As he wrote his mother, "I love this ranch. It is wonderful. I love the sea, and I love the mountains and the hollows in the hills, and the shady places in the creeks and the fine old oaks, and even the hot brushy hillsides—full of quail, and the canyons full of deer. It is a wonderful place. I would rather spend a month here than any place in the world."

So he built a home there commensurate with his ardor for the setting.

The design mind behind the extraordinary splendor of San Simeon was Julia Morgan, the foremost female architect in the world. A formal, stern presence in round spectacles, she was far more grandiose and flighty in her mechanical drawings. Morgan had refurbished the *Examiner* building demolished in the earthquake of 1906 and was completely trusted by Hearst. Ordinarily the newspaper baron roughed it out in the hills, but he wanted something more comfortable. Morgan took that broad mandate and designed a castle stuffed with the finest art and antiques money could buy. There were decorative wrought-iron works, tiles, imitation antiques, wood carvings, fine stone masonry, marble fountains. Hearst was on board for all of it, spending months collecting pieces overseas and in the east, sending it all via train and ship to San Simeon, where dangerously laden freight cars were lifted up the hill despite no working pier or paved roads.

The main building was the 115-room castle, known on the ranch as Casa Grande. It featured a foyer the size of a hotel lobby and was decorated with Flemish tapestries above Italian Renaissance choir stalls and large tables with bronze sculptures and silver candlesticks. There was antique furniture covered in slips but functional for use. Everywhere were ornate pieces, mostly of Spanish and Italian origin. As Morgan wrote to antiquarians in Madrid, "They comprise vast quantities of tables, beds, armoires, secretaires, all kinds of cabinets, polychrome church statuary, columns, door frames, carved doors in all stages of repair and disrepair, over-alters, reliquaries, lanterns, iron grille doors, window grilles, votive candlesticks, torchères, all kinds of chairs in quantity, six or seven well heads. . . ." Surrounding Casa Grande were several other buildings that became guest villas, all equally opulent and stuffed with treasures from the Old World, providing incredible views of the Pacific and the Santa Lucia Range, at least when the sun burned through the fog.

Outside was a mile-long pergola, the longest in the world, for strolling or horseback riding. Stone sculptures with large bulbs on their heads provided illumination. Everywhere were enormous gardens outlined by marble lampposts, festooned with well over half a million perennials—roses, camellias, azaleas, lantanas, geraniums, star jasmine, rhododendron, and on and on, grown in three state-of-the-art green-houses. Nearly one hundred thousand trees were planted on the estate, including six thousand pine trees brought in to obscure a view of a reservoir that displeased Hearst. He continually was moving trees around, but they were never hewn. The process was called "boxing." A trench was dug at the drip line some eight to ten feet deep. Concrete was poured in, and when it set, the entire mass was dug out, put on rollers, and transported elsewhere on the property or by truck to some other locale. It was monstrously expensive and time-consuming—one 150-year-old oak took six months to move twenty-five feet—but Hearst never let either obstacle stand in his way.

· · ·

Hearst fulfilled not merely his own tastes at San Simeon but those of his mistress, too. One of Eleanor's most reliable tennis students was the actress Marion Davies. Born Marion Douras in Brooklyn in 1897, Davies changed her name when she hit the Broadway stage, starring in several musical comedies. She moved west to break into movies and wound up a devotee of tennis. She paid Tennant an astounding 1,000 dollars a month as a retainer to have Teach drop everything whenever Davies called.

It was pennies to Davies, who was carrying on an open affair with the richest man in America.

Although he maintained his New York and San Francisco residences, by 1930 Hearst spent at least two hundred days a year at San Simeon, according to *Fortune* magazine. The sylph who took over the *Examiner* in 1887 had ballooned to a proper size for an emperor, bluff and hearty and, at six foot two, weighing well over two hundred pounds, giving him a commanding presence beyond the potency of his bank account.

Davies was three and a half decades his junior but was inexorably drawn to his force of will and godlike charisma. Davies was bubbly and irrepressible, a friend to all even after imbibing more than her share, which she did often. A *shikker* with a stutter, Davies turned her speech impediment into comedy and was determined not to let enormous wealth change how she treated people, and to humanize Hearst. She called him "Popsy," and he called her "Mopsy," and together they strove to make San Simeon a familial destination, even among the museum-quality furnishings. "I started out a g-g-gold digger," she once said, "and ended up in love."

Hearst and Davies loathed East Coast society, finding it stuffy and boring. So their parties were laden with Hollywood types: huge names like Chaplin, Fairbanks, and Garbo to up-and-comers like David Niven, Jimmy Stewart, and Jean Harlow—the "younger Degeneration," in Marion's lingo. Carole Lombard was a frequent guest, once wearing so much perfume to the barn that the ranch's 106 cows refused to let down their milk. An invite to San Simeon soon became as coveted as an Oscar nomination in the colony. Hollywood was divided into "those who had been guests at San Simeon and those who had not," in the words of Hearst biographer W. A. Swanberg.

Hollywood cast no aspersions on Hearst living so openly with his mistress, though the couple was careful not to flaunt their love in public, fearing the spectacle of a horribly public divorce. They never took photos together, for example. Hearst was also revered on the coast for his California roots and helped the nascent power structure in Hollywood feel comfortable and find its footing. Hearst's empire "was not built on celluloid," and the fact that other titans made the pilgrimage to San Simeon to pay homage helped make the state a destination rather than a way station.

Among the rotating cast of actors were politicians from Winston Churchill to Calvin Coolidge, business titans like Howard Hughes and J. Paul Getty, and prominent newsmakers. Charles Lindbergh landed the *Spirit of St. Louis* on the property during his postcrossing tour of America. Gertrude Ederle was welcomed in '26, the year she became the first woman to swim the English Channel, and became a regular, even pushing Hearst to build the Neptune Pool, having found the previous one too small. The airship *Graf Zeppelin* landed in 1929, disgorging slack-jawed German tourists and crew who marveled at stables larger than their aircraft.

And always present were the mythmakers—Hearst's crew of reporters and editors who seemingly materialized from nowhere. Aileen Pringle, actress and friend of Marion, said, "You would come downstairs and find probably thirty men standing around in blue suits. It would be a surprise. They arrived during the night." It was the Davos of the Depression, a gathering of those whose fortunes and talent and industry allowed them to withstand the worst economic downturn the nation had ever known.

. . .

Construction projects never ended at San Simeon. "If he ever stops building, I think he will die," Alice wrote her mother from the estate. In 1932 the indoor Roman Pool with its rooftop pair of tennis courts was completed, the spectacular blue-and-gold tiling offsetting the green of the grass courts above (there were also hard courts there). The tennis playing, already a fun part of life there, amped up with the new courts.

Tennant had already made a handful of trips to San Simeon, giving instruction to both Davies and Hearst and whoever else asked. She described the arrival process at the estate to her biographer, Nancy Spain. "There's a box, something like the box in your changing of the Guard, one of those small bungalows. The sentry comes out and asks who you are, and presses a button and the gate opens. And then you start driving up this hill for miles. It was just like fairyland and there was just enough fog that night to wrap the castle in fog. And it killed me. I couldn't talk. And when I can't talk that's something . . ."

The drive up could be hairy—literally: Exotic animals of all stripes wandered freely around the estate and often blocked traffic on the lone dirt road, where a sign warned that ANIMALS HAVE THE RIGHT OF WAY. If an animal lay on the road, the approaching car had to wait until it moved. As one of Hearst's columnists wrote of the experience, "The emus, gnus, kangaroos, llamas, cassowaries, and other dull ones . . . refuse to budge from the road, still warm from the day's sunshine, never dreaming that the approaching automobile might hurt." A buffalo herd was a frequent menace, but there were hundreds of wild horses, and camels, and deer, goats, cattle. There were dangerous predators like lions and tigers, too, though fortunately those were kept in caged enclosures.

Hearst loved animals so much that he refused to see them hurt. David Niven related a story that when the master of the house was told the mice in the kitchen had to go, he ensured they were trapped and set free in the garden—only to have them scurry right back to the kitchen for their next meal. He and Marion kept several generations of dachshunds at the ranch, and visitors commented that the dogs were treated even better than the guests.

Tennant would take an elevator down from her room to play tennis with Charlie Chaplin, a devoted enthusiast, every morning at 7:30, and the courts were full all day thereafter. Hearst was an avid player, though due to his bulk and age (nearly seventy) not a particularly spry one. He would take to the court in a three-piece business suit and a Stetson, and stand in the middle of the court, assuming his opponent would hit it at him out of respect (more of Hearst bending reality to his vision). The actor Joel McCrea recalled that he "didn't run around much, but if he could reach it and hit it, he did"—and hit it hard.

Hearst had telephones installed everywhere and a switchboard with operators standing by twenty-four hours a day, ensuring the boss could reach any outpost of his far-flung empire at whim. Naturally, one was courtside, but tennis was one of the few activities that superseded business in HearstWorld. Tennant remembered that "Hearst would play and play, and servants would trot out to say that Paris or Berlin was calling but he'd say 'tell them to call back—let's finish the set!'"

Alice arrived in '33 just before Christmas, and she was an immediate hit with the San Simeon swells. She and Eleanor drove from Los Angeles in Tennant's slick Chevy coupe, after the teacher had convinced a reluctant Jessie it was perfectly fine for her daughter to be mixing with famous show folk and captains of industry. "There was the castle," Alice recalled, "huge and brilliant in the twilight. I was sure I was dreaming."

They entered the enormous arrival hall, where Alice met her hosts. Davies wore her standard evening wear of black velvet and diamonds, while Hearst introduced himself in his unexpectedly high-pitched voice. Around 9 P.M. it was off to dinner, announced by one of the hosts with a cowbell, as though they were about to eat around the campfire after a hard day punching cattle.

Instead, they were ushered into a room Alice likened to a "cathedral." The dining room set had been brought over from Italy, where it was part of a church. Hearst and Davies walked in with Alice, though at other times Hearst, with Davies on his arm, would appear—godlike—out of a section of the wood paneling in the Assembly Room, which concealed his private elevator. They always sat across from one another at the center of a table that could sit several dozen. Amazingly, Alice sat right next to Hearst, with Eleanor across from her.

On this night Alice recalled there were fifty-two guests. They included the likes of Chaplin, Harlow, Bing Crosby, Paulette Goddard, child star Jackie Cooper, and a plenitude of talent, many of whom complimented Alice on her play at the Pacific Southwest tournament. "I found myself gulping for air," she recalled.

There were bottles of all kinds on the table, condiments and preserves from across the country, cheeses from around the world, and paper napkins, to remind guests that they were dining at a ranch, not a castle. The glasses were beautiful blue Venetians, the china lovely Blue Willow. The room was lined with a dozen Christmas trees, brought in from Seattle for the holiday (there were plenty more around the castle).

Alice would compare the meals to the elegance she later experienced crossing the Atlantic on ocean liners like the *Queen Mary*. Mostly it was French cooking, with escargots, turtle soup, and truffles on the menu.

Marion Davies put everyone at ease. "She was a delightful hostess. Just delightful. She wasn't formal, but she was very gay and very warm," the Hearst reporter Adela Rogers St. Johns recalled. Even with Chaplin around, Davies was usually the life of the party. "You see, Marion was a clown," Rogers St. Johns recalled. "This was her great hold [on Hearst]. She was the funniest woman I have ever seen."

She was also sneaking booze every chance she could. Hearst had imposed two-drink limits in the castle, in an effort to curtail Marion's drinking problem. She had been a heavy drinker since her teenage years in New York. The women's room—"the loo," she called it—became her private sanctum, where she hid bottles in the toilet tank, and where she gathered friends to drink with her.

Alice was exposed to Marion's private saloon.

All the women told their stories about various and sundry things that were a little strong for me when I was 17 [*sic*—she was nineteen]. They would talk about their abortions, and to me this was sinful. But, I listened and I certainly got an education. They told about how they went on diets and they would eat and then they would throw up, so they would not get fat. There was very little off-color things. They never told naughty stories or anything like that. They just had all these things when they were sort of going up the ladder, joining the chorus lines, and some in the Ziegfeld Follies. They told them with great glee when they were starving to death. They loved this life they had in New York. There was a special kind of camaraderie with all the chorus girls.

Tennant admired Marion's capacity for holding her liquor, and she adored the martinis the San Simeon barkeeps made. She instructed Alice to watch them perform their mixology magic so that she could replicate them back in the real world. It wasn't hard, Alice recalled, as it was basically straight gin. "It was about a little speck of vermouth, [just] wave the cork."

Alice didn't remember that there was any drink limit, though as an athlete and a teenager she wasn't partaking. But she would get a bartending license years later, and it was thanks to her exposure watching the drinks get made, with "very elaborate shakers," in order to service Tennant. "They had things like Daiquiris and Bacardis, Ramos Gin Fizzes, Alexanders—kind of sweet drinks which most of the women liked," she said in an oral history of San Simeon.

After dinner came the entertainment. Almost every evening in the castle's fifty-seat theater, Hearst presented a new feature film, which had been chauffeured up to the ranch that afternoon from Los Angeles, or one of the films he had produced with Davies as his star, which were kept on hand at the castle. On this night Alice remembered watching Davies in *Peg o' My Heart*, in which she played a lively Irish lass making her way in a stuffy English manse. "It was mostly Marion's movies and they were awful," Alice said in 1977. "I should not say that, because she had such a knack for comedy and he had her doing all these things in picture hats and she was not any good at it, but I guess [Hearst] wanted her to be his dream star, and I do not think she liked it."

Afterward, "sprawled on priceless rugs in one of the castle's fourteen sitting rooms," they discussed the movies. Alice was a true cineaste, a die-hard moviegoer who possessed a knowledge of filmdom that impressed the stars, who knew little beyond their own work. She argued with the director Raoul Walsh about a particular actress, and Alice turned out to be correct.

"I was the greatest movie fan that ever lived," Alice said in the oral history. "We played this game of 'who are they,' which was naming the initials, you did not have to say man or woman, of the silent movie stars. And so we would go on all evening. This was a great dinner conversation thing, because all of these people were silent movie stars. Mr. Hearst would say, 'Ask Alice, she knows everything.' I studied like you would have to be a doctor. I was the final authority on the silent stars."

She stayed up well past her bedtime on this first night, till three A.M., before at last retiring to the room she shared with Tennant. She took the elevator up with Hearst himself. "We had read so many tales in the paper that he got Thomas Ince [an early movie tycoon who died under mysterious circumstances aboard Hearst's yacht] killed and all this sort of stuff," Alice remembered, "that I was a little nervous. He had such a high squeaky voice and put his hand on my head and he said, 'Sleep well, child.' And sort of patted me on the head. From that time on, I was at ease."

Other nights brought other entertainments. "Mr. Hearst could yodel very well indeed," Alice said, and there were stories. Chaplin would perform his "Life of Napoleon" and play the violin. And after a few visits, Alice would be prevailed upon to sing for her supper.

Card games abounded—bridge and hearts and especially poker. Eleanor remembered big pots—"30 or 40 dollars!" But Alice said on one visit she sat down in a poker game and won 11,000 dollars! The figure seems exceptionally high, and it was disputed by San Simeon employees. Regardless, she refused to take any money, telling her victims she never would have sat down to play had she known the stakes.

Hearst was impressed by her forthrightness and, according to Alice, attempted to give her a car as a gift, which she refused, impressing him further. He promised that if Alice ever captured the US Nationals, he would give her the car as an earned reward.

. . .

On her first morning in paradise Alice played doubles with Hearst, against Tennant and Chaplin, who cheated mightily, according to Miss Marble, who "tried to hit him with the ball." Watching Hearst chug about the court worried the onlooking Davies. "Let them win," she implored Alice, who in her naivete and competitiveness chased everything down and led her team to a 10–8 win. "You're the best partner I ever had!" beamed Hearst.

Marble would take a lesson each day with Tennant, and also another former star staying there, Elizabeth "Bunny" Ryan, a dominant doubles player in the 1920s whose volleying techniques Alice copied as best she could. Then she would watch the movie stars take lessons, and get on the court for some action, pairing with Hearst or Davies or whichever celebrity called "dibs." By hitting with far weaker players Alice learned to change up her one-dimensional attacking pace, a tactic that would seep into her tournament tennis.

Alice had ingratiated herself so quickly into the group that Hearst and Davies gave her a pet name—"Pinky." Tennant was "Becky." Pinky and Becky had an extraordinary Christmas Eve, according to Tennant:

> After dinner our names would be called and we would be summoned one by one to the Doge Suite. It was like a department

store. There were racks and racks of beautiful dresses, terribly smart outfits, stunning polo coats, magnificent fur rugs for the car, perfectly lovely light wool rugs from Scotland, electric clocks in leather cases, luggage, a certain amount of jewelry, and Marion and Mr. Hearst greeted us. . . . Marion said, "Popsy, I think we ought to have a celebration with Pinky and Becky for Christmas Eve!"

He poured a glass of champagne for all of us and we drank to each other's health, and it was very pleasant. And I thought that was the end of it. I didn't know what the department store was. I thought it was a great privilege, and it would have satisfied me as just an experience. But they said now you have to pick out your own present. I said, "Marion are you kidding?" She said no, "pick out a lot. Take a lot of things because there are a lot of attractive things here and you're an easy size. I picked out a lot of things that would look good on you." I asked her to show me what she'd like me to have. That was the sort of thing Marion Davies would do.

Davies's generosity was a thing of legend. She tried to give Eleanor a 2,000-dollar fur robe just for driving her to an appointment. Alice remembered, "I would say to her, 'Gee Marion, that is a beautiful ring,' and she would say, 'Here you take it . . . I have a dozen more.'" On this occasion neither could refuse, and the two women grabbed half a dozen or so outfits. Downstairs they held a fashion show for the assembled guests, all of whom were trying on their gifts. It was an early version of the "gifting suites" modern celebrities get to indulge in.

Alice's most memorable evening wasn't about swag, however. In addition to her movie expertise, Alice had written a thesis for her Berkeley boards on her favorite playwright, George Bernard Shaw, who came to San Simeon for the only overnight stay in a private residence in America he ever made. He was a regular contributor to Hearst papers for many years, and though their politics differed, he and "W. R." admired one another.

The only thing Alice knew that particular night was that a special guest was coming whom she would be interested in meeting. That several famous women took it upon themselves to doll her up should have tipped her off. Davies chose a "dress the blue of my eyes, with a low back," and did her hair.

"Jean Harlow made me up," she told the San Simeon oral historian. "Dorothy Mackaill—who was a very interesting English movie star—did my nails. Somebody made sure I had the right accessories, and I went downstairs. We were all waiting to see who this guest was. I looked over and there was a man with a beard. He came over and said, 'Young lady, I admire the moles on your back.' And I thought to myself, 'That dirty old man.' I was about to say something when Marion came over and with her stutter said, 'That is your dinner partner, that's George Bernard Shaw.' . . . I could tell him the names and the characters of every one of his plays, so he had a chance to talk about himself the whole time, which he adored. I made a tremendous hit, especially with Mr. Hearst because he did not know what to do with the man."

Tennant later noted that Alice's sharp memory had at last come in handy.

Another admirer was one of the giants of early twentieth-century journalism, Arthur Brisbane. He was best known for his widely read column, "Today," which *Time* described as "a column that vies with the weather and market reports for the size of its audience, probably beating both. It is said to be read by a third of the total U. S. population. Obviously this is an exaggeration, but half that many would be some 20 million readers, 'Today' and every day."

He was also known for being the brains behind the Hearst operation and for ridiculously profitable business ventures with the Big Boss. Brisbane was making an incredible fortune through Hearst—260,000 dollars a year for his newspapering, plus revenues from their combined real estate holdings.

He was around Hearst's age, so Alice didn't take much notice when the old man doted upon her and asked all manner of questions. Turned out Brisbane was interviewing her. His front-page nationally syndicated column of December 3, 1933, introduced Alice to a wide audience beyond the sports page and revealed that Brisbane was quite smitten with the tennis great.

> What a girl Alice Marble is, with everything the Venus de Milo has, plus two muscular, bare, sunburned arms marvelously efficient. Her legs are like two columns of polished mahogany, bare to the knees, her figure perfect. Frederick MacMonnies should do a statue of her. And she should marry the most intelligent young man in America, and be the perfect mother, with twelve children, not merely the world's best tennis player, which she probably will be.

It seems that when Brisbane talked of marrying Alice off, he may have had someone in mind—his son Seward. Alice would travel to Brisbane's mansion in Florida for the Christmas holidays with the editor, who had recently lost his sixteen-year-old son, Hugo, to illness (Brisbane's wife, and Hugo's mother, Phoebe, was so disconsolate she never left her room during Alice's time in Florida). The great man had to walk up the steep stairs to the Marble front door in order to get Jessie's permission for the trip, but "she was so impressed with him" that the okay was swiftly granted. Arthur paid all of Alice's expenses and even gave her the forty dollars she forfeited by taking off work at Wilson Sporting Goods.

While enjoying the Miami sunshine, Alice entered into what she termed a "wild romance" with the other of Brisbane's sons, who "was about 6'3" tall." That would be Seward Brisbane, the second of six Brisbane children (one of whom was coincidentally named Alice).

Needless to say, given her traumatic incident of a few years earlier, and her later insistence that she remained otherwise virginal for several more years yet, it's open to question how "wild" this affair actually was. She also never mentioned this in either memoir. On the other hand, given how inconsistent her memoirs turned out to be, it's entirely possible that she let slip this unvarnished truth to a random interviewer from the Hearst San Simeon State Historical Monument and elided it from her "official history."

Whatever the case, nothing came of it, though Alice might have lived a far more leisurely and luxurious life had she pursued Seward.

Alice stayed at San Simeon about a week on that first trip, rushing home in order to return to her secretarial job. But she returned subsequently several times over the next few years, often for several weeks at a time. One visit she drove Tennant's car up to the ranch for her, as Eleanor had gone ahead. "I was driving slowly, watching for animals," she later wrote, "when a set of bony knees came into my vision." She was surrounded by a herd of giraffes and was unable to move until a groundskeeper came to rescue her. The man related that the same "lazy" beasts had stranded Winston Churchill for over an hour.

Alice got to fly in to San Simeon as well. Roscoe Turner, a well-known World War I ace with a classically curled mustache, flew her up over the mountains to the ranch. It was faster, of course (Brisbane noted in a column that the 520-mile round trip from San Simeon to LA by air took three hours, as opposed to the twenty hours by train and auto), but also riskier—aviation was still in its infancy, and the winds off the mountains played havoc with pilots. Not long before, two of Hearst's newsmen were killed while flying to the ranch in inclement weather.

Making the trip trickier was Alice's fellow passenger—a lion cub en route to Hearst's zoo. "Don't worry," Turner assured her. "This little guy is safe as a kitten." Alice was distracted from the fraught journey by the cub. "The little thing wanted to play with me all the time," she said.

Chapter Fourteen

....

FALLING DOWN

A lone figure in a wheelchair. A desolate, windswept pier in Le Havre, France.

Mere months before, she had been the belle of San Simeon. Now, Alice sat all alone, gazing out at the choppy, cobalt-dark English Channel. No one gamboled on the boardwalk on this unusually chilly late-spring Normandy afternoon. The sea before her was likewise empty. She shivered as a damp breeze scythed through her. She was drawn, sallow, the result of three desultory weeks confined to a hospital bed. Underweight and listless, her body racked with pain, Alice was left to contemplate her uncertain future, far from home and without a soul to talk to.

The year that had begun with such optimism had darkened, as suddenly as the light dropping away over the Narrow Sea.

· · ·

On January 10, 1934, a top-hatted executioner dropped the blade of a guillotine on Marinus van der Lubbe, who had been convicted of setting the fire that burned down Berlin's Reichstag the year before. "His head fell in a basket of sawdust," reported *Time*. The Nazis were in firm command of Germany, to the surprise of most and the disgust of somewhat fewer.

Like most Americans, Alice thought the news from Germany very far away and paid it little mind. The coming season seemed poised to belong to her. The almighty Moody had been dethroned at Forest Hills, and Marble's game was trending steeply upward. "She is marked with the unmistakable form of a champion," opined the *Miami Daily News*. "Her stroking is perfect in its technique and freedom from apparent effort. Her net play striking in its dash, its power, its precision."

But underneath her smooth veneer on the court, Alice felt oddly weak. She was so talented that she was able to win the Northern California championships despite being off and soon after was found to be anemic again. She had been ordered by doctors to devour liver, a dietary measure thought at the time to increase blood count after her sunstroke had played havoc with her system. Tennant talked about these "wacko prescriptions" with scorn to Nancy Spain and would snort with rage remembering this period a decade later, convinced if Alice had more closely remained under her watchful eye in this period, all would have been fine.

Things weren't all dire. Her job at Wilson was going well. Her brother George had followed Dan into the police force, and the two of them made a resplendent pair in their uniforms, giving Alice even more cause for worshipping them. And according to *The Road to Wimbledon* she had acquired a new boyfriend, a "delightful English beau" named Leslie, who was an avid music fan, like she was. One day they went with Alice's mother to the home of another enthusiast, who turned out to be a man named Henry. By amazing coincidence, Henry happened to be the suitor Jessie had turned down those many years ago to marry Harry Marble instead.

Meanwhile, Alice was already such a known and beloved figure in the Bay Area that when her kid brother, Tim, then sixteen, got bitten by the family dog and had to get treated for potential rabies, the *Examiner* ran a story about it. The great DiMaggio had reeled off his famous sixty-one-game hitting streak the year before for the Seals but in 1934 nearly ended his career by tearing knee ligaments stepping off a jitney. With DiMag down, Alice Marble was the Bay Area's number-one sporting icon.

Tennant had rented a place northeast of LA in Gladstone. But much of her time was still spent puttering up and down the coast as the tennis lessons demanded. There was much of this demand, fortunately for her bank account, but it meant she couldn't travel with Alice when she got the call (telegram, actually) to go to Europe.

Alice had been picked for the Wightman Cup team, this time not requiring an endurance test in an inferno to earn selection. She would be playing number-two singles, behind only the captain and reigning national champ, Helen Jacobs. Even better, this time Britain was the host, and that meant Alice would play the palace, or as tennis folk called it, the All England Club at Wimbledon. And as a cherry on the crème brûlée, the USLTA had set up some warm-up action, including entry in the French hard-court championships, and a one-day Cup-like series against a French team, to be played in Paris on the fabled clay at Stade Roland-Garros!

Alice was over the moon at the prospect, and while Eleanor worried, as she did any time her protégé was out of her control for more than a weekend, she had to be proud of the success she had seen as a coach, building up her student as she did from a virtual teardown project to the cusp of greatness. Alice wanted her to go, but Eleanor couldn't ignore her stateside commitments.

Alice spent her usual time training with Beese White in Montecito and got the usual addition to his tennis lessons—an astrology reading. White was a devotee of the art, counting the famous astrologer Evangeline Adams as a close friend, and one of his brothers, Stewart Edward White, wrote extensively on channeling with the spirits. White also felt, strongly, that Tennant should accompany Alice to Europe. The stars didn't like what might happen otherwise.

Astrology was, to use a modern phrase, having a moment in LA. The Depression was forcing citizens into ever more desperate pathways of finding hope and meaning in their miserable lives. Llewellyn George, considered the dean of American astrologers, and equally popular mystic Blanca Gabriella Holmes, helped people chase the blues away with positive readings, no matter how dubious.

Oddball sects and cults are associated with the Los Angeles of the 1960s and '70s, but they were far more prevalent in the Decade of Depression. Most prominent was the Mankind United Cult, which snapped up some 250,000 members at its height. Its size gave MUC a patina of credibility with the public, but the shuttered storefronts teemed with pop-up orders of all manner and sizes. Carey McWilliams, future editor of *The Nation* and longtime LA social activist, did a street-level investigation of the craze. "I have attended the services," he wrote, "of the Agabeg Occult Church where the woman pastor who presided had violet hair; . . . of the Great White Brotherhood; of the Ancient Mystical Order of Melchizedek; of the Temple of the Jewelled Cross; of Sanford, 'food scientist' . . . ; of the Self-Realization Fellowship of America," and dozens more. As one observer put it, quacks fled to LA when feeling the heat in the east, as it was the "first metropolitan center west of Chicago, America's last stop."

The ladies consulted a medium named Beulah Lewis, who gazed into Alice's aura for some time before delivering her verdict. "All these beautiful colors," she intoned, "and all these beautiful stars and things from the sky appear. And the sky rocket comes down and like all sky rockets looks black and not too good."

Eleanor stared at her for a long moment. "That's very interesting," she said. "I can't quite analyze your symbolism."

With that, they drove over to Union Station, where Alice boarded the train with a fellow player, Jo Cruickshank, hugged Eleanor goodbye, and blasted off like a rocket to meet her destiny.

On the train Alice got to meet the biggest star in all of tennis. Big Bill Tilden was "sitting in the club car eating a huge steak" when she spied him and went over to thank him for his recent kind words in the *Examiner*, pulling the clipping she had saved from her bag. They chatted well into the night, the great Tilden full of sincere praise for her game.

Upon arrival in New York, Alice checked into the Roosevelt Hotel (in *Courting Danger* she remembers her hotel as the palatial Waldorf, with its secretaries on every floor and fine art in every room, but contemporary press accounts had her staying on East Forty-Fifth and Madison at the Roosevelt, whose owners had recently gone bankrupt), while Cruickshank wandered down to the Vanderbilt Hotel on Thirty-Fourth and Park Avenue. Sarah Palfrey and Carolin Babcock stayed in separate locales as well, leading George Currie to jibe, "How these tennis girls love to stick together!"

Alice made headlines by opining that she thought her recent doubles partner and reigning queen of tennis, Helen Wills Moody, wouldn't play again that year—or perhaps ever—because of her back injury. "Miss Marble's information apparently is the final word on the question," said *The New York Times*. "[Marble] stated that she had not talked personally to Mrs. Moody but that she had got her information from the California Tennis Association." "She won't play again for psychological reasons, too," Alice taunted. "Her old rivals have improved tremendously; if she were to come back their old awe of her would no longer exist." She wasn't an old rival but rather an evolutionary advancement, and there was little doubt she was confident she had the game to beat "Poker Face." Moody responded the following day. "I always seem to hear about myself from points miles away," she said, insisting that she would play again, though perhaps not that season.

Alice went on to talk up her own game, noting that she no longer worked as hard on the court, a tribute to Beese White and his methods, and that her serve and forehand were at top level. She confessed that becoming a "radio singer" was a dream that she'd "give up tennis" for, noting that she'd been "taking lessons all winter from a famous Russian opera star."

But her main concern was whether the Brits would allow her bare legs to sully the All England Club. "We'd like to wear shorts," she said. "The Prince of Wales has said he thought we ought to, and the Duchess of York has approved. But Queen Mary has the real say." The queen had reportedly expressed displeasure at the idea. "I suppose we won't . . . but I noticed the British girls wore them in our national tournament."

Alice continued to hold court while "dangling on the arm of a chair in her suite." She told the assembled press she had packed six pairs of flannel shorts just in case, but because she "couldn't sew a stitch" they remained monogram-free, unlike the ones worn by the other girls. "But I can cook now!" she told the *New York Daily News*, apparently anxious to display some domestic capability. Also in her suitcase was a letter of introduction to the Prince of Wales himself, though she doubted His Royal Highness would stoop to meet her.

Reporters noted a ring on the finger that indicated engagement, but neither Leslie nor Seward Brisbane nor Harold Dickenson had pinned her down. "That's just a good luck ring," she told them. She also opined that marriage and tennis wouldn't mix. "You can't do both."

A different lucky piece of jewelry, one that Tennant had given her, had gone missing. It was a gold racket with a head of pearl, studded with diamonds and rubies, a small, pricey, meaningful accessory that Alice always wore when she played. Losing it seemed like a bad omen, and she wasn't feeling all that great still, despite the liver diet. Was Beulah's prophecy ringing in her ears? She headed into the night, down to the harbor to catch the midnight sailing of the German liner *Bremen* for her first crossing to the Old World, praying she wouldn't get seasick.

She wasn't a victim of mal de mer, but Alice wasn't feeling herself. She shared a cabin with Cruickshank, "a big, gawky girl with great enthusiasm," who was out late letting her hair down each night while Alice climbed into bed, exhausted, at an early hour. She managed to stay fit on the six-day voyage by hitting balls against the gym wall and walking the decks, but she clearly wasn't right. Jacobs asked her point-blank if she was feeling okay when she met the team off the train in Paris (the *Bremen* docked in Cherbourg). "I was pale, and there were dark circles under my eyes," she admitted.

On May 19 she played in exhibition doubles with a Frenchman, Marcel Bernard, against Palfrey and the great Aussie player Harry Hopman, losing the match despite Alice's fast service, which brought gasps from the crowd. Alice learned her draw for the French hard-court championships, in which she and her teammates were entered, was an easy one. And she found out she would be matched with a woman named Sylvia Henrotin in the exhibition series a few days later.

Still feeling under the weather, she asked the French team doctor to examine her. Her hemoglobin count was just fifty, low even by her anemic standards, but she was reassured that she was fine. "I wished he told me I had the flu," Alice said, not a light request given her family history. "Ignoring her doctor's orders," the *Daily Mirror* wrote, reflecting the sexism of the day, "Alice Marble, America's most attractive player in the Wightman Cup team, took part in Thursday's Franco-American match in Paris."

Roland-Garros was the foremost clay-court stadium in the world (as it remains), and the setting overwhelmed Alice. "I hated the French courts, the French players, and most of all, the French language," she said. Just trying to decipher the score, given by the umpire as *quarante–quinze*, not forty–fifteen, made her head swim. May the twenty-fourth, a Thursday, was an extremely hot afternoon in Paris. The high stadium walls trapped in the heat, which mixed with Alice's already weak feeling to send her into a daze when she took the court against Henrotin, a notable doubles player.

Alice was seeing shadow images, the racket slipping from her hand repeatedly, her tongue hanging from her mouth. Henrotin was ahead 4–1 in the first set and pushing for more when she hit a ball to Alice's forehand. "I ran for the ball, reached out . . . and knew no more until I came to at the American Hospital in Neuilly."

She had collapsed, passed out on the court. A hush came over the crowd. An AP photo captured Alice getting carried to the locker room in a sitting position by a pair of men, their hands under her knees, one bowing from the effort. Alice has her head down and is clearly in distress. As United Press put it, "She was carried to the dressing room in a state of collapse." Alice had to default the match. "The heat . . . proved too much for this girl from the country of tremendous heat waves," wrote Ulyss Rogers in the *Daily Express*.

Alice wrote in her memoirs that she didn't come to until she was in a hospital bed, but an AP reporter found her in the locker room as she revived, "stretched out on a locker room bench" and asking for a doctor as she "still felt badly" and "complained of severe stomach pains." But she was copacetic enough to throw her captain under the bus.

"I didn't want to play today, because I felt sick, but Helen Jacobs insisted, so I did my best." With that, "Jacobs immediately barred all visitors to the locker room."

She was taken to the American Hospital, where she was put under the care of Dr. Robert Dax. Initial reports from the hospital downplayed the severity of her condition. It was a "mild fainting spell rather than a serious condition" read one, and "a gall bladder ailment" according to another. Not to worry, said the AP—she was "resting easily." "The intense heat, reflected by the red clay courts, was just too much for her," intoned the good doctor. The British press confirmed Alice's mild condition. "It is expected that the trouble will yield to special treatment and prolonged rest," reported the London *Daily Telegraph*.

But Alice's back and stomach were killing her, which hadn't been the case with her sunstroke the year before. "I felt like I had been speared," she said. Dr. Dax amended his diagnosis—pleurisy, an inflammation of the lungs that was painful but ultimately not serious. She was to be ready for the Wightman matches across the channel on June 15 and 16—that wasn't an issue. None of the other Cup players reached by reporters said they thought Alice's condition was that serious. Palfrey, Babcock, and Cruickshank all "expressed the belief she yet might play in the cup matches."

But her temperature soared, and her condition refused to improve. "What is the mystery about Alice Marble?" wondered the *Daily Mail*. Dr. Dax ruled her out for the Cup, then for the rest of the tennis season, but had no answer for what was wrong. She was medicated and crying heavily when she wasn't in a narcoleptic daze. A nurse told her she "was going to die," which may have been a drug-induced vision but strangely comforted Alice—at least the nurse seemed to know something, unlike the medical staff. The rest of the Wightman team tearfully departed for England, where they would go on to win the Cup again without Alice (at a party in London for the team hosted by American ambassador

Robert Bingham, Jacobs met and fell for Bingham's daughter, Henrietta, with the two moving in together almost immediately and conducting an affair that lasted over a decade).

At last, after nearly two weeks of mystery, Dr. Dax had news—and it was a hammer blow. "You have tuberculosis," he said. "I'm sorry, but you will never play tennis again."

"You're a sadistic SOB," Alice wrote she replied to Dr. Dax. Heartbroken, she prayed she would die in the night. "But the next day came. And the next. And the next."

Tennant was cabled to meet Alice in New York, and at last, on June 17, twenty-four days after her face met the Roland-Garros clay, she was bundled aboard a train for Le Havre, where she was to take the *Aquitania* back to America. The nurse who accompanied her on the train got back on the return to Paris, leaving Alice alone on the dock in a wheelchair, trembling and fearful in the blowing ocean breeze.

At last the liner steamed into view, and at length Alice was trundled aboard, a pair of crew members wheeling her up the gangplank. They left the wheelchair at the foot of her bed and departed, leaving Alice to weep bitter tears at her fate.

Chapter Fifteen

....

The Lady Vanishes

Alice spent the first three of the six days at sea in bed, staring out the small porthole in her cabin, watching the clouds scud across the blue ocean sky.

Fortunately, the American consulate had thoughtfully sent an advocate, a lawyer named Paul Fuller, who was headed home on the *Aquitania* as well. "They asked me to look after you," he told Alice, and his light manner and sophisticated palate pulled Alice out of her gloom. It was only at length that Alice discovered Mr. Fuller was traveling back to America to bury his son. The contrast to her own situation weighed on Alice. "At least I'm alive," she thought.

But it was hard. She gamely told a *Brooklyn Daily Eagle* reporter as she packed aboard the liner that she would definitely be back the following year, while blaming the French style of play for her collapse and not breathing a word of her tubercular diagnosis. As Fuller wheeled her down the gangplank in New York Harbor, Alice saw Tennant, who had dropped everything and rushed across the country to greet her protégé at the dock, not something most coaches (or family members) did for their players in that era.

When Alice appeared, Eleanor burst into tears, an unnerving sight given her usual stoicism. "I'm so sorry," Eleanor gasped out. "If I'd gone with you . . ."

The two women were still embracing when a man from the USLTA intruded on the scene. He welcomed Alice home by insisting she join him at the association offices, where she could make an accounting of her expenses and return her unused advance.

"You stupid damn fool!" Eleanor exploded. "Can't you see this girl is ill?!" She put Alice in a taxi. "If you want us, we'll be at the Roosevelt!" Tennant yelled at the startled official, and the cab peeled off.

They stayed in New York for over a week, as Tennant waged a pitched battle with Julian Myrick in one room while Alice pretended to sleep in another. "She's been a bad investment," Myrick said, displaying nary an ounce of concern for Alice's well-being. The ocean voyages, hotels, hospitals—it cost the USLTA a fortune, "and she didn't even finish a match." Tennant volleyed back, blaming the torture session at East Hampton for Alice's condition and threatening to take the whole matter public.

In the end Myrick caved, forgiving the "debt," but that wasn't good enough for Tennant, who insisted Alice would return to become a champion, as it was "her birthright." Myrick returned her a "very cynical smile," in Tennant's words, "which I never forgot." Years later, Tennant was still angry at Myrick, although they had reached a detente when Alice indeed became a champion. "He was a very rich man and lived in a well known pot of jelly, he had these three lovely daughters and he would not have treated them in that fashion."

On June 26 Alice took the train back west, stopping long enough to tell Universal News Service columnist Dorothy Roe she was taking a sabbatical in favor of "radio crooning." "I'm a love song addict," she told Roe. But there was nothing but sad ballads in her heart. She arrived in San Francisco weak and in need of help. Her older brothers carried her up the steep stairs on Twelfth Avenue to her old bedroom, everyone crying all the way. "Enough," ordered Tennant. "This looks like a wake. She will be alright."

Alice found her mother in even worse condition, in recovery from a broken hip, but the underlying cause was bone cancer. "Seeing her mother try to climb the stairs made Alice weep," Tennant said.

Eleanor had her own family health issues. Her widowed sister, Gwen McKay, had heart trouble, so Teach took a place in Beverly Hills with her so she could remain close to her celebrity clientele. But as events would soon prove, her mind was on her protégé up north.

It was an uneasy time in the Golden State. Ten million were unemployed as the Depression fell heavily on the west. The first wave of "Okies," Midwestern farmers displaced by the enormous dust storms and drought of that year, descended upon California, raising resentment among locals. There were enormous labor strikes by longshoremen and teamsters in Oakland and San Francisco, shutting down the ports for months and leading to violent clashes as employers sought to break the walkout. On July 5, "Bloody Thursday," the *Examiner* reported that "police clashed with protestors across San Francisco, causing a pair of fatalities and leaving downtown and the port thick with tear gas residue."

The unrest pushed the social justice warrior Upton Sinclair, famous muckraking author of *The Jungle*, to switch from Socialist to Democrat and run for governor, signaling a leftward shift in the state. His platform was simple—"EPIC," or End Poverty in California. This included state control of factories, alongside Soviet-style farm cooperatives. He ran against the incumbent, Frank Merriam.

The Hollywood moguls joined forces with Alice's pal William Hearst to finance a giant war chest to defeat Sinclair, forcing many of Eleanor's clients to speak out in favor of Merriam. They also employed a dirty tricks campaign, producing fake newsreels that showed Soviets entering California in order to vote for Upton, hiring hoboes and destitute Okies pulled from freight cars to walk around with VOTE FOR SINCLAIR signs, and even threatening to pull the movie industry from LA and move to Florida if that damn Socialist was elected.

"A sense of Armageddon hangs in the bland California air," wrote *The New York Times*.

The apocalypse wasn't happening in the Marble house, where all was deathly still. For endless nights Alice stared at her ceiling, bereft about her mother and her own downturn in health. Realizing Jessie couldn't provide proper care in her condition, and her brothers had families of their own to worry about, Alice wrote Eleanor a desperate letter, asking for advice or a path out of her predicament.

Tennant responded by immediately driving north, bringing along a specialist who advised Alice she would recover faster in a warm, dry climate, which San Francisco decidedly was not. Eleanor browbeat Jessie into letting her take Alice south with her. Jessie, defeated, led Alice to Eleanor's car, kissed her daughter on the cheek, and turned back into the house without a word.

Alice assumed she was headed to Eleanor's house in Beverly Hills. Instead, upon reaching the Southland, Eleanor turned east instead, heading past Pasadena to Monrovia, a small burg at the foothills of the Sierra Madre Range, roughly twenty-five miles from LA. This was to be Alice's new home, a resting home for tubercular patients called the Pottenger Sanatorium.

Dr. Francis Marion Pottenger was from Ohio but moved out to California upon becoming a doctor and getting married. His wife passed away from tuberculosis in 1898, and Pottenger devoted the rest of his life to studying and treating the dreaded lung disease. In 1903 he opened the Pottenger Sanatorium for Diseases of the Lungs and Throat on Charlotte Avenue in the moderate climate and dry air of Monrovia. Originally built to treat eleven patients, by the time Alice checked in in late July 1934, the capacity was over 120.

Thousands of TB sufferers passed through (or passed away at) Pottenger's. Mabel Normand, a silent-screen actress whose work Alice was well familiar with, died there in 1930 at age thirty-seven. Pottenger lived on the grounds and was constantly testing and evaluating potential new cures and treatments. At heart, he believed in isolation, fresh air, and doctors on standby. He also believed in regular payments. Pottenger's wasn't cheap—Alice's room and board came to 300 dollars a month (nearly 6,000 dollars today), a sizable sum, especially during the

Depression—and he was loath to let patients leave until they were good and healthy.

There was a main two-story hospital building, with a handful of cottages where the staff lived and worked. There were flowering shrubs and gardens all around and a pond at the center of the compound. The mountains towered over the forty or so acres of property, making for a lovely scene that has been preserved in numerous postcards from the era.

But Alice found Pottenger's hateful from the start.

She was there for a six-week stay, which mainly consisted of staring at her ceiling while in bed, listening to the radio, eating badly, and slowly going mad. Gwen came to visit and taught her embroidery, and she wrote frequent letters to Jessie, the two convalescent Marble women commiserating in their misery. Once a week Dr. Pottenger would examine her, grunt out a few generalities, and return Alice to her lonely bed.

The only other constant was Eleanor Tennant. She proved her unquestionable loyalty to Alice by driving almost every day the fifty-mile round trip, rising before dawn in order to go and return in time for her crowded teaching schedule. She couldn't miss a single lesson, for Eleanor was footing the bills at Pottenger's for Alice, another sign of her devotion. As tennis writer Norah Gordon Cleather put it, "Teach, the loyal coach and saviour, slaved for long hours each day, coaching young players in the broiling sun of California courts, in order to earn enough money to pay Alice's doctor bills, never doubting her friend's ability to recover and become a champion."

After six weeks of this special torture for a formerly elite athlete, Alice packed to leave. But Pottenger wouldn't let her go, saying she needed another six weeks. This became a ritual—six weeks would pass, each feeling like a year to Alice, and she would be dying to get out, only to be told she needed another six weeks.

Another patient clued her in. "They tell everybody they'll be here six weeks. I've been here two years. They'll never let you leave."

She lost hope, not even bothering to pack after the next six weeks (eighteen in total) were up. Her clothes no longer fit, anyway. As Tennant put it, "They had kept her drinking milk and eating starches and here's this nice athletic body disintegrating into a lump of fat, which I loathe and despise. It doesn't do anyone any good to carry an excess 30 pounds of fat, like a sack of flour." Alice had a few symptoms of active TB, mainly fatigue, but wasn't coughing up blood or running high fevers or exhaling a rattle while breathing, the classic signs of someone with "consumption." But Alice's protests to the staff fell on deaf ears.

One day a letter arrived, but not in her mother's handwriting. Alice was stunned to discover not only the sender but the message therein:

> *Dear Alice,*
>
> *You don't know me, but your tennis teacher is also my teacher, and she has told me all about you. Once I thought I had a great career in front of me, just like you thought you had. Then one day I was in a terrible automobile accident. For six months I lay on a hospital bed, just like you are today. Doctors told me I was through, but then I began to think I had nothing to lose by fighting, so I began to fight. Well, I proved the doctors wrong. I made my career come true, just as you can—if you'll fight. If I can do it, so can you.*
>
> *Carole Lombard*

Incredibly, one of the world's foremost movie stars had taken the time to write Alice and urge her to push on toward recovery. She was flabbergasted, and yet she was unable to get any traction with the doctors. Pottenger wouldn't even tell her what was wrong.

In September Alice turned twenty-one. Just as she started feeling especially sorry for herself, the sound of a Mexican band filled her room. Eleanor had hired a mariachi group to serenade her. Alice sung along, her contralto mixed with sobs. "It was pretty rugged on her," Eleanor said.

Five months passed, and Alice was at last allowed daily trips outside to take the air, for all of fifteen minutes. In a small, if self-defeating, act of defiance, she took to smoking a cigarette in her daily walk to the pond. She missed voting in the California gubernatorial election, which was won by Frank Merriam, helped mightily by Hollywood's interference.

One day Alice picked up a popular inspirational book called *The Message of a Master*, by John McDonald. It told of a man who fought back from a complete breakdown (personal, professional, financial) by "right thinking," the period term for optimism. Essentially, it was the early twentieth-century version of a self-help book for those who believe in the power of positivity.

Her new attitude came on the heels of Lombard's letter. "If I didn't try, if I didn't fight back as Carole Lombard had, how would I know what I could do?" Alice reasoned.

(Alice didn't know it at the time, but Lombard had written to her while in her own state of mourning and shock. She was romantically involved with a popular singer, actor, and musician named Russ Columbo. On September 2, 1934, Columbo was shot to death by a friend, a photographer named Lansing Brown, who accidentally fired one of Columbo's dueling pistols. The ball ricocheted and struck Lombard's beau in the head, killing him. Columbo was twenty-six.)

At last came a reckoning. Eleanor came for her usual visit, but this time, it was her last. In Alice's recollection, after six or eight months (depending on the memoir) she demanded Eleanor take her from the sanatorium. According to Tennant, Alice insisted she had TB and wouldn't move, but Tennant angrily replied that she was already into the sanatorium for six months of fees, some 1,800 dollars (over 34,000 dollars today), and added that, dammit, Alice didn't have tuberculosis. "I'm giving this sanitarium [*sic*] back to the Indians," she said, and the two women decided then and there to bust out.

That part wasn't dramatic. According to Alice, Eleanor helped her waddle to her car, and that was it. Tennant's story, at least, is far more colorful. "I took all the pictures down in nothing flat," she told a reporter. "I took her phonograph. I took her radio. That place was cleared out in about 20 minutes and I had to walk a block to where the car was. But I took it all in my hands and ran with it." As Eleanor put it, after getting Alice dressed she half carried her down a flight of stairs, "except that we both laughed so much I had to put her down." At last they made it to her "old black Ford," surprisingly not having been challenged by a staff member. "I had to have a cigarette after all this malarkey," Eleanor said, and lit one for her accomplice as well. "So we're moving," she said, and she drove back to Beverly Hills, where Alice moved in with her and Gwen.

Starting the next morning, Alice began her long, slow road back to the top.

Chapter Sixteen

....

TRIUMPH OF THE WILL

Her first day it was as though she were learning to walk all over again. She could barely make it around the block. As she stated in *The Road to Wimbledon*, only the thought of children pointing and laughing at the whale in the tentlike frock kept her moving.

This was going to be tough.

Alice had ballooned to an unhealthy 185 pounds. Eleanor's first order of business was to put her charge on a diet. Fats and starches were out—rare steak and steamed carrots were in. "She must consider her body a perfect body," Eleanor said. "It wants to be made well and it shall be." Tennant didn't trust doctors. She was a big believer in the power of faith, part of the religious searching she had done as a child, and Alice was still in thrall to McDonald's power of positivity, so even though just contemplating the physical and financial path she needed to tread was "sheer agony," she put one foot in front of the other, every single day.

"Every time I was ready to give up," she wrote, "I remembered Carole's letter."

She was soon able to walk the neighborhood without fear of passing out. She added skipping rope back to her daily exertions, and it would become a habit for the next couple of decades. She used a cable band to build up her left arm with curls to equal her overdeveloped right arm. She also incorporated handstands into her routine. "It's grand for the spine, arms and wrists," she explained.

Alice had another, more fun recuperative device. She sang for an hour each day, ostensibly to build up her lungs and diaphragm, though the practical connection is somewhat dubious. "Singing teaches you to breathe correctly," she informed a reporter. "Faulty breathing is one of the chief causes of lack of stamina. Besides, singing is a healthy pastime. I recommend it to all tennis players." Regardless, it gave her something to look forward to, and the house in Beverly Hills cascaded with her pleasant contralto. Eleanor even arranged for a Russian opera singer named Nina Koshetz to give Alice lessons in breath control. Soon, Alice was well enough to begin the process of repaying her benefactor, taking over as Eleanor's secretary and booking clerk, the proceeds going toward the massive debt she had incurred in the sanatorium.

At the same time, Eleanor was still incurring costs. She needed to pay for doctors to examine Alice and ensure she would get better, as Tennant believed she would. The first sawbones she approached "was a quack," in Eleanor's inimitable dialect. "He was a chiropractor. I got down to the basic facts of life. I told him that I had been under a great deal of expense, so I would have to pay him a very modest fee. But at the same time I mentioned that many people in Hollywood would ask me from time to time who was the best antique dealer, dressmaker, grocery store. . . . In fact, they'd often ask for the best doctor. So he named a good low fee. And when Alice goes to see him, there's no x-ray, none of the things that have frightened her in the past, he just taps her lungs and says, 'Hocus locus, meenie focus, and you'll be very well and able to jump over the moon.' And Alice's eyes showed a dilation in the pupils for the first time in months. And she settled down to a course of manipulations with this fellow that improved her circulation out of this world."

Eleanor was dubious, to put it mildly, but seeing Alice feeling well enough to maybe get back on the tennis court made her swallow her suspicions. Plus, the price was right. Alas, the doctor also took Alice off meat, recommending she eat only "avocado pears and mashed potatoes. . . . Now when you take Marble off meat . . . you take her right eye." Alice was too shy to call the doctor to tell him enough, so Eleanor did, despite the cheap price he had quoted.

The next doctor, Ernest Commons, came at Lombard's recommendation. He was more expensive, with a slick office on Crenshaw Boulevard, but also was a medical doctor. He took an X-ray, and a blood count, and had good news—Alice did *not* have tuberculosis! She may have had it briefly, for her lungs were indeed scarred, but whatever her past condition, she was now healthy enough to go back to tennis, if she was up to the long struggle to regain her former level.

Alice was up for it, no doubt about that.

· · ·

We led a simple life, the two of us," Tennant recalled to the London *Daily Mail* in 1939. Whether that life included something more than the standard coach/student/roommate relationship, a physical one, is something Alice and Eleanor steadfastly refused to admit. For certain, Eleanor was constant as the Northern Star in her belief that Alice was still championship material. As the English tennis writer Laddie Lucas wrote, "When Teach gets a presentiment of that nature it frequently becomes a reality."

Alice wrote penetratingly of Eleanor's personality. "Teach always held something back of herself. Like a cat, she gave affection when she chose, allowed others to draw near only when she chose, and then ever so briefly. She'd withdraw in an instant, and leave you wondering what you had done. I stopped being hurt by it. Teach had her own secret agenda, and the strongest will I've ever known. She *willed* people to do what she wanted."

What Eleanor wanted was to earn top dollar teaching tennis, and having a celebrity clientele consisting of many of the biggest names in Old Hollywood greatly helped that cause. Her classrooms were several courts across Los Angeles, none more chic than the brownstone cement court at the home of Marion Davies on Linden Avenue, a stone's throw from the Beverly Hills Hotel, where Eleanor's LA odyssey had begun.

Eleanor charged Marion just a dollar an hour for her lessons in exchange for the use of the court, which was surrounded by orange trees and hothouses full of orchids rewarding players with pleasant aromas while they sweated in the velvety Southern California sun.

Groucho Marx was a regular player, tossing in trademark bon mots while he hit. "Pull up a tree, Teach, and sit down," he'd say, or "I don't know why you're complaining—I play as well as any man twice my age." Errol Flynn was "the best player of them all," according to Alice, unsurprising to anyone who watched him swashbuckle his way through films like *Captain Blood* and *The Sea Hawk*. Brits David Niven and Ronald Colman were classic gentlemen, emitting the mannerly quintessence of Wimbledon, if not the tennis talent. "Colman cooked a dinner for Alice and myself," Eleanor told a British reporter. "A meal such as you have never tasted in your life." Mickey Rooney brought his mom to the court; Mrs. Rooney was so impressed by her son's teacher that she suggested Eleanor take over Rooney's acting career, too. Edgar Bergen took his dummy, Charlie McCarthy, to the courts. He would have Charlie talk trash while others played, throwing his voice across the orange trees.

To Tennant, the worlds of tennis players and actors weren't far apart. "Their footlights are our tournaments," she would say, and indeed, the performance under pressure and in front of crowds was quite similar. There is a reason performers of every stripe—singers, rappers, actors—are drawn to athletes, and vice versa. Game recognizes game, as they say. And the intense physicality and raw realness of athletics simultaneously can attract and shame the actor. As the director Jean-Luc Godard put it, "Cinema lies, sport does not."

The one thing the stars had in common? "They all loved Alice," according to Tennant.

And then there was Lombard. She had been talking with "Allie" on the phone, but the two still hadn't met in the flesh, until one day when Eleanor told Alice without fanfare or buildup they were "going to Carole Lombard's for dinner." Her brothers and mother, the Peters family (Carole was born Jane Peters), were there, and Mom ordered her kids about "as though they were still five years old." Alice was nearly paralyzed with starstruck worry that somehow she would offend one of the members of Carole's family and never see Lombard again. But she managed to get through the evening sans faux pas and soon became fast friends with the Hollywood starlet.

She was Paramount's great female star at the time, the "Queen of Screwball Comedy," idolized by fans for her work in *Twentieth Century* and the then soon-to-be-released *Hands Across the Table* with Fred Mac-Murray. She was gearing up to play her most notable role to date, that of a socialite who hires a derelict to be her butler, only to fall for him, in the 1936 film *My Man Godfrey*. The butler would be played by Lombard's ex-husband, William Powell, and Lombard would be nominated for a Best Actress Oscar for her comedic chops.

Carole was beautiful and elegant and everything Alice aspired to be, except for the tennis part, though Eleanor always insisted "Carole could have been a great champion but she didn't have the time." Alice was often the prettiest woman in any room she was in, but not when she was with her blonde buddy. Lombard was very down-to-earth: a bawdy dame given to profanity, always up for a good time and not hung up on her own beauty. Once Alice asked her brother why Carole swore like a sailor. "To keep men away," was the response.

It didn't work. The fellas swarmed around Lombard like locusts.

Lombard was no pushover, that was certain, and possessed a core of steel, attested to by her comeback from a near-fatal auto accident. Alice treasured a scene in the film *Nothing Sacred*.

Carole's most important contribution to Alice may have been financial. She was extremely generous toward a girl she looked upon as her little sister (Alice was five years younger), buying her clothes and other gifts with no thought of repayment. She paid for a dermatologist to deal with Alice's persistent acne. And through her regular payments to Tennant, along with extra money passed along when needed, she eased the burden on both tennists, in the lingo of the day. She even gave Alice a dog, Jackie, a Scottie/dachshund mix so tiny "I could carry him in my pocket."

Lombard also was instrumental in coaxing Alice back toward her destiny. Tennant would arrange large doubles tournaments for the film folk, mainly women, on Davies's court, and Alice started helping out, giving a word of advice to Lombard, or shagging her balls. Soon enough, she picked up a racket again.

It was time to return to her true love.

Alice's first full match was a doubles affair, with her partner Louise Macy, a fashion journalist and editor at *Harper's Bazaar*. They tangled with Tennant and Lombard on Marion Davies's court. Alice recalled being "more nervous than she had been during the Nationals." Then Eleanor lobbed a meatball of a serve, and Alice whacked a sizzler back over the net for a winner. She was just fine.

As her blood count increased, checked regularly by Dr. Commons, so did her stamina. Soon she was up to two sets a day, plus her regular lesson with Tennant. When Lombard came to play, she would hit with Alice and root her on.

Teach was determined to rebuild a prizewinner, even though the student failed to see what she had to offer as she "waddled around the court short of breath, short of speed, short of everything it took to be a champion." But Tennant was powered by belief—she had faith in Alice's ability to get back to the top and, even stronger, a burning belief that she was the one to get Alice there.

By the spring of 1935 Alice was a new woman, fit and trim and— tentatively—ready for action. Eleanor took a seasonal gig in the desert, ideal for Alice's still tender lungs, in Palm Springs, "an arid stretch of Indian country burnt brown by the sun, yet distantly dominated by the soaring bulk of snow-bleached mountains," as described in one contemporary account. The brand-new Racquet Club of Palm Springs opened up a whole new set of "moving picture celebrity" students who wintered there, like Paul Lukas, along with holdovers like Flynn who followed Teach. Palm Springs in those days wasn't hugely developed—"one street and one movie theater," in Alice's recollection, though she also recalled gambling at the 139 Club, where the small stakes and hot chili were a draw for her. She and Teach lived in a small apartment above a drugstore about a mile from the club.

Alice worked in the pro shop, fending off the club bros like Flynn who talked dirty around her and made suggestive comments in her presence.

"Alice, I need a jockstrap!" the irrepressible Errol yelled at her one day.

"What size?"

"The largest you have, of course!"

Far from being shocked, Alice appreciated being one of the boys, as she had in the dugout of the San Francisco Seals. She wrote in her memoir about being uneasy among men at this time, still scarred from her assault of seven years prior, and the kidding from the fellas contrarily set her at ease.

Another of Tennant's students was Joan Crawford. She once screamed at Alice for daring to watch her lesson, chasing her from the court. Alice respected her toughness, if not her manners. Tennant adored Mommie Dearest, once saying of her, "She is a very fine mother to her children."

On another occasion a small, curly-haired child saw Alice whacking the ball with abandon and bet she couldn't do it while on a bicycle. Challenge accepted! Naturally, the top-ten player had little trouble returning balls while on wheels, and the next day's papers reported that none other than Shirley Temple had lost the bet.

Since they didn't get to spend time at Harwood White's manse that winter, Eleanor and Alice crashed for a couple of weeks at a local estate, one belonging to a family made rich by the Beech-Nut chewing gum empire. Once again, Alice, while deeply in debt to Eleanor and from a poor background, was spending considerable time in proximity to great wealth.

Rested and relaxed from her sabbatical among the swells, Alice was ready to play competitive matches again. She entered a tournament at the Racquet Club, one stuffed with top players, including Carolin Babcock, whom Alice met in the finals. Babcock, who hadn't seen much of Alice since she collapsed at Roland-Garros, was astonished at how fit she looked. Perhaps it was Dr. Commons's recommended addition to her tennis gear—a leaf or two of cabbage to wear under her trademark visor. It was an old ploy to beat the heat (Babe Ruth, among others, swore by it), and Alice obeyed her doctor's command. Whether it was the roughage or the adrenaline, Alice walloped Babcock in straight sets to win her first title since October 1933. Alice celebrated into the night, though her dog, Jackie, who was fed a score of cherries from cocktails, got more tipsy then she did.

After the tournament, Alice and Eleanor returned to LA, determined to make up for lost time. In May the United Press sent a reporter over to have a look at the progress made by the "taffy blonde with the serious eyes." "She is knocking the cover off the ball," he reported. "I feel swell," Alice said while "wiping sweat away with a huge Turkish towel." She professed her desire to head east once more, play in the US Nationals, and make the Wightman Cup team.

The first step was the California State championship, held in Berkeley in June. It was Alice's first trip back north since she fled for the sanatorium nearly a year before. "Appearing sun-tanned and supremely confident" she lost just two games in her first two matches.

Before the third-round match against Dorothea Schwartz, she was introduced as "Alice Marble from Los Angeles." "Both she and the audience got huffy about it," reported the *Los Angeles Times*, and the native San Franciscan was left wondering if she could, in fact, go home again. On set point in the opening stanza Alice hit one well wide, but the "blind linesman," in the words of the unbiased reporter from the *Times*, called it good. She went on to win 10–8 and cruised to victory from there. The eight games she lost in that set were more than in the nine other sets she won en route to the final, where she crushed her pal from San Francisco, Margaret Osborne, in straight sets, despite a "sore arm" that left her unable to unleash her usual "fire-ball service."

Lombard was there to hand Alice the trophy and did so again the following day when she captured the doubles crown with Frances Umphred.

Alice was back. And then she wasn't.

Julian Myrick reentered her life, once again to her detriment. The tennis kingpin sent out a decree stating that Alice would not be able to enter any eastern tournaments unless "she first submitted to a physical examination in New York." Tennant claimed that Myrick required as many as a dozen exams before he cleared her. The timing of this was transparent. A trip to New York meant Alice would miss a major tournament, thus spoiling any chance for her to qualify for the Wightman team. On Independence Day, Eleanor came out swinging in the press.

"Why Mr. Myrick should so suddenly become vitally interested in Alice's health is beyond my comprehension, inasmuch as it was he, more than anyone else, that urged her to keep playing two years ago when she was tired and ill, and eventually caused her breakdown."

Dr. Commons had signed off on Alice playing in the east, but after Myrick's decree, he turned unnecessarily chivalrous. "He advised that [Alice] forget tennis this season," Tennant explained. "He believed that she might suffer some nervous reaction if forced to go through all the red tape of an examination in the East." Alice reluctantly agreed and gave up on the rest of the 1935 season. It was particularly frustrating, as winning the state title had guaranteed a certain amount of expenses for Alice to travel east, and her sizzling form convinced multiple backers to contribute to her touring fund. She would be forced to miss her second straight US Nationals.

Universal News Service captured her bizarre situation: "Playing the best tennis of her life; rated an even bet were she matched with either Helen Wills Moody or Helen Jacobs, and yet 'on the shelf' by order of her physician, who admits she is physically sound. This is the strange case of Alice Marble." Instead of a summer battling with the best players in the nation and the world, Alice would have to make do with practice and a frustrating wait to prove herself once again.

Chapter Seventeen

....

THE COMEBACK KID

Sweat poured from Alice's brow as she pulled off her damp clothes, with Tennant's eager help. "Eleanor's hands were trembling as much as mine," she remembered. For long moments, there was a silence—"a shyness," in Alice's words. "We were afraid of killing the magic of the moment." The two gazed at one another in a magical reverie.

At last, Tennant shattered the stillness.

"Hit to her forehand and work the net," she said.

Coach and student were in the locker room at the West Side Tennis Club. Beyond the closed door, a packed house was buzzing over the tremendous women's final they had been witnessing. The match was locked at a set apiece. The combatants, Alice and Helen Jacobs, were taking a break before beginning the decisive set, one that would resolve which of them would be national champion of 1936.

Alice had come so far to get here, a truth she at length acknowledged after taking in some of Tennant's robotic strategy advice. "Teach, two years ago they said I would never play tennis again. Now here I am in the final set of the final round of the national championship. I want to win—God, I want to win—but if I don't, I haven't lost."

Tennant's voice was "husky with emotion" when she replied, "No, you haven't. Go and have fun."

• • •

In the fall of 1935 Tennant was officially made the tennis pro at the spanking new Palm Springs Racquet Club. Actors Ralph Bellamy and Charlie Farrell were the founders behind the club. Farrell was a brawny, athletic type and a regular at San Simeon, so he knew Eleanor and Alice well and was a great admirer of their tennis abilities.

Mostly Alice and Eleanor attended parties together. They dined and drank with Hollywood swells and tennis greats. During Thanksgiving week they enjoyed "one of those delicious Hungarian dinners," as the *Los Angeles Times* described it, at the Palm Springs Hotel. On December 7, ironically (given the import of that date six years hence), Alice and Eleanor attended a Hawaiian-themed party at El Mirador. No one officially reported them as an item, of course, but the fact is they were out together almost every night, despite their eighteen-year age difference.

Both Alice and Eleanor steadfastly refused to admit to a physical relationship, though rumors dogged them. From the first moment they were together, Alice had been warned that Eleanor was a "lesbian." In the 1920s the epithet would have carried a hip cachet on Broadway or in Hollywood, but that severely changed in the 1930s. In part, this was due to the Depression: The "cultural experimentation," as *The New York Times* put it, "of the 20s was blamed for the collapse." Anything with the whiff of the relative social permissiveness of the Roaring Twenties was suddenly the target of a backlash as the nation convulsed economically. Codes were enacted banning homosexual imagery from the movies, the stage, and advertising. Anti-sodomy laws were passed and aggressively enforced. Bars and clubs were stripped of liquor licenses if they served or employed gays.

In this environment came the publication of a new book called *Nightwood*, written by a journalist and artist named Djuna Barnes. It was the first major work to feature explicit lesbian sex scenes, and that, along with its high-quality prose and gothic imagery, helped make it a sensation, praised effusively by the likes of Dylan Thomas and William S.

Burroughs. But its taboo nature was what made it sought out by readers who had seen easy access to campy and overtly homosexual art wiped away. Any inclinations Alice and Eleanor may have had to be open and free were nonstarters in an environment that made a work like *Nightwood* an underground classic and not a celebrated bestseller.

. . .

As the ladies twirled about the society scene, they were blessedly hidden from the ever more desperate times around them. Hundreds of thousands of mostly unwelcome Okies now were storming California. The LAPD sent dozens of officers to the Nevada line to board incoming trains and evict the immigrating hoboes, and roadblocks were set up on major thoroughfares leading into the state. Others attempted to get in through Mexico, but the border patrol was vigilant in turning them away.

Jobs weren't quite as scarce as before, as LA became an industrial center beyond Hollywood. Automobile and defense industry plants sprouted all over the Southland—Firestone, Goodyear, GM, Ford, Chrysler, Lockheed, Douglas, and North American all had factories there. When WWII erupted, they would make the city an even more desired destination, as arms makers stepped up production to meet the suddenly increased demand. But in 1936 the precious gigs made those who had them fiercely protective, and interlopers, like the Okies, were treated harshly. Most new citizens found LA an inhospitable place. As Woody Guthrie sang in his "Do Re Mi,"

> *California is a garden of Eden, a paradise to live in or see;*
> *But believe it or not, you won't find it so hot*
> *If you ain't got the do re mi.*

Meanwhile, there was a new reckoning for the film stars Alice and Eleanor palled around with. While the movie colony remained the area's main drawing card, the Depression forced a new look at the falsity of the image Hollywood transmitted to the world. As the writer Matthew Ellenberger put it, "Like some frightening god of wrath, the motion picture industry remade the city in its image and transmitted that image to millions—urban sophisticate, worldly, at home in the nascent 20th-century culture with its corporate, impersonal organization and the cult of personality." LA was now Lotusland, or Pasteboard Babylon, or The Fabulous Empire of Oomph, and the novels of Nathanael West, Christopher Isherwood, and Raymond Chandler depicted a defiled paradise, one no longer synonymous with glitz and glamour but rather a mean and cynical place, if still blessed with endless sunshine and the fragrant aroma of jasmine.

Alice didn't see it that way. As she wrote in *The Road to Wimbledon*, Hollywood wasn't a den of iniquity, but "a quiet, rather lazy out-of-doors country-like town, where almost everyone wore slacks and went to bed at ten o'clock." Of course, Alice almost always went to bed at that hour, so she wasn't really aware of what she was missing on those nighttime streets.

While the sun shone, Alice trained hard for the biggest tennis tournament in the area, the Southern California championship in May. She cruised to wins in local tourneys and exhibitions (mostly sponsored by her old employer, Wilson, who supplied her with rackets) in the run-up, scarcely losing a set, much less a match. She was mostly practicing against men, including a new addition to the Tennant stable, a local high school kid named Robert Riggs whom everyone called "Bobby."

The future gambler, raconteur, and Wimbledon and US National champion was just a seventeen-year-old wiseacre in those days, a rebellious minister's kid dubbed the "bad boy of tennis" as much for the "boy" as the "bad." Even then he played a game devoid of power but had good footwork, excellent control, and sublime patience for a mere teenager. A local doctor and tennis enthusiast, Esther Bartosh, sponsored him early on, rounding up other donors when it appeared Riggs had a shot at the big time. They took Riggs to Eleanor, who was always keen to help develop "promising young players," especially those who didn't come from means.

Her tutelage was less about strokes than it was tactics and theory. "Teach even entered me in business school," Riggs recalled in his memoir, *Tennis Is My Racket*, "saying it would be valuable to me later on. Four or five mornings a week, I went to school. In the afternoons, I practiced. Before long, the school got to be too much for me, and I quit. But I never quit practicing." He was so devoted he would hitchhike twenty-five miles to see Eleanor, arising at five thirty every morning to do so. That dedication made it easier for Tennant to loan him the money to pay off loan sharks and creditors from dice games where Riggs was always losing.

At last Bartosh got him a car, and for a while he would ferry Alice around town with it. Alice found Riggs mostly irritating, both on and off the court, his soft game being so anathema to Alice's far more "physical" approach. She also resented being sent by Tennant to purchase clothes for Little Bobby. "She'd take him to this tailor and she'd buy him shirts and socks and whatever he needed," Tennant wrote. "Alice would get very very tired of him. [She would say], 'He's nothing but a selfish little guy—I don't see why I should waste my time buying him clothes.'"

Tennant, like President Roosevelt, was adept at playing her minions against one another—in this case it was literal. "Having Alice and Riggs at the same time was very healthy," she once said, "because each would fight for supremacy in my estimation of their games, and I never hesitated to say and play it up when one would be off or not playing very well—I'd say, well it's a funny thing Bobby Riggs sure played tennis out of this world yesterday. Or to Bobby I'd say, Alice sure could take you. And it always stimulated their adrenal gland and their practicing together—the two of them—was very very helpful."

So prepared, physically and psychologically, Alice easily won the Southern California title, besting Dorothy "Dodo" Bundy (daughter of May Sutton Bundy and cousin of May Doeg, one of Alice's early opponents back in San Francisco) in the final. Riggs won the men's bracket, making it a double for Teach. It was almost a banner couple of weeks for the Marbles, but Dan, the "burly San Francisco policeman," lost in the finals of the AAU handball national championship, played in nearby Beverly Hills at the private court of the legendary silent actor Harold

Lloyd. Dan "seemed to give up" in the second set as the defending champ, Joe Platak, the "slim Chicago swatter," reeled off nine straight points, and the "fans booed loudly." Disheartened, Dan asked Alice to ensure that someone in the family win a national championship that year. Alice said she would see what she could do.

This time, she would have an ace in the hole—her teacher right alongside. Eleanor was traveling east for the first time with Alice, the ultimate destination Forest Hills and the US Nationals. In both her memoirs Alice writes that they left in June, but the *Los Angeles Times* reported on their departure—May 23. They set off in Eleanor's "big snazzy Buick" on a road trip, stopping in multiple burgs along the way for clinics and demonstrations, picking up some touring cash where they could. Alice had decided not to play in the California state tournament, which would have guaranteed her the association stipend. She and Eleanor figured the road money was greater, and they were correct.

On May 25 in Salt Lake City, Alice split sets with male champ Grant Evans and was the only female player in a spirited 10–8 set of doubles. Four days later she "made a tennis survey" of the Quad Cities region, saying, "The need of this section of the country is more professional coaches. And more practice." Tennant was described in an article about the stopover as "the designer of tennis shoes for the Servus Rubber Co., Rock Island [Illinois]," a little-remarked-upon aspect of her resume. While in the neighborhood she checked in on her designs and each night wrote a series of instructional articles for the Hearst papers, dictating while Alice typed them up. Then on to Chicago for a two-week engagement overlapping with the men's national clay-court championships. And on to Skokie, St. Louis, Kansas City.

Eleanor gave her clinics to as many as five thousand people at a time, according to Alice, which seems fantastic. But there is no doubt she had a gift for mass instruction, bellowing into a hand microphone "stern, willful, yet kind and often patient" advice, in Alice's words. "She could make the laziest pupil run, and the one with the least coordination hit ball after ball over the net." Big Bill Tilden himself would recall that "I had the pleasure of conducting a series of tennis clinics with

Eleanor. . . . I can say without hesitation that I learned more tennis from her than from anyone before or since."

On June 19 they listened, astounded, to the radio as Max Schmeling, a heavyweight contender from Germany thought to be completely washed-up, shocked the world with a twelfth-round knockout of the indomitable Joe Louis at Yankee Stadium. If that could happen, the sky was the limit for Alice.

Then on June 23 a reporter caught up with Alice in Pittsburgh while Eleanor gave "demonstrations in department stores." A photog snapped a winning picture of Alice, her magnificent gams crossed, her smile wide, and blonde hair in a bob under a rakishly tilted felt hat. She described her layoff from the game as "a bore but it no doubt did me a lot of good." They were headed back to Cleveland the next day, where "two great teachers will work on me and thus give me a last minute bit of schooling before I enter the series of eastern events."

Cleveland—more accurately, Willoughby, a rural suburb to the northeast—was the vital destination, because of that second "great teacher," Mary K. Browne, the same player who had boosted Alice's spirits during her first, disastrous trip to the US Nationals back in 1931. They stayed in her house at Field Day Farm and played on her cement courts, the two teachers exchanging theories on the game while Alice played guinea pig.

It was the real beginning of a decades-long friendship, one that would supplant the one Alice had with Eleanor in time. "I immediately felt at home," she wrote upon meeting Mary once again, "and sensed that I always would be so with Brownie." This despite the fact that Browne was even older than Eleanor and had a full twenty-two years on Alice.

All seemed right with the world as they talked under the stars as the crickets chirped up a racket. Then, Julian Myrick stuck his infernal nose into Alice's destiny yet again.

. . .

A telegram arrived from California, informing Alice that the USLTA had refused her entry into all of the eastern matches. She was still a fragile jewel likely to shatter on their precious courts. Calling Myrick a "little weasel," Tennant picked up the phone and vowed to give him what for. But Mary stopped her and took a more diplomatic approach than what the volatile teacher had in store. In fairness, Tennant had put years of effort and psychological self-worth into Alice's career, not to mention a ton of money, so she can't be blamed for wanting to unload on the biggest obstacle to their shared success.

Mary prevailed upon Dr. Commons to send a telegram to Myrick vouching for Alice's health, but the association was unswayed. So in a series of phone calls Browne talked Myrick into a risky trial—Alice would prove her fitness by playing a series of matches against men. Tennant responded with expletives, but the confident Alice, grateful for the lifeline, readily agreed.

The three musketeers drove east, to Forest Hills, where for four consecutive scalding days Alice whipped the guys rounded up by the USLTA. It was hardly Don Budge or Bill Tilden Alice played—even she later admitted her opponents weren't very good, and Alice practiced regularly against far better players, like Riggs. The fourth adversary quit down 5–2, telling Myrick, "If she's sick, I'm at death's door. . . . She's hardly sweating." ALICE MARBLE VICTOR OVER MERE MAN, read a headline in the *Los Angeles Times*.

Myrick had been outflanked by Alice's talent.

Freed from her shackles, Alice attacked the summer tourneys with abandon. The "sunkist star" dominated in New England, winning twice at Longwood, both in singles and then the mixed doubles national championship, held that year at the Massachusetts club, teaming with Gene Mako to upset Don Budge and Sarah Palfrey. Possibly most impressive, playing with England's Kay Stammers in the semis of the women's doubles, she lost the decisive set by the incredible score of 21–19! Despite the defeat, Alice proved once and for all that stamina under a "broiling eastern sun" was not going to be an issue.

She then disposed of Carolin Babcock in a mere thirty-five minutes to take the Seabright title. The *Times* called it "a masterpiece of effortless, clean hitting and finished racquet manipulation that made a profound impression on the large gallery that filled the stands. The ease and restraint with which she turned back Miss Babcock's forcing shots with beautifully timed forehand drives was an object lesson in fluent stroke production and the conservation of energy."

The sight of Sylvia Henrotin (her opponent when she collapsed in Paris) in the final at Rye brought about some minor PTSD, and Alice lost that contest in straight sets. "You have to get rid of your ghosts," Tennant demanded afterward. Helen Jacobs then defeated her in the finals at Essex Country Club in New Jersey, the last warm-up before the US Nationals. Jacobs had won four straight national championships, so the fact that Alice took her to three highly competitive sets was a good sign in her mind.

For the two weeks surrounding the big tournament at Forest Hills, Alice and Eleanor camped out at yet another palatial manse belonging to admirers. Gilbert Kahn, the son of noted financier Otto Kahn, had gotten to know the ladies while chilling out in Palm Springs and invited them for the fortnight to stay at the family estate, called the Oheka Castle, in Cold Spring Harbor on Long Island.

It was an eastern San Simeon minus the patina of Hollywood glamour (though the castle was used as an exterior in the film *Citizen Kane*, breaking the irony meter), second only to Hearst's playground as the largest private home ever built in America. At 127 rooms and 109,000 square feet, there was plenty of room for Tennant and Marble, those jet-setters of the prop plane age (especially as they again shared a room). There were indoor and outdoor courts, an eighteen-hole golf course, swimming pools, a marina, and an extraordinary view of Long Island Sound.

Kay Stammers, a top British player who, like Alice, was constantly being described with adjectives remarking on her beauty, also was a guest for the duration. Alice called her "honest and scatterbrained and could tell a bawdy story with the dignity of a queen." Alice recalled that "men competed shamelessly for her attention, but she held them all at bay adroitly." One exception was Spencer Tracy, whom Kay would later date. Another was the future president of the United States, John F. Kennedy, who squired Kay while his father was US ambassador to England. Kay would say of Jack's attitude toward women, "He really didn't give a damn. He liked to have them around, and he liked to enjoy himself, but he was quite unreliable. He did as he pleased."

The Kahns provided a car and driver to ferry them to and from Forest Hills every day, following later to watch every point. Meanwhile, their butler thoughtfully provided several fresh leaves of cabbage for Alice to wear under her visor, while the maid gave her a bit of Scottish heather for luck. Ironically, the oppressive heat wasn't her problem, but a summer cold was, and after several people remarked upon how terrible she looked, Alice deigned to wear makeup on court for the first time.

She was seeded third after Jacobs and Sarah Palfrey and listed on the draw sheet as being from Palm Springs. Two days after the stars of the Berlin Olympics received a ticker-tape parade through a raucous Canyon of Heroes in Manhattan, play began in the far quieter and cleaner West Side Tennis Club. Alice cruised through two matches before running into trouble on the stadium court against Katharine Winthrop. She "slumped badly against her opponent's hard driving attack," wrote the *Times*, "and was twice within a point of losing the chapter at 4–5 and 15–40. The Palm Springs girl rose to the occasion at this critical juncture, went on to win the set at 8–6, and was never in difficulty again."

In the quarterfinals Alice had another tough chore, besting Gracyn Wheeler 11–9 in the second set. Helen Jacobs won her match, too, but jammed her thumb badly in the process. It didn't seem to bother her much two days later in the "true final" against Stammers, inevitably called a "comely British girl" by the *Times*. Her comfortable win was not nearly as easy as Alice's, who demolished Helen Pedersen 6–1, 6–1.

So it would be the dominant champion of the past four years against the roaring newcomer, and interest was at a fever pitch. Jacobs was the 5–1 betting favorite. The match was held on September 12, a Saturday, at 2 P.M., prime time for the viewing public, who were scalping five-dollar grandstand tickets for as much as seventy-five dollars. A sportswriter named Mel Heimer captured the moment. "As the thousands of fans poured into the hooked horseshoe that is the West Side Tennis Club's stadium, disgorged by the Long Island Rail Road trains, autos, subways and even bikes, one of the thoughts uppermost in most minds was 'Can Marble come back in the tournament that counts?'"

Alice and Eleanor stopped en route to Forest Hills at a roadside restaurant, where the finalist consumed her usual prematch meal of rare roast beef with sliced tomato, and two cups of tea "with plenty of sugar."

"Jake" came onto the court with a heavily bandaged right arm, evidence her earlier spill still bothered her, while Alice had cabbage under her visor lid and the good-luck heather in her shoe. Both players wore shorts and blouses, Alice's adorned with the lucky pin Tennant had given her, the one lost back in 1934 and since recovered.

"The blonde, beautifully proportioned Marvel," as the *Daily News* described Alice, got off to a "quavering, uncertain start," spraying twenty-five errors in the first set and sending the capacity crowd of thirteen thousand fans, most of them pulling for the upset, into a litany of groans, "taking it for granted the match was over," according to legendary sportswriter Grantland Rice.

But Alice courageously stuck to her tactics. In a letter to Dan before the tournament, Alice mentioned that Tennant and Browne had trained her specifically to defeat Jacobs, and it worked. She refused to get into a power struggle, instead beating her "veteran opponent at her own game," cutting down on the errors while not letting "Helen II" play her favorite shot, the "chop stroke" from deep in the back court. Instead, Alice lured her to the net, where she repeatedly passed or lobbed her. "There was real genius in the way she opened up the court," wrote another sportswriter for the ages, John R. Tunis.

It was "ear-splitting tennis excitement," wrote George Currie. "The crowd was on tip-toe with the umpire begging for quiet during the rallies when the blonde Californian swept the fading four-time national leader on the distaff side almost off the court in the second set."

After winning set number two, she and Tennant repaired to the locker room for a change of clothes, where they seemed unable to summon the words to meet the moment. Neither spoke while Alice "ran cold water on my wrists while she made tea." After nearly three years of hell and heartbreak, idleness and indignation, she was on the cusp of the greatest American title in the sport.

Later Tennant told reporters she urged her charge to "keep relaxed and don't worry. You have the world by the tail and a downhill pull." Thus buoyed by Eleanor's odd, British-inflected argot and relaxed by the knowledge that win or lose she had achieved her goal of getting back to the top of the tennis world, Alice went out for the ultimate set.

She bested Jacobs in that third-set war of nerves, during which the defending US and Wimbledon champ cracked. "[Jacobs] never knew where to expect the attack, was caught on the wrong foot repeatedly and her whole game broke down," while "Miss Marble's performance in the final set was one of the finest exhibitions of virtuosity and politic generalship this tournament has seen in years," wrote Allison Danzig in the *Times*. "The defending champ tried everything in her varied bag of tricks, but Miss Marble had the answer every time," noted Ellsworth Vines, writing in the *Examiner*.

At match point Alice chased down a perfect lob and walloped an even better smash past Jacobs. "Game, set and match!" yelled umpire Louis Shaw. A couple of weeks shy of her twenty-third birthday, Alice was the national champion. The final tally was 4–6, 6–3, 6–2. In just over an hour Alice had proven herself the "New Queen of the Courts." "Is it really true, Louie?" Alice asked Shaw, before nearly knocking Tennant over in her rush to embrace her coach.

"The weather was beastly hot but I never tired," Alice said afterward, looking straight at Myrick, who watched from his box seat. "Was he ever red," chortled Eleanor. Alice kissed the trophy, a large silver jug, to the photographers' delight. In other photos she appears to be near tears as she is presented with the jug. "I put everything I had into every shot," she told the *Brooklyn Times-Union*. "I have no alibis," said Jacobs. "My injury wasn't the reason I lost—Alice was."

It was "the most stunning comeback in tennis history," thought the *New York Daily News*, under the headline MARBLE WHIPS JAKE. They called her "Comeback Girl" and "High Stakes Marble" and said "Marble is Marvel" and noted, "Alice Marble, crushed to earth, shall rise again (to revise an old saying)."

While the praise tumbled in for Alice, it also was vindication of years of sacrifice and hard work for her coach. All the years of pushing and prodding and hauling from one end of the country to the other, of driving fifty miles a day on primitive roads to visit her sick charge in the sanatorium, of lending her money and finding her doctors and fighting her battles, of subsuming her own life in favor of her protégé's—at last, it was all worth it. As the English writer Laddie Lucas put it, "In Alice Marble's recovery from that illness and in her subsequent return to the very highest class of tennis was born this close friendship with Eleanor Tennant. It will remain in my mind as one of the most moving tales in all sport."

Back in San Francisco, old friend Curley Grieve had hung out with the Marbles as they listened to Alice win the championship over the radio broadcast on KFRC. In the aftermath, Dan, rather than being ecstatic, "unleashed a bitter broadside" on Julian Myrick, who he said "broke [Alice's] health." Jessie was more diplomatic, warmly congratulating her daughter for "the fine fight for her health." Grieve did note that Jessie "was not a tennis fan." Meanwhile, Helen Moody, reached across town by the industrious sportswriter, was coy about the changing of the guard atop her sport. "It is always a surprise when the champion is beaten" was all she would say.

The new champ returned to the Kahn manse on Long Island for an enormous shindig with five hundred guests. Emil Coleman's orchestra was on hand to perform, and the bandleader coaxed Alice to the microphone for a few songs, including "Pennies from Heaven." Tennant was so thrilled, she let Alice stay up past midnight before sending her to bed.

Alice was deluged with telegrams—from Carole Lombard, Marion Davies and William Hearst, Dr. Commons, and Freeman Gosden (the radio comedian who created *Amos 'n' Andy*), among others. Many asked for the racket she had used to win the nationals, but there was little doubt where it was headed—she gave it to Lombard. She was also asked by some Hollywood moguls, since she was "very pretty," if she would "like to go into pictures."

She answered no.

Chapter Eighteen

··

The King and I

Alice spent a couple of whirlwind weeks in New York after her title, being toasted by the press and squired around by her new best friend, Julian Myrick. "[He] had to love me," Alice said, noting that her triumph over disease and adversity had swiftly turned her story into a national slice of myth. After all, as the gossip columnist Norma Abrams wrote, "Between the time she reluctantly traded her Louisville Slugger for the strange, cat-gutted implement, and a few days ago when she smashed match point past Miss Jacobs to end the latter's four-year reign, Alice has travelled a rough road." Abrams was talking to Alice when she was told Myrick and other association officials were waiting to talk to her. "Oh, pouf!" was Alice's recorded response.

Lombard called to insist she had made everyone at her house pray for "Pinky," the movie colony nickname for Alice, before the match.

Pinky went back to California, and with her fans apparently too busy for prayer, she lost her last major tournament of 1936, reaching the final of the Pacific Southwest in LA but losing to Gracyn Wheeler in a tough match that Eleanor chain-smoked nervously throughout. Afterward she said she thought Alice "played like a Rolls-Royce heel."

While such a reaction seems like overkill in the big picture, winning this particular tournament was always more important for Eleanor than for Alice. Her Hollywood clientele was watching closely in the stands, and she felt Alice's play directly reflected upon her ability as a teacher. "Teaching celebrities and making champions you have to be very careful," she explained, "because if your pupils go into a tailspin, it's always your fault and you end up mumbling to yourself. You could get in the starvation line if you wanted to."

But the final was secondary to an encounter Alice had before one of her earlier matches. Alice went to say hello to her pal Lombard, only to find herself face-to-face with Carole's new beau—none other than the "King of Hollywood" himself.

Clark Gable.

·   ·   ·

He was born William Clark Gable, and everyone knew him as "Billy" until the movies made him larger than life. He was hardly matinee idol material, especially on the way up—famously huge, floppy ears; grotesquely large hands; the sallow skin and decayed teeth of the undernourished poor. But his rough exterior and hardy but gentle mien were catnip for the ladies, and male fans saw in him the sensitive but capable gent they saw in themselves.

He made a career of finding older women who kept him and paid his bills while he worked toward stardom. Josephine Dillon, an actress and his first wife (of five), fixed his teeth and his face and took care of him until he ran off and married someone even wealthier, a Texas socialite seventeen years his senior named Maria Langham, known as "Ria." "His career and ambition always came first," lamented a heartbroken Dillon.

He hit it big while with Ria and wasn't shy about stepping out on his benefactor, whom he needed less and less. His affair with Joan Crawford (married at the time to Douglas Fairbanks Jr.) was so blatant that Louis Mayer threatened to kill their studio contracts if they didn't knock it off. Gable traded Crawford in for Marion Davies—William Randolph Hearst apparently didn't mind. Later the King fathered a child out of wedlock with the actress Loretta Young, a multi-Oscar winner and strict Catholic whose blonde hair and athletic build caused many to confuse her with Alice. Young was sent on an extended "vacation" to deliver the girl, Judy, then claimed she was adopted. Gable never acknowledged the child in any way.

He and Lombard had met a decade earlier, and both appeared in the movie *No Man of Her Own* in 1932, but they had only recently gotten together. She was overseeing the annual Mayfair Ball benefit in Hollywood, and something clicked the night of the event. He asked her up to his hotel room, and she reportedly replied, "Who do you think you are, Clark Gable?"

Soon they were inseparable, though at first Gable insisted on keeping the affair on the down low. Lombard recalled, "We used to go through the god damnedest routine you have ever heard of. He'd get somebody to go hire a room or bungalow somewhere, on the outskirts, like at the Beverly Hills Hilton. . . . Then somebody would give him a key. Then he'd have another key made, and he'd give it to me . . . then all the shades went down and all the doors and windows [were] locked and the phones shut off. . . . But would you believe it? After we were married he couldn't ever make it unless we went somewhere and locked all the doors and put down the window shades and shut off all the phones."

Lombard was a rarity for Gable, a younger paramour, though she was the more bankable star and thus had more money for the moment. They called one another "Ma" and "Pa," or "Poppy," and Alice's immediate impression upon meeting Gable was to be reminded of her late father—indeed, Gable was a woodcutter, as Harry Marble had been, for many years before he traded in lumber for floorboards. "He gave me one of those heart-stopping crooked grins," she recalled.

Impulsively, she asked the King to introduce her match, but Gable turned her down, saying he was too shy. "I don't like crowds," said the most popular actor in the world. "I'd be too embarrassed to walk across the court in front of all those people."

Lombard asked Gable if he didn't think Alice was pretty enough for the movies, a pressing line of inquiry on both coasts, it seems. Alice laughed it off, hoping they would forget, but days later, she was at MGM, Lombard pushing her in front of a camera for a screen test.

"She sings!" cried the star.

Alice was dressed in a velvety black dress, a matching black wig plopped atop her trademark blonde tresses, and told to sing the sultry love number "Bill." It was, predictably, a disaster. Her voice was fine but the lights and cameras and overall bizarreness of the setting undid her. Gable threatened to buy the reel for when he needed a good laugh, then sympathetically told Alice of his brutally bad early turns on film. Alice was relieved but embarrassed enough to enter a charm school to better learn to walk and talk like a woman in the public eye, which she certainly was.

Alice could get starstruck like anyone else but for whatever reason was completely comfortable with Gable, which drew him closer—he was put off by the flattery offered by most fans, and Alice's genuineness and straightforward manner appealed to him. And of course, he respected her athletic prowess. He wasn't the tennis enthusiast Lombard was (Alice called him an "adequate" player) but tilted to his paramour's interests as she did to his, which were outdoor pursuits like shooting and horseback riding. The couple teamed as a doubles duo to play Alice and Bobby Riggs when they weren't shooting a film at the studio, and Gable was often around as Lombard took lessons from Tennant, with Alice teasing him for his legendary frugality.

According to Alice, Gable was ashamed of acting, considering it not a manly enough profession, compared to his father's days in the oil fields or his own in the forests. This despite his 1934 Best Actor Oscar for *It Happened One Night*. But Lombard drew him out of his innate shyness. "She's more fun than anybody," he said once, "but she'll take a poke at you if you have it coming and make you like it. If that adds up to love, I'll take it." The quartet (including Tennant) would have splash fights in Lombard's pool and grill steaks on the patio, and Alice would pinch herself for once again being in such proximity to fame and wealth.

Meanwhile, she couldn't afford to open her own checking account.

. . .

After celebrating Lombard's birthday in early October with some mid-night tennis ("Alice Marble wielded a mean racket," wrote Louella Parsons) at her Bel Air home, Alice went north. On October 17 she arrived in San Francisco on the Southern Pacific Lark to a hero's reception. Mayor Angelo Rossi was waiting at the Townsend Street train station with a "beautiful bouquet" of flowers (in addition to politics, the mayor was a florist) and a couple of limos, which Alice, wearing a "black tailored suit," and her family rode into city hall for an official reception, then back home to the house on the hill. Dan rode his police motorcycle at the head of the procession. Fans and tennis officials lined the route.

"I never said that San Francisco is not my home," she said to press questions about her loyalty to the Bay Area. "But I travel around quite a bit and it appears that my home is where I hang my hat." She was hatless that day but upon arrival at the Marble house discovered she was no longer car-less. A beautiful green Chevrolet coupe was at the curb, its nose pointing downhill at a sharp angle, straining the emergency brake. It was the promised gift from William Hearst and Marion Davies. By winning the national title, Alice had fulfilled her end of the bargain; now the power couple did likewise.

Alice was a woman in demand. That very afternoon, she dedicated new courts and played doubles on them, and that night she played yet another match at the Palace of Fine Arts. She played several exhibitions around town, including a memorable doubles match where she paired with a player named Henry Culley against the all-star duo of Helen Moody and Don Budge. Despite the disadvantage, the two tight sets were so dramatic and well played that the "fans started barracking for another set," according to the London *Daily Express*. "The umpire twice rebuked them, then gave in," apparently finding a way to convince the greats to play one more set. Alice and Culley won that one easily, 6–1, suggesting that Poker Face and her redheaded partner tanked in order to get out of there already.

Her siblings were doing well. Alice got home in time to receive the great news that her old battery mate in Golden Gate Park, her little brother, Tim, had achieved what had been Alice's dream—he signed a minor league contract to play shortstop the following season with the AA Mission Reds, who had played in the same stadium as the Seals. Both teams had by now moved to the spanking new Seals Stadium at Sixteenth and Bryant in the Mission District, where the Seals remained far more popular.

Dan had recently made the papers for his role in arresting a quartet of strikers looking to make trouble in the ongoing labor unrest in the wholesale fish industry. The "fish strike" was one of many ongoing battles between organized labor and management as the Depression continued to make life difficult even for those with precious jobs. Employers, knowing how desperate people were to keep their paychecks, squeezed employees in every area. Inspector Marble would also handle a notable case when he was tasked with finding three of Helen Wills Moody's favorite rackets, "stolen from her car in San Francisco." He never did track them down, which those inclined to believe he was sabotaging the rival of his sister found suspicious.

Alas, Jessie Marble was quite ill. She was officially diagnosed with cancer and was in far worse condition than she had been in 1934 when Alice was also sick. She was less than one hundred pounds, with a pallor of ash. Alice offered to stay home instead of departing for Palm Springs, but Jessie refused. "Go and live your life," she said. Hoping she would see her mother alive again, Alice headed back south, reuniting with Eleanor and pushing on to what had become their winter home in the desert. Alice answered enormous piles of fan mail and watched as President Roosevelt avoided the 1936 "period of upsets," winning a crushing reelection over Alf Landon.

At year's end Alice was surprised to discover she was not a champ but a bridesmaid. The nation's sportswriters thought Schmeling's upset of the Brown Bomber was the year's best comeback story, with Alice second in the voting. Alice also finished runner-up in the Female Athlete of the Year voting to Helen Stephens, world-record setter and gold medalist at the Berlin Olympics in the hundred-meter dash. She finished behind Olympic gold medalist Glenn Morris in the Sullivan Award ballot, awarded to the year's top amateur athlete. Even in women's tennis there were slights. Fred Perry, the British great, ranked her fourth in the world, despite her extraordinary nationals performance.

What did a girl have to do? But Alice didn't give much thought to the slights, because as 1936 saw its last dawn, Jessie Marble passed away.

Chapter Nineteen

....

BLOW-UP

She was known around San Francisco as the "Mother of Champions," but her heart couldn't take the long battle anymore. Officially Jessie died of cardiac failure, but it was the cancer that landed the telling body blows. She passed on New Year's Eve 1936, at age fifty-nine, having out-lived her late husband by almost exactly seventeen years (Harry had barely made it to New Year's Day before succumbing). Alice would loathe the holiday the rest of her life.

Her last letter to Alice was nearly indecipherable. "I love you, Petsy," she wrote in a spidery scrawl. "I'm praying for you. God Bless, angels keep. Mother."

Jessie's death presaged a difficult year for Alice in 1937, though you wouldn't know it from her highly enjoyable spring. She and Tennant were living the good life of the national champ and her Svengali. There was a plenitude of events, exhibitions, opportunities. Once a week in Beverly Hills, Alice and Eleanor threw their home open to friends and celebrities for a home-cooked buffet, giving the maid the night off to let Alice have a crack at making her favorites, one of which was a salad brought to her attention by a Mexican chef. In addition to lettuce, raw egg, black pepper, and lemon juice, there was "very crisp and chilled" garlic toast broken and sprinkled over it. "Now wash your hands," she detailed to a reporter, "roll up your sleeves and plunge in to mix the salad. Finish off with a liberal sprinkle of Parmesan cheese. Very good with spaghetti." She also grilled her idiosyncratic burgers—stuffed with scallions and parsley, then seared while melting butter and squeezing two lemons over them. Gable and Lombard kept returning for nights of Marble Burgers and tennis ("Alice . . . says he's very sweet and just bursting with vitality!" burbled one press notice), so the food must have been pretty good.

That spring, a pair of famous women planned for historic trips. In Oakland, the aviatrix Amelia Earhart took to the skies in preparation for a historic attempt to circumnavigate the globe by airplane. Earhart's initial leg of the journey would take her east, which was the direction Alice was about to travel as well. May brought Alice's second trip to Europe, and this time, Tennant would be going with her. Trips east and across the Atlantic sans Eleanor hadn't worked out very well in the past. Neither expected a repeat of Alice's collapse, but knowing that the woman who ran her life from baseline to baseline would be alongside filled Alice with great comfort.

New York was the stopover point before boarding a liner for England. Alice worked out at the Courthouse Club on East Sixty-Fifth Street with Francis T. Hunter, "formerly the 2nd ranking player of the country," who had reached finals at Forest Hills and Wimbledon. Hunter won three hard-fought sets but marveled, "The champion appeared to be almost as fresh at the finish as at the start." Hunter had hit with Alice in California earlier that winter—she was markedly improved and ready for England.

Meanwhile, Tennant rounded up several fat wallets—Gil Kahn, Freddy Walberg, Jack Straus (president of Macy's), Rosalind Bloomingdale (known as "Roz" to Alice and Eleanor)—to bankroll their trip and give them a letter of credit at the Bank of England. "It was really a pleasure for me not to be digging down into my own jeans for the money," Eleanor said.

They departed on the RMS *Berengaria* on May 4. Tucked in Alice's immense load of luggage (twenty-one bags' worth) was a Ciné-Kodak Model E 16mm camera, the latest piece of tech wizardry, a portable camera made for tourists that Alice would tote all over England, causing *Tennis Illustrated* to assume "it would take a whole boat . . . to carry back her load of pictures." Eleanor had drummed such discipline into her protégé that Alice boasted of knowing exactly where anything was packed in the nearly two dozen suitcases. "I decided that if knowing where my socks were would help me win Wimbledon," she wrote, "I was willing to go along with it."

The liner crossed the Atlantic even as another vessel made the trip in the opposite direction; the airship *Hindenburg* was due in to the mooring at Lakehurst, New Jersey, on May 6. Traveling the conventional way, Alice worked out every morning, walked the deck and played Ping-Pong every afternoon, and took advantage of the ship's sumptuous buffet at night.

Her facial beauty had, in her own admission, "lagged behind" her attractive athletic build. But the screen test she had taken the previous winter had helped in that regard, if not in getting Alice screen work. A makeup artist working on the set had tutored Alice on the positive benefits of a little primping. As a screen reporter noted, "He said to her, 'off with those eyebrows. They're too low down. We'll pencil you some brown ones. . . . And wear your hair longer to slim your face.' Alice says it's a nuisance having to paint on two long eyebrows a day, but heeds his advice. [She] used light lipstick, suntan powder, American perfume 'tweed' and favors red finger nails."

There was an ulterior motive to the makeup. As Alice wrote later of that Atlantic crossing, "My hormones were at full tilt." But Tennant's leash remained short, and Alice was faithfully in bed by ten o'clock—alone.

They docked in Southampton on a drizzly May Tuesday, the eleventh, Coronation Eve in England as George VI prepared to take the throne abdicated by his brother, Edward VIII, five months earlier. Alice was "wearing a blue straw pill-box hat at a jaunty angle in keeping with her reputation as the most fashionable of tennis stars" along with "bright scarlet fingernails." Besieged at the dock by the English press, Alice declared herself "as fit and well as I ever was. I cannot tell you how much I am looking forward to Wimbledon."

Tennant's optimism about her girl's chances changed with the fickle English weather. To one reporter she bragged, "Now that Alice has regained her health, nothing can stand in her way. She is the best women's player in the world today." Few would argue, but then, as now, there were other factors at work, like Alice's inexperience on grass surfaces and in Europe, where the players thought and played differently. Tennant acknowledged this to *Tennis Illustrated*. "I don't expect great things of her," she said of Alice. "Even the ball is different [in England]. . . . The courts are totally strange. Grass courts are a rarity in California and much faster than the hard courts Alice usually plays on. . . . Alice is [also] not used to tennis in wind and rain."

There was indeed a learning curve. Alice was used to warming up before her first service, even if the match had started. She tried that at her first warm-up tournament in Surrey, only to be told, "You can't do that 'ere," and lost a point. Angered, she only lost three more the rest of the match, which she won love and love on "a court ideal for water polo."

The weather and its effect on the grass courts also gave her trouble. At Richmond rain throbbed down, to the point Alice assumed play was done for the day and went shopping. Only upon returning to her hotel did she discover that the club umpire had declared the soggy courts fit to play. Alice was fortunate to be allowed to replay her match the following day. She lost in the final at Surrey to a woman named Freda James, a loss predicted by Tennant, who told a reporter, "That missy, Freda James, is sure going to leave some egg on Alice's face." Alice wore spikes for most of the match, realizing too late that they allowed little purchase. "Miss James played throughout with her socks over her shoes," noted the *Daily Mirror*, and by the time Alice did likewise the match was lost. A large photo in the *Mirror* showed Alice on all fours, having slipped and fallen, her racket about to bounce up and hit her in the face.

It was on to Middlesex, where the weather turned so hot one player went barefoot. It wasn't quite the inferno of Maidstone '33, but Alice and Anita Lizana of Chile were left gasping in a match won by Señorita Lizana on the day of her engagement, 9–7, 9–7.

"I do not think the Californian has become properly acclimatized yet," thought the *Daily Express*, "for at times she showed about as much energy as a snail climbing up Nelson's Column. . . . She went off as quickly and completely as milk does in this weather."

Alice's tricky tour continued the following week in Weybridge at the St. George's Hill courts, "the most favored tennis arena in England as regards sylvan loveliness." Alice forgot her admission pass before her first match, and the gateman refused her entry until Tennant came to the rescue. Yet again she made the final, only to lose again in three hard sets to a woman who would become her bête noire, the Polish Hammer, Jadwiga Jedrzejowska, better known as JaJa (Alice once pronounced it for an English reporter, who phonetically wrote it up as "Eeadjeffska").

The result was repeated in a final warm-up tournament at Kent, with JaJa beating Alice again, though not before Alice won over the crowd with a pair of incidents in the semis. She insisted a call was wrong on match point, letting her opponent have an extra moment on court before Alice finished her off. Her sportsmanship was warmly applauded. Earlier, battling the heat, she flung off her cap, "it fell to earth, and Miss Marble scrambled like lightning after it. Too late, Alice! Out of the cap fell—green cabbage leaves." She stuffed them back in, caught by the alert reporter from the *Express*.

It was time to play Wimbledon before she lost her head, too.

During these weeks in Blighty, Alice charmed the locals. While Tennant's colorful idiom left many a British reporter gobsmacked, Alice was "refreshingly bright and plainspoken." They catalogued every aspect of the Marble persona, from her early morning runs in a private Kensington park to her favorite drink (orangeade), to clinical breakdowns of her "American Twist" service style. When she went out to sing numbers like "Deep Purple" in a West End nightclub, the Fleet Street gang perked up their ears. And of course, they talked about her shorts. And her legs. And the way her legs looked in her shorts.

One reporter, Caroline Cambridge, went into forensic detail about Alice in Hemingwayesque prose:

Her eyes are hazel to grey. Hair parted in the middle. Generous wide mouth. Ready laugh. Good contralto voice. Prefers sporting clothes. Shorts well cut but pleatless, made of increasing whipcord serge. . . . Shirts are open-necked. Shoes widely laced to the toe. Evening gowns all have jacket or bolero. She likes printed cotton ones. Doesn't care for furs or jewelry except sporting variety. Always wears a tennis girl brooch of diamonds and sapphires in platinum ring that fits her engagement finger. Is superstitious about them. Also her horoscope. Goes in for the science of numbers. Likes staying on 'dude' ranches in California where you ride horseback and only see cowboys; Indian tea without milk or sugar; doing accounts; air travel; driving own sports car; dancing; genuine people; the green look of this country and the way we just sit around. Hates staying up late, swimming, our climate, wasting time, and the color grey.

One event the press wasn't invited to was a match with the Duke of Windsor, formerly the king of England, Edward VIII, the man who had just abdicated the throne so he could marry an American woman, Wallis Simpson (they had married less than a fortnight earlier, on June 3 in France). The two partnered in doubles, winning a "spirited match." The duke was a "rather dissipated, melancholy romantic" in Alice's eyes, but his new wife made a more positive impression. "Wallis took wonderful care of him, and I was touched to think that love had the power to alter monarchies." The couple made a better impression than King Gustaf of Sweden, with whom Alice played that spring as well. The duo lost a doubles match, which "Mr. G" (as everyone called him) blamed on the fact that Alice was having her period.

England has always been etched by class divisions; yet the tennis club that carries the name of the country has always been somewhat less elitist than others in London. It was hardly a place for the rabble to squat, but its beautifully manicured lawns and gardens along with the tea room and exquisite service in the club dining room were open to a wider caste of society than many more exclusive clubs that didn't also host the world's most famous and popular tennis tournament each summer. Club members enjoyed a number of perks, not the least being two full books of tickets to the "World Championships." Ironically, the one most favorably talked about was the cheap price to bring friends in to play (just two shillings). For all of its fame and wealthy trappings, compared to other clubs in London the All England Club was actually one of the most affordable, less than fifty pounds per year, but getting an invitation to join was the trick—the club only took in a few new members each year.

That isn't to say there wasn't snobbery and elitism. Fred Perry, three-time winner of the men's singles title, became the first British champion in two decades when he won in 1934, but as the son of a cotton spinner, he wasn't made welcome at Wimbledon. "[I was] regarded as a rebel from the wrong side of the tramlines," he wrote in his autobiography. "I still get angry when I think about the shabby way I was treated." The man he vanquished in the final was personally congratulated by club officials and presented with a bottle of champagne. Perry was given a gift certificate worth twenty-five pounds to a local jeweler, anonymously placed on his locker room chair.

The late-thirties vibe of the club and the "World Championship" was captured nicely by *Time* magazine. "'Wimbledon Week' is a fort-night in which five tournaments are played simultaneously before well-mannered, tennis-wise London crowds who stand in queues all night for tickets, [and] drink tea and ginger beer under the old green stands be-tween matches. . . . [In a country] where golf, polo, jai alai, jujitsu, and baseball are unknown, tennis amounts to a sort of outdoor Esperanto perfected by that spry, cosmopolitan band of young men and women who, in white clothes and becoming sunburns, buzz around the world to play it."

The tournament was always special for the players fluent in Esperanto, even from the first—the treatment by the host membership, the trappings of royalty seen everywhere during the tournament, the lush greensward of the courts. And inscribed over the entrance to Centre Court some appropriate lines from Rudyard Kipling's "If":

> If you can meet with Triumph and Disaster
> And treat those two imposters just the same.

Alice had proven to be the very model of Kiplingesque stoicism in the face of good fortune and bad. Now she was the top seed in her first visit to the All England Club. Her main competition figured to be Jacobs, the defending champ; German-born but Denmark-residing Hilde Sperling, who was tall, swift, and unconventional; Stammers, who was "not at her best after six weeks of illness, following shock due to a motoring accident," according to English tennis writer Ulyss Rogers; and JaJa, the slugging Pole.

• • •

Fat raindrops pelted the awning of Alice's hotel, as they had for several days, postponing the start of the sixtieth Wimbledon. There were no more clothes for which to shop, so Alice sat in the hotel lobby, tinkling at the piano in the lounge, warbling "I've Got My Love to Keep Me Warm." As she finished the Irving Berlin number ("I will weather the storm / What do I care how much it may storm? / I've got my love to keep me warm"), a man wearing a uniform, bedecked with battle ribbons, approached. It was Commander James Frye, a WWI naval officer turned Wimbledon official. "How would you like to have a look at the All England Club?" he asked. Alice swiftly rounded up a few other players and they motored over "in a black Rolls" to the club, located nearly eight miles south of London, with its now-famous postal code—SW19.

"Our voices unconsciously dropped when Frye led us through the players entrance," Alice recalled. They walked under the famous Kipling arch and out to the royal box, looking onto Centre Court, its golden green lawn "shimmering in the rain." Alice later swore she heard the sound of ghostly players, her racket-wielding forebears, rallying on the fabled court.

"I felt the hair rise on the back of my neck," she said.

A few days later, nerves sufficiently soothed, Alice took the same walk through the players entrance for the first time in her career as a participant to hit with corporeal opponents. After cruising in her debut match at the All England Club, Alice had a major struggle with a Brit named Mary Hardwick in the second. Hardwick, who would become a major part of Alice's story in the near future, "came on the court with her fair hair done up in more glorious curls than ever. . . . It was curls versus cabbage," in the words of one London paper. The fourteen thousand fans on Centre Court watched rapt as the local girl took a first set that lasted forty-five minutes, 11–9. Alice "leveled the sets with fiery tennis," using a service "sent down with such crashing pace that Miss Hardwick had to stand two feet beyond the baseline to take it. No woman in this country had ever hit a ball with so much power." The "statuesque champion of America" played brilliant tennis in the third set as well, to win the match 9–11, 6–4, 6–3.

The fourteen thousand fans weren't the only ones who got to witness the "story of courage in a women's match that will go down in the history of lawn tennis championships," in the judgment of the *Daily Mirror*. This was the first Wimbledon to be televised, and after a couple of days of static, the match came in as clear as 1937 technology allowed, "so good that you rubbed your eyes. . . . You could see Alice Marble's shorts, her dignified walk, her smashing cut service, the crowds, the creases in the linesman's trousers. . . . Like it or lump it, televising of outdoor sports has come to stay."

In the quarterfinals, Alice drew Sperling. The new prime minister, Neville Chamberlain, watched through raindrops as Alice squeaked out the first set before Sperling took command, winning the second and going up 3–0 in the third. Tennant told Alice to "get up to the net as soon as you can and hang on to it with your eye teeth," and she turned the tables, reeling off the last six games. Alice's sensational volleying was the key, her perfect touch allied with an ability to hit the controlled shot with unmatched pace. "Having seen her volleying art in full flower across the Atlantic," wrote A. Wallis Myers in the *Telegraph*, "I felt that, given the fine turf of Wimbledon that plant imported ought to flourish here." When in doubt, Alice simply bashed the ball straight at Sperling as hard as she could, rather than try to place shots that Sperling invariably ran down. "The way Miss Marble clouted that ball must make every American child thankful that she is not a schoolmistress," wrote one reporter.

"It was the most marvelous lawn tennis I've seen played by a woman, not excluding Moody or Lenglen," exclaimed one royal onlooker, the Countess de la Valdene.

To defeat her next opponent, Jedrzejowska, Alice would need to marry that heavy pace with great control. But that particular mixture is difficult to achieve, much less sustain, and it eluded Alice when she needed it most in the semifinal.

On July 1, as the British air ministry warned pilots and passengers not to take photos "prejudicial to the safety or interest of the State while flying over the British Isles or British territorial waters," Alice was bombed out of Wimbledon by JaJa's mighty forehand. "She volleyed a good deal, but injudiciously," thought one reporter. A poor backhand volley cost her a set point, "a mistake the price of which proved to be the price of the match," in the eye of *The Daily Telegraph*. Her Polish opponent capitalized with "sheer force . . . thumping home forehand drives that would have been too severe for [Don] Budge." JaJa took the opening set 8–6, and Alice wilted in the second, losing it 6–2.

"I turned to putty, like papier-mâché in the rain," Alice said later. "I believe it was the first time I was ever outhit." Her Palm Springs pal Charlie Farrell watched with a grim expression as Alice went down in straight sets. She held it together before retreating to the locker room, where she broke down and wept.

The fortnight wasn't a complete loss, however. Alice's volleying excellence made her one of the great doubles players of the era, and she captured her first of five "world championships" in those disciplines, winning the mixed event with Don Budge (unlike today, the doubles tournaments before WWII were not roundly ignored but were matters of high interest).

Nevertheless, as Alice and Eleanor stood on the deck of their liner back to America, her loss in the singles still stung despite the doubles trophy she packed in her huge cache of luggage. "I have to wait a whole year for another shot at Wimbledon," Alice whinged.

"There are a few things to think about before then," Eleanor retorted. "Forest Hills, for instance."

· · ·

Back in America, where the nation puzzled over the stunning disappearance of Amelia Earhart somewhere in the South Pacific, things continued to go south for Alice.

"Miss Marble!" JaJa exclaimed to a reporter with the *St. Louis Post-Dispatch* who didn't bother to clean up her Polish accent. "Ach! She plays so bee-oot-iful tennees—like da arteest's peecture!" JaJa didn't possess Alice's on-court aesthetic appeal, unable as she was to hit the ball without grimacing horribly, as though in agony. The woman the London *Daily Express* called the "fury of the courts" always ate apple tarts before her matches, as she believed they were "good for the service [and] makes you strong."

Alice and the "coy lass who talks and acts like on her first date" tangled twice more in the summer. She at last bested her Polish nightmare at Seabright before losing yet again to her before the largest crowd ever to watch a match at the Westchester Country Club in Rye. Everyone looked forward to a return engagement at Forest Hills in September. "A renewal of the rivalry between Miss Marble, the defending champion, and Mlle. Jedrzejowska, champion of Poland, would exert an abnormal appeal," wrote Allison Danzig in *The New York Times*.

But it was not to be. Alice was awarded the kickoff match of the tournament, at one fifteen on the stadium court. Fans packed the club, coming in from Penn Station on the extra trains mounted by the Long Island Rail Road, or on the Eighth Avenue Independent Subway trains marked "E" or "GG" to Continental Avenue in Queens. Good, hot weather drew enormous throngs. "All records for mid-week crowds at the American Championships have been broken," reported A. Wallis Myers. "Purveyors of hot-dogs and candies have been sold out."

Alice disposed of her first three opponents but was shockingly bounced in the fourth round by Dorothy Bundy. Alice cruised to a first-set win, but "Dodo" found previously untapped reserves to come back and best Alice for the first time in her career. The *Times* captured the stunning finale. "As Miss Marble's final daring backhand drive across the court overreached the sideline and was called out . . . Miss Bundy, in the moment of her greatest triumph on the courts, stood quietly at her baseline with a look of regret on her face. Instead of throwing her racquet exultantly in the air . . . Bundy seemed to be saddened that she brought about the defeat of her fellow Californian."

Alice did capture the doubles title with Sarah Palfrey, but it didn't ease the sting of another singles loss. She moped her way through a week of being feted despite her defeat. There was a dinner at the Kahn estate in Cold Spring Harbor, with guests including Gordon Auchincloss, Nelson Doubleday, Averell Harriman, and some sixty other couples, all of whom were listed in the "paper of record." Two nights later the investment banker Donald Stralem gave a dinner honoring Alice in the Starlight Roof of the Waldorf Astoria, with the usual society crowd in attendance.

One of her rich banker admirers, Freddy Warburg, gave her a beautiful silver cigarette box, so Alice could cheer up by poisoning her tender lungs in style. But even that lovely gesture was sullied when Freddy's father, Felix, passed away just hours after chatting with Alice. The death was a bookend to the one that began 1937, that of her mother. It was a year that couldn't end quickly enough for Alice.

Alice was just one year removed from being the greatest story in sports, the Comeback Kid who had bested illness, and two years away from the game to reach the ultimate height. In the seeming blink of an eye, she was now "Alice in Blunderland," a flash in the pan who may have caught a hot streak the year before but wasn't a serious threat to the game's best over time.

She would just have to work harder, get better. Fortunately, she had Eleanor Tennant to make sure that damn well happened.

Chapter Twenty

....

THE TAILOR

Alice may have had a rough year on the court, but her fashion sense, stylish verve, and what was considered her all-American appearance were making her a favorite of the designer world. ALICE MARBLE ENTERS A NEW FIELD! was the headline when Alice announced she had created a new clothing line. "They have all the details you want sport clothes to have," opined the fashionista known as "Babette." "All you have to do is meet Alice Marble and you understand why her clothes have so much personality. The best description of her is an ideal American girl—genuine, straightforward, no false nervous energy, no mannerisms, and absolutely no affectation."

As the fabled Wanamaker's department store in Philadelphia noted in ad copy, "She has some very definite ideas about clothes." In her down time between tournaments Alice had been hard at work with pencil and sewing machine, experimenting with ideas she had for designers to implement; Alice produced the "famous California suit" in brown gabardine, the "favorite California fabric," for Maison Schiaparelli, the Versace of the Depression. And every one carried not only her name but an important appendage: "Of California." She insisted on visiting anywhere her "costumes" were shown in the Golden State, often drawing a crowd and selling units by force of her presence.

Meanwhile, others, like the well-known San Francisco clothes empress Carolyn Kelsey, bayed to work with her on their products. Alice lent her name to a Kelsey collection that was sold in department stores across the country. For example, Horne's of Pittsburgh advertised "The Typical American Girl" collection, with copy reading, "So perfectly does she dress for the American scene, so sound is her clothes sense, that this tall, rangy blonde young woman has become the ideal of American fashion creators. . . . And Alice Marble fashions are presented to Pittsburgh exclusively by Horne's." These included the Alice Marble Gabardine Suit ("Soft English-drape jacket with sculptured bustline and new longer, modified hip. Navy blue or black . . . $29.75"), the British Blade sports jacket, and the All-American Wardrobe Suit ("The fitted Shetland topcoat Alice Marble wears over the matching two-piece suit! . . . $49.75").

Or there was the "Minute Woman" shoe Alice designed personally for specially designated shops, like Coward Shoe of Boston. "On your feet all day?" asked the ad copy. "Housewife or business woman, you want a shoe that lets you forget your feet. Here's a seamless one-piece military Oxford that's an ace for comfort—with the tailored smartness you never tire of. . . . This shoe is made of polished supple calfskin, with a sturdy men's weight sole that flexes with your foot." She also designed her own tennis shoe, one with a special "non-slip" sole, for Converse, working "personally with our designers," as the ad copy for the shoe company crowed. It featured "hundreds of deep slots in the unique *molded* sole, placed at the proper angle to provide instant, sure-footed traction on every type of court," along with "ankle-fashioned contours with reinforced web back-stay . . . ventilating shank eyelets . . . and a reinforced pebbled toe strip."

In the coming years Alice would become almost as well-known for her clothing as for her tennis. In a time when athletes weren't expected to show any dress sense, Alice was iconic for hers and, alongside her fellow San Franciscan Joe DiMaggio, wore those clothes more attractively, with better posture and fit, than any athlete of the time (arguably of any era until Michael Jordan came along).

Alice was paid a modest wage for her designs and a small licensing fee for arrangements like the one with Horne's. Athletes had yet to fully leverage the value of their names on products, with rare exceptions like Babe Ruth and DiMag, who was still years away from his peak in that department. Alice also endorsed a long line of Wilson rackets, for which she got the free use of them, though the restringing was up to her.

Or rather Eleanor, for what Alice made went straight into Tennant's pocket, as Alice attempted to chip away at the mountainous debt owed her coach, by now into five figures. Alice was a polymath, skilled in many areas, but it seems part of her boundless energy was driven by a need to earn enough to pay her debts. Alice wasn't paid anything for being national champion in 1936, remember, or for winning the mixed doubles title at Wimbledon. Only through employment off the court could she begin to repay Eleanor, who was continuing to pick up all of Alice's expenses on a day-to-day basis. So anytime she sang in a club or appeared on a radio game show or sold a new design for women's tennis clothes, the money didn't even make a pit stop in her bank account— which she didn't even have: It went right into the one Eleanor had set up for their combined usage.

The money coming in via Eleanor's teaching had taken a hit when Alice fell to Bundy. "Teach" now had the top-seeded players of both genders under her wing, as both Alice and Riggs were ranked number one in the country to end 1937. But Alice's loss in the '37 US Nationals had dented Tennant's business among the fickle crowd. "I lost many pupils when Bundy beat Marble," she complained. "I very carefully folded up my tent and moved to another area until I put Marble back on the map."

That meant hard work at Beese White's estate, and more in La Jolla, and in Palm Springs. The coaches added a topspin to Alice's forehand, weaponry to combat the JaJa howitzer. "I can bang the daylights out of the ball now," she bragged to the *Examiner* in March. It was another chisel to the stone by the sculptor, Eleanor Tennant.

Alice's future doubles partner, Sarah Palfrey, once noted that Tennant "advised Alice on all matters; what to wear, what racket to use, and how to improve her strokes." That could be expanded to include how to drive, what spice to use on meat, how to talk in social situations, and any of a thousand other areas of comportment, large and small. "Tennant taught her not only a new forehand but also numerology, bodybuilding, cooking, how to act in the company of screen celebrities and the fundamental points of Bahaism," said *Look*. Alice even sounded a bit like Eleanor now—her voice was deeper and her dialogue not so inflected with argot, but Alice maintained a vaguely British accent and proper tone that was clearly Eleanor's.

For Eleanor such complete control was a boon for Alice. "Alice had perfect timing and rhythm and no inhibitions," she said after Alice's career was over. "There was a reason why. . . . Because for eleven years she didn't have to worry about income tax or making a living, because it was my good fortune to make a home for [her]. As a matter of fact her mother died not many years after we started to work. So Alice lived in very pleasant surroundings. All that she had to do was go out and play tennis, take her singing lessons and enjoy life. And that showed in her tennis game. The players who have struggles, who have fears, they show it by not giving vent immediately to their serves or their overheads. You can always tell a bit of repression."

"She convinced me I was good at nothing *but* tennis," Alice lamented much later, "and I focused entirely on my sport, just as she intended." But that was a viewpoint from years in the future. In the moment Tennant provided a crucial buffer between reality and Alice's outsize dreams. It's not ever a realistic goal to become the best in the world at anything, and to actually accomplish it means passing on any number of distractions. Tennant not only allowed that paradigm but demanded it. She was a father to replace the one Alice never really got to have, and a mother to replace the one who wasn't well or interested enough to do the job. Eleanor was completely devoted to Alice and her every waking hour, someone who knew her down to the marrow, because so much of Alice had been created by her.

In her tennis history *Love Game*, the writer Elizabeth Wilson likens the Marble/Tennant relationship to that of longtime ballet partners Rudolf Nureyev and Margot Fonteyn. The veteran dancer had taken the wondrously gifted but raw Nureyev and shaped him into a great artist but also one who was fully dependent on Fonteyn to achieve those heights. What the two duos had with each other was "better than sex," more intense and personal, based not on passion or lust or even love but the perfectly aligned meeting of goals and the all-consuming desire to achieve them. Eleanor had the chops to be a great champion, but circumstances prevented it. What she wanted most was to be responsible for the creation of the all-timer she would have been, and Alice wanted to be that lump of clay molded into a champion and a life greater than that of a poor farmer's daughter.

As the two sailed to England in May 1938, that mind meld was still intact. But Alice was "longing for someone to love me." She wrote about relieving her sexual tension in the darkened cabin aboard the spanking new *Queen Mary* "in the way every adolescent learns."

· · ·

The *Queen Mary* docked in an England gripped by fear of a new war. Europe certainly hadn't forgotten the horrifying carnage of WWI, but here they were, racing toward more of it, prodded along by the rise of fascism and Adolf Hitler's insatiable demands. In March Der Führer had annexed Austria to expand Germany's southern border, and now he was insisting on taking the Sudetenland in Czechoslovakia to the east. The British and French were arming to stop him if he did so.

Alice and Eleanor weren't much touched by the dread that settled over the nation. Eleanor had gotten them invited to a series of manors and estates at which to crash while playing the English tour. Noël Coward got in touch and invited Alice to sing a pair of songs at a charity benefit for orphans. The American women had journeyed over on the *Queen Mary* with Roz Bloomingdale Cowen, divorced wife to the department store magnate, and her children, including Alfred, a twenty-two-year-old former football player at Brown who became friendly with Alice. The high-society companionship was old hat to the poised and open Alice, and she played well in the lead-up to Wimbledon, though her new forehand remained spotty. That included a crushing victory over JaJa, a display *Daily Mail* sports reporter Stanley Doust called the "best lawn tennis I have ever seen," and yet another defense of the Wightman Cup, held at the All England Club. Alice played first singles and was defeated by Stammers, "cool as an iceberg" in the words of the *Daily Mirror*, in the first match in three pulsating sets, a famous victory for the home side, after which the women were "completely engulfed in a tide of youthful autograph hunters" at the club gates when they tried to leave. Alice rebounded to win her other singles match and clinched the Cup with a doubles victory while paired with her new favorite partner, Sarah Palfrey. "My baby Alice is now a killer," Eleanor crowed to the press.

But did her newly murderous tendencies affect her allure? The *Daily Mirror* put it to the test, running a contest asking its readers to determine the "Glamour Girl of Tennis." Alice was among fifteen contestants, including Moody, Jacobs, and Stammers. Readers were invited to rank them with scores from one to ten in several categories, including vivacity, poise, style, confidence, sociability, figure, and sportsmanship.

"The reader whose voting list most nearly coincides with the votes of the majority and who sends the best letter in support of the No. 1 choice will be the *Daily Mirror*'s guest at Wimbledon for a day during the championships."

Unsurprisingly, it was the hometown gal, Kay Stammers, who was voted top Glamour Girl by the *Mirror*'s portion of the London populace. Alice finished a distant sixth though was the recipient of the most poetic letter of support, courtesy of Miss Geraldine Brett of South London:

> Alice Marble, glamour girl,
> Looks like Venus, but she's real
>
> I love to see her on the courts,
> Cute and smart in week-end shorts.
>
> Every time she hits the ball
> Men feel small, she's so tall.

Alice plays a sporting game,
Really she deserves her fame,

But I hope when she has won
Lots of prizes, she'll have fun
Ere she leaves our Wimbledon.

Not everyone was so enamored with Alice's "week-end shorts." Father Clement Parsons, parish priest of St. Albans, took to the *Mirror* to declare shorts on women to be "offensive to the ordinary standards of Christian morality," encouraging "sensuality among young men." The wearer of the "shortest shorts" was asked to respond. "I laughed like anything when I read the article," Alice said. "It was most amusing. I don't know why shorts should have the effect on young men that the reverend gentleman makes out. I used to wear skirts, but what happens when the wind blows?"

She added, "He has his ideas, and I have mine."

· · ·

Legs bared to the public, Alice took the Centre Court at Wimbledon on June 22, the ryegrass green as a billiard table and not yet worn to chestnut brown by a fortnight of match play. She won her first match love and two, feeling as "gloriously right" as did another famous Yank athlete that day—Joe Louis, who avenged his shock defeat at the hands of the "Black Uhlan of the Rhine," Max Schmeling, pulverizing the German at Yankee Stadium in the first round and winning a decisive symbolic victory over the Nazis in the process. Inspired, Alice cruised into the semifinals and a showdown with Jacobs.

Helen Jacobs, aka "Helen II," handicapped Alice's game in a piece she wrote for *The New York Times*.

Alice Marble has the game to win—whether or not she has the temperament remains to be seen. . . . There is no question that she has the most versatile service in women's tennis. She can hit the flat, sliced or top-spin service with equal ease. She is somewhat confined to the flat forehand drive, although it does not require great effort for her to hit a top-spin drive. Her backhand seems always to carry a slice, but when in an attacking position she can make the flat shot as well. It is her ability to play in the fore court, as well as her ability to play the shot that brings her opponent in, that equips her for the all-court game. . . .

Of my own chances at Wimbledon I prefer to say nothing.

They were pretty good, as it happened. Battling injury and sickness, Jacobs entered the tournament unseeded, and before her second-round match she fainted in the locker room from dehydration. "Only a sporting gesture by Miss Joan Ingram, who agreed to play the match the next day, prevented Helen from losing the match by default," reported the *Mirror*. Given the reprieve, Jacobs crushed Ingram and sailed to the semis and a hotly anticipated date with Alice.

A driving rain caused a forty-minute delay before the match. Regardless, Alice wore her finery, entering the court in a Lombard-designed jacket over her fabled shorts and salmon-pink cardigan, "blond curls protruding from under a baby blue jockey cap." The actress had sketched out the jacket design for the occasion, one that impressed Gable enough to bring the drawings to his tailor, who produced it. Gable's patched pockets and bumpy tweed jackets had inspired Alice to design a similar one for women. Jacobs wore a severe red sweater and white pleated skirt. Despite the soggy grass, "hundreds were packed in the free standing room around the center court and refused to leave. Their expectations were not in vain," enthused the *Times*.

Jacobs led in the first set 5–4, but Alice was about to tie it up when she netted an easy smash. "As long as life lasts," wrote Thomas Hamilton, who sent his reports back to *The New York Times* by special wireless, "those present at this afternoon's matches will remember the roar that went up when Miss Marble . . . smashed the weakest of all lobs into the net—she then kicked the ball high in the air, and well she might, for Miss Jacobs then came up irresistibly to take the set."

In the second Jacobs once again led 5–4, and once again Alice was on the verge of knotting matters. But Jacobs pulled off the "greatest passing shot of the afternoon" for ad, as "Miss Tennant's cigarette went out and fell from her mouth," according to the *Daily Express*. Then "Marble's forehand betrayed her for the last time in this Wimbledon," and she was out of the tournament.

"A roar went up," wrote the *Express*. "Alice in despair threw her racket out of the court; it bounced and bumped. But its owner went to the net again, shook hands, tried hard to laugh." SKIRTS OVER SHORTS, read a jubilant headline in the stodgy *Daily Mail*.

"Although she has probably the finest game of any woman playing today," thought Hamilton, "[Alice] seems unable to escape from the jinx that keeps her from the heights." Hazel Wightman, eponymous sponsor of the Cup tournament, dressed Alice down while in the presence of the legendary sportswriter Herbert Warren Wind.

"You lost the match when you started dramatizing yourself all over the court when you netted that drive," Mrs. Wightman said, referring to the missed smash in the first set. "You slipped and fell down on the shot, right? You didn't brush off your shorts and get back into the match," Mrs. Wightman boomed. "No, you patted your fanny, and got a nice ripple of laughter from the gallery. So you continued to pat your fanny, and while you were amusing everyone you netted two more simple shots and gifted Helen the set. Your mind wasn't on your tennis. It took you two full games before you were back to business, and after that you never caught up. Even a girl with your natural equipment can't allow anything to break her concentration."

Wightman kept going to Wind after Alice trudged from the club. "The gallery ate it up when they saw an attractive girl like Alice kick the ball after a bad shot or whack it into the backstop. But that's where Alice was wrong. She was thinking of the impressions those displays were making on the galleries and it was hurting her tennis."

Wightman recalled later, "She took it very well, a lot better than 'Teach' did when she got word that I was tampering with her pupil."

It wasn't a wasted trip, for Alice and Palfrey won the women's doubles, and the Marble/Budge duo was unstoppable in mixed, giving

Alice two titles to take back home. But the popular perception was summed up by a Wimbledon official named Samuel Bearle, a man "in his cups" as one attendee whispered to Alice. Bearle tipsily talked about the "Wimbleship Championship" before introducing Alice at the Champions Ball by calling Alice "the girl who is so very nice, but never wins."

Alice hung around for the ball despite the slap, singing her standby, "Deep Purple," and dancing with the US ambassador to the Court of St. James's, a bootlegger and movie magnate who had high political hopes for his eldest son, Joe Kennedy Jr., and whose second son, John, had just turned twenty-one. The old man, Joseph Kennedy, was notoriously isolationist and would happily let Hitler have what he wanted in Europe, but even he recognized the obvious.

Alice said Kennedy warned her while they waltzed, "If you are ever going to win this thing, you better do it soon. There's going to be a war that will make all of us forget about tennis."

Chapter Twenty-One

....

Brief Encounter

Frustrated and tense, Alice was in need of a break. Roz Bloomingdale Cowen suggested a pop across the channel to Le Touquet, a French casino town facing Blighty from the other side, and Alice leapt at the idea, as did Eleanor, who fancied some roulette and baccarat. A fashionable spot loved by the "smart set" in Paris and London, it was particularly popular in the twenties and thirties when the Duke and Duchess of Windsor, Winston Churchill, Noël Coward, and P. G. Wodehouse were regulars. If nothing else, it promised a seaside frolic and a break from tennis for a few days. Hopefully the Nazis wouldn't invade while Alice was in France . . .

Alice never named the hotel where she and Eleanor and Roz and Alfred stayed, but someone with the surname Bloomingdale would almost certainly have put down at the Westminster, a hot spot since it opened in 1924. A grand redbrick art deco masterpiece on the outside, it was brass and mahogany and plush red velvet carpeting on the inside, a playground for the wealthy, the connected, the wannabes.

Alfred quickly met a woman who towered over him and whose bust nearly burst her seams, leaving the shrimpy Alfred in danger of "losing an eye if the threads failed," as Alice recalled. The two made a date, and Alfred prevailed upon Alice to cover for him with his mother.

After taking in a movie alone (Alice didn't gamble, unlike Eleanor), Alice went back to the hotel. In the lobby she met a debonair man in a tuxedo who deployed the ultimate pick-up line—he told her how great he thought she was at tennis.

The other men mentioned as paramours in her life—and, of course, Eleanor—never actually had relations with Alice, according to her memoir. This man, who revealed himself as a Swiss banker, one whom Alice called "Hans Steinmetz" (admitting up front it was a pseudonym for reasons that will become clear as her story advances), did. Alice said she lost her virginity on the beach outside the hotel. "Hans," more of a louche playboy than businessman, had been at Wimbledon to see Alice play, and the two fell immediately into a torrid affair that lasted while they were in the bubble of the luxurious gaming resort. For the first time since coming under Eleanor's spell, Alice lost herself in someone else.

Alice tried, apparently, to keep the affair secret, fearing Teach's reaction. In the memoir she notes that young Bloomingdale warned her, saying, "You made the society pages. Teach may know." This detail opened the door for me to check said society pages; a researcher in England worked with me to help hunt down press notices of the tennis star making time in the gambling resort, perhaps with the handsome banker.

Predictably, I suppose, there was nothing in the English press. I performed a check of the multiple French papers that have digitized archives—likewise nothing. *Rien.*

Whether or not it was reported upon, Eleanor did, according to Alice, know. In *Courting Danger* Alice writes that ultimately, Eleanor threw a fit about losing control of her puppet. She insisted Alice break off the affair and "pray you aren't pregnant." Her argument bordered on the operatic. "Who was there for you when you were sick, when everybody thought your career was over, and even when you didn't believe in yourself?" Tennant asked crossly.

"You were," Alice replied, "miserably," as she would later put it.

"Who stuck by you last year when you couldn't win a tournament?"

"You."

"Tell him it's over. Or find another coach."

So Alice broke it off, she wrote, making her personal life miserable, though her professional life didn't suffer much. She returned to the US in late July and promptly won the Seabright tournament for the third time.

. . .

Never before has the turf looked quite so inviting and luxuriant at the West Side Tennis Club," opined the *Times* on the eve of the 1938 US Nationals. "Wimbledon could hardly provide a truer stretch of greensward than the one that presented itself to the eyes of the opening day crowd of 6,000 spectators in the stadium, and the grandstand court, with four feet of space added behind each baseline, was perfect. A huge new scoreboard directly to the south of the marquee and facing the tea garden reflected the thought given to the interests of the gallery. Thereon were posted the court assignments of the various matches and the progress of the score of each one as reported at short intervals by telephones."

For the first week, the improvements in Forest Hills were the talk of the town. Then the rain started, and the wind. For a week play was put on hold and the ideal "stretch of greensward" demolished by the infamous monster hurricane of 1938 (they were not given names until 1950, and female names until 1953) that devastated New England and eastern New York. Queens was spared the worst of the storm, but not a weeklong epic downpour that put the tournament on ice.

Day and night, groundsmen did what they could to protect the courts, watched by optimistic folks who refused to abandon hope that play would resume despite the howling conditions. "Clad in raincoats, slickers, topcoats and rubbers, they waited patiently in the stands or beneath the shelter of the stadium for hours," reported the *Times*. "Many of them had their shoes and trouser cuffs splattered with the red clay ooze of the parking spaces. . . . All morning the telephone trunk lines of the West Side Tennis Club had been clogged with incoming calls and thousands, unable to get a connection, started for Forest Hills without knowing whether or not there would be play."

That went for the players as well. Oheka Castle was being sold, so the Kahns moved to the other side of Sagamore Hill, living in a slightly less palatial manse in Oyster Bay, close to the home Theodore Roosevelt, the current president's cousin, had lived in for much of his life. Alice camped out there, passing on an invite to dodge raindrops and watch Seabiscuit race at nearby Belmont (the fabled horse finished third that day, five weeks before beating War Admiral in their famous match race). She did leave the house to get in workouts at the Heights Casino in Brooklyn and go to the movies with Budge and some other players. One flick they saw was the ironically titled *Carefree* with Fred Astaire and Ginger Rogers.

Few were carefree that nervy fall of '38. Even as Alice & Co. waited while "puddles on the tarpaulin grew into lakes," Neville Chamberlain was in Munich, appeasing Hitler by letting him have what he wanted in the Sudetenland. Anything to avoid war. The Japanese were pillaging their way across China, having invaded the year before. In Manhattan, an unknown radio performer named Orson Welles was prepping a script for a radio broadcast scheduled for the day before Halloween, a recreation of *The War of the Worlds* that would panic an edgy nation.

Three French players at Forest Hills, Jacques Brugnon, Yvon Petra, and Bernard Destremau, were called home by emergency cable, told to return at once for military mobilization. Petra's father was a general in the army, and his two brothers were in the ranks already. Several players wondered aloud if they would ever see the Frenchmen again.

For those inclined to see signs and omens in everyday life, like Alice, the monster hurricane was a portent of bad things on the horizon.

Fortunately, there were few bad signs in her tennis. Alice had played well in the lead-up to Forest Hills. The doubles championships were held that season outside Boston at the Longwood Cricket Club, and Alice captured both the women's title (with Sarah Palfrey) and the mixed (with Don Budge), giving her four major titles on the year. In the wake of the double, she came to New York to ready for the nationals, taking time out from practice to appear on a variety show on WABC hosted by Ted Husing that also featured the "comedy of Henry [aka 'Henny'] Youngman."

She began play at Forest Hills on the still-pristine courts by crushing her first three opponents. In the quarters she dropped her first set, to Stammers, but followed up with "one of the finest exhibitions of shot-making the tournament has ever seen" to blow out the Englishwoman in the third set at love.

A full week passed as the heavens opened before Alice finally took the court against her doubles partner, Sarah Palfrey. Having shared a side of the net with Alice, the "doll-like Bostonian" devised a winning strategy despite the difference in heavy artillery, playing a "beautiful, heady match" that won the first set and kept Marble spinning off balance throughout. Palfrey was on the verge, up 5–2 in the second and possessing two match points, when Alice snapped into gear. "Shots that had been heading wide suddenly started to nick the lines," she said, still not sure exactly why her game turned suddenly at the brink. "When the ball left [Palfrey's] racket, I knew instinctively where it was headed."

"From that point on the Californian played as brilliant tennis as she ever has shown at Forest Hills," wrote Allison Danzig. It was the magical feeling of being "in the zone," and before Palfrey knew what happened, Alice had stormed back to win the second set, 7–5.

As the packed gallery went "bananas" and a captive audience listened on WNYC radio (locally) and WABC (elsewhere), Alice eked out the deciding set by the same score, blasting serves to Palfrey's backhand then racing in to "smash with gusto." Palfrey, "a valiant retriever and defender throughout, seldom yielded a point without a struggle," wrote one reporter, "but Miss Marble was playing tennis that was simply invincible in its power and control." Alice secured the match with a winner, her 122nd point of the match. Palfrey also notched 122 points—just not in the correct sequence. "Palfrey lost under heartbreaking circumstances," wrote Danzig.

By contrast, the final was a night at the movies. Alice took on Aussie Nancy Wynne, or "Husky" Nancy, as *Time* body-shamed her (while the

Daily News drooled, "If they paid off on curves instead of points, the beauteous Alice Marble woulda won Wimbledon"). A "happy-go-lucky girl who works half the year as a stenographer and smokes cigarettes constantly," Wynne was a low seed who had clowned her way through the bracket. She "delighted the crowd by waving to friends between points and playfully tapping herself on the head when she missed a shot," but for all her antics she found herself facing Alice, who was not in a jocular mood.

A packed house of fourteen thousand fans, many of whom had paid outrageous prices of up to twenty-five dollars for a ticket, were barely seated when the match was already half-over. "Both players played uncompromisingly," Danzig wrote, "throwing caution to the winds, and Miss Wynne, unable to get her strokes under control, was stampeded into summary defeat."

Incredibly, the first set was over in just seven minutes! Alice won it at love, and though she dropped three games in the second, a mere twenty-two minutes after the umpire called, "Play," Alice was hoisting the cup. "From start to finish she flew around the court, attacking unmercifully in a remarkable exhibition of sustained power under almost perfect control." Wynne had "almost conceded defeat from the start."

Alice didn't even bother to shower.

She had regained her US championship in smashing form, easing the pain from losing both Wimbledon and the burgeoning relationship with the alluring "Hans" over the summer. Tennant had her pupil where she wanted her—close to the summit of the sport but still with a shining goal to pursue: the world championship, the Wimbledon singles title.

But war was clearly coming, and there wouldn't be many more opportunities. If Alice didn't win in 1939, she might never achieve the one victory that had eluded her (and Eleanor) since the two women had formed their partnership.

Surprisingly, given Alice's reputation for focus, her response to the do-or-die pressure of the coming year wasn't to practice harder but to take on an entirely new challenge.

Chapter Twenty-Two

PITCH PERFECT

The New York tabloids have always done headlines well, and this one in the *Daily News* was a doozy:

ALICE MARBLE SWINGS FROM SINGLES TO SINGING!

Alice had kept up her interest in singing, taking sporadic lessons from the well-known maestro and coach Ted Streater (given credit for teaching Kate Smith, whose voice and magnificent breath control Alice admired enormously). Lombard encouraged her to sing for an audience, but though occasional articles mentioned her desire to become a "radio singer" and she had indeed sung on stage as an ambitious amateur, Alice's professional singing debut came on December 1, 1938.

Unlike previous years, Alice and Eleanor hadn't immediately trained it back to the West Coast after the nationals. Instead, they hung around New York, soaking up the celebrity scene and cashing in on paydays where possible. They traveled to Louisville and Washington for exhibitions, Alice appeared on radio programs, even filled in as a guest commentator on a football game broadcast. She kept her tennis chops up at Courthouse on East Sixty-Fifth Street with several male partners.

Meanwhile she enjoyed a bit of the nightlife, especially while Budge remained in town. In October she hit the swanky El Morocco nightclub in a "wine-colored dress with puff sleeves." She apparently missed the main event of the evening, however, which was a brawl between tennis star turned actor Francis X. ("Marks the Spot") Shields and former Yale football star James Coleman. Seems Coleman "didn't like Shields's face" and the two traded insults before stepping outside, where the racket man downed the gridiron great with a single punch, earning Shields the tabloid title of "Champion cafe society fighter."

From nowhere came the opportunity Alice desired most. An agent asked if she would audition to sing cabaret style at the Waldorf Astoria Hotel. Flabbergasted but excited, Alice came to discover that Emil Coleman, the bandleader who backed Alice at Gil Kahn's parties, had recommended Alice take over for Cobina Wright, a "pretty 17-year-old" who was wrapping up a stand at the hotel on Park Avenue at Forty-Ninth Street. So Alice walked the few blocks in the biting New York cold to sing in front of Coleman and Lucius Boomer, the fabled president of the Waldorf.

She broke into "Thanks for the Memory," the song Bob Hope had made famous earlier in the year in the film *The Big Broadcast of 1938*. After just a few bars, her audience of two walked out. "Was I really that bad?" Alice wondered to herself. She needn't have worried—Boomer walked back in and said, "You'll do fine. You start in eleven days."

Holy crap. This was real.

When asked by the press why she was doing the residency, Alice answered bluntly, "I have to make a living." Despite her tennis success and high-society living, Alice was basically penniless. At least she had Eleanor to bankroll her. Other top players had to compete and train while living on the pittance granted them for expenses by the USLTA. Alice received it, too, though all the players were expected to keep quiet about it. The public, and more importantly the rich benefactors like the Kahns who opened their homes to Alice, were supposed to believe that tennis remained strictly amateur—as if a billionaire was suddenly going to turn up his nose at the sport if it was discovered the players got a small amount of expense money.

Even that money wasn't necessarily theirs to keep, as Alice had discovered after she collapsed in Paris and the USLTA's first order of business was an attempt to claw back the money it had fronted her for the trip to Europe. A recent article in *Newsweek* detailed the expenses Helen Wills Moody had to return to the USLTA after defaulting from the 1938 nationals due to "bouts of neuritis." She refunded $1,309.45 to the USLTA, money that was supposed to last her the entire summer and into October.

"Thus," wrote the magazine, "for the first time in US tennis history, an amateur player openly admitted receiving payment and named the exact amount. The public, which has long assumed that such dealings go on, was shocked only by the meagre evaluation of Mrs. Moody's services."

Even the greatest stars lived on the slimmest of margins, so unlike the riches earned even in the early days of the Open era, much less today. Their extreme talents and efforts weren't rewarded with hard currency. "All she gets," wrote one sympathetic reporter of Alice, "besides tournament expenses and bruised knees, is a silver cup—if she wins. Not much? Well, Alice Marble says all work and no pay is fun."

It wasn't, so of course Alice took the gig at the Waldorf. Doing well at it, and not sullying her name, was another thing. She did possess a good voice, the pleasing contralto she inherited from Jessie, one that had "a mellow quality" that fit the "dinner and supper hours," according to the *Brooklyn Daily Eagle*. "I'm a quiet singer, not a speedy one at all," Alice noted.

But she needed more than just a good voice. It seems odd to modern minds, but singing at the Waldorf for the rich and powerful, rather than on the radio for the masses, wasn't a particularly welcome move in the eyes of her many fans west of Park Avenue. The "decadent" nightclub scene didn't mix well with their image of a proper sportswoman. There was also the not-insignificant matter of the fact that Eleanor most certainly did not approve. "For once I ignored Eleanor's protest. . . . Teach hated it," Alice wrote in *Courting Danger*. Anything that didn't involve a racket was wasted time as far as she was concerned.

Eve Symington, a beautiful society lady, had stunned the swells back in 1934 by singing for her supper—or more accurately, singing to raise money lost by her husband during the Depression. She was a smash, earning up to 1,000 dollars a week doing so. The "socialite singer phenomenon," as *Life* called it, sprang up in her wake. "A few of them want money, work hard," sniffed the Luce publication. "But most want publicity and glamour and do little work. None of them tries the tougher Broadway night clubs where their names would mean little. Staid society, already aghast at the publicity appetite of today's debutantes, thinks the trend is deplorable."

Still, for that kind of dough Alice was willing to risk the brickbats of the 1 percent. And at heart, there was also the pure delight she received from belting out a number. "Singing is something I do all by myself and that appeals to me," she told the *Daily News*. "In tennis, if an opponent plays badly, it spoils my pleasure in the contest. Nothing spoils this pleasure." Just to make sure, she embarked upon what she told a reporter was "two weeks of the most intensive practice, athletic or non-athletic, I have ever known." Guiding her was the voice coach Al Siegel, mentor to many of the most notable singers of the day, including Ethel Merman and Bee Palmer.

The reporters called her a "handsome beauty," "Fair Alice of the Court," a "lovely canary bird" with eyes either "roguish blue" or "green" or "steel-grey" or "hazeltine" depending on who you read, or perhaps the light she sat in while talking to reporters. To prepare for the spotlights Alice submitted to a "face-shelling," a medieval form of beautification boasted about in *Life* that was aimed at clearing up her problematic skin. "The peeling took only five days," she bragged. "Who looks at her face?" wondered Walter Winchell with sexist snark unremarkable for the era.

The 1930s were the golden age of love songs, often tinged with melancholy, as that "low-down, dirty decade" seemed to demand. Cole Porter, Irving Berlin, and Richard Rodgers songs dominated the national consciousness, and Alice's slow, deep contralto worked well with the longing and fear of the future present in so many songs of the day. For her performance at the Waldorf, her initial lineup of contemporary ballads, rather than classic torch songs, included "I See Your Face Before Me," a hit composed by Arthur Schwartz and subsequently recorded by the likes of Bing Crosby and Frank Sinatra; "Two Sleepy People," from Hoagy Carmichael; and "This Must Be Love." "Thanks for the Memory" and "Deep Purple," the sentimental standby that was one of Babe Ruth's favorite songs, were also on the ten-song set list.

But would she get to sing them? When her booking hit the papers, the USLTA sent Alice word that her side gig at the Waldorf may run afoul of the organization's strict amateur guidelines. The absurdity of penalizing Alice for making money off her voice, and not her backhand, apparently was too strong even for the over-officious ruling body, and after the powers that be "sat in judgment over the enterprises of the champion," Alice was given the "O.K." All the way from London, the *Telegraph* dripped sarcasm at the decision. "None of Miss Marble's songs, the committee discovered, was tennis-minded. They dealt with 'love,' but not with 'love-sets.' So all is well, and Miss Marble may continue to warble in public." Julian Myrick sent a telegram magnanimously giving his blessing, saying, "I hope you hit the Metropolitan."

She played the Sert Room at the Waldorf, so named for the fifteen panels by Spanish artist José Maria Sert depicting portions of *Don Quixote*. *The New Yorker* helpfully reminded its readers the Sert was "must-dress" (as opposed to the more casual Empire Room) and "there are songs by Alice Marble, of all people." It sat five hundred and was packed for Alice's opening night—December 1, 1938.

Coleman's band would also back the dancer Paul Draper, whom Alice called a "superb artist," on the bill. The Gilbert Kahns were there, of course, as were Stuart and Eve Symington, and at a table hosted by Paul White, William Shirer and the Edward R. Murrows, in from London for a spell. Also there were Mr. and Mrs. Shipman Payson, she the former Joan Whitney, daughter of Payne Whitney, of *those* Whitneys. Don Budge led a large contingent of tennis players and officials to see Alice sing; according to the writer Mel Heimer, they were "startled to realize that their net queen and this slim, vibrant-voiced chanteuse in the flame-colored evening gown were one and the same."

Alice wore a diaphanous scarlet tulle gown, along with wool panties underneath to combat the cold. "I've never been in the east before during the winter," she said, even as a blizzard turned the streets outside the Waldorf white. "The snow looks beautiful but I wouldn't touch it for anything."

The reviews were mostly kind. "I don't know whether my mother would have liked the sad little songs I sing," she said, "but people seemed to like them." "The audience could not have been more enthusiastic if Miss Marble had been [opera star Kirsten] Flagstad," wrote Dorothy Kilgallen. "She has a nice contralto voice and uses it well." *The Hartford Courant* wrote, "There was general interest in the appearance of the net champion in a new role and the scores who have seen her in tournament play applauded her songs."

Other parties weighed in. One gossip columnist praised her "husky Marlene Dietrich voice" but wondered why "the No. 1 Glamour Gal of the tennis courts prefers to be just another torch singer." Then there was the *Life* writer who said Alice's singing "expressed the usual sentiments of dainty femininity . . . her ancient female willingness to be clubbed and dragged off to a cave." Alice probably put the general reaction best when she said, "I wasn't as bad as some people thought I was going to be."

As her two-month stand at the Sert went along, Alice was surprised to discover how physically taxing the performances were. And being up late was not in her vocabulary, either. But she adapted nicely. It helped that her commute was nonexistent, the Waldorf having given her a suite of rooms upstairs, making her temporary neighbors with the actress Gloria Swanson, who also did some singing. Swanson passed along some free advice. "I like the quality of your voice, but you remind me of the English actor who, when he says 'I love you,' sounds as if he's asking for a weak cup of tea." In other words, Alice was too stone-faced on stage. In tennis betraying emotions was a cardinal sin, but nightclub chanteuses needed to be more transparent.

Meanwhile, after cranking out some practice and singing exercises each afternoon, she held court with fascinated reporters, who asked about her favorite movie star (Clark Gable, natch, though with a strong love for Mickey Mouse), her supposed romance with screenwriter Gene Markey ("I've never met him"), and how she kept her figure, what Alice called her "rumbleseat problem" (constant exercise, plus Eleanor gave her a deep massage every couple of days to "keep the muscles from getting ropy").

She trod carefully when it came to talking about suitors. "Of course I like to go to dinner and the theater with men," she said, without commenting further. "The last man I went out with was Donald Budge at the hockey game last week," she parried to inquiries about her love life. "No, I have no romance. No time for it."

One perceptive female reporter hinted (which was all she could do, given the era) at the distance between her appearance and her apparent disinterest in sexuality, asking, "If you had to choose between being a typical lady athlete and a glamour girl, what would it be?"

According to the article, Alice was silent for a full thirty seconds, finally replying, "Goodness, that's a question I simply can't answer."

An all-star panel did it for her. Alice was voted one of the "Glamour Queens of 1938" by an august group including society hostess Elsa Maxwell, Grand Duchess Marie of Russia, and various style experts. "Beauty authority" Gloria Bristol said Alice made the list "because in a year of hothouse sophistication she has kept the freshness of the athletic girl before the public mind." If that was a backhanded compliment, consider the one given to Orson Welles, who made the "Glamour Kings" list thanks to his "clean-cut ugliness creating a new standard of masculine attraction," according to the duchess.

When her engagement at the Waldorf was up, Alice received other offers to sing. But having accomplished that dream, it was time to concentrate on fulfilling the one she had yet to achieve—winning it all on the "world's most famous lawn," the one in London's southern suburbs that sparkled in emerald green.

Chapter Twenty-Three

....

My Favorite Year

Alice is ready to commit tennis murder!"

Eleanor had always startled the Brits with her straight talk and Californian argot, but they really fell into a tizzy about that one. Alice was the popular choice to at last win at Wimbledon (and thus become "world champion," as the victor at SW19 was known in those days). But the fans liked their champions modest.

No one could argue that Alice was killing off the competition in the run-up to Wimbledon 1939. The twenty-six-year-old blew out all comers, not losing a set while revolving between her "ten new rackets" that the London *Daily Mail* noted she had journeyed to England with, along with her "jaunty carriage . . . and, as befits a leader of tennis fashions, some cute new outfits that will get the other girls talking."

American athletes were having a strong summer in the Old World. A USA team won the Henley Regatta, the world's premier rowing competition held annually on the River Thames, golfer Johnny Bulla came in second at the British Open golf tournament, and an American riflery team beat England for the Pershing Trophy, a prestigious target-shooting match between the former WWI allies, for the first time since the competition began in 1931. Yankee fingers were crossed not only for Alice but for her new doubles partner (since Don Budge had turned professional)—Riggs, who was making the trip for the first time.

"Bad News" Bobby had spent the first part of the year trying to clean up his act. His antics had made him persona non grata with the California tennis associations, so he blew town, figuring to have better luck with some Midwest sponsors. He moved to Chicago—in winter!—to take a job with the United States Advertising Company. His first duty was to walk the bitter, windswept streets asking people if they were happy with their current brand of dog food. He hated the job but rounded up enough backers to send him to England on the *President Roosevelt* alongside his teacher (Eleanor) and practice partner (Alice). He kept talking about how much money he was going to collect by betting on himself to win Wimbledon, but the women, used to his logorrhea, tuned him out. He was given a shot at the title with Budge absent, but as a British writer noted, "The trouble is that you can't tell when he's trying. He walks about the court with his toes turned out like Charlie Chaplin and in general gives you the feeling he is playing entirely for his own amusement, so that it is hard to form a definite idea of his ability."

Alice and Eleanor stayed at the Hyde Park Hotel during the warm-up tournaments and the fortnight at Wimbledon. The management had hosted Alice before and liked her immensely, so it wasn't out of the ordinary when they showed her to a specially remodeled room done up specifically for the tennis star. "It was light and airy," Alice said, "the wallpaper a riot of tiny pale flowers." Alice examined the suite, beaming, and it was only after several minutes that she realized Tennant was still standing in the hallway. She was pointing at the door.

"It's 803," she said uncomfortably. "That totals eleven, which is an unlucky number for Alice. We must have a different room."

Alice was devout; Eleanor, a wanderer. But both were superstitious and gave credence to the tenets of numerology. But the room was so perfect! Alice hit upon a simple but inspired plot. She asked the manager to change the room number to 802—just for the duration of her stay, of course. "Within the hour, the offending number was replaced," Alice wrote triumphantly.

Alice had arrived in England not wanting to be caught without proper attire, so just in case, she brought virtually everything she owned. "A wardrobe of tennis clothes is as important as a wardrobe of lounge wear," she told the *Daily Mail*, who reported she had traveled with "eight dresses, ten pairs of shorts and four blazers." She also had a pile of new designs and made a pop down to Harrods, the fabled department store, to see her tennis outfits on sale in the "inexpensive frock department" for thirty shillings, or about three dollars. "I haven't seen better tennis clothes than the two outfits designed by Alice Marble," wrote *The Observer*'s fashionista, Alison Settle. "One is in seer-sucker, being pleated shorts made to look like a one-piece dress, and the other a very, very fine pique, an actual dress with little shorties to go under."

"Alice Marvel," as she was known in the London press, played in shorts despite telling the press that the look was growing stale. "Henceforth it will be skirts or, to be correct, tennis dresses for women." She said this with the knowledge that several stores had asked her to design a longer hemmed look for the following year's season. "Even the most elderly and unsentimental male tennis follower felt a little pang of sorrow when she broke the news . . . that she might wear a divided skirt this year," opined the *Daily Mail*.

But when it came time for practicality, Alice kept her long legs bare. ALICE WILL WEAR SHORTS AFTER ALL, read one headline. "Look at Alice Marble," raved the London *Daily Mirror*. "Neat and immaculate although she's in the thick of battle. How many girls can play like her and still look charming?"

While the press was focused on her attire, the English masses couldn't get enough of her persona. She was asked to write a few words of tennis instruction for one of the Fleet Street editions, the *Sunday Chronicle*, and her copy was so well crafted and readable that the paper immediately begged her for more, even though, as she complained in one article, "Words seem to take away the thrill of actually playing when you've got to type them." Her first bit of guidance went like this:

"I can't help it. It's got to come out some time, so it might as well come out now. KEEP YOUR EYE ON THE BALL!"

It got more finely detailed, and colorful, after that.

"I always feel when I'm hitting the ball that I'm slapping it in the face and throwing my racket after it."

"The low bound on grass makes me feel I'm on stilts, so I must over-exaggerate the crouch while hitting the ball—otherwise I'll find myself topping the ball."

"Five years ago I weighed 25lb. more than I do today (which is about 133lb.) and when I wanted to be a tennis champion I had to kiss that weight goodbye. You must decide at once whether to be on or off the starch wagon!"

The pieces were so well received that they ran long after Alice had crossed the ocean back to America.

The consensus among the experts was that this was, at long last, Alice's year to capture Wimbledon. "In racing backing fillies is a chancy business," wrote Hubert Winterbotham of the London *Times*, "but if ever there looked a certainty for the women's singles it is Miss Alice Marble of the U.S.A." She was top seed and 2–1 betting favorite at "the tennis Mecca eight miles southwest of London." "I was at the peak of my game," she remembered. "I could feel it, and everyone could see it. Excitement changed the atmosphere every time I walked onto a court."

But in the back of her mind there was a twinge of unease. All signs pointed to this being the last Wimbledon for the foreseeable future. BRITAIN IS READY FOR WAR! screamed a headline in *The New York Times*. Hitler had ignored the Munich pact he signed with Neville Chamberlain and invaded Czechoslovakia in March. Next up was Poland, with whom Britain and France had ironclad treaty agreements. An invasion by the Wehrmacht would mean war, and all of Britain was in rearmament mode. The nation was ready to send a generation of young men into battle for the second time in a quarter century. A percentage of those young men so large it was too awful to contemplate never returned from that first march into conflict on the continent, remaining in the ground "In Flanders Fields," as the famous John McCrae poem read:

In Flanders fields the poppies blow
Between the crosses, row on row,
That mark our place; and in the sky
The larks, still bravely singing, fly
Scarce heard amid the guns below.

We are the Dead. Short days ago
We lived, felt dawn, saw sunset glow,
Loved and were loved, and now we lie,
In Flanders fields.

The tennis world tried to shut out the drumbeat, but it was difficult. The great German player Gottfried von Cramm, number one in the world in 1937 (when he lost a memorable Davis Cup match to Budge), was absent, "pale and thin" after an eight-month prison sentence in his native country on a "morals" charge (von Cramm was homosexual). He felt healthy enough to aim for the US Nationals, but he was denied a visa because of the time behind bars.

Budge at least made it to Wimbledon, though he wasn't playing. He practiced with Alice at the All England Club, making her "work like a Trojan" because, as Eleanor put it, "Alice must get tough." At one point, Budge asked the coach if he was making her "run too much."

"Gee, no! Pour it out!" Eleanor responded.

"When a man plays a woman," Tennant told a watching reporter, Stanley Doust, "it is no use his being just a little Lord Fauntleroy." She yelled to her charge, "Go to it, Pinkie, and shake your stumps!" After three hard sets, Alice, sweating profusely but smiling broadly, had some tea.

The weather was as gloomy as the national mood on Monday, June 26, as the tournament began. "Raincoats and even occasional hot water bottles were pressed into service," reported Thomas Hamilton. The sun was out when Alice began play, though she eschewed her usual cabbage leaf in gaining a sloppy win over J. S. Kirk. "There were inexplicable occasions when her ground strokes wouldn't go in and her overhead game became equally erratic." Perhaps the presence of Queen

Mary, whom, Alice wrote in an English paper, "we tennis players regard in the light of a patron saint," made Alice nervy.

Riggs was having a tough slog as well, getting through but having to work much harder than he preferred. "Everybody tells me I look careless out there," he told reporters. "Actually I'm trying harder than ever in my life." He blamed his new rackets for the missed timing. Both of Eleanor's protégés went through to the quarterfinals, but about the only real joy of the first week came when the top-seeded doubles team, a pair of Germans, was sent home by the unseeded American duo of Don McNeill and Eugene Smith. The huge crowd "cheered like they never had before" when the Jerries were beaten. Smith, a high school Shakespeare teacher from Berkeley, "just happened to be in England on his own, gaping at old cathedrals," when McNeill's regular partner was injured.

Alice would have to get past her toughest rival, Jedrzejowska, to advance. For the only time in their rivalry, she wiped the floor with the Polish Howitzer. "They traded tremendous drives with a vim seldom seen outside men's tennis," wrote one reporter. JaJa was forced to mix in some drop shots, as Alice had actually matched her for pure power, made all the more impressive by the fact the women of the day didn't rotate their hips to aid in blasting their shots. The result was "some of the most brilliant volleys ever seen from a woman's racquet at Wimbledon." With Queen Mary in attendance, Alice disposed of her rival 6–1, 6–4. "Before entering the court I won the match in my mind with my tactics clearly outlined," Alice told the Sunday Chronicle. If JaJa was distracted by the impending Nazi invasion of her homeland, she never let on about it to the press.

Somehow Alice was even more dominant in the semis, against Hilde Sperling, who was eagerly talking up her Danish residency and scarcely mentioning her German heritage. Their match was the second of the day, after hometown hero Kay Stammers upset Palfrey in a three-set thriller. Multiple rain delays had stretched the match to well past the four-hour mark, and it was raining when it ended, so Alice assumed she had time. She ambled over to the hospitality tent, socks over her shoes (a lesson she had learned well). Suddenly starving at the buffet, she downed several sandwiches and some cake, when the loudspeaker rang out:

"Miss Marble and Miss Sperling to the Centre Court. Play begins in five minutes."

Feeling as though she "had a ten-pound weight in her belly," Alice raced for the court. But clearly, the food provided an energy boost, for she went out and demolished Sperling love and love, the match lasting less time than even her pummeling of Nancy Wynne in the US Nationals the previous fall. "The San Francisco girl showed her overwhelming supremacy from the very start," wrote *The New York Times*, "and the gallery, sensing what was coming, leaned forward with all the anticipation of a crowd at the Yankee Stadium when a pitcher gets as far as the seventh inning and no man has reached first base."

It was the tennis equivalent of a perfect game. "Sperling was rendered completely helpless against the storm of drives and volleys that were rained on her," wrote the London *Daily Telegraph*. "The American, with sweeping drives of tremendous pace and power to the far corners of the court, scarcely met a challenge from a player reputed to be one of the finest retrievers in the game." Alice was into the second set before she realized she was still wearing her warm-up jacket, but despite being bloated and encumbered, nothing could stop her. Sperling managed just nine points in the first set and, incredibly, just five in the second. "Miss Marble seemed to delight in toying with her," wrote one reporter. Hubert Winterbotham, England's foremost tennis writer, thought it "possibly the most perfect display of feminine lawn tennis ever seen."

Her prematch snack barely digested, Alice hit the locker room, where she encountered the usually stoic Sperling in tears. "I've never been beaten like that," she whimpered, and the sad scene soon had Alice in tears as well.

Riggs had made the final as well, and on July 7 he bested Elwood Cooke (soon to marry Palfrey, Alice's doubles partner) in a five-set "grueling test of endurance." Riggs would claim that he was inspired to pull out the match by his bets, though the story changed some. In his 1949 memoir, he wrote, "I went to an English bookmaker and inquired what the odds would be on Riggs to win. 'Three to one' he quoted. 'Well,' I asked, 'what odds would you give me on a parlay that Riggs wins the mens singles[,] mens doubles and the mixed doubles?' The bookmaker stared at me, then turned away in disgust. 'I can't consider it' he said with finality. I pressed but he wouldn't even quote odds on it. 'It's out of the question,' he insisted. So I wound up betting ten pounds on myself to win the singles."

Forty pounds was a nice payout, but over the years the story took on larger proportions. Riggs said he placed a parlay bet on himself to win not only the gentlemen's singles but the two doubles events he was entered in as well. And the bet grew to one hundred pounds, not ten. As Bobby later said about himself, "Over the years . . . I've found it difficult to separate fact from fiction."

After Eleanor's two students had a ceremonial tea with the queen (imagine Riggs and Her Majesty sitting down together for a cuppa), Riggs and Alice played a long match in the mixed doubles as darkness fell. They were victorious in the gloaming, but the win set up a three-match afternoon for Alice the next day.

At least the weather would be cooler than her marathon at Maidstone six years earlier. But it wasn't pleasant—drizzly and windswept conditions prevailed, and at times Alice squinted through a driving rain to see the ball. There was a worse problem. At some point during the mixed match with Riggs, Alice had stretched for an overhead and pulled something in her abdomen. Adrenaline saw her through, but the following morning she was in agony.

Tennant called in the hotel doctor, who taped Alice up while Eleanor "grumbled about the room being unlucky despite the number change." It was a horrifying turn. Here she was, on the cusp of at last breaking through at Wimbledon, and winning three titles in a single day—and she could barely sit up. Tennant tied her shoes for her. In a 1950 article in *Guideposts* magazine, Alice said she asked the doctor to take off the adhesive, not wanting to feel the pull during the match.

Alice sent Tennant from the room and wept. Presently she thought of Jessie, and how she had always prevailed on her children to "trust in the Lord." "Then I did a strange thing," Alice wrote in *Guideposts*, "because I had never done it before." She got down on her knees to pray, a penitent position she didn't use. "We didn't kneel formally," she explained. Now she asked "God not to let me make a fool of myself on the court that afternoon." She said she didn't pray to win, just not to let her supporters down. "I rose feeling calm and sure in spite of the pain."

Neither Alice nor Eleanor ate or spoke before they left for the All England Club. "Teach impatiently brushed aside autograph seekers on the way to the dressing room," Alice recalled.

An enormous throng of more than twenty thousand had camped out in the rain all night to secure precious tickets, hoping to see one of their own, Stammers, best the seemingly unstoppable American. Now the odds were much more in her favor. Alice didn't serve or hit overheads in the warm-up, not wanting to reveal the pain. Despite her discomfort, when she shook hands with Stammers, their athletic disparity was palpable. The *Daily Express* wrote that "in her jockey cap, shorts, with her strong shoulders swaying like those of a man, [Alice] created a contrast to dainty, very slim Kay, who looked almost petite beside her."

There was no coin flip to determine first service; the traditional racket-toss method was used. Stammers pointed to the *B* for Bancroft on the butt of her racket handle and called, "Up," gambling that the racket would land with the letter in the regular position and not upside down. She was correct and elected to receive the first service, unknowingly putting Alice in an agonizing position. The two women curtsied to Queen Mary, and the umpire called, "Play."

"I shall never forget as long as I live that first game," Alice wrote in *Guideposts*. "Each swing of the service made me want to scream." Naturally, the score went to deuce four times, prolonging Alice's nightmare. At last she pulled out the game, discarding with a flourish the cardigan she wore at the outset.

"Then, from the moment we changed courts, I did not, for an instant, remember the torn muscle."

Whether it was divine intervention or adrenaline or painkillers (she insisted she didn't take any until after the match) or simply muscle memory, Alice went on to destroy Stammers. "The score of 6–2, 6–0 scarcely revealed the overwhelming superiority of Miss Marble," wrote Hamilton. "Critics here spoke of her as being in the class with the late Suzanne Lenglen and Helen Wills Moody when they were at their greatest." Alice's "cyclonic attack" was just too much for her "comely" opponent. "She hit them so hard Miss Stammers made no effort at pursuit," wrote Frank Menke.

And when she wasn't overwhelming Stammers, Alice was frustrating her. "There is nothing to be done against a player who, after being passed in midcoast by a lovely drive down the sideline, runs back and replies with a perfect drop shot off the backhand," thought the *Times*. "That was the type of thing Miss Marble was doing all afternoon." Stanley Doust marveled how "her drives were like those of Budge in forthrightness allied to shots of such delicacy that are only possible by a woman's softer touch." The *Express* thought, "It is no overstatement to call her brilliant." One awestruck English paper burbled, "No woman ever played like that before; none ever can duplicate the astonishing performance. This was the ultimate in perfection."

"I have no excuse," Stammers said afterward. "I could make no impression on her at all." She was asked if she had had an attack of nerves. "No, I had an attack of Alice," she replied.

"The marvelous Marble girl" met her beaten opponent at the net. The photo of Marble and Stammers shaking hands at the net, Alice still perfectly fresh, ran in papers worldwide. The West Coast press got their hands on it through the miracle of "radiograph," a precursor to fax technology that allowed images to be sent by radio waves. Stammers hugged Alice and said, "Time to meet our Queen." The two players walked to the royal box, where Joseph Kennedy sat with Queen Mary, who was dressed all in white, her hat "perched atop her snowy hair." Alice shook her hand, and during their short conversation the queen said, "Thank you for a fascinating match. And I like your hat." Not exactly the Sermon on the Mount, but it made Alice tremble. In fact, she broke protocol and turned her back to the queen instead of shuffling backward away.

"Standing in the door of her dressing room as she left the courts," wrote *Newsweek*, "Miss Marble . . . beamed, 'I have realized two lifelong ambitions—I have won Wimbledon and I have met Queen Mary. She said my match with Kay Stammers was the finest she had ever seen played. I owe Eleanor Tennant, my coach, much of my success. Three specialists told me I would never play again but I refused to believe it and so did she.'"

Alice, in her best thirties-era "aw-shucks" mode, added, "I proved that you can win—if you care."

Alice was on an incredible high, but there were still two more matches to play that day. Her doubles partner Palfrey looked aghast when she saw Alice struggle to sit down in the locker room. "For god's sake don't tell anyone!" yelled Tennant. Nevertheless, Alice and Sarah cruised past Helen Jacobs, on the downslope of her glittering career, and Billie Yorke, losing just one game.

Alice was more worried about the mixed doubles, as she didn't love playing with her old antagonist Riggs, the "arrogant rascal." But Bettin' Bobby took up the slack for his injured partner, racing around the court. The pair survived a tough first set to take out a British team 9–7, 6–1. One hundred and eight minutes on Centre Court was all it took for Alice to become Wimbledon (and thus "world") champion in all three disciplines, as was Riggs, who won the men's doubles with Cooke. He became the first player in Wimbledon history to win all three titles on his initial entry at the All England Club.

Alice also became the first female player to hold the two most prestigious titles, Wimbledon and the US Nationals, at the same time. And certainly no one—not Wills, not Lenglen—had ever "annexed," as they put it in the London papers, all six titles, counting the doubles, at once. It is a feat only matched since by one player—Billie Jean King, in 1969.

It was equally an astonishing triumph for Tennant. Noted at this time for her "greying hair," her "intellectual brow," and her "charming smile," along with "a big supply of cigarettes," the great coach told the press, "It's the most rewarding day of my life." A reporter for the *Daily*

Express eyed Eleanor as she "sat in the stand, calmly watching each stroke, surveying with curbed emotion and suppressed pride, the grand culmination of five years' strenuous effort in the making of a world champion. . . . Eleanor has nursed, dieted, coached, and trained a young flabby, pale-faced twenty-year old girl who gave us all a fright at Auteuil five years ago by falling in a dead faint on the court."

To Alice and Riggs, to whom Eleanor seldom delivered praise without a leavening barb, she said simply, "You've both made me very proud."

The day got better and better. Alice was recipient of a champagne toast at the hotel when the phone rang. It was Gable calling from Los Angeles. "Honey, what wonderful news!" the King told Alice. "We're so proud of you." His famous voice echoed over the long-distance cable. Lombard got on the line. "Hello, world champion!"

The Champions Ball at the Grosvenor House Hotel was packed with over 1,500 celebrants. Alice entertained with her "beguiling, husky contralto," singing "This Can't Be Love" and "Stardust," two of her standards. Palfrey accompanied on the piano when she wasn't chatting up John F. Kennedy, who was at Harvard with her younger brother, John Palfrey. "She had a lovely singing voice," Sarah said of her doubles partner. JFK's father, Ambassador Kennedy, gave Alice the "big hug" he had promised her if she won, made during one of the nightly phone calls he made to her hotel room during the fortnight, ostensibly to "wish her luck."

Alice also danced with Riggs, towering over her other doubles partner as they twirled the floor. While dancing, Riggs—according to Alice—told her he had "bet every dime he had" on himself to win all three titles, another version of the "Riggs the Rake" tale.

"We danced as if we could delay the dawn," Alice remembered.

. . .

Disdaining monuments of brass,
Fame chooses Marble for her song;

Though Wimbledons unnumbered pass,
her shorts will keep her memory long.
                        —*PUNCH* MAGAZINE

Alice and her legs weren't long for London after Wimbledon. She packed up and left for Dublin and the Irish championships a couple of days later. A reporter visited her suite at the Hyde Park Hotel, finding "her rooms were in an interesting stage of disorder. There were trunks covered with labels that lured the imagination to far places; there were flowers and parcels and books; there were cardboard frock boxes which had just come from the shops." Alice removed the string from one of the boxes to reveal a "full-length coat in checked tan and white rough tweed."

"Don't you think that's lovely?" she asked the reporter. "But it's not for me, it's Miss Tennant's."

Eleanor now had Alice shopping for her, instead of the other way around.

Alice was so big the fabled Irish tenor John McCormack couldn't wait for her to get to Dublin—he traveled to London to pass along his secrets of musical note holding to the best singer-swinger in the biz. "I believe she will be a better singer than tennis player," thought the original Johnny Mac, but Alice said he "tried to make a soprano out of my froggy contralto . . . and it just wouldn't work."

McCormack watched as Alice sang for the first time in England, on the BBC program *Starlight*. It was a particularly noteworthy show as it was televised from the new Beeb studio at Alexandra Palace, London's "birthplace of television." "Miss Marble wore an elegant white evening dress and on the screen appeared in head and shoulder close-ups," reported the *Telegraph*. She waved a white scarf in her left hand as she sang "This Can't Be Love" and "Get Out of Town" in her "deep contralto, almost mannish voice, with a faintly husky timbre. . . . She sang them wistfully and seemed to be a trifle nervous. But she had reserved a charming smile, given after each song." The *Daily Mail*'s theater correspondent wrote that "Miss Marble has a deep, magnetic voice and she knows how to use it. Her performance takes her nearer to a Hollywood career." In the US a performance like that would have earned her a few hundred dollars, but "here things are different," as the *Express* explained. She was paid nothing. McCormack was clearly impressed, for after the gig he hosted Alice and Eleanor at his estate in Dublin.

Meanwhile back in Hollywood, the agent Frank Orsatti gave the movie star thing another volley, telling the press that he had signed a contract for "the shapeliest of all movie stars," though there was no such legal document, just an agreement to give Alice more screen tests. According to Orsatti, the contract stipulated that she was forbidden to portray a tennis player onscreen and that any acting "will not interfere with her amateur status as a tennis player."

Alice didn't have much to say about the new development. "[Orsatti's cable] is very brief and does not give many details. I cannot even tell you what studio it is or what is the figure. . . . I shall perhaps sing and for the rest I shall act just the same as any other actor in Hollywood—though I have no experience."

"She is a capable actress and has a good singing voice," said Orsatti. "She should be able to sell herself on her ability as an actress."

Despite the lingering effects of the injured rib muscle, Alice romped to victory in the Irish championships. Then it was back to the Atlantic, for a pleasant crossing on the *Champlain*, where she won the shipboard Ping-Pong title with "some of the finest table tennis the French liner's staff has ever witnessed," according to the *Brooklyn Daily Eagle*. Her play was deemed too good for the women on board, so Alice "put on slacks" and "polished off the male ping-pongers just as easily as she went through the field at Wimbledon."

She arrived in New York Harbor on July 26, resplendent in a black-and-white dress and new wide-brimmed hat, purchased on one of her London shopping expeditions. "I feel like a million bucks, and I want to look it," she told Eleanor.

A large crowd was gathered to greet her on the wharf. Her name was chanted, reporters swarmed her, flashbulbs popped like it was

Independence Day. She signed hundreds of autographs and posed for photos with any fan who asked for one. As she waited for her piles of luggage to clear customs, she denied rumors that she would turn professional. She mentioned there were "a half dozen" offers to sing while in London, but it wasn't "in good taste" to do so during Wimbledon. And she gave her immediate summer plans.

"We're off to the races—Seabright, East Hampton, Rye and all of them right on through the Nationals."

Alice and Eleanor were occupying Roz Bloomingdale Cowen's plush suite at the Sherry-Netherland hotel (the Cowens were summering at the shore) at Fifty-Ninth and Fifth Avenue. It was tough to concentrate on tennis. Alice was deluged with offers—radio appearances, nightlife appearances, writing commentary on every issue under the sun—making it hard to get in any practice. Orsatti stepped in and established some order, but there were other issues. One of her pet desires was speechifying on how she had overcome her illness and poor upbringing. She had a title for her talk—"The Will to Win"—and had the writing chops but needed a professional polish and more time to concentrate. She sought the assistance of an Eleanor even more powerful than Tennant—the first lady, Eleanor Roosevelt. One of her speechwriters, Amy Scherer, helped Alice with the text, then arranged for a group of powerhouses in the arts and politics, including Mrs. Roosevelt herself, to gather at Roz Bloomingdale Cowen's summer place for a trial run.

"No tennis opponent ever made me tremble" the way she did that afternoon, but her inspirational speech was well received. The first lady said she was "impressed" and vowed to go back to the White House and "straighten all the dresser drawers."

Alice would give some version of that speech well over a thousand times over the next decade and change, and countless more into her dotage.

The hectic schedule of appearances proved too busy for Alice to play Seabright, which began just after her arrival on domestic shores. Instead, Alice decided to brave the courts of Maidstone at East Hampton, last played during her marathon in the blazing heat six years earlier. It wasn't nearly as scalding this time out. In the quarterfinals she lost her first set of 1939 but took out Pauline Betz (who would shortly thereafter begin an affair with Spencer Tracy) nonetheless on the way to winning the tournament. Julian Myrick had, at last, given up his throne atop the tennis world, and he wasn't on hand to watch Alice exorcise the ghosts of 1933. She and Palfrey won the doubles title as well.

The partners tangled in the singles final at Rye. It had been Tennant's suggestion, of course, that the two team up, and they had turned into the best doubles team of the prewar era. "Our games and temperaments were completely in sync," Palfrey reflected. "She received serve on the backhand side and I on the forehand. Her American twist serve was super, as were her volleys and groundstrokes, especially the backhand return of serve." Once again the outmanned but game Palfrey provided a test for her partner, but Alice won in straight sets, remaining unbeaten on the season.

One tournament with Riggs as her partner was quite enough, thank you very much. So for the nationals doubles championships, held once again in Chestnut Hill, Massachusetts, Alice teamed with the great Australian player Harry Hopman to win the mixed crown, while she and Palfrey won yet again in the women's doubles. She had now won eleven doubles titles in the two tournaments that towered above the others, the US Nationals and Wimbledon.

In late August the Wightman Cup rolled around, held this year at the West Side Tennis Club. Tickets were a bargain at $2.75 each. Alice was top singles, of course, though she had to wait a couple of days to play, thanks to a deluge similar to the one that she endured the year before. Erudite New Yorkers killed time with David Loth's new magisterial biography, the "first in a quarter-century," of the forgotten Founding Father Alexander Hamilton. Less well-read sports fans stopped by their local RCA Victor television dealership to watch the first baseball game ever televised, on August 26, between the Reds and the Brooklyn Dodgers. The "Ole Redhead," Red Barber, described the fuzzy action, which was less vivid than the televised tennis at Wimbledon had been.

Alice took out Mary Hardwick to begin the competition, but the Brits tied the score at two matches apiece. Alice would need to beat Stammers to fend off the threat. It was a far more difficult day than the cakewalk at Wimbledon. Kay "lashed out with determination" to take the first set, but "at several opportune moments sent her shots outside of the lines by inches." Alice slipped through the small crack to seize the match and won with Palfrey to ice another Cup, the ninth straight won by the Americans.

If her play during the Cup was less stellar than her Wimbledon showing, perhaps it was because she spent her spare time posing for the cover of *Life*. The American institution sent its most famous photog, the legendary Alfred Eisenstaedt, to capture the cover portrait of Alice looking ready to put away whatever feeble shot her opponent had to offer. Inside the weekly, photographer Gjon Mili, pioneer of the "fast-action camera," captured Alice's blurring serve and smash. The shots "show the strain under which she plays, how her muscles grow tense and how she puts all her strength into each shot." Mili lowered the West Side net one foot, allowing for his lens to get a great look at how Alice started overhead like a baseball windup and smashed deep for the baseline, rather than swinging down on the ball.

The August 28, 1939, issue was, of course, a milestone for Alice, though she was rather circumspect about it later in life, seldom mentioning the great honor. Perhaps that was due to the (uncredited) copy that threw cold water on Alice's image.

"Newspaper writers like to think of Alice as a glamor girl," sniffed *Life*.

They prattle about her beautiful clothes, her night-club singing, her movie offers. They call her the "streamlined Venus of the tennis courts." All this is nonsense. She is a pretty girl who looks well in shorts. Her arms and legs are too long and muscular, and she plays too much of a slam bang game of tennis to be glamorous. As a kid in California, the daughter of a cattle rancher, she was a real tomboy, spent her afternoons shagging flies for the San Francisco Seals baseball team. At 14, when she took up tennis, she didn't like to play with girls because they played too gently. Even today, at 26, she is somewhat of a tomboy, hits a tennis ball harder than do most men. In fact, if she had her way, she would play only in men's tournaments.

Alice, of course, had never said anything like that.

If she had, it would have made news, for Alice's every move was breathlessly covered. But she was more interested in a tennis tournament that went on while the Wightman Cup stole all the headlines. One of Alice's friends, Jimmy McDaniel, another Californian, was playing for the national title. But since McDaniel was Negro, no one in the white world much cared about him or the match.

Black tennis in the era was very well organized, if not as well publicized as, for example, Negro league baseball. As *Time* put it in an article called "Jim Crow Tennis," "They have their own American League and National League, their all star baseball game. They have their own national golf association . . . but at no sport are they more firmly organized than at tennis." The American Tennis Association (ATA) was the governing body for 150 clubs and twenty-five thousand players, many of them "upper-crust negro doctors, lawyers, teachers, preachers [who loved] a chance to shine socially. . . . Eager to show the snooty USLTA that negroes can be developed into high grade tennists, the colored race—especially its intelligentsia—has become extraordinarily tennis conscious."

The annual ATA championship was held at Hampton Institute, the venerable college in Virginia's Tidewater, before a crowd of 1,500. The '39 match was legendary due to its matchup, one that pitted the brash, young (twenty-two) McDaniel, an aggressive lefty, against the best-known Negro player, Reginald Weir, the "Bill Tilden of his race." Jimmy was known as the "Bobby Riggs of Negro tennis," partly for his brashness, partly because while in high school he had played Riggs, who took a lot of heat for deigning to hit with a black opponent (Riggs edged McDaniel 7–5, 13–11).

Weir, the son of a violin teacher in Washington, DC, had achieved the ultrarare accomplishment of captaining the tennis team at a white school—City College of New York, in his case. Swift and playing a thinking man's game, Weir had been Negro champion for three years running in 1931–33 before taking off for medical school. He won again in 1937 and was hoping to end his competitive career with one last hurrah.

But it was not to be. Playing amid "seesawing shrieks of delight and dismay," McDaniel was too young and talented for Dr. Weir, winning in straight sets. "Besieged by dusky damsels, Champion McDaniel was swept off the court, and signed his autograph until his hand went numb."

Given how the *Life* article bludgeoned her, Alice would surely have just as well skipped the cover shoot and been courtside in Virginia instead.

A lesser but still popular magazine, *Look*, gave her a much better write-up, though still imbued with the sexism of the time, calling Alice a "honey-haired, streamlined sweetheart who makes you wonder who ever thought up the nickname of 'muscle molls' for women athletes." Alice was also "electrifying," with "fierce vivid power" and "proportioned like something out of the Louvre." Of course, her wearing shorts at Wimbledon was mentioned. "When word got around how fetching she looked, the famous lions at Trafalgar Square all but jumped off their pedestals and went out for a look."

· · ·

The same issue of *Look* offered readers a poll asking, "Do you favor a third term for FDR?" Two of every three respondents answered no. A whopping 61 percent said they would vote against Roosevelt regardless of opponent.

Much of that had to do with the increasingly loud isolationist movement that was sweeping the States, even as Germany invaded Poland on September 1, 1939, kicking off World War II in Europe. Joe Kennedy wasn't an outlier. A disturbing number of Americans sympathized, at least somewhat, with the Nazis' racial ideals, while others simply wanted no part of European bloodshed. As famous a figure as the great aviator Charles Lindbergh was exploring a presidential run based on his "America First" campaign, which used anti-Semitism and xeno-phobia as not-so-subtle background reasons for staying out of the war.

"What probably will be the last big national tennis tournament to be held anywhere until the end of the new world war will start today on the turf of the West Side Tennis Club," said the *Times* on September 7, by which date Germany was already on the cusp of conquering Poland. Meanwhile, every German player invited to the US Nationals had de-clined. "No reason was given for the refusal," according to the *Times*, but the answer was obvious—the Nazi government had prevented their travel.

Alice did her best to stay cocooned in her bubble of athletic celebrity, and Eleanor did what she could to keep the news out of Alice's mind. Looking "absolutely invincible," she swept aside all challenges in the first three rounds. Mary Hardwick at last put up some semblance of a challenge in the quarters, taking an 8–6 set, but Alice took her down in three. To make up for that blip, she demolished poor Virginia Wolfenden, a San Franciscan who idolized Alice, 6–0, 6–1, in the semifinals.

In the final Alice took on Jacobs once again, but her more formidable opponent was the gale-force wind that played havoc with her pace. "The gusty cross-currents" carried papers and dirt and other detritus onto the stadium court, while "it was impossible to know where our returns would go once they left our racquets," Alice said later. Combined with the gray, foreboding sky, it was easy to make the connection between the day and the portent of war just over the horizon.

A large and rabid crowd turned out despite the conditions, eager to catch one last day of championship tennis "until the roar of cannon shall no longer drown out the ping of racquets in the Old World." The throng was firmly for Jacobs, the massive underdog; though, as in the McDaniel-Weir match, she was actually the more accomplished, having won the national championship four times, the French Open twice, and Wim-bledon once, with fifteen Grand Slam titles overall including doubles play.

The crowd doubled down after Alice won the first set, 6–0. Des-perate to get their money's worth, they cheered lustily as Alice lost the plot up 5–3. With her mental excellence and "match play courage,"

Jacobs pieced together a rally that won her the set, 10–8, as Alice "struggled to keep the ball on the court" in the wind.

"Players with considerably better stroke equipment than Jacobs possesses have gone out against Miss Marble and been blown off the court," wrote Danzig, "counting themselves beaten before the striking of the first ball. . . . Jacobs is made of far sterner stuff."

The comeback "threw the stadium into bedlam," and the standing ovations and chants of "He-len! He-len!" weren't able to be contained by the umpire straining for quiet. Eleanor could scarcely be heard over the din, but at 3–1 to Jacobs in the third she screamed, "Get off the dime!," to her protégé—Tennantese for "Stop screwing about and concentrate!"

Alice jammed her trademark cap down tighter on her head and went to work. "The blond champion collected her disintegrating forces to hammer her way to victory over as game an opponent as she has ever faced," reported the *Times*. The last game was a microcosm of the razor-tight match, a "furiously disputed" twenty-point epic that saw Jacobs twice fight off match point before at last succumbing to Alice's hammer blows. "It was her turn to show the fiber of which champions are made" and a victory worthy of capping her undefeated 1939.

(Except she actually played in one more tournament: the Pacific Southwest back in Los Angeles. She won that, too, of course.)

She gave her title-winning racket to Lombard, as usual. "Now Miss Lombard has more racquets than Al Capone had at his best (or worst)," wrote one wag. Another took in the arc of her career in flowery terms. "Alice Marble lives simply because the age of miracles is not yet gone. . . . Even the nearness of the grave never dimmed the bright flame of ambition."

This time Alice ran away with the AP Female Athlete of the Year voting, with fifty-four of the eighty-three first-place votes. She was the number-one player in the world, by wide acclaim, and hadn't lost a match, singles or doubles, in over a year. That was somehow not enough for the Sullivan Award voters, however, who gave the nation's top amateur athlete trophy to Joe Burk, the rower who had done so well at the Henley Regatta. "I thought Alice Marble deserved it," Burk said. One tennis expert even listed Alice among the ten best male players in the world.

"In these days of what Chesterton called 'a world of flying loves and fading lusts,'" wrote Mel Heimer with typical floridity, "Alice Marble has proven herself a real person and true champion. She seems to be composed of equal parts of Joan D'Arc, Victoria Regina and Helen of Troy."

"The Girl Who Would Not Give Up," as Dale Carnegie called Alice, was in midstride, in the midst of a legendary career, despite the years lost to disease, one that could supplant Lenglen and Moody on the all-time list.

Meanwhile, over in Germany, Propaganda Minister Joseph Goebbels gave a New Year's Eve speech predicting that 1940 will "be a hard year, and we must be ready for it."

PART THREE

Chapter Twenty-Four

....

Gone with the Wind

In December 1938, *Photoplay*, the biggest and most influential movie magazine of the time, published a breakthrough exposé titled "Hollywood's Unmarried Husbands and Wives." The story detailed unwed celebrity couples who were virtual spouses but hadn't visited the altar and were thus living in sin. Charlie Chaplin and Paulette Goddard and Robert Taylor and Barbara Stanwyck were prominent on the list, but at the very top were Clark Gable and Carole Lombard.

"They go everywhere together, do everything in pairs," gossiped the article. "They handle each other's business affairs. They build houses near each other, buy land in bunches, take up each other's hobbies, father or mother each other's children. . . . Yet to the world, their official status is 'just friends.' No more."

The piece caused a sensation. It was far more revealing about what actually went on in Hollywood than anything that had been printed to date. The issue sold out instantly and caused an extreme stir among the moral guardians (Daughters of the American Revolution, Knights of Columbus, National Legion of Decency) of the nation. As one writer put it, "Their demands could be summed up in four words: 'Get those tramps married!'"

So Gable and Lombard did. They slipped away to distant Kingman, Arizona, and tied the knot on March 29, 1939. Gable was clear to marry his beloved "Ma" as his divorce to Ria Langham had at last become final. But he was pressed for time—he was due back on the set of the biggest production in MGM, and perhaps Hollywood, history: *Gone with the Wind*.

The genesis of the making of *Wind* is Hollywood legend. Margaret Mitchell's 1,037-page Civil War epic had been a bestseller since publication in 1936. Filming it, however, was a daunting proposition. Irving Thalberg, the production chief at Metro Goldwyn Mayer, told his boss Louis B. Mayer that "no Civil War picture ever made a nickel," and passed on the rights to the book (Thalberg also had, not long before, dismissed talkies as "a passing fad," so perhaps Mayer should have known to go the opposite way).

Instead, Mayer's son-in-law, David O. Selznick, scooped up the rights to the novel for the sum of fifty grand, a fine lump of cash but peanuts given what was to come, and produced the film under his independent shop, Selznick International Pictures. Mayer still took on a co-production role and took half the profits as his fee for loaning his top star, Gable, to Selznick, who paid Gable his 7,000-dollar-per-week salary. The King was lukewarm on the role at first, but Lombard brought the novel home and encouraged him to take it.

Every step of the production was fodder for the press, most especially the search for the actress who would star alongside Gable. For nearly two years the public played a guessing game, answering innumerable polls as to their preference for lead actress, gobbling up countless items of gossip and rumormongering, no doubt despairing that anyone would ever get selected. At long last, Selznick's brother Myron brought a young actress named Vivien Leigh to a dinner party at David's house, introducing her as "your Scarlett O'Hara."

"I took one look and I knew that [Myron] was right," Selznick recalled. (Selznick also was responsible for a part of the movie's most memorable line, adding the word *frankly* to the originally scripted "My dear, I don't give a damn," ensuring a quote that would outlive everyone involved in the picture.)

The release date was set for December 1939, and though filming was often frantic, Gable managed to slip away quietly in order to wed Lombard at long last. The rest of Hollywood was aghast, not at the marriage but at the secrecy and normalcy of the event. "I have felt a tremendous disappointment sweep the town at the unspectacular, gag-less nature of the Lombard-Gable nuptials," wrote Don Worth in *Motion Picture*. "Hollywood felt surprised and cheated that Lombard didn't pull some kind of outrageous gag, or give out some kind of dynamitish statement either at or immediately following the ceremony."

The two had by now mostly decamped from Lombard's Bel Air rental home for a ranch in Encino, which meant Alice saw less of her favorite couple. But in late 1939, they shared some quality time. Alice booked a two-week singing engagement at Cafe LaMaze on the Sunset Strip in October, followed by those screen tests and meetings at MGM that her agent, Orsatti, had set up. Not much came from them, but at least she got to see Gable finishing up his work on the lot portraying Rhett Butler.

War was convulsing much of the world, but in America, there were more important matters to obsess about. As Gable's biographer, Warren Harris, put it, "By December 1939 the average American Joe and Jane Public were probably more interested in *Gone with the Wind* than in the wars raging in Europe and China." The Hollywood publicity machine had been in overdrive promoting the picture for years, and in a perverse way, even the war news from Europe played into the martial themes of *Wind*.

The Southern California fall was a fun and relaxed time for Alice. According to Ed Sullivan, Alice had been seen squired about town by Welby Van Horn, a tennis ace whom Riggs had defeated to win the 1939 US Nationals in Forest Hills. She had also turned down several offers to go pro, played several rounds of golf (her instructor, pro golfer Charles Lacey, told reporters she regularly drove the ball two hundred yards) at the Hillcrest Country Club, and welcomed the opening of LA's opera season by escorting Tennant to a grand party in Beverly Hills for the stars of *Rigoletto*. Gable and Lombard were there, as were Walt Disney, Spencer Tracy, Jimmy Stewart—anyone who was anyone, basically. Alice definitely qualified as "someone." She was included in that year's *Who's Who*, a chronicling of the nation's movers and shakers. For $2.98 you could even buy an "Alice Marble Doll" for your junior tennis player at home.

So it shouldn't be a surprise that when the time came for Gable and Lombard to journey to Atlanta for the grand opening of *Gone with the Wind*, according to Alice's memoir *Courting Danger* (but not *The Road to Wimbledon*), they invited Alice to come along.

Gable was at his crankiest in the days before the premiere, refusing to make the trip south until Lombard informed the King that he was acting like a child. Besides, the blonde had just purchased a new outfit for the premiere. "Think of it as the honeymoon we never got to take," she cooed, and Gable was convinced. As a minor act of rebellion against Selznick, whom Gable had grown to loathe, and MGM, under whose restrictive leash he continued to chafe, the actor flew to Atlanta alone on a chartered flight, instead of on the TWA mainliner Selznick, Lombard, and the rest of the cast took. That plane, true to the subtle nature of the proceedings, had "Gone with the Wind" stenciled on its side. Before takeoff, Lombard grasped the hand of a nervous publicity man who had never flown before. "If we're going to crash, we might as well go down together."

There is no record of how Alice got from Los Angeles to Atlanta. She almost certainly didn't fly with Gable or Lombard. It was a three-day train journey, and commercial flying was extremely rare before the war. It's possible she drove, though that would have been a much longer journey in those days before an interstate system made it simpler to traverse the nation by road. There was no reporting on either end of her departing California and arriving in Georgia.

The scene in Atlanta was the most raucous the city had seen since the 1864 battle depicted in the movie. Estimates vary, but somewhere between 250,000 and an even million people crowded into the Peach State as the mid-December premiere approached. Confederate flags flew everywhere. Hawkers peddled Rhett caramels and Melanie molasses and Tara pecans. MGM flew in press from all over the US and Canada and overseas as well, at least those not consumed with war coverage.

The stars and their entourages arrived in Atlanta on December 14, and the seven-mile motorcade downtown was lined by enormous throngs. Gable and Lombard sat in an open Packard convertible, while Leigh rode in the next car with Selznick. Aged veterans of the War Between the States, wearing their old gray uniforms, saluted as the actors passed. When Leigh heard a military band strike up "Dixie," the British ingenue blurted, "Oh they're playing the song from our picture!"

As Alice tells it in *Courting Danger*, "Clark refused to stay in the big hotel where the rest of the cast stayed, opting for the quieter Georgian Terrace." Gable and Lombard did indeed stay on the ninth floor of the Terrace hotel, but so did Leigh, Olivia de Havilland, Selznick, and the other major parties involved (except Hattie McDaniel, who wasn't allowed to enter the whites-only hotel). The Beaux-Arts masterpiece, which is still welcoming guests at the corner of Peachtree Street and Ponce de Leon Avenue (across the street from Atlanta's modern-day arts palace, the Fox Theatre), held the gala events in its ballroom, including a formal-dress ball much like the charity dance scene in the film.

According to Alice in *Courting Danger*, she had an adjoining room with Gable and Lombard. At one point, Lombard rapped on the door and beckoned Alice. Gable was taking a bath, and Lombard pointed out the window. Across the street were dozens of open windows with binoculars peeping out, all trained on Gable's bathroom.

"Don't you want to go in there and draw the blinds?" Alice gasped.

"What, and spoil their fun?" Lombard responded. "Let them look. Besides if they see his 'manly weapon,' they'll find it's a dinky little thing!"

Alice dined out on this story often. Lombard certainly was bawdy and relished defrocking the King's sexual mystique. "He's a lousy lay" was a standard Lombardism. She and Alice were close enough to have that sort of gossipy chatter.

The date of the premiere, December 15, 1939, had been declared a state holiday by Georgia's governor, Eurith Rivers. The initial showing was at Loew's Grand Theater, an art deco pile farther down Peachtree, at Forsyth Street. It sat close to 2,500 people, which was ten times too small for the demand that night. Tickets were an astounding ten dollars (the average price for a movie in 1939 was about a quarter), and scalpers got as much as 250 dollars for them.

As Clark and Carole exited their limousine, the throng let loose with an enormous rebel yell. Their walk down the red carpet was interrupted a dozen times by photographers jostling for the choicest shot, by radio announcers asking asinine questions, by fans lunging over the rope lines for the opportunity to get a handful of the King and his Queen.

Gable grabbed the long microphone from the tuxedoed emcee and laid down the law. "Ladies and gentlemen. Tonight I am here just as a spectator. I want to see *Gone with the Wind* the same as you do. This is Margaret Mitchell's night and the people of Atlanta's night. Allow me, please, to see *Gone with the Wind* just as a spectator." Gable and Lombard went inside the theater and sat with Mitchell and her husband, John Marsh. It was the first time Gable had seen the completed epic in its entirety.

Did Alice see it that night with them, as she had said all those years later? It wasn't a question I expected to ask. The Georgian Terrace hotel, where Alice says she stayed, is still open and just across Peachtree Street from the Fox Theatre, now the city's most historic showcase for films, musicals, and concerts. I happen to live just a few minutes' drive away, so visiting it was an easy trip for me and one that added an extra layer to the facts of Alice's story. While artifacts and photographs from that single evening in 1939 dot the Terrace, there is no sign of Alice anywhere. The hotel didn't keep full records of its guests, so there is no record of whether Alice stayed in an adjoining room to the "it couple." Likewise, the nearby museum at 10th and Crescent, dedicated to Margaret Mitchell's life and work, has no evidence of Alice's presence among its fine collection of the premiere.

Alice, supposedly Clark and Carole's guest, didn't stroll the red carpet, or sit in the theater with them. She wasn't photographed entering Loew's, nor was she interviewed. It is highly unusual that the presence of a persona of Alice's magnitude would go completely unremarked upon during the most closely covered public event of the era. Saying that, there isn't any record of Alice or Eleanor being elsewhere at the time, and it is certainly conceivable she did attend, if on the considerable down low.

Whether she saw it at the premiere in Atlanta or her local picture palace, and whether she was there with Gable and Lombard or saw it with her brother Dan, as she had many other classics, Alice felt *Gone with the Wind* was not only the best movie she had ever seen but "the best movie ever made."

"Clark seemed pleased when I told him so."

Chapter Twenty-Five

....

The Searchers

Alice was in California as 1940 dawned, living with Eleanor in a Beverly Hills apartment (137 B South Peck Drive), keeping her books and schedule while Tennant gave lessons around town. If she resented the fact that she had gone from celebrated Wimbledon and national champion to unsung secretary in a matter of weeks, she never mentioned it. Unfortunately, that was the way of the world for great tennis players of the day.

One afternoon Alice got a call that a player at the Beverly Hills Country Club was asking for her. As he came off the court Alice got a look at him. He was wearing "high-top black basketball shoes (he had weak ankles), rumpled khaki pants, a sweater fastened with a big safety pin, and a badly stained tennis cap." Only someone of considerable wealth and import could dress this way at a swish club.

Will du Pont, heir to the chemical and munitions family fortune, was certainly that. And he would become an important figure in Alice's life for the next quarter century.

Du Pont was rail thin, with a natty mustache and a casual demeanor about him that belied his extreme work habits. He had taken a considerable inheritance and turned it into an enormous fortune. In his spare time he was one of the most influential sportsmen in the state of Delaware, where he lived. He was a particularly important horseman, owning several farms in the Maryland and Pennsylvania countryside and racing Thoroughbreds across the country. He also loved tennis and was in California to seek advice on building hard-weather courts for his estate and for the public to use in Wilmington (remember, everything on the East Coast at the time was grass).

He was also, in Alice's words, "an unhappy man." His wife, Jean, liked Will's money but took little interest in his person. As he wrote in a letter to Alice, Jean thought "we 'tennis nuts' have a certain form of insanity." He took out his frustration with his language—"Dirty Willie" talked like a stevedore, not a man of society. But he was pleasant and gentle for the most part. He had a meal at the apartment on South Peck every day for the three weeks he was in California. He would drink a copious amount of bourbon, according to Alice, take a swim, then retire at seven thirty, in order to be up at three A.M. to tend to his East Coast affairs. The grateful houseguest later sent Alice and Eleanor nylon stockings, a recent invention of the DuPont company.

The meals Alice and Eleanor (and Will) ate were prepared by S. T. Bratton, Eleanor's occasional maid, who had just given up a job working full-time for Tallulah Bankhead. Her cooking was exceptional, and Du Pont warmed quickly to Alice, if his senses pricked up at Eleanor's obvious obsequiousness. Eleanor had never forgotten her poor upbringing, and financial hardship was always just around the corner in her mind. Alice, despite coming from a similar lack of means, just didn't view the world in that manner, for better or worse.

For example, Tennant badgered Alice to turn professional, seeing the handwriting on the wall for the more prestigious but war-threatened amateur tournaments. The 1940 edition of Wimbledon had already been canceled, and the Luftwaffe was gearing up for a summer of softening the British landscape through endless bombardment that would presage a cross-channel invasion (to be called "Operation Sea Lion"). Eleanor also remained keen on a movie career for Alice, seeing dollar signs. But Alice wanted another national title, and the studio life just wasn't for the

"Glamour Girl," no matter how many fans and reporters swooned over her. It fell to Carole Lombard to reroute Tennant by suggesting Alice and Eleanor get out of town and see the countryside, stage clinics and exhibitions, and make some dough before the summer tournaments in the east.

Wilson Sporting Goods, under the far-seeing stewardship of L. B. Icely, a forgotten but important figure in the realm of sports marketing and sponsorship, saw the opportunity and ran with it. A thirty-stop tour was set up, hitting large cities and out-of-the-way burgs that seldom saw any top-level tennis up close, especially in the summer, when the top echelon of players were playing across the Atlantic. Provided they arrived safely in each town, on schedule, it was a win-win setup.

Before departing, Alice ironically told the *Los Angeles Times* she wanted to stay amateur "forever." "I have no designs on a professional tennis career," though she was embarking upon a tour that was for all intents and purposes the same thing. Then she hopped in the passenger seat of a spanking new Studebaker, provided free of charge by Wilson for Tennant to ferry their star athlete around the country in style, and Eleanor peeled away.

In the back seat was Lily Yeates, one of Alice's voice teachers, who was headed home to Minnesota, where the ladies would stop after a southern swing. They took off on Route 66, the famous road connecting Chicago and LA, built to skirt the Rockies in order to ease travel difficulties for the nascent trucking industry and allow rural farmers to transport their goods to the big city. Over the past decade the bumpy, dusty westward lane had been choked with Okies fleeing the Midwest, to the point John Steinbeck, in his classic novel *The Grapes of Wrath*, called Route 66 the "Mother Road."

The heavy usage persuaded the federal government to fully pave Route 66, a project that provided thousands of jobs for unemployed laborers. Route 66 was considered "continuously paved" by late 1938. The women took advantage of the smooth road to make excellent time in getting to Arizona, where they did a clinic in Phoenix. Next stop—

Shreveport, Louisiana, and the three rowdy women worked their way across the desert and prairie scrub of the Southwest, a change from the easy driving on 66.

That didn't stop Alice from unleashing her need for speed. She took the wheel and gunned the Studebaker for all it was worth, going over one hundred miles per hour, before Eleanor, supposedly dozing in the passenger seat, muttered, "You're going too fast." Alice, ever obedient, eased back to about sixty and rounded a curve, where a large truck was taking up most of her lane.

Alice whipped the wheel over and the car hit a ditch, flipping several times before coming to a stop "pointing back toward Phoenix." Alice bashed her head pretty good against the windshield but miraculously escaped with just a badly jammed neck and a headache. Eleanor and Lily were even luckier, coming out unscathed. The brand-new car was totaled, but Wilson came up with a replacement, and the tour continued. At most stops Eleanor would find a chiropractor to manipulate Alice's neck.

No sooner had they arrived in Louisiana than Alice went into the hospital to get her neck checked out and was advised to stay for a week to ensure it healed properly. The press was told Alice had "strep throat" and was hospitalized. She emerged into the Shreveport humidity smartly dressed, in a "peppermint striped blouse and check brown box coat." Wrapped around her head was "a smart net turban of white, gold, and brown." No one commented on the fact she couldn't turn or lift her head. "We kept [the accident] out of the papers, somehow," Alice noted.

The ruse worked, as the press stuck to less newsworthy chatter. In Atlanta she bragged about her baseball bona fides. "Lefty O'Doul is still my most special boy friend," she said. "He's swell. Wires me everywhere I go." She played an invitational in Chattanooga, where the local papers ran a picture of her—from the waist down. In North Carolina they went wild for "Eleanor Tennis." Up the coast to Philly, where Alice lost to a couple of male players, "heartbreaking" the large gallery. When asked about romance, she answered, "No, not at this time."

Then it was on to the Midwest. They dropped off Lily in Minnesota before turning back to Chicago, where Alice won both the singles and doubles (with Palfrey) at the national clay-court championships. Ohio, Indiana, Missouri—everywhere they went, they were put up, sometimes in grand style at the palatial homes of the well-to-do, sometimes in the modest homes of the average fan. Either way, Eleanor was usually able to bank the ten dollars Wilson was paying for daily expenses.

As Paris fell to the Nazis, Alice arrived in Wilmington for her first visit to Will du Pont's enormous estate. Alice got to see the state of the Du Pont marriage up close and witnessed how unloving it was. Will confided that he wished for death on many occasions. Instead, he was divorced later that winter.

By late spring Alice and Eleanor were in New York, looking ruefully at the harbor. Usually they would have boarded a plush liner for England and Wimbledon. At the moment, however, German U-boats were wreaking havoc on shipping in the Atlantic. Instead of lobs and smashes, bombs were dropping on the All England Club (in October several huge ones would demolish the grandstand at Centre Court, causing *The New York Times* to snakily opine, "Some nameless Nazi hero has now dropped bombs on Wimbledon and has damaged the center court stands. What could be more fitting? The totalitarian creed has no use for free competition, sportsmanship, good manners, good-will, the things that Wimbledon always stood for. . . . [The bombs] struck a legitimate military target, a nest of decadence that must be removed if the Nazi way of life is to triumph"). Roland-Garros, the home of the French Open where Alice collapsed in 1934, meanwhile was to be used as a holding camp for the rounded-up Jews of Paris before they were sent east to more permanent concentration camps.

Alice couldn't ignore what was going on abroad, but she was hardly well-informed or scholarly. She did a stint on a new radio show called *Information Please*, where panelists attempted to answer questions sent in by listeners. It didn't go very well, leading *Look* to decry not just Alice but women guests in general.

"Ordinarily *Information Please* is a sassy and erudite free-for-all. But let a woman appear as a guest expert and the popular radio program

One of the earliest surviving photos of Alice is this one, taken in Philadelphia just before she turned eighteen, in 1931. She is still wearing a skirt, a sartorial choice that would notably change shortly thereafter. | *Associated Press*

Alice with her coach, mentor, and close companion Eleanor Tennant.
| *Associated Press*

On a torrid day in Paris in 1934, Alice collapsed on the court at the Roland-Garros stadium. The initial diagnosis of heat exhaustion was changed to tuberculosis, seemingly putting an end to her immensely promising career. | *Getty Images*

Alice embarked on a grueling comeback to tennis over the course of two years, thanks in part to an intense physical fitness regimen that included playing multiple sports. Her secret weapon in her shocking return to the top of women's tennis, however, was singing.

| *International Tennis Hall of Fame*

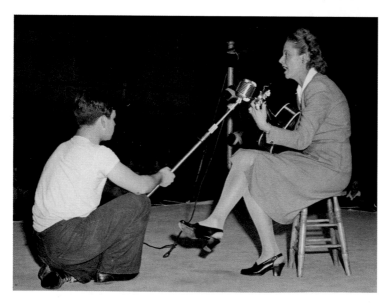

Alice is presented the cup for winning the 1936 US Nationals in Forest Hills over Helen Jacobs. | *Associated Press*

Alice arrived in San Francisco in the fall of 1936 and was given a hometown-hero greeting, which included Mayor Frank Rizzo meeting her at the train station, a motorcade through the city, and a reception at city hall. | *Fang Family* San Francisco Examiner

On her first trip to England, in 1937, Alice was as much a tourist as a tennis player, snapping tons of photos with her new camera. | *Getty Images*

After crushing defeats in the 1937 and 1938 Wimbledon singles tournaments, Alice was the overwhelming favorite to win the 1939 title. Her powerful serve and superior net game were tailor-made for the grass courts. | *Associated Press*

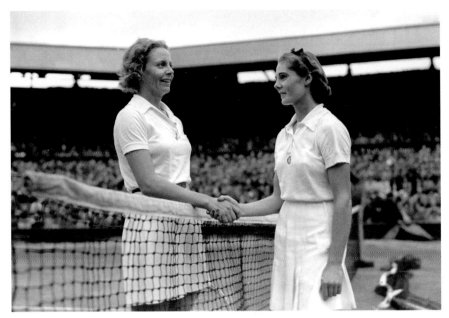

Alice demolished Kay Stammers in the 1939 Wimbledon final, looking as though she had just begun her warm-up when she greeted her beaten opponent at the net. Alice lost just two games despite playing with a painfully torn abdominal muscle.

| *Associated Press*

Alice also captured the 1939 Wimbledon doubles title, along with her regular partner Sarah Palfrey. The duo would win six major championships at Wimbledon and Forest Hills. | *Associated Press*

After winning all three titles on offer at Wimbledon in 1939, Alice danced with her mixed doubles partner Bobby Riggs, who had also captured three championships in England. It was the last tournament held at the All England Club until after WWII.

Getty Images

Alice returned to America as World Champion and was at the height of her fame and prowess. She would go on to win the US National Championships later in 1939, sweeping to the AP Female Athlete of the Year award.

Getty Images

LIFE

ALICE MARBLE

AUGUST 28, 1939 **10** CENTS

REG. U. S. PAT. OFF.

The ultimate evidence of Alice's celebrity—appearing on the cover of *Life* magazine in August 1939.

| *Getty Images*

Alice had a lifelong love affair with singing, to the point she crooned professionally at nightclubs on both coasts. Here she belts out a tune and plays piano in a less formal setting in San Francisco.

Fang Family San Francisco Examiner

Alice and Eleanor Tennant toured the country relentlessly, giving clinics and speeches about proper living and the importance of athletics. Usually they wore tennis togs, but here they are captured more formally dressed during an appearance at Smith College in Massachusetts.

International Tennis Hall of Fame

Alice hangs courtside in Los Angeles with her friends, the Hollywood power couple Clark Gable and Carole Lombard. Also seen is the gambler and café owner Felix Young. | *Getty Images*

Alice and Clark Gable chat about her game at the Pacific Southwest tournament, where most of Hollywood turned out to watch the matches every winter. | *Getty Images*

The epic film *Gone with the Wind* premiered on December 15, 1939, in Atlanta. Alice wrote in her memoir that she was the invited guest of Gable, who starred in the movie as Rhett Butler, and Lombard. No evidence exists of Alice's presence, though the premiere was heavily photographed, including this picture of the couple seated in the Loew's Grand Theatre, along with *Wind* author Margaret Mitchell and her husband, John Marsh. | *Associated Press*

Carole Lombard was tragically killed in January 1942 when her plane crashed shortly after taking off from an airfield in Las Vegas. Lombard was en route back to Los Angeles after raising money for war bonds in Indianapolis. Here a search party lowers her body from snowy Potosi Mountain. Clark Gable had to be restrained from going up to the crash site; he would accompany Lombard's body back to California. | *Associated Press*

Alice turned professional in 1941, touring sixty-five cities over four months. At each stop she played singles against Mary Hardwick, an Englishwoman marooned in America by the war. The women also played mixed doubles with legends Bill Tilden and Don Budge.

| *Associated Press*

The flags of America and Britain fly high over the Madison Square Garden court at the opener of the 1941 Pro Tour. Alice would best her English opponent Mary Hardwick in a closely contested match.

| *Associated Press*

Alice dines with her friend Don Budge, the top male player of the era immediately preceding WWII.

| *International Tennis Hall of Fame*

In late 1941, Alice was appointed as assistant physical director of the Office of Civilian Defense and given the task of making America's women fit and ready for war. Here she is flanked by the male head of the physical fitness division, Olympic rower John Kelly, and the overall director of the OCD, New York City mayor Fiorello La Guardia. | *Associated Press*

Alice traveled the nation for the OCD, giving numerous speeches (like this one on the steps of the New York Stock Exchange) and meeting with local officials to set up physical fitness programs. But the cause was lost in the sweep of the war, and Alice quietly resigned in the spring of 1942.
| *International Tennis Hall of Fame*

Alice continued to work tirelessly for the war effort, including raising money for crucially needed ambulances, which were mostly sent to Britain. | *Associated Press*

Alice was much in demand for radio appearances that went beyond singing, often competing in trivia contests or being part of a celebrity panel. She was also briefly a college football prognosticator, picking games over New York City's WNEW radio at a nearly 70 percent clip.

| *Getty Images*

In 1944, Alice played in a mixed doubles match in Harlem with stars Robert Ryland and Reginald Weir. It was a sign of her devotion to the cause of integrating tennis, which would rise to greater heights in the coming years.

| *Getty Images*

Alice's very public support of Althea Gibson in her fight to play at the top level of tennis was a key factor in Althea's entrance in the 1950 US Nationals at Forest Hills. Here the two walk together after Gibson was victorious in her historic first match.

| *Getty Images*

Sincerely,

Alice Marble

Member of the
WILSON SPORTING GOODS CO.
Tennis Advisory Staff

Alice had a decades-long association
with Wilson Sporting Goods, makers
of her signature tennis rackets and her
sometime employer in California.
International Tennis Hall of Fame

Even as she aged, and despite many health setbacks, Alice maintained her high-level game, especially her dominant serve.

| *Getty Images*

This print of Alice, created by Harry Warnecke and Robert F. Cranston in 1939, hangs in the National Portrait Gallery in Washington, DC.

| *National Portrait Gallery*

deteriorates into a tea party. The men's chivalry rises to the surface, they become polite, suave, smooth. The women do one of three things—generate timidity, act bored, or giggle."

Alice preferred the popular sports quiz on WABC. The listing for the program read, "Those who say they know declare that while males are superior when mere muscle and speed are involved, when brains count in sports, it's the women athletes who have the edge. This theory is tested to a shadowy extent on Choose Up Sides, when Tennis Star Alice Marble comes up against Eddie Collins; now general manager of the Boston Red Sox after an active career!"

Showing her knowledge did extend to sports, anyway, Alice wiped the floor with Collins.

Fortunately, she didn't encounter quite as much sexism on the tennis court. She and Eleanor pulled into Arthur Loew's estate in Glen Cove, called Pembroke, the latest in the long series of incredibly plush headquarters. The Loews' limo took her around to the summer series of events (and when the weather was nice and the tennis on the shore, Loew would take Alice to the courts by sailboat).

Her transport thus sorted, Alice crushed Jacobs 6–1, 6–0 to win in Rye, winning no cash but "outright possession of a pair of handsome candelabra and a large armful of gladioli," and swept to easy victory at Essex, Massachusetts. She then went to Brookline to win yet another pair of national doubles titles, with Palfrey in women's and with Riggs in mixed. Alice was now up to thirteen "majors" in doubles alone.

She was after her fifth singles title in the "big two" when play began in September, after several days of rain in Forest Hills. "The war has definitely left its mark upon the men's championship," wrote the *Times*, with most Euros and the potent Aussie contingent unable to make it. The women were likewise underpowered, though Alice was "the logical favorite to win" regardless of who was able to transit war zones to play. Daily headlines detailing the ins and outs of the German bombing of England and Britain's heroic resistance filled the papers and the minds of most tennis fans. A far smaller gallery than usual turned out to see Alice blow out Jacobs to win her third consecutive national championship, and fourth overall. "There was never any question of her superiority," wrote Danzig.

The question was, What would Alice do now? Jacobs was hanging up her tennis shorts, and shortly after losing at Forest Hills she joined the WAVES, the Women Accepted for Volunteer Emergency Service, a naval reserve unit that allowed females to join up and aid what was certain by this point to be a world war. The WAVES didn't see combat but by 1943 earned equal pay and rank to men, and they filled crucial communication, aviation, and support duties.

Jacobs achieved more than most. She was one of just five women in the entire program to attain the rank of commander. She served with Naval Intelligence during the war and appears to be something of a touchstone for Alice. Helen was a WWII spy and also an oft-published author (she wrote multiple works of fiction as well as tennis memoirs and instructional guides). "Jake" was also a publicly out lesbian, although only after her career was finished. Jacobs didn't possess even a fraction of Alice's star quality, though she was a great player in her own right. She won four national singles titles minus any of Alice's glamour and society lifestyle. Yet whereas Alice's life contained mystery and enigma, Jacobs was an open book, one who achieved everything she wanted without concern for social mores. She was out when that was a death sentence for commercial opportunity and played an important role in the service when most gays were forbidden.

Alice tried her best to join up. The Selective Training and Service Act had just been passed, requiring all men age eighteen and over to register for the draft. Alice read about this and was jolted with a patriotic urge to enlist as well.

Alas, no one would take her. The army, navy, marines, and coast guard all turned her down, with extreme prejudice. The reason? Her tuberculosis history. Never mind that she was clearly fit enough to win at the highest level of sport, or that her doctor had pronounced her fit and in fighting trim. The services could still be choosy in 1940, and besides, Alice was still just a girl, then, if a well-known one.

She and Eleanor were back at the Sherry-Netherland by now, and

Alice was feeling low. Tennant brought up turning pro once again. She'd been in touch with L. B. Icely at Wilson Sporting Goods. There was plenty of dough to be made and a tour that just needed her name on the marquee. Left unsaid, but hanging omnipresent in the room, was the still considerable debt Alice owed Eleanor. Here was a chance to pay off most, if not all, of it.

Alice had been extremely fortunate to have essentially given power of attorney over her life to Tennant, who removed all money concerns. Her opulent lifestyle among the rich and famous gave the allure of having made it, and her popular appeal had her living the glamorous life of a 1 percenter. But beneath the sheen she had nothing. All of her revenue, from her tennis to the road tours to her fashion designing, went to pay off the marker held by Eleanor. Alice's debt still ran to many thousands of dollars, and short of a false marriage to one of her wealthy admirers, she realistically had only one recourse of paying her teacher off.

Out of fight and options, this time Alice agreed. She would no longer be eligible for Wimbledon or Forest Hills, but with the world ablaze, best to seize an opportunity when it presented itself—for another might not come.

Chapter Twenty-Six

....

THE COLOR OF MONEY

Colonel John Kilpatrick, the president of Madison Square Garden, surveyed the landscape and declared as recently as November 1939 that "pro tennis is dying." But, he added, there was one exception: a certain long-legged blonde from California who packed them in wherever she went. "Miss Marble can turn pro and revive the game. She has beauty and grace and—er, ah—what is called oomph these days. She'd pack 'em in. She could make fifty thousand as easily as she could hold a tennis racket."

"There have been extremely few women players who were big box-office attractions," noted *The New York Times*. "Miss Marble rates with [Moody and Lenglen]. She may not have been as great a player as these two on unswerving consistency of form over a period of years but she excelled them in the virtuosity of her command of all the strokes in the game."

On November 12, 1940, Alice put Kilpatrick's prediction to the test. She held the public announcement of her decision to turn pro at the Sherry. An Acme photographer caught Alice appearing to wipe away a tear, but her dominant emotion was excitement. "I am genuinely thrilled and excited about going to work. For the first time I will have the time and money to do the things I have wanted to do. . . . One of my chief ambitions in life is to be a concert singer and I also want to do something in radio. I may have talent for singing or I may not. Now I will have my chance." Eleanor hovered behind her, likely already tabulating how much each stop could be worth in extra fees for clinics. She had negotiated a $25,000 contract for Alice, plus a cut of the gate. Another photo snapped of Alice pictured her in a different mood, smiling widely as she wrote "$25,000" on a mirror with her lipstick.

Wilson was the bankroll behind what was planned to be a long tour across the country, stretching into Canada and including Havana and Nassau as well. The promoter, a Chicagoan named Jack Harris, was a former Wilson rep who grew close to many players. He had mounted a world tour the year before, only to have the Nazis storm Poland, canceling the tennis. Now he was trying again, with not just Alice but two enormous male figures.

Don Budge wasn't quite the box office draw Alice was, but he was the world's best male tennis player by unanimous acclaim. A rawboned, good-natured redhead, the son of a Scottish footballer turned Oakland laundry truck driver, Budge was quite certain of his own value, believing he belonged with Ruth and Dempsey and Jones on the roster of all-time great sportsmen. For all of his bravado, a large part of his appeal was his humility. He once shattered the rules of etiquette at Wimbledon by casually waving his racket at the queen, rather than formally bowing at the waist. He got away with this stunning breach of tradition thanks to a persona *Time* described as "amiable, homely, naive, [a] wholly likable young man of 22, who would wave at a queen quite as naturally as he would offer a pretty girl an ice-cream cone." He worked well with Alice in doubles, though he once disdained drop shots as "girls' tennis." He was something of a hepcat—an amateur drummer who owned an uptown laundromat in New York. He had been a pro since 1939, but this represented his best chance to make some serious dough, which, despite winning the "Grand Slam" in 1938, he and his wife, Deirdre, needed badly.

His regular opponent on the tour was Harris's ace in the hole—Big Bill Tilden, now forty-seven years old but still spry and able to compete with the younger, fitter players. He was six foot two, with long legs and broad shoulders, so the "Big" was fitting (though he was just 155 to 160 pounds, so "Pipe Cleaner" would work, too). So was his other nickname, "Mr. Tennis." During the era of godded-up athletes he was right up there with the aforementioned Babe and the Manassa Mauler, thanks in part to his seven US National titles and three Wimbledons. He also got that way by being a showman. He knew the key to getting audiences vested was to involve them, so he was always talking to the gallery or putting on a showy display. He had tried his hand at being an actor, like Alice, and as with her, nothing came of it.

Big Bill smoked incessantly, loved to drive, and was a big card player, though for tiny stakes only. Like Alice he had a regular diet of steak, potato, and peas, the only vegetable he ever ate. He never wore whites on the court, preferring jet-black or ruby-red shirts. Likewise, he refused to wear suits, often putting on a baseball warm-up jacket over a shirt and tie if it was a formal occasion.

He was also in the closet, though in his case the door was left widely ajar. Everyone in the sport knew his proclivities, which as he got older ran to younger and younger boys. By the end of the war he would become virtually unemployable, an outcast jailed on multiple occasions for contributing to the delinquency of minors. But for the moment, Harris and Wilson were hoping Tilden would pull in the nostalgic fan, to go with the ones besotted by Alice and, to a lesser extent, Budge.

As for the identity of the woman who would tangle with Alice at every stop (and play mixed doubles), Harris was coy. "The player in question has written home asking family permission," he said, "and I am 90 percent sure that she will sign." Indeed, Mary Hardwick did sign shortly afterward, adding a bit of British pluck and war appeal to the tour.

A recent Gallup poll revealed that a large majority of respondents agreed that America was bound to be drawn into the war eventually; a slightly smaller majority even agreed that it was more important to stop the Nazis than to stay neutral (Japan wasn't mentioned; even then nobody thought of Japan as a likely enemy). Much of that attitude could be chalked up to admiration for the English. The bravery and resilience of the Brits in facing the Nazi menace that summer had stirred the world, and Alice had gone out of her way to help. Two days before the pro announcement, Alice made a charity appearance "by way of doing her bit for Britain," giving her "Will to Win" speech and tennis lessons to raise the 1,050 dollars required to purchase a new ambulance for the British-American Ambulance Corps and 300 dollars more for "upkeep." "Packing her smoothly flowing story of her own life with hosts of tips on good tennis," reported the *Times*, Alice talked about her comeback from ill health, "doomed to the life of an invalid," with "the audience all but cheering her swift-paced and dramatic story."

Meanwhile, the social whirl continued. She was a bridesmaid in Palfrey's marriage to Elwood Cooke, the sixth-rated player in men's tennis. Palfrey had taken one look at the strapping Cooke and immediately fell in love. Snag was, she was married at the time, so she flew to Reno to obtain a quickie divorce. Typically, the large photo in the papers was of Alice, looking quite fetching in a black silk dress with touches of white and a corsage, not Mrs. Cooke.

• • •

Not content with upstaging her tennis star pals, Alice sought to disrupt the all-male field of football handicapping. It was the heyday of radio, when families gathered around their living room sets to hear entertainment, news, and sports programming. The station buildings in New York especially were the centers of the radio world, with the biggest stars of the day—Bob Hope, Jack Benny, Arthur Godfrey—putting on live programs, while in between shows the lobbies were full of sound booths broadcasting the stars of the singing world belting out tunes. Alice often stated that she wished to have a radio career when her tennis days were over. She meant singing on the air, but a different opportunity came in the fall—she was hired by WNEW to serve as a college football analyst (few cared about the pro version in those days, certainly compared to the collegiate game). On Friday nights at 7:45 she came on to give her picks for the next day's action; on Saturday nights

she gave a fifteen-minute review of the games—and her prognostica-
tions. "I may be sticking my neck out," she admitted, but she knew football, harkening back to the days in San Francisco when her brothers
"dragged me to all the games." She did indeed know all about the exploits of stars like Tom Harmon and Frankie Albert—in her debut on
October 11, she correctly picked the winners of thirty-one of forty-five
games, with three ties.

Just after Christmas, Alice was onstage at the Loew's State Theatre,
singing alongside other acts, including a tap-dance extravaganza, and in
the *Times's* unique syntax,"the Six Honeys, acrobats, and the Three Sailors,
comedy." There were four shows a day; plus, Alice had a small part in a
vaudeville revue, leaving her out of gas and with empty pockets from
taking crosstown taxicabs several times a day to get from the theater to
practice and back again.

She made her pro tennis debut on January 6, 1941, in a ballyhooed
match at the Garden, defeating Hardwick in a sensational match, 8–6,
8–6, before more than twelve thousand fans. "Surpassing anything she
had shown in America as an amateur," Hardwick made the crowd "roar
with its approval of the brilliant opposition to Miss Marble by the industrious, hard-hitting British girl." Playing on a canvas court they would
roll up and take with them across the country, Alice was down 4–0
before she "came on to eke out the decision." The match was "as fine an
attraction as any one could have hoped to see," according to the *Times*.
"It was the best game of my life," Hardwick said after the match.

Meanwhile, Tilden served "cannonball aces in a manner to recall
the halcyon days when none could stand before his withering speed and
confounding mastery of spin," but it wasn't enough to defeat Budge. The
close matches augured well, for the future box office was dependent on
the public turning out to see some competition. This event pulled in
over twenty-five grand, the tip of the iceberg as far as the promoters
were concerned.

The combatants then left for Chicago, where Alice had an even
harder time subduing the "plucky British star," winning in three tough
sets, 9–7 in the third. Truth was Alice was exhausted. Icely congratu-

lated her on "letting Mary win so many games," when Alice had been going full steam. She let the sports magnate have it, saying, "I do not give anyone games." She was even madder when she discovered, at the third stop in Minneapolis, that Budge had signed for 75,000 dollars—three times more than Alice! She was supposed to be the star here!

"Some deal you made," she told Eleanor icily.

"I'm not playing," she told Icely, through Eleanor.

For the first time in her life, Alice was about to embark on managing her own affairs. The fact that she was being paid a pittance next to Budge's salary certainly put her on the moral high ground, even in those less equitable days. The fact that the tour was booked for sixty dates and canceling it now or replacing Alice would be virtually impossible gave her the upper hand in negotiations. Meanwhile, Tilden was an actual employee of Wilson, while Hardwick's husband was, too. All three, it was revealed, were making more than Alice, the headliner.

Icely tried to call her bluff, threatening to sue. Eleanor tried to talk her down.

"What's wrong with you?" she said to Alice.

"You!" Alice retorted. "Icely made a fool of both of us, but mostly you. You made the deal."

The Minneapolis *Star Tribune* caught wind of the coming strike, writing of "rumors . . . of friction in the tennis troupe." About an hour before Alice was supposed to go out on court, as the stands at the Minneapolis Auditorium began to fill, Icely capitulated. He agreed to give Alice the same deal as Budge was getting, including his cut of the gate. When it was over, she would earn a cool hundred grand (or about $1.7 million in today's money) for the tour, allowing her at last to get out from under with her business manager.

"I thought Teach was the business manager," Icely told Alice ruefully.

"I think I'm old enough to manage my own affairs," she replied.

"It was the first time I interfered in Teach's handling of my tennis," she wrote in *Courting Danger*. "I wanted control of my life. I wanted to choose my friends, lovers and career, but I was bound to Teach, because of all she had done for me. Would I ever be free of that debt?"

Free of the idea of working for less than her compatriots, Alice went out and crushed Hardwick in Minnesota, two and one.

· · ·

Alice worked hard for her newly earned dough. The tour was relentless, scarcely leaving time for anything but tennis and travel. Alice often helped out with Tennant's same-day clinics as well, leaving her tired by the evening feature against Hardwick. Despite that, she almost never lost. It wasn't until the tenth stop in Boston on January 23 that Hardwick at last bested Alice, in three sets. It was Alice's first loss of any kind in an incredible 235 matches, dating back to her defeat at Wimbledon in 1938. Hardwick didn't make a habit of winning—she only took three of sixty-one matches, a Washington Generals–like record.

Tilden wasn't doing much better against Budge, though in part that was due to an injury he sustained in a car accident after the January 15 stop in Milwaukee, forcing him to miss several dates. He was already taking a beating from Budge, both on the court (as expected) and behind the scenes, where the redhead regularly mocked Tilden's flamboyant homosexuality and called him "chicken queen," slang for gay men who prey on young boys. "He had a high voice and an effeminate way of standing with his hand on his hip," Alice recalled, which became a point of focus for some of the uglier natures in the game (and Budge was generally considered one of the nicer fellas). "Who is this fruit?" Ty Cobb was reported to have said upon first encountering Tilden. "He talked to me only once about his homosexuality," Alice wrote, "trying to find the words to express his torture. He didn't need to; it was written all over his face."

Alice's sexuality remained hidden, less a secret that she kept than a nonissue she ignored in public. Still, that Tilden's struggles for acceptance had an effect on Alice's reticence in talking about her sexuality is undeniable. "She saw what happened to Tilden," Rita Mae Brown told me. "She saw the prejudice and so she was circumspect regarding all her affairs, regardless of gender."

Alice's triumph was to not let her private life spill out onto the court, and to Tilden's credit, he kept up excellent tennis with much more clatter ringing in his ears. "Bill is unbelievable," Alice told United Press during a tour stop in LA. "He is 48 . . . but every time he steps out against Budge, he firmly expects to beat him." Tilden would spend most of his day conducting business with Wilson, where he had a regular job, played tennis at night, then hopped in his car to haul to the next gig, even after his accident. "He thinks nothing of driving 900 or 1,000 miles a day and then playing five sets of tennis," Alice marveled, though the distance between stops was seldom that much. She also liked the fact that he always picked up the check at dinnertime.

Those road trips would, by the time it was all over, encompass some twenty-five thousand miles, an "accomplishment Marco Polo would have been proud of," said the official program printed up for the tour, which included bios of the players and an accounting of the "Safari" they would embark upon. The players "must not go to the movies" while on tour—"they are bad for the tennis eye." Cards were permitted, "bridge, hearts and rummy," though "poker is more or less taboo—too exciting." Shopping had to be rationed as well, as "pushing through the crowded aisles of big stores tires the player out."

The dates ground away, as the foursome took their canvas court—a portable prelined sheet made of sailcloth and dyed green that could be unrolled and stapled to virtually any surface—for the entirety of the journey. As described in the official tour program, "it weighs a little over half a ton. . . . And is stretched taut by means of 16 blocks and falls. Just in case you didn't know, a 'block' is a pulley, and a 'fall' is a rope running through the pulley. Stretching the canvas is a ticklish job, requiring expert handling by our property men. Too much, or too little, strain at any one point, and there is a 'loose spot' which may result in one of the players taking a dangerous spill."

They played atop a skating rink in Los Angeles's Tropical Ice Gardens, kids skating while the stars hit. They played atop a dirt floor in El Paso, their footfalls leaving impressions in the makeshift court. Alice described a bizarre scene in Minneapolis, where the balls wouldn't bounce at all, until a local youth ran into the bowels of the arena to close all the windows. It worked, and Alice and Hardwick brought the hero on court to play with them. In Trenton, New Jersey, a particularly low balcony and Hardwick's particularly high toss on her serve allowed a kid to snag her ball before Mary could serve it.

"I say, we both can't play," she told the boy.

To end January the women played the capital, Washington, DC (technically College Park, Maryland), where before the match they shared some birthday cake with a very special celebrant—President Roosevelt, who turned fifty-nine on January 30—and a group of celebrities at the White House. In February they hit in Havana, Nassau, outdoors in Miami, and on clay in Fort Worth. March was the west, April the Midwest and Canada. At long last, the parade ended in Birmingham on May 10, the sixty-first stop in a touch over four months. Alice suffered from malnutrition and exhaustion and was put on glucose for several days to recover. Tour officials estimated that nearly 1,000 dollars' worth of tennis balls had been used, and "that little white pellet" had been hit over the net 4,628 times per night, or some 324,000 times in total. Pity the poor slob who totaled up that statistic.

The foursome reconvened at the Polo Grounds on June 15 for an event called the Father's Day Sports Parade. The stands were jammed with over fifty thousand to watch a cavalcade of athletes—a baseball game featuring pros turned servicemen, a touch football game featuring greats like Sid Luckman, a pretend fight between Benny Leonard and Lew Tendler, who fought a pair of epic brawls in 1922–23, and even a relay race won by Polo Grounds ushers over their archrival ushers from Ebbets Field in Brooklyn.

Alice and Hardwick dueled between second and third base. A caption in *American Lawn Tennis* magazine said it best—"Unique in Every Way." The final score was rather unique as well—Hardwick won 6–4.

There were other appearances, but with a little financial security at long last, Alice took a breather. But come the fall of 1941, she started to get restless. With the German invasion of Russia in June, Europe was now at arms from Moscow to the English Channel. British pluck and airpower had forced the Nazis to cancel Operation Sea Lion, the invasion of England, but the Brits were essentially the lone holdouts in Western Europe. The Japanese were menacing Southeast Asia, to the point that the Roosevelt administration had to embargo oil and other precious goods in order to tame Japan's imperial quest.

And what was Alice doing? Putting on the odd exhibition at military bases in the northeast, playing with socialites, hitting the town—generally acting as though there was nothing amiss in the world. It bothered her, and her inability to join the service—any service—still gnawed at her.

Then one day the phone rang in her hotel suite.

"This is the White House calling. Please hold for President Roosevelt."

Chapter Twenty-Seven

....

Pain & Gain

One of Franklin Roosevelt's first initiatives after winning his third term as president in November 1940 was to announce to a national conference of doctors, educational leaders, and physical trainers that a program to "toughen" the country's citizenry would be enacted as soon as possible. It would be under the guidance of John Kelly (like the future President Kennedy better known as Jack), who won fame winning gold medals in the sculls in the Olympics of 1920 and 1924.

The idea began with Kelly, who noted that FDR had mentioned in a speech that in comparison to disciplined European nations, the US "was too soft."

"The wealth of the country," Kelly said, "is in the strength of its men and women. The manpower of Europe is already toughened. We had better wake up, or they will force us to our knees if we ever come to grips."

"Stamina, endurance and vigor" were the objectives, according to Kelly, who hastened to add that the government would not make anyone run who didn't want to, lest the whiff of fascism (similar programs were heartily endorsed by the Nazis) repel Americans. Sports and individual fitness programs would be the initial focus of the program, in Kelly's view, along with physical examinations that would "reveal deficiencies," such as scoliosis or poor teeth, and steps to overcome them.

Kelly's comments and announcement of a national fitness council "evoked a large response," according to *The New York Times*. "An extraordinary interest was shown in letters by women," Kelly noted.

Enter America's Queen of the Courts.

On recommendation from his wife, Eleanor, FDR was calling to offer Alice the number-two position in Kelly's fitness council, concentrating on women. It fell under the auspices of the Office of Civilian Defense (OCD), which was run by New York mayor Fiorello La Guardia.

Here was Alice's chance to pitch in. She crossed the river to the "summer city hall" in Queens, where the mayor escaped the sweltering environs of city hall for the cooler breezes of the Long Island Sound. There, La Guardia swore her in as assistant director of civilian defense in charge of physical fitness for women. She made Mary Browne her number two. The job entailed a four-month tour of the country, giving talks on the importance of fitness.

It also entailed an FBI background check, which Alice recalled involved a pair of agents in "identical dark suits" firing off a multitude of questions. When she noticed the repetition of questions, she wrote in *Courting Danger*, she brought up what she called her photographic memory. Intrigued, the agents asked Alice to play spy at the various functions she would attend as part of her job and pass along anything suspicious. She said they gave her a Spanish-language typewriter and a PO box to mail her reports, which in the end, as Alice admitted, amounted to not a whole lot.

As it happens, Alice's work for the feds was either so secret as to be highly classified to this day, or else it was such a nonentity it wasn't worth writing up. Whatever the case, she does not have an existing case file in the FBI archives. I filed several Freedom of Information Act requests, none of which turned up anything. The only piece of information of use was that as Alice allegedly wasn't any kind of suspect but rather was to be put to use by the bureau, a file on her wouldn't necessarily have been opened.

What was important in the end was she was cleared to take the job with the OCD. Her work from her office at 715 Fifth Avenue kept Alice firmly in the national spotlight. She was the national guru on physical fitness, and she adapted her standard speech on overcoming sickness and personal adversity to include more all-purpose advice. In the speech, titled "Civilian's Bit—Stay Fit," she came across as a wartime life coach, saying things like, "Every woman who joins in the program would discover a new and greatly increased capacity for a happy life." And, "Today each of us should be geared to do his utmost to make America strong and it is imperative that we maintain a high degree of physical fitness." To do so, Alice outlined a plan to get America walking more, sleeping better, and eating right. She would work with local organizations to pump up the sporting outlets in every community. She would instill pride by conducting mass group exercises, with all participants wearing outfits she had specially designed for the cause. She would insist on improving America's posture, which "accomplishes more in producing permanent changes than all the apparatus in gymnasiums." And she would have all Americans get periodic examinations of their eyes, teeth, and feet.

She concluded by saying, "Our message is simply that physical fitness is fun, and I'm going to ask for 50 million women assistants to help me make civilian defense a success."

The Depression had indeed left a nation of people woefully unprepared for actually fighting and winning a war. Alice harkened back to her days in England when she noted that nation's general fitness in contrast to America's. "One of the factors that has made it possible for England's civilian population to adapt itself to the enormous changes and hardships of every day life during the past two years has been traced to their national hobby of walking and hiking parties as well as cycling excursions."

It was hard to argue with any of her suggestions. It was true that "people who play together know how to live and work together for a common purpose. Physical fitness is not only an emergency necessity, but a long-range objective for happy, purposeful living." Alice's personal story of comeback and the appeal of her muscular fitness lent credence to her speech. And the fact that she clearly had written her own speech, and delivered it admirably in her forceful contralto, won plaudits from all who heard it.

For all this she was to be paid one dollar a year.

Alice did things other than speak for her one hundred cents. On a Friday night in November, "New Yorkers walking their dogs in Central Park were startled when martial music shattered the quiet and park roadways resounded to the purposeful tread of marching feet." Alice had arranged to march with Mayor La Guardia, "staunchly leading Manhattan's sedentary legions on an inspirational hike" from the Seventy-Second Street band shell to the Fifth Avenue gate at Fifty-Ninth Street. As the *Times* put it, "The sedentary were still at their fish and soup when the Mayor was introduced" at 7 P.M.

Alice, "vigorous in sports coat and rakish overseas cap," spoke after the mayor. "We have come out tonight to show you what fun you can have getting physically fit." She also wore heels so she had to kick them off to jump rope. In a press photo, she is seen jumping while "The Little Flower," jowls flapping in the wind, leans in, hands folded on knee, in rapt attention to the tennis star turned fitness guru.

Alice broke down the sports the average New Yorker could take up—badminton, ice-skating, cycling. She hit a few tennis balls, then La Guardia "squared his shoulders, set his sombrero, and with detectives and uniformed men sidearming screaming children and overeager boys and girls in their teens, set out for the south gate." Alice "towered over the Mayor at his right."

At the gate the mayor got in his big black limo and peeled out.

"How's your wind?" he was asked.

"Nothing to it," the mayor panted.

An even more powerful politico—the first lady of the United States—was with Alice on December 2, the last Tuesday before America entered the war. Alice was in Philadelphia for "Hale America Day," showing off her dress design for "health-minded and patriotic Philadelphians" as well as the first lady. Eleanor Roosevelt told Alice she liked the way the outfits captured the figures of a girl athletic group called, simply, "AJ." The event at the Philadelphia Convention Hall featured "folk dances, Negro spiritual singing, and mass athletic drills."

Alice queried Mrs. Roosevelt on her exercise routine. "Very little," admitted Mrs. R. "I walk from the White House to my office, about a mile. Then when I get home at night, I go for a twenty-minute swim. Friday night, I go to Hyde Park and spend two days working in my garden. This is fair exercise, because I'm so tall I have to stoop a long way."

"That's quite . . ." Alice started, but Mrs. Roosevelt was on a roll. "Weekends I also get up early and go for a ride, but still I don't get anywhere near enough exercise." Alice thought her workouts needed a little improvement but on the whole were better than famous hostess and columnist Elsa Maxwell, who came out against all forms of exercise in a syndicated newsprint diatribe against Alice and her campaign of exertion. "She's a fool!" cried Alice.

Fittingly, Alice was playing tennis on December 7, 1941. She was at Pembroke, Arthur Loew's Long Island estate, playing with her host and Paul Lehman, one of Wall Street's Lehman Brothers who was taking a leave from stocks and bonds to serve in the navy. Shortly after noon, Lehman excused himself from the competitive match to take a phone call. "Hurry back," Alice called. "We can win this set." Instead, Lehman, ashen at the news of the Pearl Harbor attack, went straight to Washington, still dressed in tennis whites.

Alice went to her office at 715 Fifth, her job suddenly given new urgency. She immediately set off on a nine-city tour, including her hometown of San Francisco, where she was to "confer with mayors and educational leaders in those communities in an effort to put into effect without delay efforts to raise the nation's standard of health." Her original plan to encourage less intense exercise "died on Sunday when Japan attacked." Now her office was endeavoring to find gyms across the nation where women could conduct calisthenic drills. Alice was brooking no excuses from the unfit. "Women who come staggering on high heels into the various volunteer services; women who want to help but are underweight and tired and hysterical, are a drag in the wheels of defense. They must get ten percent stronger before their willingness to do their share in this crisis can be of value."

In early 1942, *The New Yorker* caught up with Alice, now back in New York, to check in on her mission "to toughen up American women so that they can handle such men's jobs as driving trucks, delivering mail, and working on munitions." Alice delivered a sermon against the national epidemic of sitting. "Women sit in offices, on subways, in cars, at home, and at the movies. The machine has made them sluggish," said Alice, "who was sitting at her desk." Noting that she played tennis at Loew's estate most weekends, the magazine wrote she "has told him a dozen times that double features are a terrible health menace, what with all the sitting they involve . . ."

"My social life has gone to the devil," Alice told the mag in her "throaty conversational voice." She had to give up singing for lecturing and was busy all day prepping radio talks and organizing activities nationwide. "I'm even drinking milk now," she said, adding that, in addition to playing tennis, she had been skipping a lot of rope. "'Rope-skipping,' she observed, looking at us narrowly, 'is only for people in good condition, or it's likely to kill you.'"

In February she unveiled a new design of hers at the Waldorf. It was a shoe, "an Oxford type, made of seamless calf, with a medium leather heel. The thick, flexible sole, similar to those seen on men's shoes, may be renewed." It was part of a "complete line of footwear suitable for women in uniform," all donated to the cause.

Shortly afterward she decamped from NYC for DC, moving to the burgeoning nation's capital, where the formerly sleepy town was struggling to deal with the sudden influx of tens of thousands of new residents. Housing and office space were at such premiums Alice decided to spend as much of her time as possible on the road. Eleanor stayed in New York; those several weeks were by far the longest stretch of time they were apart since Alice had collapsed in France in 1934.

Busy as she was in the immediate aftermath of Pearl Harbor, her OCD job didn't last past spring. While in theory her lectures were sound, in practice everyone was working. "Women spent long hours on assembly lines beside men who would soon leave the work force for the military," she wrote. "The few hours between work and sleep were devoted to family, leaving no time for exercises." Alice's office quietly folded up shop, and, rather than take some make-work job for her one dollar, she resigned effective May 1.

Brownie went into the Red Cross, where she was sent to faraway places, including Australia. Meanwhile, Alice moaned, "I'm just a working girl" to an AP reporter. She was at loose ends, her debt to Eleanor considerably lessened by her astute negotiations of the previous year, but there wasn't much more coming in, either. Tennis touring was out, due to the war. Singing was at best an occasional gig, and that, too, had dried up. Her designs brought in some money, but she needed a day job. She talked about possibly directing a radio program ("there aren't many women" in that job), or hosting a sports program ("there aren't any really good ones, if you think about it").

"You don't need a copy girl, do you?" she asked the reporter. "I can run."

New York was electric that spring with war fervor, but Alice found it hard to get worked up.

She had already lost someone important to the war.

.   .   .

While the rest of the world was fighting fascism, Clark Gable and Carole Lombard were fighting each other. The cause was Gable's latest costar, the luscious twenty-one-year-old Lana Turner, whose pinup photo would soon adorn footlockers and bulkheads throughout the military. At the moment she was costarring with Gable in the new movie *Somewhere I'll Find You*, and Lombard didn't like the look on her husband's face when he came home from the set. So she left, taking off on a tour to raise money for war bonds. Gable was noticeably absent from Union Station when Carole left for Salt Lake City.

Lombard had left a pneumatic blonde dummy, a forerunner to a sex doll, on Clark's bed. "So you won't be lonely" read the note. He spent three days building a male riposte, expectantly erect, to welcome her home. The joke thawed things, and Gable called her to coo. "They sounded like lovebirds," said his secretary, Jean Garceau. "I'm really nuts about him," Carole confessed while on tour, "and it isn't all that great lover crap because if you want to know the truth I've had better."

After Utah and Chicago the tour went to Indianapolis, a short distance from Lombard's hometown of Fort Wayne, on January 15, 1942. Her mother, Elizabeth Peters, was with her. Lombard gave a rousing speech at the Indiana statehouse, yelling, "Heads up, hands up, America! Let's give a cheer that will be heard in Tokyo and Berlin!" while giving the "V for Victory" sign. For eight hours she sold bonds and signed autographs. "I'm like a barker at a carnival," she moaned, but she was doing great business. The Treasury Department had hoped for Lombard to raise $500,000, but she passed that before lunch, en route to $2 million.

Two more stops on the bond tour were scheduled, but suddenly Lombard was overwhelmed by a desire to get back and see Clark. Since Pearl Harbor, airports across the country had been blacked out and runways lit dimly. Air travel was a risk in 1942 under the best of conditions, but Carole was determined to be in LA, ASAP. Her mother, and MGM PR man Otto Winkler, whom Carole had comforted on the flight to Atlanta for the *Gone with the Wind* premiere, tried to talk Carole out of flying, but she just couldn't face three days "on the choo-choo train." At last, Winkler tossed a coin, Carole won, and they boarded a flight leaving Indy at 4 A.M. It was scheduled to arrive in Burbank at eight that night—such was air travel in that era.

The plane was a DC-3, TWA flight 3 (at that time "TWA" stood for Transcontinental & Western Air), and as the party of three boarded, Elizabeth again begged Carole not to fly, that the numerology was foreboding. Lombard told her mom that if she kept up that numbers jabber she would have her committed. Mrs. Peters calmed down as the plane made stops in Wichita and Albuquerque. The pilot kicked passengers off to make room for servicemen at each stop. Carole was asked but refused, not wanting to stay overnight in New Mexico, of all places. The resulting row delayed the flight, and as gloaming settled on the west, the flight was diverted from Boulder, where there were no lights at the airfield, to Las Vegas. They landed in pre–Sin City at 6:30, refueled, and took off at 7:07. Arrival time in LA was 8:45.

The plane didn't make it over nearby Mount Potosi, better known to locals as Table Rock Mountain. In the dark it smashed into a cliff near the summit, exploding into a fireball clearly visible in the town below. There was no chance for Lombard, her mother, Otto Winkler, the crew, or the fifteen servicemen on board—all were killed immediately. The pilot, an eleven-year veteran of TWA named Wayne Williams, was blamed for the crash.

Gable was alerted to the disaster that night and raced to Vegas. The MGM general manager, Eddie Mannix, arranged for Lombard's decapitated corpse, and her mother's, to be brought down from the mountain and returned to LA for a small funeral. Gable rode the train with the caskets, weeping.

Alice was at Pembroke, again on the tennis court, when Arthur Loew was notified of the tragedy. He told Alice and Eleanor, who were devastated. "Losing Carole was like losing a sister," Alice said. "We had such a wonderful kinship, an intuitive understanding of each other." She remembered their recent phone call, with the usual gossip and talk of Clark and the war.

"God bless," Alice had said to sign off.

"Angels keep," Carole replied.

Now she was gone.

FDR sent Gable a condolence telegram and later awarded Lombard a medal as "the first woman killed in action in the defense of her country in its war against the Axis Powers." On the nineteenth every Hollywood studio paused at noon to play taps, followed by two minutes of silence. Gable bought a motorcycle and drove hell-bent through the canyons, brooded, drank heavily. Joan Crawford invited him to dinner and he went on and on about Lombard until 3 A.M. "Clark you have to stop drinking," Crawford told Gable. "I know I must," he said, and wept.

He got off the sauce, at least for a while, and started agitating to enlist. To Alice it seemed like a death wish.

Chapter Twenty-Eight

....

SUMMER OF '42

Alice was agitated as well. Now with no job and having precious little money stored away, even after the pro tour, she returned to New York—and moved right back in with Tennant.

She became a full-time Manhattanite just as the City That Never Sleeps developed a full-blown case of the jitters. The threat of German invaders, bombers, and saboteurs pervaded the city. Some sixty thousand volunteers of the Aircraft Warning Service scanned the skies at six hundred different observation points. Most of them were men, but they reported unidentified aircraft to female plotters in the information center, who charted them on a master map of the sky. Eleanor Roosevelt visited one day, then wrote in her syndicated column "My Day" that "ladies are never considered to be able to keep a secret. . . . Yet complete secrecy is maintained" by the women in the war rooms.

In February the SS *Normandie*, a captured French shipping icon set to become an American troop transport, was set ablaze under mysterious circumstances in New York Harbor. As thirty thousand civilians made the trip to Pier 88 to see the impossible sight of the great ship toppled and blackened ("It was as though the Empire State Building had slowly teetered and fallen sideways in the street," wrote the *New York Journal-American*), the city longed to catch the Nazi agents responsible. When it turned out to have been caused by the sparks of a careless welder's torch, the collective exhalation whipped flags up and down Broadway. Similarly, in March, several artillery shells landed near Wall Street or in the East River. Attack! screamed New York. Mistake! said the army. One of its batteries that had arrived to protect the city had used live ammunition during an exercise.

And there were the air-raid drills, conducted in those early days of 1942 without sirens or blackout screens or shelters, none of which were available in these early days of war preparation. On April 30 a major Midtown drill was held, with civilians meant to flock to the subway or basements. Instead, a huge crowd in Times Square frolicked in a "New Year's Eve without lights." Mayor La Guardia said if it had been an actual raid, there might have been "wholesale slaughter." In July, baseball's All-Star Game, held at the Polo Grounds in Harlem, ended seconds before another blackout drill. The players raced to the center-field clubhouse as the lights went out. The crowd was told to stay seated for the twenty minutes of the drill. Thousands lit cigarettes to help pass the time, accidentally giving potential bombers a glowing target. La Guardia was criticized by the army for the incident.

Alice had many skills and didn't scare easily, and her talents didn't sit idly on the sidelines for long. She took on a couple of new service-adjacent roles, joining the public relations department of the American Women's Hospital Reserve Corps, where she was made an honorary lieutenant. She drilled ceaselessly, turning her athletic walk into a military swagger, and studied nursing and emergency care, in case those bombings really did come and there were wounds to bind and patients to stretcher.

She also took what was essentially a sales job in uniform, organizing schools and clubs to sell Navy-Marine Corps Relief Society emblems in order to raise money to build aircraft carriers and torpedoes.

"I'm working harder than I ever have," she told the Newspaper Enterprise Association. "There's a job to be done—we'll do it," she said with her typical straightforwardness. There was a gender-pride component to it as well. "This is an important age for women," she told the AP. "For the first time we're in a man's war and doing a man's work. I'm happy and grateful to be part of it."

Her tennis playing was reduced to four or five sessions a week, mostly with beefy Jack McDermott, a fifty-two-year-old stockbroker who could still move and "keeps me running," Alice said. There were still occasional exhibitions and clinics, too, but as she said, "Unless a sport is doing something for the war, there is no excuse for it."

Baseball, in the estimation of no less than President Roosevelt, was doing plenty for morale simply by continuing to play despite the new situation. That suited Alice, who remained a tremendous fan. One day during that summer of '42, she was sent by NEA editor Harry Grayson to the Polo Grounds to find a story about the baseball Giants. Mel Ott, the great slugger turned Giants manager, recognized Alice and got to talking with her. When he discovered she was a former player, he asked, "Why not work out with us?"

Alice pitched a few, just like the old days when Tim was her catcher at Golden Gate Park. She shagged flies like she did back at Rec Park. Ott called her fielding "flashy." Then she stepped into the batter's box. "I missed the first one by—conservatively—five feet," she confessed to her readers. She finally got a tick on one at pitch four. "C'mon Alice, smack it!" yelled one of the fans watching the pregame workout. Which she did—a clean liner over third. "That's a hit in any league!" yelped one of the players.

"Then and there, I discontinued my hitting," she wrote. "Why ruin a pleasant memory?"

· · ·

Alice had certainly grown in sophistication from the days when she scarcely knew the world beyond the tennis court and what Eleanor allowed her to see. Roz Bloomingdale Cowen had accidentally spurred a period of enlightenment in Alice, harmlessly introducing her as "my friend Alice, whose knowledge is a mile wide and an inch deep." It wasn't said with cruelty, but the fact was Alice had done nothing but swing a racket, work out, and hang with movie stars for most of the last decade. So despite the war and her duties to the volunteer services, Alice decided it was time to broaden her horizons. She took night classes in literature and philosophy at NYU, read more widely, went to the theater, and, most crucially, for many reasons, began to learn a foreign language.

Her tutor was a unique woman named Margarita Madrigal. She became famous for a period for her lessons, not only in Spanish but other languages, and the ease and speed with which her students grew fluent. Known as "Tica," she came to the US courtesy of the University of Mexico, on a survey of the study of Spanish in the US. "It is important for Americans to learn Spanish and know what Latin Americans are really like," she told the *Brooklyn Daily Eagle* in 1941.

She worked out of the Third Avenue YMCA, but her private classes were where the bold-faced names learned the language—author Sherwood Anderson, newsman H. V. Kaltenborn, and Roz Bloomingdale Cowen, through whom Alice got invited.

"I went from beginner to advanced Spanish in six months," Alice recalled, and that wasn't the only lesson she learned from the short, dark teacher. Margarita used her guitar as part of her lessons, believing that singing was a crucial shortcut to comprehension and dialect. She named her axe "Valentina" and told a reporter that the guitar was always asked to join her at parties. "Bring 'Valentina,' they say. She is invited."

Margarita told Alice she would give her guitar lessons. One Thursday, Alice sat on the floor, stringing her instrument, though this time a guitar, not a tennis racket. Tica came up behind her to help, murmured a Spanish phrase meaning "You are ripe and ready to fall from the tree," and soon they were engaged in lovemaking right there on the floor. "Who knew how to please a woman better than another woman?" Alice recalled thinking at the time.

Eleanor, as one might expect, wasn't pleased. The crack in her armor that Alice's affair with "Hans" had opened became a wide chasm when she discovered her charge had begun a lesbian affair. "I didn't realize I was too old for you," she fumed. But there wasn't much she could do at this point. Alice was, at long last, increasingly ready to free herself from

Tennant's steely grip. Eleanor had her standard withering sarcasm and English-accented scorn to deploy, but now that tennis was a casualty of war, she had little tangible to hold over her protégé. Except their increasingly strained love, or what modern-day observers would call codependency.

In this case, she needn't have worried. Margarita had a live-in lover, who soon fled their apartment in tears, leaving Alice to assume she would slide into that spot. But the fickle Spanish teacher caught the eye of a translator named Doris Dana, who would later become the lifelong partner of the Chilean poet Gabriela Mistral, winner of the Nobel Prize. Tica left Alice for Doris, and, as Alice wrote in *Courting Danger*, "it was my turn for tears."

....

A Guy Named Joe

Tanks rolled down Fifth Avenue.

Overhead, multiengine bombers flew noisily, turning figure eights over the city. American flags waved from seemingly every window. Confetti floated down to land on the service hats of some half a million soldiers and sailors who were marching across town from Washington Square Park to Seventy-Ninth Street during the New York at War parade. An estimated 2.5 million people lined the streets, screaming patriotic slogans and enjoying some three hundred floats, depicting scenes like Hitler, wearing a dark suit that screamed "gangster," being led to the gallows, followed by an enormous bust of FDR's patrician head, albeit without his patented cigarette holder, which at that scale might have sliced open the preceding float.

It was June 1942. Slowly, New York was adjusting to a wartime footing. The nighttime city was under a "dimout" footing. Windows over fifteen stories high were required to be veiled to hide the shine of lights inside. Streetlights and traffic lights used lightbulbs of reduced wattage. Exterior lighting from the Battery to the Bronx were turned down, if not off. The New York Times Tower turned off its wraparound electronic news bulletin board for the first time since its inception in 1928. Even the torch on the Statue of Liberty went nearly dark, its 13,000-watt lamps replaced by a couple of 200-watt bulbs, the minimum light needed to prevent planes from smashing into Lady Liberty.

During the day, the city was adorned by red, white, and blue bunting. Men in uniform were everywhere, some of them merely boys, gaping like tourists at the gray towers soaring to the sky above them. Others were older gents recently transferred from business to service, walking briskly with their briefcases newly filled with papers of federal origin, their urgency spurred by the enormity of the task ahead—planning a war on two fronts, with the Axis powers well ahead and on the front foot.

America was being counted upon by the free world to reverse the situation in the Pacific, where Japan held a huge swath of empire radiating out from the Home Islands south to the Philippines, north to Mongolia, and threatening Hawaii to the east. In Europe, the Nazis were at the English Channel, the Mediterranean Sea, and the Volga River in Stalingrad. The situation was perilous, and though "war fever" filled the streets, the informed populace realized it was going to take some time to beat back the forces of fascism.

Not everyone in uniform was male. Some 350,000 women served during WWII, both at home and abroad. As Alice walked the streets of Fort Manhattan every day, she flinched at the sight of so many other women doing their part for the war effort. She had been lending her name to money-raising efforts, to be sure, and entertained the troops at every possibility. But these women in uniform were heroes. "I wanted to do something important, something to serve my country, like Helen Jacobs," she wrote.

"Instead, I was writing comic books."

But Alice wasn't working on the funnies. She was part of the launch of the most iconic female superhero ever created.

. . .

Wonder Woman was created by a man named William Moulton Marston expressly to advance a feminist agenda. The press release announcing her arrival read, in part, "'Wonder Woman' was conceived by Dr. Marston to set up a standard among children and young people of strong, free, courageous womanhood; to combat the idea that women are inferior to men, and to inspire girls to self-confidence and achievement in athletics, occupations and professions monopolized by men" because "the only hope for civilization is the greater freedom, development and equality of women in all fields of human activity."

Alice didn't write that release, but she easily could have, for it represented her beliefs as though she were tied in a lasso of truth and had been asked what she thought about the male-female power imbalance. So it had to be karma that brought her and Max Gaines together. Gaines was a pioneer in comic book publishing. His All-American Publications put out titles featuring classic characters like the Green Lantern, the Atom, Hawkman and Hawkgirl, and Bulldog Drummond. All-American had recently merged with the better known Detective Comics (or "DC Comics") and were sister companies, though for some time they put out comics under separate corporate banners, including the adventures of the best-known hero of them all, Superman. Gaines happened to read an article in *Family Circle* magazine that quoted Marston praising Superman and comic superheroes in general, as they fulfilled "our national aspirations of the moment—to develop unbeatable national might, and to use this great power, when we get it, to protect innocent, peace-loving people from destructive, ruthless evil." Gaines hired Marston as a consultant, and the man who a few years earlier had given a press conference stating that women would one day rule the world told the publisher that he needed a female version of Superman. Wonder Woman tiptoed into the national consciousness with a few cameo appearances in other titles, but by mid-1942 Gaines felt it was time to give her her own comic book.

Alice was seeing a lot of Will du Pont at the time. He came to New York every Thursday on business and would infallibly have dinner with Alice. Tennis was always part of their activities. During the war, the duo played weekly with Bishop Fulton Sheen, the golden-voiced Catholic proselytizer who talked about faith to millions of listeners on his Sunday night NBC radio show, *The Catholic Hour* (Sheen later brought the program to television). He had recently called Hitler "the Anti-Christ" and told his flock that the war effort was not merely a military or political struggle but a "theological one."

"The Bishop was the worst tennis player I've ever seen," Alice said of the father, while also noting his fondness for drink. He particularly enjoyed a concoction called a Horse's Neck—brandy, ginger ale, and a long rind of lemon peel. During one match Alice smacked a forehand directly into the bishop's cassocks, so to speak. He groaned and left the court for a time, ashen. When he returned, he saw Alice cackling and wondered what could possibly be funny.

"I was thinking of my mother," Alice replied. "When we got hit, she always told us to rub it."

"The Bishop told that story from coast to coast," Alice later wrote.

When not hurling double entendres at clergy, Alice was busy fighting off Du Pont's repeated proposals of marriage. Alice wasn't just playing hard to get—the industrialist's wooden, gloomy manner and workaholic tendencies made the idea of marrying him difficult to conjure. Before Alice turned pro the year before, Du Pont had offered her 100,000 dollars not to tour, and to marry him instead. She turned him down then and did so again in '42, though she continued to see him socially and stay in Wilmington when the need arose.

"The scenario was always the same," she wrote in *Courting Danger*. "We'd go to dinner, walk back to my apartment, and he'd ask me to marry him. My answer was always the same. 'No, Will. You're very dear to me, but I can't marry you. I'm not in love with you.'"

Perhaps not, but it is clear she allowed herself to behave as though she were. Rita Mae Brown, who grew close with Alice near the end of the tennis star's life, told me bluntly, "I know she was kept for years by Will Dupont [*sic*]," accepting Du Pont's money in exchange for sex on demand, as well as arranging her schedule to accommodate that of the billionaire. If Will couldn't make Alice Mrs. Du Pont, he surely could buy a reasonable facsimile. Brown's mother was friendly with Will's sister, also named Alice. "The relationship was not openly discussed but tacitly acknowledged," Brown added. It was an affair that would last, on and off, for decades.

Du Pont had been married in 1919 to the daughter of a railroad baron, the combined wealth causing the press to dub the ceremony the "Wedding of the Century." His first wife, Jean, bore him four children before their 1941 divorce (the youngest child, John, would gain infamy for the murder of wrestling champion Dave Schultz in 1996). While the breakup of his marriage had many factors, Will's daughter, also named Jean, blamed Alice and held a grudge that would span decades. Will was buying Alice train tickets to spend weekends in Delaware quite often in 1941–42, according to his correspondence with her, in addition to their weekly engagement in New York. "Dear Pinky," went one letter to Alice, "I enjoyed yesterday so much and want to thank you for the swell breakfast as well as the tennis. Enclosed are return train tickets to Wilmington. My man Hugo will pick you up from the station as usual." Only some of the missives end with "love, Will," but his point was made with money.

· · ·

One Thursday evening in 1942 Alice and Will went to a cocktail party in Midtown, and Du Pont introduced her to Gaines. While chatting, Gaines happened to mention that Alice's tennis exploits reminded him of his new superhero, one who traveled incognito under the alias Diana Prince. Alice wondered aloud if it wouldn't make sense to include illustrated stories of real-life "Wonder Women" alongside the fictional tales of Princess Diana of the Amazons. Gaines loved the idea and hired Alice on the spot as an associate editor, tasked with researching and writing scripts for the biographies.

All-American, "Licensors and Publishers of Flash Comics, Green Lantern Quarterly, and Mutt and Jeff Comics," according to its letterhead, was based at 225 Lafayette Street in Manhattan's Little Italy, but Alice worked out of the DC Comics office on Lexington Avenue in Midtown, typing her scripts in a bullpen surrounded by other writers.

Wonder Woman #1, debuting in June 1942, sold for ten cents down at the local candy store. INTRODUCING MISS ALICE MARBLE AS ASSOCIATE

EDITOR OF *WONDER WOMAN!* screamed the masthead. For the dime the reader received a sixty-eight-page spectacular, featuring multiple stories, including the origin tale of Wonder Woman, aka Diana Prince. Wonder Woman also joined a circus to investigate a rash of elephant poisoning; battled double agent Paula von Gunther; and fought a bullfight while stopping a Japanese invasion of Mexico. Alice could relate to her perpetual motion, certainly.

Alice seemed to have been a role model for Wonder Woman in at least one crucial way—her outfit. During her scattershot early appearances, Diana wore long, flowing culottes that stopped just above the knee, what today we would call a skort. But upon receiving her own comic book, Wonder Woman wore form-fitting shorts, just as Alice had in transforming women's tennis on the sartorial side. One can picture Alice getting a load of Wonder Woman's original get-up and exclaiming, "You can't fight crime wearing that!"

But the unquestioned highlight of the debut issue was the four-page biography of Florence Nightingale, the "Angel of Crimea." Alice's script was illustrated by Sheldon Moldoff, who drew the first six of Alice's historical bios.

Like all writers, Alice was responsible for promoting her work. She gave away copies of *Wonder Woman* #1 at women's functions and tennis clinics and sent them gratis to nurses at army bases across the country, along with her cover letter:

7/20/42

Dear Army Nurse:

I am happy to present you with this complimentary copy of "WONDER WOMAN."

"WONDER WOMAN" is the only comic strip character of its type, that is, a female "Superman." "WONDER WOMAN" first appeared in one of our monthly magazines—"Sensation Comics"— about nine months ago, and already it is one of the most popular features in the entire comic magazine field.

You will note that "WONDER WOMAN," in her everyday existence, is Diana Prince, an Army Nurse, on special duty as secretary to "Colonel Darnell" in the Office of Military Intelligence in Washington. She only becomes her dual personality, "WONDER WOMAN," when it is necessary to help Major Trevor, of the Army Intelligence, (with whom she is secretly in love) foil the misdeeds of the enemies within our borders.

I should like to call your particular attention in this issue to my story on Florence Nightingale—in our next issue, I tell the story of Clara Barton.

I hope you like this first issue of "WONDER WOMAN." After you have read it, won't you be good enough to write—if you have time?

Very Sincerely Yours,
Alice Marble

A heroic nurse was not just the subject of Alice's second script—Clara Barton, "Angel of the Battlefield"—but number three as well. Edith Cavell, the British nurse who allowed hundreds of Allied soldiers to escape Belgium in WWI, for which she was shot by the Germans, was Alice's star of #3. "Patriotism is not enough!" Cavell says in the strip, before she is executed. "We love and serve our country so that it may serve God and man!"

Alice's workday in researching these women wasn't as easy as simply clicking on Wikipedia and selecting a few "top moments" from their lives. The research was done at work and at home, where she and Eleanor pored over reference books and works of history, looking for details that not only were important but would pop when illustrated. For example, Clara Barton dashing under fire to deliver much-needed bandages to battlefield surgeons at Antietam when drawn by Moldoff, with whom Alice worked closely to condense and sharpen the material.

In the months to follow, women famous (Joan of Arc, Susan B. Anthony, Helen Keller) and more obscure (Emma Willard, Evangeline Booth, Elizabeth Blackwell) were among her bios.

Her last script told the story of Lucretia Mott, the abolitionist, in issue #20, which hit newsstands in late November. The entire run of nineteen biographies (she skipped one issue for reasons unexplained) made her a tidy sum—Alice would claim 50,000 dollars, half of what she had made slogging across the country the year before with the other three tennis pros. Wonder Woman required considerably less physical effort. But Alice was "restless and discontented with my life." She was an athlete stuck at a desk job. Around this time Gaines and Marston decided to shift their emphasis from strong women to married women. "Wonder Women of History" was replaced by "Marriage a la Mode," which highlighted marriage customs and ceremonies from around the world.

Ironically, according to a story Alice would tell for her entire life, she was heading in a similar direction.

• • •

Despite the war, or more accurately because of it, Manhattan's nightclubs were experiencing a boom time. Between the servicemen, the enormous support bureaucracy, and the camp followers, money was flowing around the "Tijuana on the Hudson," as "anyone with a $100 bill to spare" raced to the "market town" of New York to spend it. "The nightclubs minted fortunes unmatched even in the lunatic 20s," wrote Alistair Cooke in *The American Home Front*.

One was famous for more than merely striking it rich. Of all the New York hot spots during the war—the Copa, the Latin Quarter, the Stork Club, El Morocco—none had the cachet of the Stage Door Canteen. A pop-up party in Times Square, the Stage Door Canteen held a nightly bash for the thousands of servicemen (and they were all men—WAVES and WACs and other volunteers like Alice weren't invited as guests) wandering around the city, waiting for orders to ship out to remote battlefields or lonely ocean voyages. It opened on March 2, 1942, in the underground floor of the 44th Street Theatre. By the end of the war there were imitations in eight American cities, as well as London and Paris.

The Canteen was the brainchild of the American Theatre Wing War Service, Broadway's contribution to home front morale and fundraising since WWI. They turned a former basement speakeasy into New York's most happening club, where any serviceman strolling through Midtown could come in and dance with a showgirl, or see stars like Judy Garland and Ethel Merman sing, backed by the orchestras of Benny Goodman and Count Basie. Alfred Lunt was in the back emptying trash cans. Lauren Bacall danced to the point she "thought she would drop," passed from marine to sailor to artilleryman in a single number. The Stage Door Canteen provided a unique combination of normalcy and glamour for the average enlistee fresh off the farm or Officer Candidate School.

It was, also, very often a place for these GIs and swabbies and leathernecks to get routed in Ping-Pong by one Alice Marble.

Alice spent many nights at the Canteen, comfortable with crowds and strangers and men in uniform. Most evenings involved some table tennis, a dance or three, and some singing at one of the several pianos in the joint, and then home to her and Teach's apartment.

One night, however, was different. As Alice tells it, she had taken a break from the "ping-pong wars" and was singing "Taking a Chance on Love" when a rich baritone joined in. "He was an army captain, tall, with dark, wavy hair and genial brown eyes. Something about those eyes made me blush and forget the words to the song."

He introduced himself as Joe, Joseph Norman Crowley in full, of Kansas and the Ohio State University and now the US Army, intelligence wing, who "snapped him up" when it was discovered he studied five languages, including German. He was a flier, apparently doing secret reconnaissance flights that he couldn't speak about.

Their first night was chaste, but when he returned three months later, in mid-1942, he took Alice to dinner. They went to Le Pavillon, the famous French restaurant that had moved over from its place at the World's Fair to a permanent home at Fifty-Fifth and Fifth (the owner and chef were war refugees and couldn't go to France if they wanted). Almost immediately they were joined by two of Alice's showbiz pals, Gloria Swanson and Mary Pickford, two veteran actresses who also did their part for the war by visiting bases and entertaining at the Stage Door.

At the dinner, Joe blurted to a fan who had stopped to praise Alice that he intended to marry the tennis star. "Captain Crowley is moving a bit fast!" Alice replied, but she was in with both feet, even though at one point Joe told Alice she reminded him of his "best friend."

"Who is that?" Alice asked.

"My dog, Rusty."

"I should have laughed," Alice recalled, "but there was something so touchingly innocent about his remark I wanted to cry."

After a whirlwind courtship, punctuated by months-long absences to battlefronts unknown, she writes in *Courting Danger*, they were married—in secret.

Alice writes that Joe had a friend, a "Navy chaplain," who married the two aboard a ship in New York Harbor. No family, or friends, or even Tennant were there, but "a hundred sailors in dress whites gathered around us on deck" for the ceremony, after which they tossed their hats in the air.

"How long do you suppose it took them to get their hats sorted out?" Alice wondered.

Of course, Tennant didn't approve. "He's in the army for God's sake!" "It's a one-night stand!" "It's lust, not love!" Though Eleanor had less leverage over Alice than ever by this point, according to her memoir, the words still pained. But, she wrote, "I didn't cry, and I didn't give in."

Alice was beginning to spread her wings and fly on her own. The war and her experiences to that point, away from the comfort of the tennis circuit, certainly had a lot to do with that maturation. But was this warrior, Joseph Crowley, really part of the equation?

First it was the banker on the beach, "Hans." Now came a man whose name she gave freely but who carried his own set of questions that deepened the mystery of Alice even further.

Chapter Thirty

··

The Road Warrior

Eleanor was starting to feel her forty-six years. She remained wiry, but arthritis had set in in several joints, making each attempt to rise from a seat resemble the evolution of man, and a lifetime of chain-smoking had sapped her wind. New York's cold didn't appeal to the California girl, so she returned in the winter to the Golden State, renting a home in Culver City to reengage with clients there, with an eye toward a more permanent return.

Eleanor had always bucked up Alice when she was feeling less than useful to the war effort by saying, "Your tennis whites are your service uniform." Now it was time for Alice to don her battle gear and, in their way, march into combat.

She wouldn't be alone. Mary Hardwick, Alice's punching bag on the pro tour of 1941, had certainly used her name and game to assist the Allied effort. Few civilians of any background had been as tireless in their efforts to raise money for the fight against fascism. Mary had been in the States when war came to Europe. A frantic cable from her family advised her to stay across the Atlantic, out of bombing range. She came from a wealthy family, had been to a Paris finishing school, and could be a "frightful snob," according to Alice, but she was also full of classic British upper-lip stiffness and get-on-with-it purpose. "She has been one of the most devoted workers in the cause of the Allies," wrote Allison Danzig, comparing Hardwick's hard work to a religious zealot.

The British government had clamped down on exporting any funds overseas, so Mary was essentially cut off from her family fortune, a large reason for her decision to turn professional, a move that dumbfounded her people back in London. "They could hardly be said to be pleased as Punch," she said.

Without money of her own to donate, she encouraged others to do so. She and Alice had raised some 43,000 dollars for the Red Cross, the USO, and British War Relief Society to this point, and Mary had just returned from ten weeks in the desert Southwest, playing exhibitions at every base in the area while putting the squeeze on the locals.

"There is no tennis in England now," she told a reporter, "and there may not be again in my lifetime, but some day the stands around the Centre Court at Wimbledon will be filled again. England will win eventually, and I'd like to feel that I have helped in some way, however small."

On August 5, 1943, Alice appeared with Hardwick at the USO offices on West Fortieth Street, alongside the stately Captain Geneva Mc-Quatters of the Women's Army Corps (WAC). The trio announced an upcoming tour that would take them to the WAC camps of the "middle West, South and East under sponsorship of the USO Camp Shows." "In addition to opposing each other in singles," reported the *Times*, "Miss Marble and Miss Hardwick each will select a partner among the Wacs in the camps they visit for a doubles match." There would also be clinics, and Alice would lecture on fitness.

Come the end of the show, "the two players will live in the barracks with the Wacs."

"It should be a lot of fun," Hardwick trilled.

"Yes, if they don't get us up at five o'clock in the morning," Alice added.

The America the women would tour was a troubled one as summer turned to fall of 1943, despite the fact that the war situation had improved. Japan's naval dominance had been lessened the year before at Midway, having lost four aircraft carriers to American bombs, and America's mammoth industrial production machine had begun to crank out ships, airplanes, and munitions in overwhelming numbers, dwarfing what the Japanese could produce to replace lost materiel. The first blooding of US forces in North Africa had produced victory, and with the invasion of Sicily the Allies now had a toehold in Europe (though D-Day was still a year into the future). The sense of gloom over war news no longer pervaded Americans when they read the morning papers.

But domestically, matters were different. Rationing was starting to pinch, hard. Food shortages began to appear, hitting all the basics— bread, milk, eggs, meat. Workers used to hearty fare to fuel their work in heavy production were having to make do with what one miner called "lettuce sandwiches in his lunch pail." The huge population migration that saw industrial centers like Detroit and Los Angeles swell with new arrivals produced critical shortages in housing and services. It also inflamed race relations in those places, as Southern blacks worked alongside, and often took jobs from, white locals. The tension exploded in Detroit on June 20, when a major race riot took thirty-four lives (twenty-five of them African-American), injured eight hundred others, and cost an estimated $2 million in damage (nearly $30 million today).

The influx of women into the workplace took its toll on their children, who were often left without care during the day and meals at night. Movie theaters became ad hoc day care centers, as working mothers dropped their children off at the picture show and told them to make a day of it. "I have had as many as 50 to 60 children left here and sometimes when I leave the closed theater they are still waiting, out on the streets, for their family," reported one theater owner in Muncie, Indiana.

The railroads occasionally saw wildcat strikes, despite a "no strike" pledge given at the beginning of the war, but for the most part the nation's transit industry functioned smoothly during the war. That allowed the Marble-Hardwick WAC tour to get around the nation without undue delays. They started in Chicago and worked their way across the Midwest to Jefferson Barracks in Missouri, where "much to the WACs' delight" they ate with the girls and "even washed their own clothes." The *St. Louis Star-Times* wrote, "A fancy suite at the Waldorf or an apartment at the Ritz are very nice but Misses Alice Marble and Mary Hardwick have found during the past two weeks that a bunk in a WAC barracks at an army camp can be just as delightful."

The ladies next turned south for army bases in Virginia, Tennessee, Georgia, and Florida. With autumn's arrival it was on to bases around the mid-Atlantic and Northeast. "They will complete their tour in time to take in the National championships at Forest Hills as spectators," reported the AP.

At night there was always some dancing and singing, and then a bed in the barracks, often a private officer's quarters surrendered by the occupant for the night. It was here that Alice received many a visitor keen for more than tennis lessons.

"It was courageous—and foolhardy—for them to admit they were lesbians," Alice said later. And indeed, homosexuals were denied entry into the armed services or were immediately drummed out with a dishonorable discharge. But as Alice admitted, "I knew their loneliness only too well."

After the WAC tour Alice raised money elsewhere. At Thanksgiving she helped drum up a million dollars in war bonds in an astonishing ninety minutes down on Wall Street. In January 1944, she played a match at the Seventh Regiment Armory at Sixty-Sixth and Park Avenue as part of the Fourth War Loan Drive, a push for more public dough that would eventually raise nearly $3 million.

Meanwhile, she checked in on her designs. Her Alice Marble oxfords, a civilian version of the shoe she had designed for the OCD, being particularly hot during the holiday season. Wilson Sporting Goods was selling her Alice Marble line of tennis rackets like hotcakes, with the "Court Queen" the most popular, though the "Tournament" model was more treasured by the cognoscenti, for its "Speed Flex Fibre Face" and, of course, Alice's signature on the shaft. For $7.95, it was a bargain for the tennis player in your life, though the war ensured that no new products rolled off the pipeline.

Meanwhile, the gossip about her love life continued, in bizarrely inaccurate fashion. Ed Sullivan, that font of misinformation, reported that Alice and Herb Harris, an actor and film producer, would "take the leap over the holidays," and that Alice and (radio actor) Ben Grauer "aren't discussing footfaults." Since there is scant evidence that the two even knew each other, just what they were "discussing" instead remains a mystery.

As the war dragged on, and obviously was not going to be over anytime soon, Alice and Mary decided to take on a near-constant tour of bases, hospitals, ports, physical training areas—anywhere military types gathered and had a tennis court available. Or even just a patch of land on which Alice and Mary could throw down their portable canvas court. "We played on the rolling decks of ships, on baked-earth courts, and in a variety of gyms, armories, and Quonset huts," Alice recalled.

Alice and Mary attracted plenty of attention during their travels. "They have discovered that a couple of personable young ladies wearing shorts and rushing about a tennis court are regarded as gifts from heaven by the soldiers," wrote the *Los Angeles Times*. There were some unexpected issues that hadn't come up on the WAC tour. For one, mixed doubles tended to include one officer and one enlisted man, but this led to some hard feelings when the "G.I.s root vehemently against the officer." The schedule, of course, was always strenuous—fly or drive or train all morning, lunch with officers, tennis all afternoon, dinner and dance with GIs, more dinner and dancing with officers, then up at the crack of dawn to make it to the next base. Meanwhile, Mary wasn't "too good an air traveler," as Bill Henry of the *LA Times* reported, "and at times couldn't take it." Alice would sing to Mary to calm her down.

But she also exposed Mary to far more air miles, thanks to the head of US Caribbean Defense Command, Lieutenant General George Brett, who was a huge fan of Alice. When the USO arranged for Alice and Mary to tour bases in Panama and Guatemala, General Brett, based in

Panama, stepped up and let the women have use of his personal plane, a B-17D Flying Fortress nicknamed *The Swoose*. The tennis stars used *The Swoose* to get around not only the Caribbean but stops in the southern US as well.

There was not just turbulence in the air. Alice and Mary had been at each other's side for months of constant, often hard-paced travel, and, quite naturally, they began to wear on one another. A sailor named John Burgoon wrote about one of the exhibition matches, when the tennists came to the Coco Solo naval base in Colón. "It was obvious before they got on the court that there was no love lost between the two. As play began, Alice's face got red and she missed quite a few shots as she became 'furious-er and furious-er.'"

While they mostly flew between bases, Alice had been driven the fifty miles from an army base in Cristóbal to Coco Solo. En route, as she relates in *Courting Danger*, the jeep she was riding in crashed, nearly sending her and her driver over a cliff. They managed to escape with relatively minor injuries, but it was another automotive near miss for Alice, who still counted her blessings that she hadn't broken her neck outside of Phoenix back in 1940.

She wrote that she couldn't play "for two weeks" after the accident, due to the damage to her hands, though the entire trip was scarcely longer than that, so perhaps that is an overstatement. Of more import, according to Alice, was a surprise trip into Panama by one Captain Joe Crowley, Alice's secret husband. It was to be a honeymoon of sorts.

"We even had the luxury of sleeping together," Alice writes. "We were discreet, but Mary, a proper Brit, seemed a bit scandalized." This description of Hardwick is at odds with another memory from John Burgoon, who recalled, "The British lady was stark naked under her short, pleated tennis skirt" while she flounced around the court, "and she took every opportunity to show herself to the crowd of sailors, who howled in approval."

Alice and Mary returned to the States in late March to a cold welcome. The two women were flown in *The Swoose* to Miami, where they were to catch a train to New York. An army courier handed Alice an envelope that held the tickets, but when the conductor came, Alice discovered to her horror that there was only one ticket inside. They had no funds, having spent weeks in Central America and bought plenty of gifts and goodies with the last of their expense money.

"Will you take a check?" Alice asked.

"Like Hell I will," replied the conductor. "I'll put you off at Jacksonville."

Alice decided her fame was her best bet. She pounded on a few stateroom doors, finally coming upon someone who knew of her. He gave them enough (thirty-five dollars) for the second ticket, but they still had just thirty-two cents between them, and a couple of long, potentially hungry days on the train. She sweet-talked a Mexican man—in Spanish, courtesy of Tica Madrigal—into buying her and Mary dinner. The señor also agreed to give them some cash when he disembarked in DC, but matters got confused and he wound up chasing the departing train, waving a pair of five-dollar bills as Alice got smaller in the window.

Another couple was prevailed upon to buy lunch, and Alice repaid them later with a rare gift—a dozen golf balls, very hard to come by during the war. But Alice had access to all manner of things—nylons, catgut, steak—that others did not, by dint of her connections and relentless work. That included not just the exhibitions and speechifying but a stint as "an agent for a mail-order house, contributor to a children's magazine, designer of women's shoes, especially those worn in war plants, and singer and guitar player," according to the *St. Louis Post-Dispatch*. She was also a tireless pen pal, writing to no fewer than fifty-four soldiers overseas, including "her beau" and Tim, now in the merchant marine, and several new ones acquired in Central America. "She didn't mention anything about writing to train conductors," wrote the *Post-Dispatch*.

Another thing she didn't mention to reporters, or anyone save Tennant, was that she was pregnant.

"I began having morning sickness upon my return" to New York, she writes in *Courting Danger*. Eleanor was predictably unstrung. "How could you?!" she roared, per Alice. "You have obligations, a career."

"Being a wife and mother is part of that career from now on," Alice replied.

. . .

One thing seems certain—the father wasn't Joseph Norman Crowley. There are no records of a Joseph Norman Crowley in the National Personnel Records Center in St. Louis, in and of itself not necessarily proof of anything (especially as some sixteen to eighteen million records were destroyed in a horrible fire there in 1973). But there is also no record of a Joseph Norman Crowley ever attending Ohio State University (or Ohio University), according to the registrar's office at both schools. There is no record of a Joseph Norman Crowley registering for the Selective Service in the state of Kansas. There is no record of a Joseph Norman Crowley in any Kansas census that would match his rough age. Though Alice said the Crowley line ended over the skies of Germany, there are no records of his death in any such incident during the war. The state of New York issued no marriage license to anyone named Joseph Crowley or Alice Marble in the years 1940–45, although I was warned those records are incomplete. Given my inability to find any contemporary official record of him, I wondered, Could Alice really have conjured a husband and such a full backstory for him out of the ether? Had she indeed done that, or was he hiding in history, waiting for me to find him?

Chapter Thirty-One

....

Bringing Up Baby

The Palm Springs Public Library in California is airy and modern, as chic a public facility as one might expect for such a wealthy enclave. But that doesn't mean there aren't musty stacks inside, with items in the collection seldom seen by borrowers.

I happened to stumble across one such buried treasure. It is a videotape of a "documentary" shot by a local outfit called Prickly Pears Productions in 1986. The subject:

Alice Marble.

Unfortunately, the technology required to watch the tape is as outmoded as Alice's old wooden racket. There are no VCRs in the library, or, quite likely, anywhere in a hundred-mile radius. Fortunately, much of the collection at the library has been digitized in the last few years, and the staff offered to get this tape transferred to a computer file for me.

The "documentary" is actually a simple interview with Alice at her home in Palm Desert. She is older now, four years from passing away, an Alice I never have seen on video in my research, which to this point has shown her younger, hitting tennis balls or giving interviews.

Her interrogator is a smiling young actress named Courtney

Gebhart. The chat takes many turns as Alice goes off on non sequiturs and down cul-de-sacs, mostly involving her life in Palm Springs and her days hobnobbing with celebrities. I hear stories I have heard before, with some of the details a little off, attributable to Alice's age and the tricks of memory.

But there are some tantalizing moments in there as well. The camera remains mostly on its tripod and still, shooting Alice and Courtney in a two-shot. But occasionally, the operator pans around Alice's home, revealing her portrait and other, simple decorations.

At one point, it catches a portion of a framed eight-by-ten photo, which Alice then grabs and holds up, allowing the camera to zoom in for a better look.

In the black-and-white picture, Alice is wearing an evening gown and is dancing with a handsome, smiling army officer. She says the shot was taken in Panama during the war.

And, she adds in a surprisingly clear voice, her dance partner in the photo is her late husband.

"Joe Crowley."

. . .

Writing off a made-up husband as a runaway story, or as an elaborate cover for Alice's public image during the war, is simple enough, but the fact she had a photo of herself dancing with this man, and kept it for some forty years, makes it hard to believe there was no relationship at all.

The photo captures the man in profile; he has a prominent nose and an army-issue haircut that is close-cropped and straight-lined. From what of his face is visible, he appears to be somewhere between thirty and forty-five years old, clearly older than the naif Alice describes at points in *Courting Danger* but hardly middle-aged. He bears a passing resemblance to Alice's friend in Panama, General George Brett, though is obviously younger than the general, who was pushing sixty.

But Brett might factor into the mystery. Alice talked at various points, including in the Prickly Pears video, about how Joe did a stint "flying a General around," which didn't square with his supposedly dangerous duties overseas. In examining the history of the B-17D bomber that was Brett's personal plane, *The Swoose*, I discovered that her pilot during the Caribbean mission was one Captain Jack Crane. Born in 1919, Crane was in his mid-twenties during the war, a little young for the figure in the photo, though he looks the part. According to his obituary in the *Los Altos Town Crier*, he left the service after the war, and lived most of the rest of his days in Northern California, not far from where Alice grew up and returned on occasion throughout her life.

It's hard to believe that the rank and similar name, down to the initials, are entirely a coincidence, but whether Alice actually had a love affair with Captain Crane or merely borrowed some of his specifics to create her "Joe" is unknown.

By the way, Jack Crane's middle name was Joseph.

The little that Alice says about "Joe" in the video is as vague and fragmented and contradictory as her other statements about this man. "He was off to the Pacific and then he was off to Europe and he was all over the place," Alice says of Crowley's wartime movements. She also mentions his arrival in Panama, noting how much he "hated flying a general around, because he wanted to be in the fight," and that while Alice "didn't want particularly to get married." She also remembers him as a fellow "movie buff," and the fact that "Joe introduced me to wine, which I had never had before," trivial details in comparison to what she said about his college and home state, perhaps. But they still are rather specific bits of business for someone who has seemed to be a ghost, if not an entirely made-up man.

But then she talks about the dinner at which Mary Pickford and Gloria Swanson appeared at her table while dining with Joe, and says that "Carole Lombard" was there—an obvious impossibility, since the actress died in the plane crash months before Alice claims to have met Joe.

There is plenty of contradictory information about "Joe" in the contemporary record as well. A United Press story on January 24, 1944, headlined ALICE MARBLE TO WED AFTER WAR, revealed that "her husband-to-be is 'a very special guy' named Joe, an army captain overseas . . . but she refused to reveal his last name." The story had the timeline correct, stating the romance began in mid-1942 "when they met at a party in New York."

"The hostess asked me to 'look after Joe,'" she told the UP reporter. "Well, I looked after him all right."

In Alice's 1946 memoir, *The Road to Wimbledon*, she states that "I hadn't known [Joe] long and it just didn't seem right to be married" during the war, especially given all the insta-marriages the war had created. Alice encountered many women who rushed into wedlock on her tours, and witnessed the pain and regret prematurely tying the knot had caused. In yet another interview, Alice said that she didn't get married to Joe, due to "religious differences."

In a 1981 interview with *The Desert Sun*, Alice says, "Joe was a lieutenant when we met," not a captain, and mistimes the length of their marriage, saying they were married for several months and that Joe "died at the end of the war," rather than in 1944. Small beer, perhaps a function of age and the faultiness of memory. But then she suggests he wasn't "Joe" at all, calling him a pilot and protectively saying, when asked about him, "I will call him 'Joe.'" She added that they were "married by a naval chaplain" and honeymooned in Stowe, Vermont, "where we skied."

"He was Mr. Right for me," she explains to the *Sun* when asked why she never married again. "After he was gone, he was too hard to duplicate."

What did the conflicting details mean? Was he a made-up husband? Did he exist at all? Was he the "one who got away," a real person like Captain Crane who, for whatever reason, slipped through her fingers? Or did he represent to Alice something more fleeting but very real—her genuine, personal connection with the troops at this time, a way to express her exhaustion at being asked about her home life, and the very trying ordeal of being a major public star during an era that frowned upon visible intimate lives that challenged a traditional, heterosexual narrative? Alice was a big box office draw during her amateur days and felt pressure from the USLTA and other associations to be America's sweetheart. When she turned professional, she had even more reason to stay quiet, and the same held true for all of her moneymaking forays. She was forever being contrasted favorably to the "muscle molls," the derisive nickname for physically strong, less-than-glamorous female athletes, regardless of whether they were actually lesbian. The armed services were quick to dishonorably discharge homosexuals on "morals" grounds, and Alice spent time around many, many servicemen and servicewomen who weren't asked and certainly weren't telling.

Were it to come out that she hadn't come out, the forward motion of her public life—by this time, the public life that had peaked and she was trying hard to revitalize—would come crashing down overnight.

There is no record of Alice even being married, though she said there was a marriage to Joe Crowley. At the same time, she was well known to have refused to marry Will du Pont, though that affair was certainly real. It would be easy to assume the entirety of her supposed marriage to the warrior was purely a cover story, except for the evidence of the photo. The mysterious officer—Jack Joseph Crane?—in the framed picture Alice kept until she died, whatever his name, was not Will du Pont.

Perhaps this man did have an affair of some sort with Alice. If she had become pregnant, a connection of that sort would explain why she was moved to keep the photo all those years. Of course, it is possible that it was some other encounter in Panama, or at any stop along her tour, that was the magic moment. And it's impossible to discount Will du Pont as the potential father, though there is no record of his seeing Alice in this period, or of her stopping by Wilmington for one of her visits.

And of course, as with the marriage and maybe even Joe Crowley himself, there is the very strong possibility that this story hadn't happened at all.

. . .

These parts of Alice's story are completely unremarked upon in the press of the time, though of course the preparations for and execution of the Allied invasion of Europe took up most of the media oxygen in the spring and summer of 1944. Even as the D-Day operation was going on,

Alice was taking part in the planning for the New York War Bond Sports Carnival, another athletic lollapalooza held at the Polo Grounds. Alice also took part in a large war bond fundraiser in Philadelphia, "crossing rackets" with Hardwick yet again, not showing any noticeable baby bump despite being—according to her timeline—almost five months pregnant.

At the same time, war correspondent Ernie Pyle was wandering the beaches of Normandy in the aftermath of the D-Day landings, where he came across, incredibly enough, a tennis racket that some soldier misguidedly had brought with him. "It lies lonesomely on the sand, clamped in a rack, not a string broken."

The breaking of the German lines in France, followed by the liberation of Paris, gave rise stateside to an outbreak of "victory fever." It seemed all but certain that the Nazis would surrender and the boys would be home by Christmas. Alice was caught up in the idea of the war ending sooner rather than later. But then, yet more automotive disaster struck. Alice writes in *Courting Danger* (but again, not in *The Road to Wimbledon*) that when she was "five months pregnant"—mid-August, according to her timeline—she was returning from a party on Long Island when she was run off the road by a "drunk driver." When she came to in a hospital room, once again she learned she had avoided serious injury—but, according to *Courting Danger*, she had miscarried the baby due to the trauma.

As she put it in a 1981 interview with *The Desert Sun*, "I was driving in my Buick on a highway in New York when a car sideswiped me. I crashed and the steering wheel jammed into my stomach, killing the baby."

Alice does mostly disappear from the public record during August, which would fit with a miscarriage five months after her March tryst in Panama. So if she was indeed recovering from a car accident (one that also prompted a miscarriage), it could have happened then. Perhaps unsurprisingly, the accident and injury weren't reported or mentioned in any press accounts.

By September, Alice was well enough to be feted at the Setauket,

New York, home (an estate called Point of View) of H. V. Kaltenborn and his wife, Olga, on September 3. On September 16, Alice and Mary Hardwick tangled at an army air base in Lake Placid, New York, and on September 19, Alice appeared on Milton Berle's radio show *Let Yourself Go* on the Blue Network (which had been part of NBC and was the forerunner to ABC).

Most intriguingly, she played a set of mixed doubles at the Cosmopolitan Club in Harlem in early September, teaming with pioneering African-American player Robert Ryland against Dr. Reginald Weir and Hardwick. Ryland was a private first class in the army air force at the time, based at Walterboro Army Airfield in South Carolina. "The army thought it would be good publicity to send me to New York for the match," he said. Two black men competing alongside two white women was hardly a common sight at the time, even in New York. It was a quiet and graceful gesture of inclusion by Alice (and Mary), who knew the stresses and difficulties of the glass ceiling, if not the color barrier.

She also gave some impromptu remarks to the overwhelmingly black crowd, saying, "Tennis may be understood by all races." "Tennis is a great sport," she continued, because "we get to know more about the other fellow's problems and understand a little better his situation," according to the Negro newspaper *The Weekly Review* of Birmingham, Alabama. In couched but clear language, she added, "Competition is keen and when we can respect a fellow regardless of who he is or where he comes from, for his ability and fineness, then that is something in anybody's language."

Her most ironic statement was that since she had given up pro tennis, "she was free to play with whomever she liked and whenever she liked." That was certainly true, and yet in a different context, it sounded more like a wish for the future than her present reality, so much of which remained clouded in secrecy.

Chapter Thirty-Two

....

The Spy Who Loved Me

*S*ecret is the best word to describe the next period of Alice's life, from December 1944 to May 1945, the portion of her wartime experience that went uncommented upon by her in her first memoir, or in any forum, for nearly fifty years. It was not until the publication of her second memoir, *Courting Danger*, that she described the extraordinary story of her recruitment into US spy services, her mission to Europe to reengage with her former lover, now suspected of working with the Nazis, and the incredible night where she nearly paid the ultimate price in the name of duty and revenge.

It is an amazing tale, full of period detail and emotional engagement, high-stakes thrills and incredible twists and turns—literally, during a life-and-death chase on a dark mountain road. It is an episode of espionage worthy of inclusion among the most celebrated of WWII.

And, as with the story of "Joe Crowley," researching what actually happened revealed a wholly unexpected mystery.

First, Alice's story, as she tells it in *Courting Danger*.

. . .

The winter of 1944 was a cruel one for Americans conditioned by the triumphs of summer that the war would soon be over. The Germans counterattacked in December in a major push that nearly hurled the Allies back to the English Channel. The Battle of the Bulge was an Axis defeat, but it ended all hope of the boys coming home anytime soon. In fact, to most civilians, it appeared that the war would go on into an indefinite future—that Germany and Japan would never, ever surrender.

It was in this context that Alice felt her own loss, as she tells the story of this period. Just before Christmas, she was interrupted from singing Christmas carols with Tennant, Browne (home for good from Red Cross duties), Will du Pont, and, surprisingly enough, her old flame Tica Madrigal and her new lover, Doris. At the door of their Midtown apartment was a courier with a telegram. It was from the War Department.

"We regret to inform you that Captain Joseph Crowley was killed in action when his plane was shot down over Germany . . ."

In a state of shock, Alice went into her bedroom, where she grabbed a fistful of sleeping pills and swallowed them, hoping for the darkness to envelop her and relieve the immense pain.

She woke up in the hospital, her stomach pumped, her faith in life shattered.

She was destroyed for a long period, only coming out of it in part thanks to a telegram from Clark Gable, who had escaped his grief by serving in the army air force, filming actual bombing missions over Germany from inside the plane, dangerous duty that nearly resulted in his death when a 20 mm shell knocked the heel off his boot and continued up, narrowly missing his skull. The gesture was reminiscent of Gable's late wife, Carole Lombard, sending a letter to Alice while she was floundering in Pottenger's Sanatorium.

If I can do it, so can you.

Buoyed by the note, Alice wrote that she shook off the depression that weighted her down and started leaving the apartment once again. On one occasion, she was approached while out to lunch at 21, the famous eatery on Fifty-Second Street, by a man from army intelligence she called "Captain Jones," though stating directly that it was a *nom de combat*. He arranged to drive her into Brooklyn the following day, where she met Jones's superior, a Colonel Linden, also a name Alice made up, she said, in order to protect his identity.

Due to the FBI background check from her days running the physical fitness arm of the OCD, the army men had discovered the fact that she had been involved with the Swiss banker, "Hans Steinmetz," in 1938. Now they wanted her to go to Switzerland under cover of tennis, in order to reunite with her former paramour and discover whether or not he was hiding funds several Nazis had stolen and stashed with his bank.

"They know they're losing the war," Linden explained, "and the smart ones are smuggling riches they've acquired—gold, jewels, paintings, currency, anything of value—into Switzerland."

"I couldn't believe what I was hearing," Alice wrote. "I almost expected someone to yell 'Cut' and the actors to relax, light up cigarettes, and start talking about their social lives. This wasn't real!"

The plan was deceptively simple. Alice would be sent to Geneva for tennis clinics and exhibitions, as she had done throughout the war. Then the hope was Hans would find her. If he didn't emerge, well, they had tried. If they did connect, they would teach Alice all she needed to know about how to get proof of his Nazi connections.

She went back to the apartment she shared with Tennant, and Mary Browne was there, too. She worked on her "squeezie" rubber ball that was omnipresent while debating if she should actually do it. When Linden called the following day, she had this melodramatic conversation with him:

"I've thought about your offer."

"And . . . ?"

"Well, I've nothing left to live for."

"You do. Your life."

"I'll take that chance."

So Alice was in. She was taken to an anonymous warehouse in

Brooklyn, a spy training academy not far from the navy yard, where some seventy thousand longshoremen and shipbuilders and harbormasters worked around the clock during the war, as vital shipping and materiel flowed in and out (to prevent foreign agents from watching the activity from above, pedestrian walkways on the nearby Manhattan and Williamsburg bridges were encased). Here, she was issued a .25-caliber pistol and trained to shoot by an instructor named Dave ("I only knew first names, and I suspected those were phony," she wrote. "I never knew enough to endanger the operation").

A burly instructor everyone called "Grunt" taught her hand-to-hand combat, calmly tossing her around to the point she had to wear long sleeves while playing tennis to hide the bruising. She also learned map reading, which was greatly aided by her ability to have instant recall of written or printed material. And the use of a hidden camera, and safe cracking. She would play tennis in the mornings, then tell Tennant she was off to take a course at NYU but would instead slip over to Brooklyn (whether by subway or taxi she didn't say) for training.

Lastly, she was given a briefing on the layout of Hans's residence. "He had often threatened to steal me from Teach and lock me up in his castle," Alice remembered of their dalliance in France, and indeed, his home was a monstrous chateau just outside of Geneva. It dated to the 1600s, though it had of course been remodeled and updated over the years. The intel boys had worked up a set of plans based on some "educated guesswork," and now they briefed Alice on the home, from the formal dining room to the grand staircase.

"Here, under the staircase, is probably where you'll find the doorway to the basement," Jones told her. "You can be sure there's a wine cellar, and that's probably where the vault is."

"Why would he keep records at home?"

Linden answered, "Discretion. Everyone on his household staff has been with the family for years. They're loyal. Employees at the bank come and go—they might be nosy, or Russian agents." He went on to explain that the Russians were after the Nazi loot as well.

Alice was issued the latest development in spy craft, a miniature camera created near war's end by Kodak, officially called the "Eastman M.B." matchbox camera but known colloquially as "Camera X." It was a metal-encased contraption that fit in the palm of Alice's hand, with a touch button to advance the shutter. It was incredibly simple, designed to be used without looking through a viewfinder or even at the camera at all. Alice had been a cameraphile for years, hauling one to England on her trips there for Wimbledon. By contrast, the spy camera was a snap to use. The spies also gave Alice a photo of her contact, "Franz," who was a goldsmith on the Grand-Rue in Geneva's Old Town, close to her hotel, the ritzy Hôtel Les Armures. Her mission was to photograph any records or ill-gotten booty Hans may have and get the film to Franz.

And she would be leaving in two days.

It was the spring of 1945, and the war in Europe had turned again. By now, German resistance was reduced to children and old men, their war power destroyed to the point that the fighting was obviously going to be over soon. The army wanted to handicap any Nazis planning to flee with their illegally banked Swiss funds to hideouts in South America or Africa or wherever else money talked. It was now or never for Alice to contribute to the war effort, in a far more tangible way than she had already.

•   •   •

She arrived in the glistening city at the foot of Lake Geneva in an army transport plane. The sun was shining, but Alice was shivering, partly from the alpine cool, partly from nerves. "People had been known to disappear in neutral countries," she wrote. She said she talked to reporters and Swiss tennis officials, then was taken to her posh suite at the Hôtel Les Armures, treated as a visiting star athlete should be.

Things were quiet for a couple of days, as Alice played matches and gave her usual talks. Then she was handed a bouquet of roses, which were from Hans. He wanted her to meet him that night!

They had dinner, and the seven years since Le Touquet melted away almost instantly. Their potent attraction remained set to high. Alice congratulated herself for waiting until the following night to sleep with him once again.

It was at Hans's chateau, southeast of Geneva on the "road to Chamonix" (now the A40 but then a far more primitive affair that wound dangerously through the mountains). Alice was both happy and sad, overjoyed at having rediscovered her first love, and so soon after losing her next. But she also was carrying around tremendous guilt for what she had been sent to do to him. Surely, there was no future between them?

Hans asked her to move out of the hotel to the chateau, for it was too public for him at the Hôtel Les Armures. Alice scoffed—*too public for him?* "For three days after, I refused to return his calls," she wrote. She toyed with simply going home. But she thought of Joe once more, and the Nazis who had caused his death and were hoping to get away with plundering millions. So at last, she packed her bags—including her spy camera and gun—and moved into the chateau.

"A day stretched into a week, then three," she writes, as she enjoyed her luxurious life, driving a borrowed Jaguar into town to play at the famous Parc des Eaux-Vives, spending time shopping in Geneva, then back to the chateau, where Hans awaited. One night they attended a swanky party at the Argentine embassy, with multiple Germans in attendance. Alice quizzed Hans about the morality of banking with the Nazis. "I don't worry where the money comes from," he said, while noting his family bank had also stored money from Frenchmen fleeing the revolution in the eighteenth century. She danced with American and Argentine diplomats, and tennis fans of all stripes, while she flushed with jealousy when the ladies danced "a little too closely" with her man. "It was all so complicated," she wrote.

They returned to the chateau, where a drunken Hans boasted that he had the Nazis "by the balls." He was holding a vast fortune of their loot in his basement safe, just as the Americans had predicted. It was protected by explosive charges, but the key "hidden in the radiator" would get him safely through the war, when he just knew the great majority of his account holders would never come to claim their fortunes. Which would then make it all his.

There was another bash the following night, this time at the British embassy. But Alice feigned sickness, wanting some alone time in the chateau. She waved farewell to Hans, whom she convinced to go on without her. It was seven o'clock. Alice would retrieve the key, get down to the safe, collect some evidence, and be back in bed by midnight, when Hans was to return. Then the next day she would simply drop off the film with her contact, go to the airport, and depart.

Easy.

Alice unscrewed the radiator cap, fished out the key, and got dressed, putting on her shoulder holster and placing the .25 inside. She slipped from the room. The house came complete with a full roster of servants, but Alice had learned that only a couple were around at night, the head butler and "another old family retainer with headquarters in the chateau." She eased her way down the main stairs, slowly opened the door, and descended the stone steps to the wine cellar, with "rack after rack of ornately labelled bottles."

Her flashlight picked out a stone wall. Dead end. Retracing her steps, Alice realized there was a small wooden door in the stone wall, with a large lock on it. She used the stolen key, bracing for an explosion, but none came. She pushed the door open, and there was a safe.

The explosives had been placed in a way to go off if anyone forced open the door. After examining the wires, Alice realized that without the key, she would have had no chance. Even better, she saw that the safe itself wasn't wired to blow up. She flipped on the overhead light, but she quickly saw it threw light back into the cellar, where anyone opening the upstairs door would see it. Instead, she fished out a headband with a battery-powered light that was also part of her spy kit. Then she commenced to crack the safe.

It took a while, but at last "the tumblers . . . clicked into place." Alice glanced at her watch. Incredibly, it was close to eleven! The time had slipped by, and now she had to hurry.

Inside the vault were large paintings wrapped in brown packaging, row upon row of gold bars ("each with the unmistakable imprint of the Third Reich, the swastika"), and boxes of jewelry of all manner. One "heavy gold" necklace still had a Star of David attached. "My anger turned to nausea," she wrote.

But Colonel Linden had told Alice the real fortune was in the currency the Nazis were stashing. Sure enough, "I saw the leather-bound ledger lying in plain sight on a shelf." Inside, "German names and columns of figures told the story of Hans's enterprise, line by line, in his bold, precise handwriting."

She took out her Camera X and began to snap away at the pages in the ledger. That particular camera could take thirty-four shots, saved on a two-foot roll of film, but Alice only took about twenty pictures, she recalled, "enough evidence to nail a lot of Nazi thieves."

Keenly aware of the passing minutes, and the inevitable return of Hans, Alice replaced the ledger, closed the safe, and returned up the cellar steps. There was a clamor coming from the other side of the door. Servants were yelling, "Miss Marble!? Miss Marble!?" and rushing about in search of her. Then she heard Hans's voice. "Alice? Where are you?"

Without thought, she bolted from the shadows. "I ran straight into the soft belly of the head butler. . . . Before he could recover, I shoved him away from me and darted for the front door. Heaving it open, I ran outside."

It was actually a godsend that Hans had returned, for his Mercedes was right there in the drive. "The keys would be in it," Alice knew, "so the servants could drive it to the garage." She raced for the car. Its owner appeared in the doorway of the chateau, backlit, his face a mask of hurt and confusion.

"Alice! Wait!"

"I'm sorry," she gasped, her voice choked with emotion. She tossed the camera into the front seat, precious film loaded in the back. The key was in the ignition. She started the Mercedes and roared off, the car's "back end slipping like a fat man on ice." She tore down the road back to Geneva, a narrow affair with sheer rock on one side and the abyss on the other. It was mostly unlit, and the Mercedes's twin arrows of lamplight barely pierced the darkness ahead.

"Goddammit!" she yelled aloud as she tried to keep the heavy car on the road. "I'm a tennis player, not a spy!" She tossed her gun onto the passenger seat as well. "A gun, a camera, and a stolen car," she recounted. "I was definitely a spy—not a good one, but a spy nevertheless. And a liar."

Self-recrimination was soon the least of her problems, for a pair of headlights appeared in the rearview mirror. And they were gaining on her.

In moments they were upon her, and then alongside. "Like a cornered animal facing its executioner, I risked a glance"—it was Captain Jones, US Army! He motioned to Alice to pull over. She was safe!

"Thank God it's you!" she said as she hugged him. "I have the film."

"Let me have it."

"Something in his voice made me grip the camera tighter," she wrote, and she answered that they should bring it to Geneva, as planned.

"Stop wasting time with that bitch," came an angry voice from the car. It was whoever was driving with Jones. "Get the film!"

They struggled for a moment, and the matchbox camera fell. Jones pulled a gun, and when Alice went for hers, she realized with a sickening pit in her gut that it was still on the passenger seat of the Mercedes. "Kill her, hurry you fool!" yelled Jones's partner. He stooped to pick up the camera, and when he did, Alice "ran like hell."

As she sprinted the "sounds behind me became remarkably clear—the squeal of the car's brakes on the road's surface, doors flung open, shouts, and gunfire.

"Then it came—the white-hot pain of a bullet finding its mark."

Alice awoke, as she so often had during her remarkable life, in a hospital room. She'd been shot, though not severely wounded, just a flesh wound. As her eyes cleared, she focused on a familiar face.

Colonel Linden.

"I came to rescue you, but was a bit late," he said grimly.

"Jones" had been a Russian double agent and had been agitating to

Linden that Alice was taking too long, so Linden let him come to Switzerland to suss out the situation. "Something didn't smell right, so I came to Geneva . . . prepared to pull you out, if I had to."

Linden had men watching the chateau, and when it all went down, they followed, discovering Jones to be a traitor as well. He and his partner were dead, shot by the Americans, but before dying Jones had exposed Alice's film. It was useless.

"I wish I could give you a Purple Heart like any soldier wounded in battle," Linden told Alice, "but it doesn't work that way in our business. You won't ever be able to talk about it."

But it wasn't over. For Alice had looked at all the pages she photographed. And when she closed her eyes, all the names and figures appeared. Her photographic memory was as good as the film. A stenographer was quickly sent for, and Alice recited as much of the information as she could remember. Linden said that the names on the list—the ones who survived the war, anyway—would be tried as war criminals.

Alice asked about Hans. Linden confessed he probably would never see justice. "He's a clever man," he said. Alice, to his surprise, looked relieved. He had offered her a life of love and leisure, and she had betrayed him, at least in her mind. Despite the good that came from it, she felt miserable.

Otherwise, she was well taken care of. She was secure on an army base (she didn't say where). The Swiss tennis officials were told she needed to leave unexpectedly due to an emergency back home, and Tennant was sent a wire explaining that Alice would be back as soon as "an inflamed cyst was removed from my back."

She wrote that she slipped back into New York on an army transport on May 8, 1945, "my arrival overshadowed by another celebration: The war in Europe was over." It was V-E Day. The Nazis had unconditionally surrendered.

And come November 1945, when roughly two hundred Nazis stood trial in Nuremberg for war crimes, Alice recognized some of the names of the accused from Hans's ledger.

"I had, in a small way, avenged Joe's death."

. . .

An amazing account. And one that, as I learned more about Alice and about her life during that time, seemed both perfectly plausible and utterly impossible at the same time. She was immensely patriotic and would not shy away from a challenge. As the writer Seth Wickersham put it, "Any great athlete will tell you the urge to redefine your limits doesn't wane with age. It gets worse and so conspires against future happiness." An espionage mission was certainly an opportunity to test herself once more. With or without a husband to avenge, the motivation to accept the assignment was strong.

My eighteen months of research and reporting, document requests, interviews, and trips crossing the country felt like they had brought me simultaneously closer to understanding Alice, her inner conflicts, and her times, and further away from crucial elements of truth about what I previously thought were the key details of her life. I understood Alice's ambitions, her fears, who she knew, and why she acted as she did better than ever. And yet for every step closer I took, other mysteries of her life remained just out of reach.

Alice's movements from that period can be fairly well reconstructed from contemporary press reports. On New Year's Day 1945, barely a week after she said she was dealt the hammer blow of learning of her husband's death, Alice was heard on the radio. It was a spectacular called *What's Next?*, with Alice speculating on the year ahead in sports with famed football coach Amos Alonzo Stagg and Sergeant Joe Louis of the US Army.

In late January she appeared at a large sporting carnival in what was becoming her second home, Wilmington, alongside another army sergeant, Joe DiMaggio, staying with Will du Pont for at least a few days. In early February an appearance at the YMCA of Passaic, New Jersey, was canceled as Alice was hospitalized with bronchial pneumonia, her troubled lungs continuing to plague her, as they would the rest of her life. But she was out in time to keep a February 9 appointment in Knoxville, Tennessee, a February 13 engagement in Montgomery, Alabama, a March 7 speech in Ridgewood, New Jersey, and a mid-March program with her former partner in physical fitness preparation, Jack Kelly, that screened numerous athletes looking for heart defects.

In mid-April she traveled to the Chicago area to play a few exhibitions; then on April 20 she jaunted over to Minneapolis, "sans tennis rackets and luggage," according to the *Star-Journal*. "She finds it easier to travel light these days." She gave several interviews, did her standard exhibition matches and clinics, and even gave the convocation speech for graduates of the University of Minnesota at Northrop Auditorium. The speech, carried live on local radio, covered her usual combination of the importance of never giving in and keeping up one's physical fitness. "You can have beautiful clothes, a million dollars, or be in love, but if your health isn't good it won't do you any good," she said, while prescribing a daily diet of "leafy green or yellow vegetables, orange, grapefruit or tomatoes, milk, eggs, one pint of milk at two of the meals, rich cereal or bread and at every meal butter or margarine."

She was back in Chicago on April 22–23, appearing on WGN Radio's *Distinguished Guest Hour* to deliver her "Will to Win" speech, then on *Melody Lane*, where she sang her favorites—"Smoke Gets in Your Eyes," "People Will Say We're in Love," "Beautiful Lady," and "Blue Skies." Airing at the same time a recorded sports show, *Jack Horner's Corner*, featuring Alice on KSTP in Minneapolis.

The next time she appears in a press notice is on May 18, playing an exhibition match in Baltimore against Buddy Geltz, the club pro at the Columbia Country Club. Buddy raced out to a 4–0 lead, causing Alice to proclaim loudly, "I'm mad, real mad," but getting angry didn't help—she lost 6–2. "The fact the gallery was with her didn't get her a single extra point," reported *The Baltimore Sun*.

According to *Courting Danger*, Alice was in Switzerland for over a month, culminating on May 7—clearly that's not possible, since she was incontrovertibly in Minnesota and Chicago in late April. But what if, in the same way she elided the names of the key figures in her story, she did the same with the dates? Move the action up to March, and there is a possible window for her to have spent a fortnight or more on a mission overseas. It could also be the case that V-E Day is a red herring, or a figment of an experience that shifted in Alice's memory, or just something she threw in for some color, giving the audience what (she thought) they wanted.

And in early June, Alice was indeed sidelined with a "back injury." Was this the cyst she refers to in the "wire to Tennant"? Was it a continuation of her cover story? Perhaps it gave her the idea for the cover story. Or, causing as it did the cancellation of a couple of New York–area appearances, was it a genuine injury, a happenstance that is merely coincidental to the fact she said she was shot in the same part of her body?

Alice's mission was supposedly grounded in her ability to operate in plain sight, her tennis celebrity giving her the perfect cover to travel and move around Geneva. Yet despite all the mentions in her memoir of "reporters" and details of exhibitions she played, a culling of the online archives of Swiss papers (numbering well over a hundred, in English, Italian, French, and Swiss German) reveals no mentions of Alice in Switzerland in all of 1945 (her Wimbledon results were well covered, along with the odd feature from years previous, so it's not a question of local writers not knowing who she was). No American papers reported on her departure or return, either, though this conceivably fits in with the covert element of the espionage, if not the "hiding in plain sight" element. Is that the be-all and end-all? Of course not. But if the reason for her recruitment was, in part, her celebrity, then where are the flashing bulbs and shouted questions that were meant to obscure her clandestine activity?

• • •

Naturally I made repeated attempts to interview Alice's *Courting Danger* ghostwriter, Dale Leatherman, about all of this. Dale had learned from Alice something of keeping her cards close to her chest; she was not forthcoming about what aspects of her ghostwriting were taken from Alice's writings and what, if anything, was her own invention. She did mention that "Alice signed off on all of it," and that while working on the memoir she (as I had) attempted to back up the story with Freedom of Information Act requests that "came back either with nothing or so heavily redacted they were useless," an experience I shared after seven separate requests. She also quoted to me a conversation she had with a friend of hers who was in the military intelligence trade, who noted that during the war almost all records were either destroyed or never created in the first place, due to secrecy concerns. As Lee Sandlin put it in his brilliant essay "Losing the War," "We forget now just how pervasive the atmosphere of classified activity was, but . . . the best information—whole Mississippis of debriefings and intelligence assessments and field reports and rumors—went up the line and vanished. . . . Everybody was doing something hush-hush; nobody blinked at the most imponderable mysteries."

It's no shock that my trips to the relevant historical archives came up empty, with no records of any Alice-related activity. The National Archives and Records Administration in College Park, Maryland, has a declassified list of personnel employed by the Office of Strategic Services, the OSS, which was the forerunner of the Central Intelligence Agency and was the espionage apparatus for most intelligence work during WWII. She is not on that list. Alice never claimed to have worked for the OSS (whose roster included people like Julia Child, future TV and baseball executive Mike Burke, and major league ballplayer Moe Berg, among others), of course, and she was never inducted into any military service, so her lack of records at the National Personnel Records Center in St. Louis is easily explainable as well.

Not so easily explainable is the lack of any hard evidence as to the real identity of "Hans Steinmetz," her quarry in 1945 and erstwhile lover in 1938. There have been several speculative stabs at who he might have been over the years, but nothing that can be reliably proven. Alice had known at least one "Hans" in her life, but it was the famed American radio broadcaster and her close friend, Hans V. Kaltenborn, better known as H. V. Kaltenborn. Is it possible that she paid him a sort of tribute by attributing his name to a key player in her story?

I discussed this story with experts on Swiss banking history, including Professor Sébastien Guex at the University of Lausanne, and the man he called the foremost historian on Swiss bankers during WWII, Dr. Marc Perrenoud. None could confirm any of the details of the story provided by Alice—a significant historical figure such as she described who was heir to a banking fortune and a playboy, the chateau outside Geneva, working with the Nazis.

Then I decided to take another pass at the Prickly Pears interview Alice gave in 1986. Therein I was given an *Anhaltspunkt,* as the Swiss (some of them, anyway—the nation has four official languages) call a clue, a potential path toward enlightenment. At one point, the interviewer, Courtney Gebhart, asked about a subject that wasn't public information at that time but something Alice must have mentioned to her before the cameras began rolling—her spy mission in WWII. Alice slickly eludes the question but says that the details will be revealed in an upcoming TV movie of her life. She holds up a sheaf of pages and offhandedly says that "this script was written by my good friend, the writer Rita Mae Brown."

The German language has another word that summed up the situation—*Gretchenfrage,* which is a question that is crucial to understanding but is evaded by the subject of the query. Gebhart had innocently posed a *Gretchenfrage* to Alice, who, like Faust (from whence the term originates), skirted the main thrust. But in doing so she opened up a line of inquiry that I hadn't considered.

My presumption to this point had been that Alice told her story to Dale Leatherman, the ghostwriter of *Courting Danger,* and Dale alone, and that any potential filmed version of the story was based on the memoir. I realized with a belated start that the key figure in deciphering this mystery was actually Rita Mae Brown, whose work with Alice clearly predated the book.

And unlike every other person I had written about in this book so far, she was alive.

PART FOUR

Chapter Thirty-Three

....

California Split

There is a wondrous time machine hidden in a basement of an otherwise unremarkable building of the south side of Kansas City. Deep in the bowels of the library on the campus of the University of Missouri–Kansas City is the Marr Sound Archives. Here there is a collection of recordings dating back to the earliest days of capturing sound. Every format is here, from hundreds of thousands of LPs to transcription discs to old-fashioned cylinders. Around the space, on the floor and mounted high on shelves, are the listening devices—record players, Victrolas, crystal radio sets. It's like walking into an original record shop that never got rid of old inventory. A century's worth of audio possibilities, all in working condition, are available to the visitor.

Most importantly, the collection includes recordings of every genre of music, news reports, interviews, and radio programs. It also has advertisements. I'm here for those: specifically, public service announcements—even more specifically, a set of interstitials cut in 1945 pleading with the American public, who had already sacrificed so much to the war effort, to dig deep once more.

The Victory Loan war bonds had raised millions over the years of

315

WWII. By August 1945, the fighting was over, thanks to the dropping of two immense new bombs, the final blows in a campaign of systematic destruction that left the Axis powers almost completely obliterated.

After Fat Man and Little Boy's atomic fury were unleashed on Japan, obviating the need for a massive invasion that would have cost countless lives, a nation took stock of the horrifying cost the war had required. In late summer Alice added her voice to another Victory Loan drive, in this case to raise money to care for wounded veterans and arrange their transport back from overseas. Star athletes from across the sporting spectrum asked an America that had scrimped and sacrificed for years to open its collective wallet once more and "buy every Victory Loan bond you can afford," in the words of boxing announcer Don Dunphy. Red Barber, the Hall of Fame announcer for the Brooklyn Dodgers, spoke in his deep southern drawl ("We get back 4 dollars for 3 dollars, why that's like finding money, it sho' is, so get yourself some of those bonds y'hear? Yessuh"), as did Dixie Walker, "The People's Cherce" and Dodgers outfielder. The heavyweight champion of the world, Sergeant Joe Louis, noted, "I'm no speaker—I'm a boxer. But I do know that Victory bonds are the safe investment they is. And I do know that what Joe Louis is going to put in every extra dollar he can get."

Another rare recording of the Victory Loan radio ads survives in the Marr Sound Archives, where I have come to slip on a pair of headphones and, thus, venture back in time. Over the hiss of the record and the thump-thump of its turning, there is Alice, using her "professional delivery." She has a far more pleasant voice and mellifluent tone than any of the other athletes, and with her elongated *o*'s and oddly formal cadence, with a hint of British inflection, and a throaty but not harsh intonation, she sounded every bit as professional as the broadcasters taking part in the series.

A generic announcer introduced the segment with, "The Treasury Department, in the interests of the Victory Loan, presents Miss Alice Marble, world's leading woman tennis player—Miss Marble?"

"One thing tennis teaches you is good sportsmanship," Alice says on the recording. "Win or lose, you learn to accept it gracefully, and with a smile. But despite all we've learned about good sportsmanship on the courts, I think we could still take lessons from the fighting men and women who've just come through this war. Good sports—you just bet they are! Lots of those who have come back are wounded or disabled. But are they complaining? No, they're not. The courage that smiles through their eyes goes far beyond good sportsmanship. 'You can't win every time,' they say, and then they tell you what they're going to do when they get out of the veterans' hospital. Well, I think it's up to us to help them get back to a normal, healthy, happy life, and buying Victory bonds is the way to do it. Let's support this great Victory Loan with everything we have and show them that we're good sports, too."

One thing I definitely learned about her in the research was that Alice was too good a writer for her to have penned that material herself.

· · ·

The months after the war ended were a wrenching shock for the country, as the overwhelming joy of victory gave way to a poignant sadness over the cost of ensuring tyranny did not triumph. The soldiers and sailors and marines who had triumphed and come home safely celebrated their luck but often struggled to adapt to peacetime, after the extraordinary experience of fighting a war. The ones whose lives were forever affected by their wounds, like the ones Alice was trying to help with the Victory Loan drive, would never be able to fully put the horror of war behind them. There would be difficulties in the sudden change from a total war footing to complete peace, with the nation beset by shortages of goods, services, and housing, while a series of labor strikes made everyday living difficult.

If Alice was affected by any of it, however, she never let on. She went on with her peripatetic life seemingly unaffected by a life-altering, gunshot-suffering espionage mission in the dying days of WWII. Alice spent the summer of 1945 touring with Bill Tilden and Don Budge, trying to wring out any last iota of nostalgia from their names. Her game was still strong—when she played an exhibition match at Forest Hills in late June, her "serves were as hard as the men's and she served several aces." If she had been eligible to play in the upcoming nationals on those West Side Tennis Club courts, which her pro tour in 1941 made impossible, Alice would have been an overwhelming favorite.

As such, she was a natural choice to instruct others on how to achieve greatness. In 1945 General Mills partnered with Wheaties to produce the "Library of Sports," thirty-two-page manuals of instruction and pep talks from an even wider array of athletic greats than were lobbying on the bond drive. The "Want to Be a Champion?" series included Alice on tennis, though her book was unusual for how it leaned toward the motivational, rather than the how-to technical side of the game. Wheaties offered a "try two for free, we're sure you'll want the rest" deal, advertising that Alice's book was "jam-packed with action pictures that show how to develop champion form." It was just a warm-up for Alice's later foray into books.

Alice is quick to credit Eleanor Tennant in *Want to Be a Tennis Champion?* But around the time the public was reading about Teach's impact on Alice on the court, their relationship was ending off of it.

.   .   .

Eleanor had had a far different, and far more difficult, war than Alice. Alice's celebrity and public impact were, if anything, greater during the war than during her playing days. Her coach, by contrast, mostly faded into the background. The years spent in New York had distanced Eleanor from her faithful Hollywood clientele. She tagged along on some of Alice's tours, conducted her usual clinics, and did what she could to remain relevant, but the simple fact was her identity had become wrapped up in Alice's fortunes on and off the court. "Teach had become as dependent on me as I was on her," Alice wrote of this period, but in reality the power dynamic in their always volatile relationship had swung definitively toward Alice. She began to realize that she wasn't really dependent on Tennant at all.

Will du Pont played a role in this. Alice's faithful pal was always there to play money manager, or gift her a new black Buick for her thirty-second birthday, or to ask for her hand in marriage, which she says he did yet again in the summer of 1946, only to be rejected with extreme prejudice once more. While Du Pont wasn't unfriendly toward

Eleanor (they exchanged gifts and made friendly wagers often during this period, though the nylon stockings had to stop due to the war. "I am afraid that the end of the road is in sight along this line for the duration," he wrote to Tennant in 1943), there was a certain jealousy as the two vied for Alice's attentions and loyalty. For Eleanor had belatedly come to accept her love for her student, according to Alice, as WWII ended.

"The woman to whom affection meant a pat on the head rather than a kiss," she wrote, "finally realized that she loved me, and her desire to hold onto me ultimately destroyed our relationship."

Eleanor's decreasing station in not only Alice's eyes but in her professional career had led her to increase her already sizable drinking habit. As Alice recalled, Tennant would "humiliate me in front of my friends," only to break down in apologetic tears later. She became "increasingly jealous, wildly accusing me of affairs with anyone who came close, man or woman." Most disturbingly, Eleanor "threatened to kill me or to kill herself."

According to *Courting Danger*, and thus perhaps to be taken with a hint of salt, Alice wrote that she "dreaded to return to their hotel suite" as she knew she would find Tennant "half out the eleventh-story window when I opened the door." It became a crushing codependency. Alice would plead for Eleanor not to jump and in return give in to various demands that both women knew weren't ever to be met.

"Why do you need other people?" Eleanor would ask.

"I'm a person, not a trophy for you to show off!" Alice replied.

The wounds were too deep, the situation too unmanageable, for it to continue. Eleanor, to her credit, gave up the scorned-lover bit and moved on and out, returning to California in Alice's new Buick. According to Alice, Eleanor cleaned out a joint bank account they shared, one set up by Will du Pont, then returned to their apartment, where Tennant "shoved me so hard I fell back on the couch." The housemaid came in and sent Alice out in order to cool the situation down. In Central Park she sat on a bench, eating a sandwich, when Tennant's former student, Marlene Dietrich, wandered past, pushing her grandchild in a pram (Dietrich had relocated to the Upper East Side upon war's end).

Alice's memoir is the only source that describes this event. The usually dispassionate, hard-edged Eleanor Tennant comes off as uncharacteristically emotional in the telling. But the fact is Eleanor did end their cohabitation rather suddenly at this time, after living together ever since Alice's escape from Pottenger's Sanatorium nearly a dozen years earlier, and move three thousand miles away, a fact confirmed by Eleanor's reappearance in California phone and tax records. If it was merely a professional split, all business, it was sudden and pointed.

In Alice's story she says that when she at last returned to their place, she found the staff had rearranged the furniture, accentuating the fact that Eleanor was gone and Alice was, for the first time since she was a fledgling tennis player at Golden Gate Park, on her own.

Chapter Thirty-Four

....

Author! Author!

One of Alice's first orders of business was to move out herself. She took a room in the Rockefeller Apartments, at 24 West Fifty-Fifth Street. It wasn't an easy place to move to—there was a lengthy waiting list that Alice jumped by dint of her celebrity. It was a breezy, well-lit building with a unique design known as the "international style." Living there held a certain cachet for people like Alice who were well-known and held to a certain lifestyle standard but weren't actually rich folks living on Park Avenue or Sutton Place.

That may have been the reason for some momentous good fortune just before Christmas 1946. She took a cab to go hit at the River Club and left her silver cigarette case, the gift of Freddy Warburg and valued at 500 dollars, in the taxi. Fortunately, the driver, one Sam Goldwyn of Brooklyn, "turned the case in to the police just as Miss Marble reported the loss," according to the *Times*. An ecstatic Alice said there would be a "suitable reward" for the honest cabbie, though she didn't take the incident as an omen to quit smoking.

Her career as a designer and style maven continued apace. The "tall attractive young woman in wintry guise" bounced around department stores in a "beaver coat, smart suit of black wool and Shepards tweed, and heelless pumps. . . . A far cry from the abbreviated white garb she flashes about the world's tennis courts." She was checking on displays of her fashions, including "her latest creation . . . a two-piece white pique. The shorts have stitched pleats and a front zipper, hidden under a band, which gives a nice, flat effect. The blouse is a simple little thing, with cap sleeves, extending just over the shoulders, which allow plenty of room for playing." When not designing, she was still endorsing products, her signature rackets and shoes and even Dr. Lyon's Tooth Powder ("In tennis . . . or a dentifrice . . . it takes a rare combination to reach the top. And among tooth powders, Dr. Lyons [sic] is the first choice, year after year . . .").

She also became, at last, in 1947, a movie star. Alice's ties to the golden-age Hollywood stars had frayed severely since she had relocated east and Tennant had stopped hanging out with the A-listers, but there she was, on the marquee, as star of a John Nesbitt documentary short called *Tennis in Rhythm*.

Nesbitt was a prolific pioneer in reality filmmaking, with a series called *The Passing Parade*. Subjects included Alfred Nobel, the "unseen guardians" of the Postal Inspector Service, the inventor of the wooden friction match, and the Bowery neighborhood of New York. His sixtieth film was about Alice, though Warren Murray handled the directorial duties. Not so much about Alice as her tennis strokes, actually—the film was a moody and expressive examination of Alice in action set to music, combining some old film of her in her prime from newsreels with newly shot material of Alice hitting at Forest Hills.

Alice would be more widely seen in a cameo several years later in the Katharine Hepburn–Spencer Tracy vehicle *Pat and Mike*. Hepburn plays a sensational athlete who golfs with Babe Zaharias and "trades forehand drives and backhand volleys with Alice Marble." "She had a bad case of tennis elbow," Alice recalled of La Hepburn, "and could hardly hold a cup of coffee between scenes. I saw the tears in her eyes every time she hit the ball, and admired her courage." For her part Alice and the other real players were considered "credible, colorful and exciting" by the *Times*, not bad for a gal a decade removed from her competitive days on the court.

· · ·

One day late in 1946 Alice was riding on a train to Pittsburgh when she fell into conversation with a bishop who knew all about her tennis greatness. As related to *The Desert Sun* years later, they talked "til four in the morning," and the clergyman assured Alice that she "would write a book." Alice had been told likewise by Arthur Brisbane, her old fan from the Hearst syndicate, who assured her "it would be an inspiration to every clean, right-thinking boy and girl throughout the country."

At Scribner's the legendary editor Maxwell Perkins took a liking to the idea. Perkins had discovered authors including Ernest Hemingway, F. Scott Fitzgerald, and Thomas Wolfe over three-plus decades at the famed publishing house, and putting his deft touch on Alice's story looked like a great victory. Perkins had worked on the autobiography of Helen Wills Moody, called *15-30*, and was a huge tennis fan, so when one of his colleagues, W. L. Savage, mentioned the idea, Perkins was all for it.

Unlike "Want to Be a Tennis Champion?" this was no how-to primer. Alice did include some tennis-playing tips but kept that to a minimum, at the advice of Perkins. Instead, she dove deep into her background, including a picaresque description of her early life on the Sierra Nevada farm and growing up in San Francisco. The main hook was her comeback story, of course, which led to Perkins deciding to call the book *The Road to Wimbledon* (which won out over other titles including "The Will to Win," "That Sissy Game," and "Little Queen of Swat"), though oddly, there isn't anything about Alice's victory at the '39 Wimbledon tournament in the book—indeed, it ends with Alice's triumph at the 1936 US Nationals, her original comeback. Considering the title, the book has surprisingly little tennis in it.

She mainly delved into topics including lobbying for major tournaments to become "open" to all, not just amateurs, and devastating indictments of the USLTA and how it handled young players in particular. The book opens by saying her story "all began with a guy named Joe . . ."

and then begins, well, at the beginning of her life, saving her tale of Captain Joseph Crowley for the last couple of pages. Perkins cut out several late chapters, telling Alice in a letter, "These last chapters, as is common in an autobiographical book, tend to become desultory and topical, and make an anti-climax after the direct narrative." As a result, the ending feels needlessly rushed.

It also reads in different voices, as though Alice's ghostwriter, Margaret Treadwell, and Perkins rewrote major portions while at cross-purposes, which left Alice upset enough that she seldom talked about the book, regardless of its popularity. Years later in an interview in *The Desert Sun*, Alice would dismiss *The Road to Wimbledon* as "poorly written and poorly edited," saying Perkins was "doddering and sick at the time" (Perkins died a year after the book was published). Alice handled the initial draft herself, at which point it was turned over to Treadwell for smoothing out.

The book was handsomely designed, with a picture of a wooden road sign pointing toward Wimbledon on the cover, and a studio portrait of a classy, smiling Alice on the back flap. *The Road to Wimbledon* was released in the summer of 1946, "certainly not without design" as one alert cynic wrote. The hardcover cost $2.75 at "all major booksellers." Advance signed copies were sent to Alice's siblings and friends—Mary K. Browne, Gilbert Khan, Harwood White, Bill Tilden, Arthur Loew, and, care of the Beverly Hills Tennis Club, the estranged Eleanor Tennant. What "Teach" thought of the book was not captured for posterity. Almost everything written about her in the memoir is complimentary, however.

Alice's connections back in Los Angeles came in handy when it came time to sell books. Russell Birdwell, Hollywood's most flamboyant press agent, took on the role of drumming up publicity, his 1,500-dollar salary paid for by Will du Pont, who sent the money to "pay the man to push your book. It is worth the gamble and I hope it will turn out most successfully." One of Birdwell's gambits was to buy space in newspapers across the country and run a fake telegram he supposedly sent to William Hearst, who was back at San Simeon after his profligate lifestyle and questionable business practices at last caught up with him during the Depression.

It was a crafty stroke, making it seem as though the reader were being let in on a secret, the making of the publicity sausage, while at the same time actually getting the word out to millions of readers about Alice and her book.

Titled "The Inspiring Story of Alice Marble," it read in part,

Dear Chief:

Infrequently, as you know, I come knocking at your door with an idea which I feel may be good for the largest number of people who seek and find inspirations in the reading of your newspapers. . . . In the midst of international chaos, in the midst of national juvenile delinquency, Alice Marble and her great true story shines out as an inspiration to all other young Americans. I wire you in the hope that you will ask your editors and editorial writers to help point up and point out this truly inspirational story of a typical American girl so that mothers and fathers as well as young people facing the problems of life in this uncertain period can be reminded that the Horatio Alger story can happen over and over again but only in the American way of life.

Yours, Russell

Two of Alice's more fervent admirers in the press, Brisbane and Harry Grayson, also put their muscle behind the selling of the book. Grayson wrote a long recap of Alice's story for his column "The Scoreboard." "A very real and admirable personality shines through its pages," he wrote, though perhaps his most creative turn of phrase was to describe the young tomboy Alice as a "roisterous hoyden."

Yet for all the push, *The Road to Wimbledon* didn't sell especially well. Exact sales figures aren't available, but Perkins wrote Alice in January 1947 that "I fear you will be rather shocked at learning that the sales are not large." In context, that probably isn't surprising—for all her popularity and success Alice already belonged to a bygone, prewar era, and her comeback story was well-known. There was enough of a market for the book that an English publisher, W. H. Allen, paid Alice $1,006.25 for "British Empire rights."

Regardless of its popularity with the book-buying public, it is a cracking read, especially the early sections about Alice's California upbringing. *The Road to Wimbledon* was very well received critically, and by more than just Alice's coterie. Alpha Phi Gamma, the journalistic society, named it the story of the year. In the *San Francisco Examiner* Jose Rodriguez notes "many surprises" in the book, the main one being that this was no typical sports star recounting the highs and lows of a career. "One realizes that in a calm, reticent and modest way Alice Marble has gone beyond her subject matter in a statement of principles which apply specifically to tennis but actually extend to all human activity." It was her "Will to Win" speech put on paper for anyone to read. Rodriguez was further impressed that "with admirable restraint, she then refuses to sermonize." A reviewer in *The Hartford Courant* wrote that her lack of writing about practical ways to play tennis was "a break for the reader." International plaudits came as well; in the London *Times*, D. C. Browning wrote that "on the worries that beset the first-class player it is a mine of information. . . . It is a very human record of her career."

One captivated female reviewer named Elizabeth North Hoyt noted that she was "fortunate to see Alice play at Forest Hills one summer and I will never forget what a human dynamo she was, flashing over the courts in immaculate tailored shorts and shirt, a beautiful body with perfectly controlled coordination. . . . [She] knows how to give the customers their money's worth, whether it be on the courts or in a book."

It was a line that would become more significant when her second memoir was published nearly fifty years on.

. . .

The same could certainly be said of the woman with whom I needed, more and more desperately, to get in touch. Since the publication of her seminal novel, *Rubyfruit Jungle*, in 1973, Rita Mae Brown has been giving readers what they want in scores of books, screenplays, articles, and every other method of storytelling.

Few women exemplified the second wave of feminism and activism, not to mention courage, like Rita Mae Brown. She was born in Pennsylvania to a teenage mother who dumped her at an orphanage as a newborn. The mother's cousin rescued her and, with her husband, raised Rita Mae as her own child. Overcoming her Dickensian beginnings, Brown won a tennis scholarship to the University of Florida, where she took part in several civil rights demonstrations. As a result, she was expelled from the segregated school. She hitchhiked to New York and spent several destitute years putting herself through NYU. In the big city, Brown became affiliated with several women's and gay rights groups, though they often let her down. She took a job with the fledgling National Organization for Women but resigned after Betty Friedan distanced the group from lesbians, whom she called the "lavender menace." She cascaded between other, more radical feminist and lesbian groups but never found her place.

So Brown turned instead to writing. *Rubyfruit Jungle* is a thinly disguised account of her teenage flowering as a lesbian and her experiences with lovers, family, and institutions, including the University of Florida (in the book she is effectively expelled for her lesbianism, not for seeking racial justice). *Rubyfruit Jungle* (a slang term for female genitalia) was an immediate hit, thanks to Brown's witty writing and blunt retelling of her sexual encounters, including with men. It was easily the most popular and important lesbian-themed work since *Nightwood* and launched Brown's career, which continues to this day.

•   •   •

Since discovering the importance of Brown to Alice's story, I tried to reach her, but this proved frustratingly, almost comically difficult to accomplish. Brown, now seventy-five, lives on a farm in the foothills of the Blue Ridge Mountains, a place not far from civilization but at the same time remote enough to keep her as cut off from everyday contact as she wishes. It is a working horse ranch, so she remains very busy and outdoors, away from the house phone, upon whose answering machine I left a steady diet of pleas to call me for an interview. Later I would discover a telegram sent to Rita Mae all the way back in 1986 by television executives trying without success to reach her. "Anxious to contact you. . . . Your phone is out of service." I shared their exasperation.

With no recourse to bygone modes of communication, and modern ones failing me (Rita Mae didn't appear to have an e-mail address), I decided upon a new course of action, one I felt Alice herself might have taken.

Direct confrontation.

Which is how I found myself on a dusty horse path on a glorious autumn afternoon, full of false bravado, marching toward Rita Mae's front door and seeking answers.

. . .

The success of *The Road to Wimbledon*, in its critical reception probably more so than its modest receipts, led to many more opportunities for Alice at the keys of an Underwood. She was given regular columns in *American Lawn Tennis* magazine and *The Racquet*, a periodical that covered squash and badminton as well as tennis. She was asked to cover Wimbledon by the London *Daily Mail* in 1946, the first tournament back at the spiritual home of tennis since Alice won in 1939, having been put on hold due to war for seven long years. There wasn't a hint of sentimentality or self-serving attitude in her reportage, just straightforward accounting of the action, which saw an unprecedented all-American final-four women's bracket (Pauline Betz emerged the winner), an achievement Alice chalked up to the Yanks being "physically fit as racehorses, thanks to practicing steadily during the war."

The following year the United Press asked Alice to cover Game 1 of the 1947 World Series between Brooklyn and the New York Yankees. She remained, as ever, an ardent baseball fan, the Yankees her team "for 25 years now." After all, she wrote, her beloved San Francisco Seals had been an unofficial Yankees pipeline for years, supplying the pinstripes with the likes of Tony Lazzeri, Lefty Gomez, Frank Crosetti, and, of course, the Yankee Clipper himself.

Joe DiMaggio was the focus of Alice's Series piece. Watching from her box seat on the third-base line (not the press box—no women allowed there in those days), she looked out at the great man in center field and mused, "Now there's a job . . . $55,000 a year plus a World Series bonus and all he does today is catch two easy flies and hit one single. Now that's living—glamor, adulation, financial success, and he didn't have to run as many steps as I do playing just one game of tennis. I am envious."

She went on to point out the irony of their backgrounds. "I trod the same earth years before Joe DiMaggio set foot in sacred center field at Recreation Park in San Francisco. He, at the time, was playing a game called tennis while I was spitting in my glove, ready for the next fly."

Alice cheered as the Yanks scored five in the fifth inning to take the opener, 5–3 (they would go on to win in seven memorable games in one of the greatest Fall Classics ever played). As the Bronx Bombers were in the midst of the decisive rally, Alice noted she had the "regular womanly reactions," a "sort of tearful feeling" for the beaten Dodgers pitcher, a twenty-one-year-old named Ralph Branca (she would have occasion to feel far worse for Ralph four years hence).

Baseball, and Alice's love for the game, would be a recurring theme in her writings. Her longest and most lyrical piece was written for *The New York Times Magazine* in 1955. "If there has to be a reason," she wrote, "baseball is still my favorite sport because it was my first, unforgettable love." She passed on the legend of dropping baseball for tennis at the behest of big brother Dan—"it was tennis or else, the latter being my older brother's five big knuckles"—but mostly wrote in colorful detail about the pastime and its players, in vivid language that was more reminiscent of great baseball writers like Roger Angell than purple prose–meisters of the era:

> Having seen it once, I will always have a picture of Williams' big hands bruising a bat handle and the ripple of his swing. Of Musial in that unlikely crouch. Of Snider going effortlessly up the wall for an impossible catch. Of Yogi Berra's slue-footed trudge out to the mound.

The ones who are big in terms of greatness have something in common: they don't fall away from the close ball unless it's a low-bridge. They jerk their heads back an inch or suck in their ribs, but they're still in there. They don't step out on the pitcher who takes too much time; they just wait, all the more menacing in their nerveless patience.

I love the language of baseball and the voices of the holler guys in the infield. The bench jockeys riding a rabbit-eared batter. The mere thought of [Roy] Campanella shrilling "hum that pea!" to dolorous Don Newcombe.

At a football game knowing gentlemen invariably advise me to concentrate my attention on the line, which is all very well and good except that while I'm watching the heaving, straining Goliaths a back has broken away for the most thrilling run of the season. . . . No such nonsense about baseball. With the sanction of one and all, my eye is on the ball and I see it all: the fast ball and the curve, the strike and the one that got tagged, the brilliant fielding play and the boot, . . . the close decision, and I am as intimately involved as every man participating in the play.

Alice even was thrilled with the negative aspects of fandom. "The man with the loudest voice and the fewest inhibitions in the stadium will be a close neighbor of mine throughout the game. So will the man with the most noxious cigar. And the one whose gestures with the beer cup become more sweeping and perilous with time. It matters not a whit whether I try to keep my box number a secret; they always find me."

Alice was lucky enough to be at Yankee Stadium on September 28, 1951 (on her thirty-eighth birthday), when Yanks pitcher Allie Reynolds tossed a no-hitter against the Boston Red Sox. "The Chief had so much stuff that day that everyone in the Stadium knew he had a no-hitter going by the fifth inning," she wrote of that afternoon in the Bronx. "It rode on every pitch, [during] which we held our breaths; it tingled in our nerve ends every time there was the clean, hard crack of bat against ball."

With Reynolds one out from his no-no, the immortal Ted Williams stepped in to face him. He hit a pop-up that, to a "roar of anguish torn from all our throats," catcher Yogi Berra dropped. Fortunately for all present, Ted hit an exact replica on the next pitch, and this time Yogi "thundered up to clutch this one in a grip that must have left imprints on the ball."

For all her excellence with the racket and the microphone and the sewing needle, it can be argued she had equal facility with the pen. She wrote and delivered speeches constantly in the years after the war and inked a regular column for United Press that one feature writer noted was "not about tennis, nor how to keep fit, nor what to wear on the court. It will be about anything that happens to pop into her head."

But by far her most impactful writing took the form of a letter to the editor.

Chapter Thirty-Five

....

DO THE RIGHT THING

Alice flaunted her nose at segregated tennis mores in 1944 when she played doubles with Robert Ryland against Mary Hardwick and Dr. Reginald Weir at Harlem's Cosmopolitan Club. Yet she didn't suffer as much blowback as one might expect. "There was no opposition" to it, in Ryland's words. "As long as you were playing in that neighborhood, you were OK. We couldn't have done that in the south, though."

In the audience that day was a gangly teenager and local tennis star named Althea Gibson, who watched Alice play with wide-eyed enthusiasm. "One of the days I remember best at the Cosmopolitan Club was the day Alice Marble played an exhibition match there," she said years later. "I can still remember saying to myself, boy, would I like to be able to play tennis like that! She was the only woman tennis player I'd ever seen that I felt exactly that way about." Alice knew who she was; Ryland recalls talking about her prospects with Alice while having postmatch drinks at the Cosmopolitan Club that day in 1944. "I told her Althea was strong, and had a good head for the game. She just lacked the experience, that's all."

Althea was born into the heart of the Jim Crow South, on a share-croppers' farm in the tiny burg of Silver, South Carolina, in 1927. Had she been raised in the Deep South, Gibson's career may never have launched, but fortunately when she was three, her family moved to New York as part of the Great Migration north, settling at 143rd Street in Harlem between Lenox and Seventh Avenues, where her father found a job fixing cars. Her childhood was the Big Apple version of Alice's tomboy youth—Althea often skipped school to play softball and bas-ketball (on a celebrated team called the "Mysterious Five") in Central Park with the boys. "When other girls were putting on lipstick, she was playing stickball," said her sister Millie.

As with Alice at that age, she was blissfully unaware of her lack of wealth. "I remember you could get fish and chips for 15¢ and soda at 5¢ a quart," she told *Time*. "And there were sweet potatoes—we called 'em 'mickeys'—that we cooked at a fire over milk crates. We'd climb over the fence to a playground and we'd swing way up, two on a swing. And we'd sneak in the movies. If there was any poverty, I wasn't aware of it. How could you think of it when you could get soda for five cents?"

Like Alice, Althea was into astrology and numerology and was a product of public courts, where she wowed locals with her ability to unload on the ball. She quit school at age thirteen in order to concen-trate on tennis, taking a variety of odd jobs to sustain her career. She was a counter girl in a Chock full o'Nuts coffee shop in Lower Manhattan, a chicken cleaner on Long Island, an elevator operator in the Midtown Hotel Dixie, a packer in a button factory, a mechanic in a machine shop. Any time work interfered with tennis, she quit her job.

Just as Alice's early days were marked by a violent temper and a lack of polish, Althea was unmannered and a poor sport, while hanging out in nightclubs and pool halls. There was the time when she strolled right up to championship boxer and Harlem legend Sugar Ray Robinson and told the fighter how she could whip him—on the tennis court. But that worked out: Sugar Ray was so taken by the high schooler's moxie he bought her a saxophone.

And as with Alice, Althea had a benefactor in Wilmington, only hers was in North Carolina, not Delaware. Hubert Eaton, an African-American surgeon there, would house Althea during the school year and ensure she got her education at Wilmington High, thus getting her off the street and into intensive practice in a milder climate.

When she arrived at the Wilmington train station, she was more of a turnip seed than any of the local gentry. "There she was with Sugar Ray's sax in one hand," Dr. Eaton said, "and in the other an old pasteboard suitcase with two belts tied around it. She was wearing an old skirt; she'd never owned a dress in her life."

But could she ever play. Althea was awarded a full scholarship to Florida A&M through tennis. She was also successful on a larger scale. This was the era of the ATA and a separate black national championship, the one captured by Jimmy McDaniel in 1939. The events were held at historically black colleges throughout the South, and the tennis was just part of a festival weekend, with dances and fashion shows being part of the spectacle. They were greatly anticipated by the black tennis community.

Althea won multiple Negro titles by dint of her potent physical game. She was five foot ten, 144 pounds, unstylish but an overwhelming presence on the other side of the net. Getting balls over or past Althea was nearly impossible, and while her backhand needed work, few could match the velocity of her forehand blasts and service—much the same scouting report that detailed Alice Marble's game.

Her game was superb and developing rapidly, ready for the US Nationals in Forest Hills, but the tournament wasn't ready for her. The outer borough neighborhood was being transformed postwar into "a swarming sector of Long Island where the backwash of Suburbia blurs into the edge of New York City," in *Time*'s description. The West Side Tennis Club was increasingly a "green refuge from the crowded reality about it." By 1950, Althea was clearly good enough to play in the nationals. As Jack Kramer said, "She has the best chance to be a champ in the manner of Alice Marble that I've seen." She petitioned the USLTA for entry.

The ruling body wasn't quite the arbitrary fiefdom it had been during

Julian Myrick's czardom, but it wasn't a progressive, forward-thinking group by any stretch. They turned Althea down, hiding behind technicalities, as many organizations did in the era. Althea, they reasoned, had not accrued the requisite match play on grass, the surface at Forest Hills. "We can't very well invite the girl until she makes a name for herself on grass—at Orange and East Hampton and Essex," the USLTA said in a press release. "And those tournaments are all invitational. We can't tell them who should be invited."

Of course they could—they just chose not to. Desperate, the leaders of the American Tennis Association, Dr. Walter Johnson and Dr. Hubert Eaton, huddled in secret negotiations with USLTA officials Ellsworth Davenport and Alrick Man. There was certainly momentum on their side. Jackie Robinson had broken the professional baseball color line in 1946, and began play in the major leagues the following spring, and was such an unqualified success that several black players had closely followed him into "white folks ball." Later in 1946 a pair of black stars, Kenny Washington and Woody Strode, became the first players to integrate the National Football League. Shortly before the push to include Althea began in earnest, the nascent National Basketball Association had integrated as well, with Nat "Sweetwater" Clifton and Earl Lloyd paving the way. There was no reason beyond prejudice that tennis shouldn't follow suit.

The ATA leaders had a few allies within the white organization, most importantly Edward Niles, a lawyer and longtime advocate for inclusion in tennis. But when the ATA officials asked what they could do to ensure Althea's inclusion, the reply from the USLTA was brief, a single word from an anonymous and unctuous bureaucrat whose name is lost to history.

"Nothing."

And it might have ended there, except Althea's childhood hero stepped in.

Alice did what she did best at this stage of her life. She put pen to paper and unleashed a broadside, in the form of her column, "As I See It," in the July 1950 issue of *American Lawn Tennis* magazine, the bible of the sport. The periodical prefaced Marble's piece with a caveat:

Miss Marble's column this month deals with an issue of such importance to the game that we felt that its rightful position was on a page specifically devoted to opinion. . . . At times we may disagree with . . . opinions, but in this case *American Lawn Tennis* wishes to go on record as wholeheartedly supporting the sentiments and opinions expressed by Miss Marble in the following editorial.

Titled "A Vital Issue," Alice's column began by noting that she was frequently asked on her lecture tour about Althea and whether she would be allowed to play in the nationals. "I couldn't answer their questions, but I returned to New York determined to find out. When I directed the question at a committee member of long standing, his answer, tacitly given, was in the negative. . . . True enough, she was a finalist in the National Indoors, the gentleman admitted—but didn't I think the field was awfully poor? I did not. It is my opinion that Miss Gibson performed beautifully under the circumstances." She went on to elucidate the lack-of-grass-court-experience excuse, ending with, "Miss Gibson is over a very cunningly-wrought barrel, and I can only hope to loosen a few of its staves with one lone opinion."

"I think it's time we faced a few facts," she continued. "If tennis is a sport for ladies and gentlemen, it's also time we acted a little more like gentlepeople and less like sanctimonious hypocrites. If there is anything left in the name of sportsmanship, it's more than time to display what it means to us. If Althea Gibson represents a challenge to the present crop of women players, it's only fair that they should meet that challenge on the courts . . . [not] the inner sanctum of the committee, where a different kind of game is played."

Alice confessed that she didn't know if Althea had what it took to be a champion, but that was not the point. "If she is refused a chance to succeed or to fail, then there is an ineradicable mark against a game to which I have devoted most of my life, and I would be bitterly ashamed. . . . It so happens that I tan very heavily in the summer—but I doubt that anyone ever questioned my right to play in the Nationals because of it. . . . She is not being judged by the yardstick of ability but by the fact that her pigmentation is somewhat different."

Alice then decried the sport of tennis for not falling in line with the other games that she loved. "The entrance of Negroes into national tennis is as inevitable as it has proven to be in baseball, in football, or in boxing; there is no denying so much talent. . . . Eventually the tennis world will rise up en masse to protest the injustices perpetrated by our policy-makers. Eventually—why not now?"

Alice ended her passionate plea for inclusion with a personal note of support. "I've never met Miss Gibson but, to me, she is a fellow human being to whom equal privileges ought to be extended. Speaking for myself, I will be glad to help Althea Gibson in any way I can. If I can improve her game or merely give her the benefit of my own experiences, as I have done many other young players, I'll do that. If I can give her an iota more of confidence by rooting my heart out from the gallery, she can take my word for it: I'll be there."

It was an extraordinary gesture—as though Babe Ruth had penned a column for *The Sporting News* in the 1930s demanding that Major League Baseball allow black players to break the color line. And unlike the entreaties made before the war to the Lords of Baseball by desegregationists, Alice's gambit worked. The ATA followed up with a press release highlighting the editorial, and Edward Niles was encouraged to push his brethren at the USLTA to find Althea a trial tournament. In short order, the Orange Lawn Tennis Club, in South Orange, New Jersey, was chosen as the test case. Althea was invited to play in its prenationals tournament, where she did well enough to convince the USLTA to include her in the 1950 nationals.

On August 28, 1950, Althea became the first African-American of either sex to compete in the nationals. She roundly defeated England's Barbara Knapp, 6–2, 6–2, to make the day triumphant as well as symbolic. "No Negro player, man or woman, has ever set foot on one of these courts," wrote Lester Rodney in his column in the *Daily Worker*.

"In many ways, it is even a tougher personal Jim Crow–busting assignment than was Jackie Robinson's when he first stepped out of the Brooklyn Dodgers dugout."

Her second-round match was with the reigning Wimbledon champion, Louise Brough. With the gallery packed with "as many as could squeeze into the grandstand, find standing room or get a view from under a fence," in Allison Danzig's description, including an unusually large number of black fans, Althea faltered early but stormed back to win the second set to even the match. The third was an incredibly tense affair, with Brough leading 5–3 only for Althea to even the set at 5–5, then 6–all. "The skies, which had been ominously dark for some time, grew blacker now and lightning flashed, while peals of thunder rolled over the scene," wrote the *Times*. "But hardly a person left the stands, so intense was the interest in the fight." At one point, a bolt of lightning struck a concrete statue of an eagle at the top of the stadium, sending it "shattering to the ground," according to one onlooker. "It may have been an omen that times were changing," Althea later wrote. Gibson went up 7–6, but then the deluge began, just in time to save Brough.

The match was halted, to be taken up again the following day at high noon. A tense encounter with reporters ensued, as one reporter recalled. "It was a trying session for Miss Gibson," said David Eisenberg of the *New York Journal-American*, "one made much more difficult by several members of her own race who decided to make themselves her personal protectors. One was a young man whom Althea later said she never had met before, another an unknown woman. Both tried to keep the press from talking with Althea, and bitter words were exchanged. The incident left Althea in a state of near shock."

The next day Brough's superior experience and savvy showed through. The huge throng was rewarded with just eleven minutes of action, enough time for Brough to win three straight games and the match, 9–7 in the third set. "It was a heavy blow to Miss Gibson," Danzig wrote, "after the marvelous rally she staged [yesterday]. Possibly, had the rain not intervened, she would have been the winner, but that is only speculation, to engross those who saw the match, for some time to come."

Certainly Althea had earned her place in the sport, regardless of her skin color. Alice had chatted with Althea the day before the Brough match, for fifteen oft-interrupted minutes. She was impressed with Althea's game, as she wrote in her follow-up column in *American Lawn Tennis*, "An Open Letter to Althea Gibson," published in November. "You were blessed with more natural ability than any woman on the courts today; you're a bold player and you have that rare spark."

In a long piece that touched on various subjects, Alice denied she had been any help to Althea's game, despite the number of people who "erroneously congratulated me after that match. They labored under the delusion that you had performed so brilliantly against Miss Brough because I coached you, which is ridiculous. . . . I can't take any credit for your performance. As Ogden Nash said, I'm a stranger here myself."

She also spent several paragraphs cautioning Althea against what "Ted Williams, the great ball player, calls the front-runners," the hangers-on and entourage fillers that swarm around newly famous (and often rich) celebrities of all stripes, people who wanted to get "into the act for their sakes, not yours." She had been startled by how many had surrounded Althea at Forest Hills. "You don't need them," she warned.

And she went into detail about these "front-runners" who had turned on Alice after her passionate, public support of Althea's right to play.

"I still don't know who my friends are—I only know who my friends aren't," she moaned. "People who fell all over their feet to entertain me when I was champion greeted me very formally this September. People who had called me 'Champ' since 1938 suddenly remembered that I was 'Miss Marble.' People who had taken ostentatious advantage of our kissing acquaintance gave me a chilly handshake or failed to notice my approach, or glared, which was even funnier. . . . They only remember a terrible article I wrote, saying a good tennis player named Gibson ought to play in the Nationals. Things are certainly tough all over, aren't they?" She ended with, "See you in 1951. On the center court, I hope."

Althea wrote back in the February 1951 issue. "I am sorry for the slurs you received and the friends you lost," she said. "I believe the new friends you gained who believed in fair play and democracy will outnumber the few old ones you lost." Then she cut to the obvious chase—"Miss Marble, if you find things really tough, imagine how I find them."

She spent the rest of the piece recounting her troubled road to Forest Hills and how those "front-runners" were mainly her benefactors, in particular Walter Johnson of Lynchburg and Dr. Eaton from Wilmington.

"Miss Marble, can you imagine being picked up out of the 'slums' of New York and placed in a house of luxury?" Actually, Alice could relate to that particular experience far better than Althea probably realized.

Writer Bruce Schoenfeld noted that Marble's letter "changed the history of the sport. In a small way, it also changed the course of American history. . . . Perhaps blacks would ultimately play in the U.S. championships, just as they eventually integrated the National Basketball Association, the Augusta National golf club, and the modern incarnation of the United States Senate. But without Marble, it certainly wouldn't have happened in 1950."

Althea's Alice-aided breakthrough hardly led to a landslide in African-American participation at the national level. The USLTA instituted a quota that held well into the Open era, allowing only the ATA champion to apply to play in USLTA events, guaranteeing not only a maximum of two black players (one of each gender) but also that they would be unable to get into the majority of tournaments, as they took place before the ATA title was won. This worked against Gibson in particular, who was too good for her ATA competition and desperately needed topflight adversaries year-round. But the lack of them hurt her in the years immediately following her breakthrough in Forest Hills. Her national ranking dropped, and one black publication called her "the biggest disappointment in sports." That made her success in the latter half of the 1950s, including titles in both the nationals and Wimbledon in 1957 and 1958 (she also won the 1956 French Open and six doubles championships), all the more impressive.

It wouldn't have happened when it did without Alice. She was rewarded for her efforts by Harvard University, who granted her an honorary degree, one of three the girl who never went to college would accrue in her life.

Chapter Thirty-Six

....

The Twilight Zone

Alice was still the ultimate multitasker, but one by one some of her creative and monetary streams began to dam up. She took language classes and extolled the virtues of learning from recorded lessons, to the point she invested a small amount in a company that produced language LPs in 1948. She was fluent enough in Spanish to write a note to H. V. Kaltenborn entirely in the language, addressing him as "Don Juan" and talking about spending time with some Latino houseguests, including her old lover, Tica Madrigal. Translated, her note read, "[Tica], to me, is like a sister. She knows me better than anyone except my dearest." The language company didn't last long, however, and she fell out of practice with tongues other than English.

She still loved to sing, and play guitar, which she brought with her on her lecture tours, sometimes to play for the crowd, sometimes to get a little hootenanny going on the train. She told an Oshkosh, Wisconsin, crowd that she tuned her guitar string just as she tuned her rackets, tightening the gut almost to exactly the same tautness. "Just one pitch lower" was the sweet spot, she said in a conspiratorial tone. One reporter talked to Alice getting off a train in Norman, Oklahoma, with "my hobby" (the guitar) in one hand and "my profession" (the racket) in the other.

But she started to notice her breath growing shorter, her control of her voice not so sharp. Singing became more difficult. When she went for a checkup, the doctor found pneumonia, which recurred often enough to send her to a specialist. This physician found a severe lung infection, no doubt residue from her earlier battles with tubercular infections. The right lung was severely affected—beyond treatment, actually. It would have to be removed. She was told her chances of surviving the procedure were "fifty-fifty."

"I'd faced worse odds," she noted.

For three days she received penicillin in the form of shots to her gluteus maximus. They were a painful reminder of the iron shots she had gotten back during her lengthy bout with anemia. "My rear felt like a pincushion," she said.

Walter Winchell went on the radio to announce that Alice was "at death's door" following the surgery, which removed the right lung and a pair of ribs to go with it. Meanwhile, a tongue depressor used at some point during the procedure wasn't properly sterilized. Her gums got infected, and within a couple of years the disease pyorrhea would set in. But Unsinkable Alice would bounce back yet again, though she was bedridden for two months, causing her to miss out on a lucrative speaking tour.

That was okay for the moment, as Saks Fifth Avenue, the most swish of the Saks department store chains, began showing her sportswear designs in an exclusive engagement, a coup in fashion circles. "The new look is as fashionable on the courts as in restaurants," she said. "Trim lines, freedom of movement and comfort distinguish her creations," read some promotional copy, "most of which are patterned from her own court costumes, self-designed at the start of her career." Perhaps, but her new dresses were longer by some three inches, going against Alice's usual penchant for showing more leg than the other women.

Meanwhile, she made a point of "doing the shops" wherever she went, always keen on finding ideas to "borrow," or finding something to wear on her own still "trim and lithesome," "tall and attractive" frame. One pre-Christmas stop in Indianapolis was accompanied by a reporter, who struggled to keep up with Alice as she "strode briskly" from store to store, "blond, hatless, as full of verve as her best serve."

She moved with speed when alone but slowed down when there were men at her side. Many years later Alice gave an interview to *The Desert Sun* and recalled her many suitors from the era in a way only a fellow mixologist would appreciate. "I remember them all by what they drank—Fernando, an artist, drank hot port in the winter and cold port in the summer; Charlie, a Yale grad, drank Tom Collins; Jerry drank Manhattans."

The exact identities of "Charlie" and "Jerry" are lost to time, but "Fernando" was Fernando Puma, a modern artist who went unappreciated in his time, perhaps thanks to his works of "Christ with his head on crooked," in Alice's description. Alice also described him as a "wonderful lover" who "liked to dance for me wearing his top hat and carrying a cane, but wearing no pants." "Tennis star Alice Marble and artist Fernando Puma are a heart toddy," wrote gossip maven Dorothy Kilgallen in her column in January 1947. By May, the *Brooklyn Daily Eagle* was reporting they were "to tie the knot soon." But he was a "brooding, selfish soul, and rude to all my friends," Alice wrote, and she ended it.

She never mentioned what Rod Serling liked to drink, or if he ever danced around bottomless, but Alice did write in *Courting Danger* that she carried on an affair with the creator and host of *The Twilight Zone* for several years. Alice was a full decade and change older than the married Serling, a notorious womanizer who, according to his biographer Gordon F. Sander, didn't have any issue bringing Alice to Hollywood parties.

Alice said she used to "type his scripts for him, and if I changed one comma he would notice, and tell me he didn't need an editor." Sander called Serling "TV's last angry man," and Alice agreed that he was a sourpuss. "Ulcers made him perpetually grim-faced," she wrote. "Sometimes [he] would sit all evening at a party and not say a word." But she was also in awe of his talent and his "marvelous mind" and noted that his crew thought highly of him. According to Alice, the affair ended when Serling moved to Hollywood from New York, even though Alice moved there soon after he did.

Confirmation of Alice's romantic escapades is almost as difficult to uncover as that of her wartime intrigue. I reached out to Serling's daughter, Anne Serling, the author of the memoir *As I Knew Him: My Dad, Rod Serling*, but she declined comment. One thing seems certain—Alice's sexuality was as fluid as her movement on the tennis court. Alice enjoyed the company of men as well as women. Rita Mae Brown may as well have been speaking about Alice when she told *Time* in 2008, "I don't believe in straight or gay. I really don't. I think we're all degrees of bi-sexual." She told me that Alice "had the great good sense to enjoy both genders" but felt the need to remain careful about publicizing affairs with either sex.

• • •

Alice was definitely bi in one regard in the early 1950s—bicoastal. She never had gotten used to the New York winters, and after her lung removal she decided to spend more time in the sun, moving back to California in the early fifties, although she went back and forth for a time in order to stay au courant in the fashion capital of the country (her work in this regard mostly dried up by the midfifties). She wasn't necessarily happy about it; she informed one reporter that "Los Angeles is an overgrown hick town." She moved into a Beverly Hills duplex with a "magazine writer friend" and got a cat, a Siamese, who refused to eat without hearing Alice's raspy voice. "I have to talk to it sometimes on the phone to keep it from starving," Alice told the *Los Angeles Times*. "After I talk to him, he goes right over to eat."

It didn't much matter that she found LA less sophisticated than New York—she didn't spend much time in any one spot long enough for moss to grow. Her relentless travel never seemed to end. In February 1947 she journeyed across the Atlantic by plane for the first time to participate (with Budge and Riggs) in an exhibition series that took them to England. While there, Alice coached several promising British girls in the finer points of the game; when asked the difference between English and

American women on the court, Alice answered, "Aggression." One student told *The Daily Telegraph* she was impressed at how quickly Alice discovered her weaknesses. "[Her] methods of coaching are most original and, in fact, are probably unique," wrote the *Telegraph*. "She spent a considerable time on her pupil's service, making her place one foot on top of the other in order to teach her correct balance. She encouraged her to hit up and over the ball instead of hitting down on it." She then took the court and "delighted a packed Wembley Stadium with her beautiful tennis." Susan Noel, an Irish player and occasional doubles partner with Alice, thought that "Miss Marble at 34 is still probably the best woman player in the world."

Others, though, weren't so easily impressed. According to Alice, Winston Churchill refused to give her an autograph until she requested Queen Mary step in and insist.

From England the pros journeyed to Sweden, at King Gustav's personal request, to help revive postwar interest in the sport. The king was quite an ardent player and fan, though he was mourning the recent death of his grandchild in a plane crash in Copenhagen and didn't get to play with Alice, as he said he wanted to do. Alice nearly met the prince's fate; the plane taking her, along with Riggs and Budge, back to London from Sweden skidded off the runway while landing. No one was hurt, but the players disembarked ashen.

Planes were still falling from the sky at an alarming rate in the late 1940s, but advances in technology that were a side effect of the war had made commercial aviation much safer and speedier than in the days when Carole Lombard lost her life. Still, the "jet set" wasn't quite yet in vogue while Alice was zipping all over the country. She flew far more often than the average traveler in the decade after the war. A typical journey, in October 1954, saw Alice flying from Los Angeles to Minneapolis, giving a lecture there, then renting a car and driving 2,200 miles over a two-week stretch to give several more speeches. She complained to the Minneapolis *Star Tribune* about the "weary hours of lonely driving" and the "inadequate food and lodgings offered by smaller towns on the lecture circuit," but added, "I love what I'm doing." She would then fly home and repeat the process in some other region of the nation. In all, she gave approximately one thousand lectures in forty-four states between 1945 and 1955.

Despite the fact she had experienced several auto wrecks and been lucky to walk away from them, Alice never hesitated to hop behind the wheel. A true road warrior, Alice estimated she had racked up an incredible 120,000 miles in that same time frame, driving across America, a staggering amount for the period that only the hardiest long-distance truck drivers could match. All that mileage was racked up on roads that remained poor in many places: pocked with potholes ("bumpy enough to churn butter" in the words of contemporary country singer Mel Tillis), not wide enough for the traffic load (the Interstate Highway System didn't begin construction until 1956), often poorly paved and lit, without anything like the roadside services, including food and lodging, that would dot the landscape in the decades to follow. Merely making it to all of her scheduled stops on time was one of her greatest feats. That's not to say she didn't encounter trouble. In 1955 she wrote that she had been involved in no fewer than nine accidents, several of which had happened in the last few years.

She was also a woman traveling, mostly, alone. Self-reliance was a hallmark of her feminist talks; to Alice the act of getting from one speech to another by herself was a political statement in a time when women were expected to be subservient to the men around them. Even in the tennis world this was the case, as with a player *The New York Times* identified as "Mrs. Robert B. Leith," who had to withdraw from a tournament because "she couldn't make satisfactory arrangements for someone to prepare her husband's dinner." Yes, the war had opened the eyes of women nationwide to what they were missing by waving goodbye to their husbands every morning. But the initial postwar decade was hardly marked by a feminist renaissance; if anything, the backlash from returning servicemen felt like a step backward. These were the years that saw Simone de Beauvoir observe that the patriarchy was increasingly baked into society in her book *The Second Sex*, and resulted in Betty Friedan writing *The Feminine Mystique*, in which she pinpointed the feeling of helplessness that smart women trapped with no outlet for their ambitions possessed and identified it as the "Problem That Has No Name."

Alice was happy to name the problems she felt plagued America— a lack of exercise, sleep, proper nutrition, and willpower. Ironically, driving as much as she did caused her to eat poorly, sit for long stretches, and miss out on a full night's rest. Her health problems would only get worse in the coming years, and the sedentary life spent behind the wheel during this period, while difficult to assess, may have increased her physical deterioration.

She maintained her willpower, however. Alice's perpetual motion made her something of an expert on automotive travel. She often wrote and spoke about the importance of (fifties-style) proper road etiquette. She shared an anecdote of driving her Oldsmobile behind "one of those big, double-jointed trucks," and after a long spell on his bumper, she passed him with a toot of her horn. Later she had occasion to signal to him to slow as heavy traffic approached. An hour later, she was eating at a roadside stop when the driver came up to her. "I watched you ahead of me for a long time, and I just wanted to say that I wish there were more like you on the road. You're a mighty fine driver."

"And though I held my breath a long, long moment," Alice wrote, "he didn't add, 'for a woman.'"

"Certainly hand signals are elemental," went another explainer she wrote for the *Times*. "The hand extended upward indicates a right turn, extended outward, a left turn; dropped a warning to slow or stop. The hand wagging frantically in all directions means only one thing: woman driver!"

Indeed, when it came to driving, Alice was decidedly retrograde. She even penned a long op-ed for *The New York Times Magazine* in 1955 titled "Plea: 'Don't Be a Woman, Driver.'" She implored women not to drive like, well, women. "The lady autoist's chief fault," she wrote, "is she imagines she's a lady—when she's not." In other words, "stop being women behind the wheel."

"I have just completed a 2,500 mile auto trip on which I came to the sad conclusion that almost everything 'they' say about us is true," she moaned. She elucidated the many examples of horrid driving she encountered in her travels: a woman in the Midwest who drives too slow and weaves around; the one in the South who made a left from the right-hand lane; women everywhere jumping lights. Once, when Alice was in the rare position of a passenger being driven to an appearance, the woman at the wheel turned around to talk—and, Alice said, ran into a tree.

What bothered the former tomboy the most was the way that women dealt with the aftermath of their road shenanigans. "Women deal with it by taking advantage of being women," batting eyelashes and throwing themselves upon the mercy of the male libido.

Using whatever abilities to their maximum was all part of "The Art of Living," as she called her speeches in the immediate postwar era. One thing Alice stressed in her talks was to "cultivate a pleasant speaking voice," ignoring the fact that overuse and other factors, including the greater efforts it took to breathe with a single lung available for inspiration, along with all the cigarettes she refused to give up, had worn hers down. Still, reviewers were unanimous that Alice had a "nice sense of humor and a winning delivery." That was important as she croaked out speeches about healthful living.

As the prosperous fifties dawned, Alice's talk altered somewhat to include bountiful tips on living well that would be the province of a life coach today. "A Sound Mind in a Sound Body" was the name of the speech; in it Alice told audiences it was "as important for people to take inventory of themselves as it is for a shop keeper to take inventory of his goods," while speaking of the "dynamic power of rest," noting she always got her eight hours, "unless a speaking engagement interferes." Punctuality was important, said Alice. "Few people waste money but many, many more waste time, a far more precious commodity. When you're late for an appointment, you are picking someone else's pocket, robbing him of invaluable minutes, lost waiting for you." And "successful, glamorous people are usually very, very hard-working. For success is made up of dull, unglamorous, hard work."

Few people could be said to work harder than Alice; she had more side hustles than she could count and never felt the ennui of all those fifties-era men in their gray flannel suits. Despite it all, there was never much money. Of course, the original sin to her lack of financial security as she passed forty years on the planet was the fact that she made it to the pinnacle of a profession that was strictly amateur (as it would be until 1968, when the Open era at last came to be the standard). She had been the best at her chosen craft in the entire world and got almost nothing but opportunities from that. She made what she could from them, but she wasn't the best designer or lecturer or nightclub singer of them all.

She had been the best female tennis player of them all, but it hadn't made her rich. Even worse, her prime was cut short by circumstances far outside her control, just as much of her life seemed to have been shaped by powerful currents that buffeted her regardless of how hard she swam.

It was a trend that would continue as her playing prime grew smaller and smaller in her rearview mirror.

Chapter Thirty-Seven

....

VALLEY GIRL

She was a gal from a hardscrabble part of the big city who learned tennis on the public courts of the nearby park, playing with whoever turned up. She helped out her family's finances by taking odd jobs and was discovered and nurtured by local players to rise to the top of her sport.

Darlene Hard had a remarkably similar story to Alice, except that she grew up in the 1950s and learned her tennis in LA and Griffith Park, not San Francisco and Golden Gate Park. So it was very appropriate that when Hard needed polishing, she turned to Marble.

With the passing years Alice could no longer lean on her New York celebrity to put a roof over her head and a meal on her table. Her name no longer carried weight with the department stores, radio and television producers, gossip columnists, and lecture-tour bookers. The wind had been taken from her sails quite literally with her pneumonectomy, and she had become alarmingly frail. Sleep eluded her, as she would wake gasping for breath. Finally, not yet forty-five years old, she took to using an oxygen tank at night to ensure getting enough air. Meanwhile, the pyorrhea contracted from the dirty insertion during her lung operation had caused her teeth to go bad, to the point she required false teeth. Years of life in the sun wrinkled her skin, giving her "character lines" that creased her once-creamy face. Her hair was worn in a tight bun, and the constant smoking didn't help her complexion or her general well-being. "I got terribly old looking, terribly fast," she admitted.

But Alice wasn't one to sit still. She wrote H. V. Kaltenborn in 1958 that she had been taking long weekend trips frequently to visit her sister, Hazel, and her husband in San Francisco, to Santa Barbara, to Rancho Santa Fe. Mainly, she felt "revived and happy to be back in a busy office. It's just great to be alive!" Alice no doubt felt lucky to still be breathing, literally.

The office she referred to in the letter to Kaltenborn was, ironically, a physician's office. In 1956 a friend remarked affably that since she had spent so much time around doctors, perhaps she should work for one. Alice thought it a good idea and found a job in Encino with Dr. John Bach, who had an obstetrics and gynecology practice on the Broadway of the San Fernando Valley, Ventura Boulevard.

At first she commuted through the canyons from Beverly Hills, but the commute wore even this accomplished long-distance driver down. She soon found a property she wanted to buy in Tarzana, on leafy Nestle Avenue, five minutes from the office. She didn't have the money to do so, however, so she turned to the one man we know of who really did know Alice and love her.

•   •   •

There are few more beautifully kept acreages in America than the grounds of the Hagley Museum and Library, set alongside a snaking offshoot of the Delaware River called Brandywine Creek. It is here that the history and legacy of the Du Pont family is kept, mainly in a vast archive cataloguing the Du Ponts' contributions to chemical technology and munitions, all set inside a gorgeous estate. Hidden amid the botanical gardens and hilly meadows of the "Brandywine's most beautiful mile" are the artifacts of the company's original gunpowder works and explosives laboratories. The picturesque surroundings almost make the visitor forget the company's important contributions to over a century of war and destruction.

Hidden deep in the bowels of the estate is the Soda House, where the sodium nitrate, a compound used to accelerate the explosive process, was kept. Today, it serves as the archive for reference materials concerning the Du Ponts, including Will. I've come here on a glorious September afternoon, but instead of enjoying the scenery I'm inside the Soda House, reading Will and Alice's correspondence.

It is in these letters that the depth of Will's financial "keeping" of Alice shines through the hints and winks and outright denials in Alice's memoir. While there isn't a complete set of letters to and fro, and even in the writing they remained proper and circumspect, it quickly becomes clear just how much Alice depended upon Will's money, especially once she moved west.

Will had actually gotten married in 1947—and to a different tennis star. Margaret Osborne (whom Will called "Meow") was a younger version of Alice, a farm girl who grew up playing baseball only to become a star tennis player with a sunny disposition and a graceful manner on and off the court. She also moved to San Francisco as a girl and grew up playing at Golden Gate Park, her home a few blocks from the Marble place on Twelfth Avenue. Osborne bore her husband a son, William du Pont III, in 1952, and went back to tennis, winning several more doubles championships after childbirth. She would win thirty-seven Grand Slam titles in all, a sensational amount, twenty of them doubles titles with Louise Brough.

Alice was only an occasional presence in Du Pont's life during this period, usually seeing him and Osborne when the couple were on the West Coast, but beginning in 1956, that changed. He had recently purchased a large tract of land in the Palm Springs area, upon which he built a ranch called Point Happy. Du Pont asked Alice if she would periodically check in on the progress of the estate he was building there, an arrangement that was a way to funnel Alice money while allowing her to salvage some pride and not feel like she was constantly writing for handouts. "I suggest I send money—up to $3,000—as a gift," he wrote Alice on March 16, 1956, so "you would not have to pay any taxes." He sent her checks every June and December and, when push came to shove, whenever she asked for more.

The money kept flowing, and not just in small amounts. Will bought Alice her Tarzana house. "In regards to your possible new home . . . I will work out a proposition with you," he wrote Alice in June, and by July Alice was writing back, "I am in my house and all is fine. . . . I love the house and am so grateful to have it." She just needed to learn some basics of home ownership, as "the Japanese gardener wanted fifty dollars just to clean up the back yard."

In October 1957 she was working hard at the doctor's office, running the shop, keeping the books, making appointments, and doing chores such as "injections, blood counts, electrocardiograms, urinalysis besides . . . keeping the two doctors and patients happy." For all her hard work, she wasn't paid much, and when she needed a new freezer, she turned to Will. "I need some money, if you will be so kind (even if I haven't earned it). The reason is I ordered a new refrigerator-freezer. . . . It's a dandy Philco, and I would like to have the appliance man send it out, but I have to pay for it first." A few months later, in early 1958, Will wrote, "I enclose check for your new car."

In 1959 Alice requested a pool to keep the Valley's brutal temperatures at bay. "In order for the pool men to start working on the pool I had to give them some money in advance. Since I am trying desperately not to take any of the money I've saved out of my savings account I got the loan of $891 from the bank. . . . I only have the loan for a month, so may I please have some money. Also, I want to have the back of the house painted, buy some plants and do numerous other little things. As I suggested in the last letter, if you think everything is costing too much you can send me whatever amount you think out of the thousand that I have been getting this time of year."

The check arrived, of course, as did one for 2,800 dollars three months later to "get rid of the mortgages on your property," and her usual "check for 1,000.00 that I give you at this time of year." In late fall Alice wrote to ask, "Do you think I might have my (Xmas) check now?"

Shortly thereafter, another missive. "It's taxes time and I wonder if I might have some money, please. I have some in my savings account but I'm trying not to touch it. Thanks very much, Will." He sent money west in February, June, October, and December of '62, and in March, June, and September of '63 as well.

It was all a drop in the bucket for a man of Du Pont's enormous wealth, and he enjoyed having Alice back in his life. In March 1957 he alluded to a rebirth of their former relationship. "I enjoyed seeing your place and having breakfast and the trimmings which went with it made it a most enjoyable visit." There were other visits, sometimes with wife Margaret and daughter Jean (known as "Mouse"), sometimes not. On at least two occasions, she drove Du Pont down to Point Happy to check on the progress of construction, and the two spent the weekend there, minus Will's wife.

For Alice, who spent years having everything in her life paid for by Eleanor Tennant, it might have felt natural to have someone to turn to for cash. But she was always a workaholic, regardless of the funds courtesy of the Du Pont fortune. So when the opportunity to coach came up, she closed the office, jumped in her car, and drove over to the courts.

• • •

Jack Kramer had seen Darlene Hard play in Griffith Park and brought her over to the Los Angeles Tennis Club, making a suggestion about a coach—Alice. Alice wasn't experienced, of course, but she had studied under the master coach, and a recent rapprochement with Eleanor had strengthened her resolve.

Tennant had, after many years, found another champion to haul to the top in her Sherpa-like manner. Maureen Connolly was a California teen with a willful manner that made Alice seem a dissembler. Her ground strokes were enough to carry her to the brink of major championships, but her serve was wobbly.

At first, Eleanor was still full of "resentment," in Alice's words, and delighted in telling her former pupil how much better her new one was. But Connolly's constant double-faulting and weak spin serve were driving Tennant to the brink of insanity, so Eleanor swallowed her pride and called the best server in women's tennis history to that point. Alice also swallowed her pride and agreed to help "Little Mo." They worked for several trying weeks in La Jolla, Alice finding the teenager "willful, cocky, and difficult to teach." But Alice's methods, including bringing in a pitcher from the San Diego Padres to instruct Connolly in how to throw a curveball, in order to perfect the wrist snap that would cause her spin serve to bite, worked wonders. By that summer Connolly was good enough from the service line to win the US Nationals at sixteen years old.

Connolly also had a turbulent relationship with Tennant, which ended the following year when Teach recommended she withdraw from Wimbledon due to a shoulder injury. Mo, surpassing her coach's stubbornness, refused, and the resulting argument ended the partnership. Connolly went on to win Wimbledon with the bum shoulder, and Eleanor was chastened. The old familiar pattern had played out again— Tennant was unparalleled at bringing out a student's best game, but her demanding personality eventually grated and the partnership ended. It is tribute to Alice's good nature that she lasted as long with Eleanor as she did.

Alice, not one to hold a grudge, didn't hesitate to put the rancor with Eleanor behind her and was surprised at the charge she got from helping great talents achieve their dreams. So it was with Darlene Hard. Alice's first step after watching Hard hit was a familiar one—she had her new charge change grips, from the Continental/Western one Darlene used to the Eastern grip that had transformed Alice's career. Darlene found she suddenly had much more control on her shots and shortly afterward found herself in the semifinals of Wimbledon as a result. She would win three Grand Slam titles in singles and make the International Tennis Hall of Fame in time, and always credited Alice's grip-change suggestion as the key to her stellar career.

Word of that positive tiptoe into the coaching waters was passed around, and it brought Alice a new student. Billie Jean Moffitt was a teenage sensation from the port city of Long Beach, the daughter of an athletic firefighter who would also father a major league pitcher, Randy

Moffitt. Yet another municipal player who proved hungrier than the country club types, Billie Jean was driven to be the best—and also driven to travel the forty miles to Tarzana every weekend to train with the legendary Wimbledon winner. She would stay overnight with Alice, whose oxygen tank would hiss at night, often preventing the teenage houseguest from sleeping.

Despite her physical frailty during this period, Alice proved a highly sensitive coach, in more ways than one. She could detect the slightest flaws in strokes, even from the side of the court, and was highly attuned to match tactics. While Billie Jean noticeably improved her serve and shot-making under Alice's tutelage, their discussions about playing under the bright lights while eating dinner left an even greater impression on the young star. "For the first time in my life," Billie Jean later said, "I sensed some kind of a legacy that I was part of." When Alice talked about performing on Centre Court at Wimbledon or in Forest Hills Stadium, Billie Jean could feel her "stomach tighten," imagining herself doing the same.

Alice taught her students to play the way she played—all-out assaults on the net, smashing the ball with abandon, winning by dint of intimidation as much as skill. And like her former teacher, she brooked no guff. Billie Jean found this out one day when Alice was feeling particularly ill with respiratory problems.

Instead of feeling any concern for Alice's well-being, or sympathy for her plight, the teenage Billie Jean was put out. "I guess I won't be coming up today," she told an insulted Alice, who informed Mr. and Mrs. Moffitt that she would no longer counsel their daughter.

Billie Jean remembers the split, although added some context, speculating that perhaps Alice was uncomfortable teaching someone who quite possibly was good enough to usurp her status in the history of the game. Billie Jean had told Alice that she hoped to become the best female player in history, which Alice thought presumptuous. After that, Alice "became less friendly and more aloof," Billie Jean said.

Billie Jean never denied that she was pretty bratty as a teen; Mo Connolly also told her she could never be a champion because she was too self-centered and egotistical. "To have two ex-champions such as Alice and Maureen blast you when you're still in your teens is pretty tough," she said. "Those two incidents left a mark on me, and I still remember them vividly." Little BJ grew up, physically and emotionally, married a man named King, and became a legendary champion, winning thirty-nine Grand Slam titles, twelve of them in singles. She was the only player after Alice to win the women's singles, doubles, and mixed doubles in one championship at both Forest Hills and Wimbledon.

In 1973 Alice's old frenemy entered Billie Jean's life. Bobby Riggs had spent two decades well off the beaten path, but the second wave of feminism brought out the cunning opportunist who once bet on himself to win Wimbledon. Now fifty-five years old, "Riggs the Rake" began denigrating female players, guaranteeing victory while allegedly placing large wagers on himself, just like the old days, with a little sexism thrown in. He beat the world's top-ranked player, Margaret Court, with contemptuous ease, stunning the tennis world. Emboldened, Riggs set his sights on Billie Jean.

The resulting circus that surrounded their match, played September 20, 1973, in the Houston Astrodome, overwhelmed the sport and became a national happening. Eleanor Tennant gave one of her final interviews on the eve of the match between her former student and Alice's. Tennant thought Riggs would win, as he would "psyche" out his opponent, much as he had Margaret Court. But she also thought Riggs "more of a clown than he used to be . . . though perhaps that's the facelift tennis needs." For her part, King told the press she was playing not merely for her gender but to bring tennis some much-needed attention, so perhaps Eleanor was on to something.

Billie Jean took Riggs apart in straight sets, winning the 100,000-dollar prize at stake and giving the feminist cause a potent shot in the arm, though tennis itself wasn't especially affected, at least on the women's side. King then got a divorce and came out as a lesbian. She was a generation removed from Alice, and certainly suffered blowback for her choices, but she was able to withstand the public backlash in a way Alice never dared to attempt.

Another of Alice's students was a hard-hitting tomboy from Encino named Sally Ride, who would later become the first female American astronaut. If Billie Jean had been a handful for Alice, young Ms. Ride was unmanageable, whacking the ball with so much power but so little control that Alice feared for her safety. "I'm fifty years old!" she would yell as another Ride rocket screamed her way. To Sally and her mother it was merely a matter of youthful lack of mastery, but years later Alice saw something more sinister, claiming Sally had deliberately tried to hit her coach.

"I had to duck like crazy," she told Ride's biographer, Lynn Sherr. "It wasn't that she mis-hit the ball. She had perfect aim. I was terribly amused she was chosen to be an astronaut. I think she probably had these aggressive feelings all her life."

Alice remained pretty aggressive, too. The sixties had become "The Sixties," especially in California, and Alice, who always had a conservative bent, turned harder right with every sit-in and inch of hair grown. She was already pious—now she became quite religious, saying, "There's nothing in life that speaking to God won't be good for." She was already patriotic—now news that a visiting Russian delegate to the United Nations was picketed by anti-communists upon arrival stirred her blood and caused an angry letter to the Los Angeles Times. "It looks to me like our domestic rabble rousers have a lot to learn in the ways and means in 'winning friends and influencing people.'" She also indicated support for a pair of stalwart Californian politicians named Reagan and Nixon (the identification with the right wing wouldn't last—by 1988 she was done with the Republican Party, writing Rita Mae Brown, "I saw every debate and felt like throwing up").

Nevertheless, she was a forgiving soul at heart, as witnessed by her renewed friendship with Eleanor. The two didn't hang out and reminisce about the old days, but they corresponded regularly, Eleanor writing "in her very bold hand, as though she were positive about everything," until failing eyesight and arthritis put an end to that.

Tennant died of cancer in La Jolla in 1974, age seventy-nine, after giving nearly seven decades to the game she discovered by stealing a boarder's racket. As her obituary in *The New York Times* put it, "At 78, arthritic and nearly blind, [tennis] was still what she cared about most of all." She remains one of the most intriguing and unique figures in the history of sports, a pioneer in personal coaching, sports psychology, and athlete management. Were Tennant to have been male and coached football or basketball, the keepers of the sporting iconography in the press surely would have ordained her a legend on par with the Lombardis and the Woodens. Instead, she became almost completely forgotten, even by tennis fans.

Alice's accomplishments were massively beholden to Eleanor's unshakable will and belief in Alice's talent and her ability to bring out Alice's best. With her death the world lost a wildly influential figure, as well as one of the only people who knew the full story of her greatest protégé and their intertwined lives.

· · ·

One of the last living people to possibly hold the key to stories of Alice's life, Rita Mae Brown, lives outside Charlottesville, Virginia, not far from the state university, and about an eight-hour drive from my home near Atlanta.

The stretch of road I take to get there, once I disengage from the interstate, just west of the Shenandoah Valley, hasn't changed greatly since the days when Alice was driving through rural areas, speechifying across the country. The roads are better, and service options a little more plentiful, perhaps, but the countryside remains covered by farms and stands of trees, the autumn sun still catching the gorgeous leaves that haven't fallen yet, and at the edge of every town there is a place of worship. Alice would have encountered every denomination in her peripatetic travels.

After many hours of driving through the scenic back roads of North Carolina and Virginia, I arrive at the entrance to Rita Mae Brown's farm. A slow drive along the gravel road reveals numerous stables and arenas, and multiple horses, calmly grazing in the hazy sunshine (Brown will later tell me that one of the equines is an offspring of the legendary Secretariat). Several dogs are lazing in the midday heat, the only one to stir a highly enthusiastic and tiny puppy, who races over to my car, then ambles off in the direction of the large house where Rita Mae, hopefully, awaits.

I've tried connecting with the author by phone for, literally, months, without success. In desperation to talk to someone who actually can shed some light on the mystery that is Alice Marble, the mountain has come to Mohammed, so to speak—I'm no longer content to be passive about getting in touch.

My heart skips as the foolishness of this plan—at last—starts to dawn on me. Before I overthink it, I pound on the door. And pound again. No reply. For ten minutes I case the joint before I'm finally convinced that no one is home. Rita Mae has stolen a march on me yet again (I will later discover she has journeyed to Kentucky on business, the inevitable downside to showing up unannounced).

Given the overall trajectory of my search to discover just who Alice Marble really was, this latest setback was hardly a surprise. Dejected, I stop outside the driveway to ponder my next move. In my rearview I see a mail truck, and that gives me what will prove to be a better idea than my half-cocked rush on Rita Mae's farm. I'm a writer. Rita Mae is a writer. We should do this by letter.

Brown has a long history of correspondence, some of which is archived at the nearby University of Virginia. So I write out more than a dozen questions, each with several subqueries, their length and breadth revealing the long and winding and obstacle-strewn path that has led me to, literally, her doorstep. With a flourish and not a little prayer, I drop the envelope into her mailbox, complete with self-addressed stamped envelope.

Sure enough, a couple of weeks after my Blue Ridge adventure, an envelope with an "RMB" sticker holding it shut arrives.

Chapter Thirty-Eight

....

QUEEN OF THE DESERT

Alice stared up at the massive globe, its circumference ringed by three iron bars, representing the orbital trajectory of NASA's initial three satellites, lights glowing to mark the world's great cities. The enormous structure was called the Unisphere, a steel rendering of the earth constructed for the special occasion of the 1964 World's Fair, which had come to New York for a pair of six-month exhibitions, with a short break in between. It was four years before astronauts on Apollo 8 snapped photos of the blue marble posed rising over the moon's horizon, its vulnerability highlighted in the deep black emptiness of space. In 1968, chaos reigned across the planet, giving added poignancy to *Earthrise* when the photo was splashed across newspapers and television screens worldwide, showing humanity a full-color, alien view of our world.

But in 1964, despite the assassination of the American president (Kay Stammers's old paramour) less than a year earlier, the placidity of the 1950s still reassured, the seething passions of "The Sixties" still tamped down, if ever more tenuously, by the comforts of Pax Americana. Alice took in the Unisphere and the rest of the displays at the fair, the jet packs and Belgian waffles and the scale model of the proposed "twin towers" to be built in Lower Manhattan, among others, secure in the knowledge that the future on display would be part of a mostly unchanged America, for better or worse.

The newly constructed Shea Stadium, home of the expansion Mets, towered over the proceedings. Alice didn't get to a game, though whether it was due to her loyalty to the Yankees isn't known. Within a dozen years construction would begin on another stadium adjacent to Shea, one that would house the US Nationals (by then the US Open) three miles north from its ancestral home in Forest Hills.

Alice had not been east in nearly a decade. Her visit to her old stomping grounds in New York was merely a fun layover for the real reason for her travels. She had been granted a singular honor—induction in the International Tennis Hall of Fame, housed in Newport, Rhode Island. After a few days in New York, examining what lay ahead, she took a trip back in time, to her glorious past.

On August 25, 1964, Alice got to look at her newly chiseled plaque gleaming in the Newport sun. The likeness, in marble, of course, captured her at her glamorous best.

But at present, Alice didn't look so much chic as sweaty. She was enshrined while wearing a white collared shirt and a pair of shorts, hardly suiting for the fashion maven of the sport. Before the ceremony, she had played doubles with her old partner, Don Budge, who was also honored that day. The match went on so long she didn't get a chance to change clothes, so the "beaded aqua gown" that she had bought just for the ceremony remained in her luggage. She was inducted in "tennis togs" instead. Despite her casual attire, or perhaps because of it, she remembered that "at the ceremony we all blubbered like babies."

Now that she had achieved immortality, Alice's next destination was paradise. "I haven't really had more than a week vacation in about eight years and I think it is about time," she wrote to Du Pont. She traveled to Hawaii, the fiftieth state in the union for just past five years in September 1964 when Alice arrived with "long-time friend May Klein," according to the *Honolulu Star-Bulletin*, which covered Alice's arrival. "Eat a couple of those ripe pineapples and think of me," Will du Pont wrote

Alice. She sent him some of the island fruit, along with the bill for the round-trip tickets, costing the Delaware billionaire $220.04.

Alice returned home tanned, relaxed, and ready to devote herself to tennis once more. She had given up the medical office job to return to the courts in a new kind of way, spurred to do so when a group of investors approached her to design a new development, the Lake Encino Racquet Club. "They gave me a free hand and no limit on the money," she told *Roto* magazine, "so I built a tennis club the way one should be built." One of the first things she did was inaugurate a "Motion Picture Tournament" featuring any celebrity she could talk into schlepping to the Valley to play, a list that included Mary Pickford and Efrem Zimbalist Jr.

She worked as the pro at the club while also giving lessons to anyone who wanted them, giving up the headaches of working with championship talents for the joys of teaching beginners. "I have 15 regulars and 450 on the waiting list" she crowed to the *San Francisco Examiner* in October 1964, giving many of the lessons on the private court of Diane Disney Miller, the daughter of Walt and Lillian Disney. In the main she taught girls and women. "I teach boys until they reach a certain age, and then I hand them over to men teachers," she said.

"I don't get impatient with anyone," she explained. "I was such a hacker when I started out myself that I know what it's like. . . . When one of them hits a ball by me, she goes home on top of the world. What they don't realize is that nothing could thrill me more than to see that my teaching has paid off."

Unfortunately, it wasn't easy: Her body betrayed Alice once again. She wrote Du Pont in bold cursive that she was getting "violent headaches" that her doctor attributed to "too much time spent teaching tennis in the sun. . . . A person gets to a certain age where this much physical activity is impossible." She had to quit the club, which didn't bother her too much, as it was about to go under. "We were losing money . . . because none of the homes have been sold and there were no members-only guests."

By this time, Will du Pont was once again alone. "Margaret will be in Reno as she wants a divorce," he wrote Alice in 1964. "She hasn't found the reason yet except I am doing the same things as usual—foxhunting, shooting and racing. Since she quit playing major tennis, she has taken up squash, table tennis and runs with a different group so our paths seem to have separated." In reality, Osborne had run off with someone else—her doubles partner, Margaret Varner Bloss, with whom she went to a Wimbledon doubles final. Now she and Bloss were beginning a new life together on a horse ranch in El Paso, Texas. Whether Du Pont's special relationship with Alice was any factor in the divorce isn't known.

The rich, mustachioed sportsman had at long last given up on knocking his head against the wall when it came to an actual marriage to Alice. He had asked her to wed him so often it became more of a running joke than an actual possibility. "He'd have to put 'have intercourse' on his schedule," Alice said, laughing at one point, mocking Du Pont's workaholic and closed-off nature.

Alice may not have wanted to marry Du Pont, but she still had no issue accepting his money. And after many years of paying Alice's bills and supplementing her income with the make-work job at Point Happy, Du Pont upped the ante. In November 1964 a trust he set up for her began paying her 6,000 dollars per year (a touch under 50,000 dollars today), "in the event I die." He set it up so it paid 500 dollars a month in order to avoid federal taxation, "though it might be subject to State Income Tax," he warned.

There was more to follow. Alice's job checking in on the Du Pont ranch near Palm Springs served to rekindle her warm feelings for the area, ones that first blossomed when she and Tennant lived and worked there in the 1930s. When Alice mentioned how she might just move to the Coachella Valley herself, Du Pont insisted on building a home on his ranch for her. It wouldn't quite be the marriage he envisioned all those years, but at least he would have Alice at hand, closer than ever before.

And Mary K. Browne would be there, too.

Alice's old friend, who had helped her so much when she was getting back into tennis after her illness, and had been her lieutenant on the physical fitness front during the war, came out to live with Alice at the Du Pont estate. Browne has remained an elusive target for me, in terms of her impact on Alice's life. She comes across as a yin to Eleanor Tennant's yang, another older woman who could steer Alice without the drama and Eleanor's gift for acerbity. It is apparent Alice treasured her wisdom and guidance, though she doesn't receive much treatment in either memoir or in any correspondence I could find, beyond what appears in the narrative.

Alice, her future apparently secure, was over the moon. "I don't think I have to tell you that each day I get more and more excited about the house at Point Happy," she wrote Will. "It's just a wonderful dream come true." As the house rose from the earth, she wrote again. "Just returned from the desert after spending most of the week there. What a wonderful experience this is, watching every detail fall into place. . . . I am the luckiest person alive."

The two tennis vets moved into their home on December 29, 1965. Then, just two days later, Will du Pont died of a brain tumor.

Alice was devastated, but that was nothing compared to the feelings of Will's daughter from his first marriage, Jean, who inherited Point Happy. Jean held a deep-seated grudge against Alice, whom she blamed for the breakup of her parents' marriage. While Will and Alice cared for each other very much, the Du Pont marriage was doomed for reasons beyond any home wrecking Alice had done. But Jean would not be swayed.

Even as the women were moving into Point Happy, and with Will on life support, Jean acted to rid herself of Miss Marble. Alice received a terse registered letter from the Du Pont heir and her attorney.

Due to the critical condition of Wm. Du Pont, Jr., who is in the hospital, we think that no changes should be made with respect to any of his property.

Consequently, this is to advise you that we cannot permit you or Mary K. Browne to occupy house #7 on the Point Happy property.

Alice and Brownie were out. Alice's lawyer recommended a lawsuit, but she didn't want to jeopardize the trust fund, and besides, she didn't have the strength, physical or mental, for legal maneuverings against a multimillionaire heiress. Instead, the two former tennis stars moved quietly to a new community nearby called Palm Desert Country Club.

There was a tennis and golf club at PDCC, but it was (and remains) a neighborhood with the recreational facility as its centerpiece. Alice and Brownie moved in in 1966, and Alice would remain there until her death a quarter century later. Alice was club champ every year until 1970. For a fun spell Alice and Brownie lived an idyllic lifestyle in the desert. "We competed ferociously on the golf course (we had the two lowest handicaps in the club), had pillow fights, and generally behaved like two happy children." Keep in mind that Browne was twenty-two years older than Alice, who was in her early fifties at the time.

But Mary, an accomplished amateur artist, chose her art over Alice and reliving her childhood. She moved to New Mexico to be closer to the painting community there, and in 1971 she passed away after suffering a stroke.

Mary was gone. Will was gone. Eleanor was on her last legs. Dan Marble, who had always been there to guide Alice, had also passed away in untimely fashion, dying while on vacation at age fifty-six in 1963. Alice was left bereft of the peers, teachers, and parental figures who had taken her by the hand, loved her, and led her throughout so much of her life.

She was in poor health, with false teeth and one lung, on a tight budget, and with only her cat, another Siamese, named Frisk, for companionship. The last two decades of Alice's life would be a trying test of her legendary ability to overcome all hurdles placed in front of her, and a testament to her skill at doing just that.

Chapter Thirty-Nine

....

DEFENDING YOUR LIFE

It was just another party, hosted by a fellow Palm Desert Country Club couple. Small talk, Sinatra on the hi-fi, fading light spilling in through the glass patio doors.

Over by the bar, mixing drinks with a smile, tucking tips into her apron, was the former Wimbledon and US National champion who lived down the block. Alice had always enjoyed putting together a cocktail. As her sixtieth birthday came and went, she more frequently enjoyed knocking them back, too. In both cases, money, or rather lack of it, was the reason why.

· · ·

Alice's can-do attitude and open, if at times sardonic, approach to life were vital traits, for she scraped through the 1970s by the skin of her teeth. She scrimped for every dime after Will du Pont died, even with the trust he enacted for her bringing in a monthly stipend. She drove a beat-up old Chevy, a far cry from the brand-new sporty numbers she drove in her heyday. She was a regular at desert tennis tournaments, sitting courtside as stars like Chris Evert raked in huge paydays. "I don't begrudge Chris a single cent," Alice told the press after Evert won the

1977 Colgate championships in Palm Springs, which took her over $1 million in career earnings. "But I do know what it is to have been born too soon." Alice frequently rued not playing in the modern era, though she claimed it was less for the money involved than for missing out on the chance to play on television (which amounted to pretty much the same thing).

Despite her financial straits she often taught tennis for free, noting that "$25 a half hour is steep. A lot of kids can't afford it." Her generosity wasn't always repaid. Once, one of her students threw a fit and whacked a couple of balls over the fence. Alice chewed him out. "Don't ever do that again!" she yelled. "And you march right out there and get those balls because they are mine and I paid for them." Somewhere, Eleanor Tennant smiled.

The holiday season had never been kind to Alice, and just after New Year's in 1975, bad juju struck her again. She awoke to find her cat, Frisk, clawing and biting her frantically. Slowly, she came to realize her house was on fire. She followed the terrified cat into the bathroom, where neighbors yanked Alice out of the window and into the garden (Frisk jumped out on her own). Fortunately, the fire was extinguished, but "I coughed for a month to get the smoke out of my lungs," Alice told *The Desert Sun*, not mentioning that she only had one. "I thought I was going to die."

Once again she was forced to bounce back from near bottom, physically. It was 1934–35 all over again, as she forced herself to walk, swim, and play tennis though it all left her gasping. But the old Marble spirit shone through, and soon she was once again coaching, singing in church, and sitting at the bar in the resort, sipping martinis with whoever came by. She had "the smirk back in my gravelly voice."

Her return to form allowed Alice to make plenty of appearances around the Palm Springs area, giving talks about gutting through adversity and the importance of wellness, even though she "smokes incessantly and isn't the least hesitant to acknowledge her liking for martinis and manhattans," according to a write-up in *The Desert Sun*.

One reporter caught her at age sixty-four, about to make a standard lecture before a local Retired Teachers Association. "I go to so many of these things—if I ate everything they put in front of me I'd be a blimp," she groaned. Indeed, she "pushed her lunch aside and whispered like a naughty child: 'I don't have to eat my carrots anymore if I don't want to!'" After all, she "spent too many years force-feeding herself carrots and turnips as part of her tournament training."

She got by on the trust fund, along with social security and an occasional column in *The Desert Sun*, which earned her "hair-dressing money." She also ran the local resort pool, for which she got a minuscule sum. "I made more money when I was 15," she complained to a local reporter. The same journalist caught a rare glimpse of an angry Alice, disturbed by a "difference of opinion" with another rec center employee. "Smoking furiously, Marble was tense. . . . 'It's just a difference of opinion, but in this case I know I'm right. When people give me ultimatums it makes me very angry.'"

As ever, she was surrounded by wealth, this time club members with "bouffant hairdos and pretty hats," but shared in little of their financial security. It wasn't much different from her days hanging at San Simeon and various Long Island estates while not actually having any money of her own.

She lived in an old tract section of the neighborhood, at 77300 Indiana Avenue, in a white house with gray trim, a rock garden in front and a small swimming pool in the back—a classic retiree's home in the desert. Her living room was lined with the hardware she had won, silver cups and gold plates and trophies of all kinds. A large oil portrait of her that was painted in England before Wimbledon and bought for her by Will du Pont hung in the living room as well. "I never looked that good on the best day I ever had," she remarked to *The Desert Sun*, gazing at her beautified image. There was a Ping-Pong table on the back patio, where she took on all comers, even after cataract surgery in her seventies. Next to it was a "signature wall," a large piece of poster board signed by every guest who came over, including the likes of James Michener and dozens of tennis stars. She would often ride a nearby exercise bike and "try to figure out the names on the wall."

In 1977 she was invited back to the All England Club for the celebration of the one hundredth Wimbledon. Unfortunately, the powers that be at the venerable institution weren't picking up the tab. Alice didn't have the money for the trip, as times were tight. "Miss Marble is not well off," reported the London *Daily Mail*. "Everything had gone to pot," she admitted. "The swimming pool, the air conditioner, the garbage disposal." So she started a Carter-era version of a GoFundMe, raising money from friends and relatives, including a donations party at nearby Indian Wells Country Club. She even took two dollars from a child at a local supermarket. She managed to make it across the ocean for the affair, where she posed for a photo with every living Wimbledon champion (Bobby Riggs was late and missed out), getting compliments on her handbag from the Duchess of Kent while attending all the balls and turning back the clock to 1939, when the tournament orbited around her. At least until the day one youngster asked for her autograph, only to query, "Are you anyone important?"

Alice didn't feel that way. She was alone, often in summer the lone resident of the neighborhood, most of whom fled the desert heat for the coast. Alice would water her neighbors' lawns at all hours, despairing at the brown patches. When she hung a nameplate on her pool director's office, people would knock and say, "There used to be an old tennis player named Alice Marble." She could only smile. There were few recognitions of her day in the sun. I tried to put myself in her shoes. "I once was Athlete of the Year—this is the thanks I get?"

When asked why she was alone, Alice fell back to her old standby, the Joe Crowley story. She maintained in public and to reporters that she was married to an "Army Air Corps Captain who died in action in the last two weeks of the Second World War," and that she "lost [my] baby in a car accident." In the same breath she would say, "If I had it to do over again I'd have a half a dozen kids. All my life I've adored kids and animals."

A feature on Alice in a local paper in 1978 described her in a way that may not have been fair or kind, and that she couldn't have liked. "Mouth set in a grim line, arms folded across her chest, she presented a far different image than the gregarious smartly-attired luncheon speaker of a few weeks before. From a distance she looked like a man. Broad-shouldered, wearing a leather jacket, slacks and dark glasses, she had short, thinning hair that caused an English hairdresser despair when he tried to style it for a number of Wimbledon balls last summer." Another profile around the same time described her as having a "short bob and weather-beaten complexion."

Her appearance understandably came second (and was in part due) to her physical trials. In 1981 she was diagnosed with colon cancer and required no fewer than three surgeries to remove the diseased tissue. She emerged from the hospital sporting a colostomy bag. Two more operations to resect her bowel followed, making it five times under the knife. For several months she was either in tremendous pain or a morphine-induced haze. But after a hard slog of recovery she was pronounced cancer-free. There seemed to be no insult to her constitution that Alice could not overcome.

Given all her travails, it was no wonder she had little appetite for small talk by then, a hard turn for such a gregarious person. One reporter attempting to interview Alice recounted his abrupt dismissal. "As her guest tries to extend their conversation in hopes of eliciting her views on the tennis scene of today, Marble candidly waves her hand in a polite gesture of farewell and, with a smile on her face and the twinkle still in her eyes, repeats softly, 'Bye . . . bye . . . bye.'"

· · ·

There isn't much going on at the Palm Desert Country Club these days. I visited on a glorious winter afternoon, one perfect for tennis, only to find the courts empty and the bar not much more crowded. Locating anyone who had known Alice from her time living here seemed unlikely. The woman behind the counter at the pro shop gave me a blank look at mention of her name. The manager of the property thought the name rang a bell but couldn't place it. Fortunately, she walked out to the bar and loudly asked the tiny assemblage if anyone knew the name Alice Marble.

"Sure, I do," responded the bluff man with the neat mustache tending bar.

His name was Rusty Brinder. Thirty-some years earlier, he had just started bar keeping in Palm Desert, and vividly recalled the grande dame (Alice was in her midseventies at the time) who every day "held court" at the club. "She wasn't playing tennis anymore," Brinder told me, "but was in the bar all the time. She was a real sweetheart, with a great sense of humor—not ever one to complain no matter what happened, very upbeat. You would never know she was a star athlete." Brinder remembers that Alice was "very popular," and "everyone knew who she was." This was despite all of her illnesses and setbacks.

"Alice could talk," Rita Mae Brown told me. "She basked in the glow of attention."

But if Alice ever talked about her role in WWII, it wasn't to Brinder. When I relate the story of Alice's espionage heroics, Brinder shrugs. "That's all new to me."

Chapter Forty

··

Sleeping with the Enemy

tried to read between the lines."

This is the first thing to jump out at me when I at last tear open the letter from Rita Mae Brown. In other words, even after she and Alice became good friends, there was no crumbling of Alice's vow of omertà. She told Brown the same story she told the rest of us.

However . . .

Rita Mae got to know Alice in a way few other people who are still alive did, and is perhaps better suited to provide some understanding of Alice and what she went through in her life than anyone. While Rita Mae only got to know Alice for a relatively short time near the end of Alice's life, in those years, the highly perceptive writer took measure of her friend and her incredible story and came to some fascinating conclusions.

"I felt Alice covered for many people who were in the war, on both sides," she writes about my questions concerning "Hans Steinmetz," the crucial figure in the alpine espionage story. "I don't think he was a Swiss banker. My hunch was he was an Austrian aristocrat, titled, financially astute. He may not have believed fervently in the National Socialist Party but he would benefit if he helped them take over Austria."

The Nazis annexed Austria in the Anschluss of March 1938, meaning it had already happened when Alice supposedly met "Hans" in Le Touquet, France, that summer. In other words, she wasn't sleeping with a neutral Swiss banker and tennis aficionado; she was sleeping with an actual Nazi (and tennis aficionado). That's a secret worth keeping, even close to a half century later. Brown adds, "Many of these people were still alive when I talked with her—on all sides of the war. She would protect them. That was her nature."

Certainly Alice was comfortable keeping secrets. It also makes sense that by 1945, an Austrian (or even German) financier with any sense of self-preservation would have long bailed out of there, with the Allies storming in from the west and the even more fearsome Red Army pillaging its way toward Germany from the east. Switzerland would be an easily reached and comparatively safe place from which to arrange a postwar future. It makes the scene Alice described at the Argentine embassy in Geneva (yes, there was one in 1945) more believable if she attended on the arm of an actual Nazi party member. The disgust she recalled at being surrounded by the Nazis would have been her honest reaction.

"I believe she accepted an OSS mission," Brown writes. "Many athletes and celebrities did as doors would have been open for them which would be closed to others. She may have started from Switzerland but I believe she covered more ground. Her fame somewhat protected her plus she could dazzle anyone."

In the time frame Alice gives, late spring 1945, there would be no travel to Austria or close to Germany unless she rode in a Sherman tank or a military airplane. There are a handful of narrow windows in her public record where it would be possible to have slipped across the ocean on a covert mission, but no confirming record—in the military, government, or press, or the memories of others—exists.

As mentioned earlier, the National Archives and Records Administration in College Park, Maryland, has no record of Alice working for the OSS, though NARA holds only an OSS personnel roster, not detailed files. Alice may indeed have been working with elements of army intelligence that were not under the auspices of the OSS. It may also be that Alice did work for the OSS, but it was "off books," or that the documents disappeared. "Unless those OSS files, the early ones, are found and made public we will never know," Brown writes. "Bill Donovan [the head of the OSS] was under no obligation to make [those files] public." If Alice was indeed seeking out a former lover who was not merely working with the Nazis but was actually the enemy, it is understandable those files will never see the light of day, if indeed there ever was anything written down officially.

"She was always ready for adventure," Rita Mae told me. "She loved this country. I have no doubt she was willing to take great risks, to die, if necessary. She was keenly aware that death would explode if Germany took over other countries. While not an ideologue . . . she knew there would be no negotiated peace until Hitler was removed from power, and hopefully national integrity re-established. At the time of her mission the reality and horror of the concentration camps were not known. Alice said that when that all came out she was devastated. . . . To her it was unimaginable yet there it was." The revelation of the true depths of the Holocaust would certainly be another reason to drive Alice to keep her dalliances with a Nazi buried deep.

What of the mission itself? "I saw the scars on Alice's back," Rita Mae writes in perhaps her most tantalizing sentence. "Were they made by her being shot during her escape? I don't know but they resembled the scars on my Uncle Ken's back, who invaded Okinawa with the Sixth Marine Division and was wounded [there]. . . . I don't know but Alice was only too happy to take her shirt off. I didn't ask."

Of course, Alice had plenty of scars from a lifetime of going under the knife. But Rita Mae's take has the ring of truth, a ribbon of sunlight piercing Alice's shadowy past.

Alas, "Alice never spoke to me of Joseph Crowley," although Rita Mae did write that Alice "did mention pregnancy, and I never pursued it."

Chapter Forty-One

....

It's a Wonderful Life

The 1980s saw a surge in interest in women's tennis after a fallow period, as Chris Evert and Martina Navratilova became the Athens and Sparta of the sport. Evert's blonde locks and sunshine smile evoked memories of Alice, racket in hand, posing for the newsreel camera. The press seldom failed to write about Evert without using some synonym of *pretty*, much as they had with Alice. As for Martina, her power-house serve-and-volley style was a direct descendant of Alice's game. The throughline was captured by longtime English tennis writer Laurie Pignon.

> In my old £12 Austin Seven, which needed a raw egg in the radiator every morning to stop it leaking, and sporting a green pork-pie hat and yellow pig-skin gloves, my first journalistic encounter with "greatness" was with Alice Marble in 1939. . . . It was she who revolutionized women's tennis. Miss Navratilova's game can be traced back to that brave and brilliant young lady. . . . So powerful was her serve and volley and so strong and successful her game that when the Americans returned to

Wimbledon after the war they all brought with them this new concept of tennis, with such remarkable effect that for the next ten years [only one] non-American reached the semi-finals.

The Evert-Navratilova rivalry boosted the prevalence of women's tennis in the culture at large, and with that came a fond remembrance of the champions of the pre-Open era. Suddenly, Alice was in again. In February 1976 a Palm Desert developer put together Deep Canyon Tennis Club, and the roads inside were named for various tennis stars, including Don Budge, Arthur Ashe, and one Alice Marble, located about seven miles from her own residence across town. It was the first glimmer of a Marble Renaissance, though she couldn't afford to move into one of the new 50,000-dollar homes on Alice Marble Lane.

Soon she was in demand once more, asked to appear on ABC's *Greatest Sports Legends* television show, or to comment from the booth when the tennis tour stopped in the Palm Springs area. She was the guest of honor at tournaments held at nearby Indian Wells, where she once informed the great German player Boris Becker that she held six Wimbledon titles. "He literally jumped as if he was hit by a bolt of electricity," said tournament official Loch Jones. "Don't worry, you're still young," Alice teased. Martina Navratilova herself insisted on Alice sitting in a special courtside box to watch her play at Indian Wells. Alice held a joint birthday bash with her old contemporary Ellsworth Vines, where *Tennis in Rhythm* was screened at a party "that had everything but a line judge." There she was, big as life, in her former superstar form once again. Even small good luck came her way—at one point she was asked to draw raffle prizes for a huge benefit in her honor and walked away with free tennis lessons from the club pro.

Asked to speak at another major party for her at Indian Wells, one that brought her sister, Hazel, down from San Francisco to attend, Alice said, "I've had a few accolades in my life. I've had 45 different honorary memberships. But what I love to hear is, 'Alice, you played great today, you're getting better.'"

That seldom happened anymore, of course, though in the mid-1980s

"Alice was looking quite feeble but moved about the room with some of her old grace," in the words of one reporter. There were other plaudits. In April 1987, the Palm Desert club courts and recreation hall were named in her honor—and Althea Gibson showed up to dedicate them. Former president Gerald Ford sent a letter of congratulations, as did Alice's former students Billie Jean King and Sally Ride. Then the mayor of Palm Desert declared April 11, 1987, as "Alice Marble Day," issuing an official proclamation as such:

> Whereas Alice Marble, a 30-year resident of Palm Desert, has become renowned far beyond the confines of this community; and
> Whereas Ms. Marble is a three-time Wimbledon champ and a three-time U.S. Open champion [*sic*] and was the first to hold three titles of each in the same year; and
> Whereas she was selected Woman Athlete of the Year in 1939 and in 1940 and was also instrumental in introducing the first black woman, Althea Gibson, to tennis; and
> Whereas Ms. Marble is well known for efforts on behalf of not only women's rights but human rights throughout the world.
> NOW THEREFORE I, Richard S. Kelly, Mayor of the city of Palm Desert, California, do hereby declare that Saturday, April 11, 1987, as
> ALICE MARBLE DAY
> in the city of Palm Desert, and I hereby urge all residents of our community to honor and pay tribute to a woman who has given so much of herself for the betterment of her fellow human beings.

Then, a reminder that for Alice, bodily harm usually accompanied her successes. Two days after Alice Marble Day, the honoree was at the club during a farewell party for Gibson, seated on the terrace chatting with a man next to her. When he rose from his chair, he offered his hand to Alice and began to help her up—but then he slipped on the marble floor. He landed with his full weight on the human Marble rather than the floor marble and in the process fractured a pair of her ribs, along with bones in her right arm and leg (in the filmed Prickly Pears interview with Gebhart, she visibly lets her bad arm hang limply).

As always, Marble shrugged off this latest affront to her corporeal being. "Old Champy bounced back fairly well," she wrote to Brown. Shortly after she regained full adhesion in all her bones, a neighborhood kid lost control of his skateboard and it crashed into Alice's foot, breaking it and requiring another period of frustrating inactivity. When time came to exercise again, she bought a pedometer and religiously marched three miles every day.

None of the broken appendages prevented Alice from one last trip to Wimbledon. She was invited back for the 1988 championships by the chairman, R. E. H. "Buzzer" Hadingham. "We should very much like to recognise your extraordinary achievements in the late-1930s at our Championships, by inviting you to attend this year's Championships as a special guest." The package included a reception given by the Duke and Duchess of Kent, a visit to the royal box, and an invite to the Champions' Dinner at the Savoy hotel after the men's final. "I guess he figured I might not last until 1989, which will be my 50th anniversary [of her singles title]," she wrote to Brown. This time around, the All England Club picked up Alice's airfare and put her up at the Rembrandt hotel for the fortnight.

Her fortunes had indeed changed since her difficulties of the previous decade. Nowhere was this more true than in her personal relationships. A pair of newcomers had entered Alice's life—typically, both genders were represented. In 1985 on a Palm Springs golf course, Alice met an African-American woman named Gloria Toote. Though Alice once described her in a letter to Brown as being "as liberal as you or I," Toote was a conservative Republican who had spent time working in four GOP administrations, including a stint as assistant secretary of the

Department of Housing and Urban Development under Richard Nixon and a recently ended advisory role to Ronald Reagan (Alice, too, was a political conservative, though like Toote she was far more liberal on social subjects).

"We are most attracted to one another," Alice wrote Brown about Toote. "She is a beautiful black woman, bright like you."

Her new male friend, W. Robert Prestie, known as "Bob," was an oddball character, a native of Saskatchewan who studied to be a Trappist monk before leaving the order for the allure of film, working as a producer in London for many years. He also toured the country speechifying, in much the manner of Alice decades earlier, giving a talk entitled "The Betterment of Mankind." There was another distant connection to Alice; in the 1970s Prestie worked for Rosalie Hearst, the seventh wife of George Hearst, the son of Alice's old friend William Randolph Hearst. Working out of Palm Springs, Prestie met a highly successful author of romance novels named Taylor Caldwell and became her fourth husband in 1978, despite being seventeen years younger than the writer.

Prestie and Alice met in the social whirl of Palm Desert in the mid-1980s. Prestie was still married to Caldwell, who had suffered a stroke shortly after signing a new book contract worth nearly $4 million. There were lawsuits and family drama pertaining to the money and the care of Caldwell, who was still alive when Alice came along and began spending large amounts of time with her husband (Caldwell died in September 1985).

"Bob is a very spiritual man, thoughtful and devoted," Alice wrote Brown, who had inquired about her budding "romance." "He is the perfect escort," she added, quite happy to have someone "carry her bag" while traveling.

"It is one of the sweetest experiences I've had. It's a touching, loving one with no sex."

Alice, though in her early seventies, was like a schoolgirl with her two crushes. "There was much of a stir," she wrote to Brown. "Between Gloria and Bob, both warm and hand holding, there were plenty of people staring [at me] the last two days. Dear God, it's good to feel alive again."

Toote was an easterner, so any fireworks she had with Alice were eventually dampened by distance. Alice and Prestie did spend Thanksgiving 1987 with Toote and her family in New York, however. The seating arrangements presumably found Alice tucked between Gloria and Bob.

Chapter Forty-Two

....

THE ALICE MARBLE STORY

On January 22, 1986, there was a meeting at the swank L'Ermitage Hotel in Beverly Hills to discuss a new film project. Gathering in the hotel were Alice; her television producer pal Berl Rotfeld, who was paying Alice for her rights to the story; executives from ABC TV and the film production arm of corporate giant Procter & Gamble; and a petite, raven-haired woman brought in to write the screenplay of Alice's life—Rita Mae Brown. "ABC hired me to write a movie-of-the-week concerning Alice," she wrote to me. "Everything I had written for TV won the night's ratings and I had two Emmy nominations." Rita Mae was promised 50,000 dollars plus bonuses and a cut of the profits for her work. P&G was planning on the film, at the moment titled simply *Alice Marble*, to be the first in a series called *Great American Women*, this placing Alice above the likes of the "Wonder Women" she had profiled in the comic books more than forty years earlier. The group spent several hours talking about the details of bringing her story to television and the next day assembled again at her house in Palm Desert.

In that forty-eight-hour span, Alice fell hard for Rita Mae.

She wasn't the first. The acclaimed writer had a celebrated romance with Fannie Flagg, author of *Fried Green Tomatoes at the Whistle Stop Cafe* (she also wrote the movie adaption, simply called *Fried Green Tomatoes*), and then a more notable affair with Martina Navratilova, which began in 1979 and ran for three turbulent years.

The couple lived together on the farm in Virginia, all while denying they were a couple. "I find it offensive and ridiculous that anybody should think that I am gay," Navratilova told a London paper while competing at Wimbledon in 1980, even as she was staying with Brown in a nearby home. Eventually the push-pull between Martina's rapidly advancing tennis career and the opportunities she felt she was missing because of her sexuality drove a wedge between them.

The two had titanic arguments, including the finale of their operatic relationship. In an interview she gave to Adrianne Blue, who wrote a biography of Navratilova, Rita Mae said that Martina stormed from the farmhouse and peeled out in her sports car, spewing gravel as she raced away from her life with Brown. The writer, not content to let the tennis star have the last "word," grabbed her pistol and heaved it at the car. It fell short, but fired upon hitting the ground, the bullet smashing out the back window. Miraculously, Navratilova was unhurt, but Brown said the incident "scared the living daylights out of me."

I asked Brown about that, of course, especially given its overtones of the scene in Alice's story when she peels away from the Swiss chateau in a sports car and soon after gets shot. "I had no intention of killing her," she wrote to me, "only scaring the bejesus out of her, in which I richly succeeded." Then, "You are under no moral imperative to report the truth. I am much more fascinating if people believe otherwise."

Brown was not only in touch with her true self; she was vivacious and possessed an acute intelligence. Little wonder that Alice fell hard for her almost immediately, writing of Brown after she departed, "*Tengo ganas por ella* . . . translated—I have the hots for her." A few weeks later she wrote Brown at her home in Virginia. "Since January 23rd I have been in the clouds, 'going to Heaven' daily. . . . Dear God, it's good to feel alive again, thanks to a certain brilliant writer. . . . Now I have to come down from the clouds and do my laundry."

Brown was over thirty years younger than Alice and lived on the opposite side of the country—a physical affair was not practical. But the two became pen pals, Alice sometimes addressing Brown as "Molly," the name of the protagonist in *Rubyfruit Jungle*, and signing off as "Champy" or "The Ol' Champion (with young thoughts)."

"You changed my life—from the neck up and the waist down!" Alice wrote to Brown about eighteen months before her death. A little ruefully, she added, "Sexually I am fine—all by my little self." A few months later she wrote again. "I read your books, your letters and dream. It's a very special bond I feel, warm and spiritual. Thanks for assuring me that you 'Felt something' or my ego would have been wounded."

In the meantime, Rita Mae got to work on the screenplay, since retitled *The Alice Marble Story*, one that told of a brave, if somewhat naive former tennis champion turned female spy working to get information from her former lover in Switzerland near the end of the Second World War, all in two hours—ninety minutes, after the commercials.

. . .

The beginnings of *The Alice Marble Story* came when Alice was contacted by Berl Rotfeld, a longtime producer best known for his show *Greatest Sports Legends*. Alice's appearance on the program led to Rotfeld becoming interested in exploring her story in more depth on screen, especially when Alice told him her war story. Alice's life rights were locked up early, and the money it brought in was most welcome, though Rita Mae wondered if she was being shortchanged. "Do you know . . . what she's getting for this?" she asked of the production executives with whom she was working. "I wonder if Berl/Burl is cutting her a fair deal. I wish somebody would buy the old girl a new car. I don't think she's terribly bright about money and even though Willy [du Pont] invested money for her I doubt, seriously, if she gets more than $10-15,000 off of it (per annum). It's none of my business but she has become quite dear to me."

Brown told me that she didn't make up anything for the screenplay. "License is part of TV but I did my best not to invent anything," she said. "I worked with what [Alice] told me." But from the first, she had concerns about the veracity of the story, as did the development executives. "My worry," she wrote to them in March 1986, "same as yours, is that Alice is not quite accurate. I'll go over to Palm Springs Monday night so I can get up at the crack of dawn. It's the best way to get clarity from her. . . . You can't get much from her after lunch. . . . If Alice is lying, sorry to be blunt, she's not going to cough up anything that can be cross-checked. She may be garrulous and fond of her spirits but she isn't dumb. I like her very much . . ."

Alice was around Hollywood stars for most of her life, but she had never seen the difficulty of launching films off the ground, an insanely arduous and time-consuming process even for the best of material, like *Gone with the Wind*. "I'm happy that I don't have to make my living in the TV field—everything is hurry up and wait," she complained to Brown in a letter in the summer of 1986. According to an interview Alice gave *The Desert Sun* in 1986, "There's a script, but it's at a standstill because they can't find the leading lady. They thought they had Linda Evans, but she's tied up in a mini series. Then they thought they had Sybil Shepard [*sic*], but she turned down an offer of $450,000." (According to Alice's letter to Brown on May 2, 1989, Shepherd had asked for $650,000, and "P&G wanted to pay $450,000," which she rejected. "Guess movie and television stars have to make it when they can," Alice wrote, a truth that applied to tennis stars once upon a time as well.) In the 1986 Prickly Pears interview, Alice said her preference to play her would be "Cheryl Ladd, because I watch *Charlie's Angels* in the afternoons and she's good." Alice then laughingly offered the part to her interviewer, Courtney Gebhart.

"They've already soaked $200,000 into the picture and we need a name star," she told the *Sun*. But there were bigger problems with ABC. The network's legal department raised a few red flags about the potential accuracy of Alice's account. Alice wrote Brown that the "meeting with the Dept. of Broadcast Standards and Practice went off well. There were no drastic changes, just clarifications." But a letter sent to Rita Mae Brown by one ABC executive, Philippe Perebinossoff, outlined five full pages of questions about material the network was squeamish about airing, asking for the sort of independent confirmation of events I have likewise struggled to find.

Examples include some bits of dialogue and narrative that Rita Mae threw in to add "drama" to the "docudrama":

Page 6 & throughout: Please confirm scripted presentation of Alice's coach, Teach, as the individual who broke up Alice and "Hans Steinmetz" and who tried to discourage Alice's romance with Joe Crowley. Was she a "Little Hitler" as she is called by Mary Hardwick in the script (page 15)?

Pages 56–60: Please confirm that the scripted training Alice received for her mission is accurately portrayed, including being taught how to bite a man's throat out (Page 60). Did Brownie find Alice's tools, as scripted?

Page 84: Is Hilde Sperling's advice to leave "Hans" accurate? Is Hilda's scripted attitude about Nazis correct? What is the basis for the rumors and stories about Nazi atrocities that Hilda refers to?

Pages 104–111: Please have Alice confirm all scripted details of her escape from the chateau, of the car chase, of "Al's" ["Jones's"] shooting Alice in the back, of a driver demanding the film and of her story of her stay in the hospital room. Did "Linden" talk about "Al" as a double agent and tell her he had a man watching the estate, that the Russians and Nazis were getting closer, that he had doubts about "Al" and that the film was exposed, and Al killed, etc. Did Alice recall much of the photographed records?

Apparently, Rita Mae and ABC were as stymied as I became, even while Alice was still alive. Given time to think about it, ABC decided it wasn't worth the risk. The network had higher standards, apparently, than the cable outlet USA Network, which aired *My Little Assassin*—the story of Marita Lorenz, whose wild, if dubious, tales of having a son by Fidel Castro and later attempting to assassinate El Jefe resemble Alice's—in 1999.

"ABC couldn't substantiate Alice's stories," Brown explains. "The legal department was nervous. They always are." The moment passed, and all concerned moved on.

But as I totally understand, the urge to believe was strong. Years later, husband-and-wife producers Harry and Renee Longstreet tried to make *The Alice Marble Story* into a feature film, grabbing the script and snagging Farrah Fawcett to play Alice. But by then the rights to Alice's story had expired. Agents from the Authors and Artists Group were assigned to find an heir who would sign over Alice's life rights, but they failed to do so. That's according to a suit filed by the Longstreets in the Los Angeles Superior Court in the year 2000. The suit alleged fraud and breach of contract on the part of the agency and sought more than 150,000 dollars in damages to recoup costs the Longstreets laid out in pre-producing the project. The suit was settled out of court, but it was Alice's legacy that paid the cost, as any film project was thereafter shelved.

Alice was undaunted by it all. "If it never happens," she wrote Brown, referring to the making of the film about her life, "I have had a great time."

·   ·   ·

During the period after Alice had her bones broken by the falling gentleman at the club, she was mostly idle at home. Never one to relax, and seeing the handwriting on the wall in terms of the ABC movie, she turned her restlessness into a new project. As early as 1983, she had mentioned the idea of writing another memoir, this time stuffed with anecdotes of her memorable life. "I'm about 70 percent sure I'll be doing it," she told *The Desert Sun*. Now she had the time and opportunity to actually make it happen, despite her injuries. "I cleaned every cupboard, drawers, files and found so much material for a book," she wrote Rita Mae Brown on October 7, 1987. She still claimed that "mentally, I'm pretty much the way I've always been. I'm one of those fortunate people who has a marvelous memory, a photographic memory," as she told the *Sun*. Writing was still the key to triggering that memory, which was why her home began to fill with small white and pink notepads scattered about. She was constantly jotting notes on them so she would be able to recall them for her memoir.

"Once I write something down," Alice told a reporter, "I remember it." To prove her point, Alice "tears the top sheet from a pad and, handing it to her guest, recites from memory, 'Peg Carroll, Peg Innes, and Jo Roshan,' names she earlier had jotted down."

It was an impressive parlor trick, but for the actual doing, Alice would need a professional writer to organize the multiple tendrils of her story. "My love, what would you suggest?" she wrote Brown. "I would love to have a writer like George Vescey [sic] of the N.Y. Times or Frank Deford of Sports Illustrated." Instead, Brown put her together with a travel and horse writer named Dale Leatherman, a friend of Brown's from her own work in raising horses. Leatherman, in Brown's words a "solid non-fiction writer," took on the task of getting Alice's extraordinary life on paper. "You've got glamor, glitter and the gutter," Rita Mae wrote Dale about Alice's story. "Can't lose."

The process often involved Alice talking into a tape recorder, speaking aloud her rambling free-form memories, then sending the recordings across the country to Leatherman, who lived in West Virginia. The process irked Alice. "I felt so self-conscious just talking into the damn little machine," she wrote Brown. But "Dale . . . says they are very helpful." The ghostwriter, operating under the working title *Angels Keep*, worked with the same material Alice had provided Brown and ABC, and did them one better: Leatherman prevailed upon Alice to write of her affair with Margarita Madrigal, what Alice called in the same letter to Brown "my first and only romance with a woman."

For her part, while Leatherman admits to a myriad of factual mistakes ("We were working in an age before Google, after all," she told me), in the finished product that would come to be titled *Courting Danger*, she, like Rita Mae Brown before her, lets her work stand as written. "Alice signed off on all of it," Leatherman says.

Courting Danger was released in June 1991 to varied reviews. "Marble reports on [her] misfortunes with a remarkable lack of self-pity, displaying the courage, candor and wit that made her a winner," wrote *The New York Times Book Review*. "Marble . . . also shows a refreshing respect and empathy for her competitors that today's contestants would do well to note." *Publishers Weekly* called it a "fast-moving, glamorous tale." Others such as *People* and *Kirkus Reviews* were struck by the "implausible" and "credibility-defying" nature of the book. The book briefly did resuscitate Hollywood interest in Alice—it was *Courting Danger* that the Longstreets bought the rights to and wanted to put on screen. But as before, the project was swallowed up by the forever capricious Hollywood development process. Yet another attempt to mount Alice's story for the screen using *Courting Danger* as a source was begun in 2017, again with no discernible results.

The pattern captures the struggles I felt in chasing Alice's story around the globe and through the mists of time. The big picture is intoxicating; the devil resides in the details. The movies aren't much for nuance and enigma and shades of gray, which are what Alice and her story are all about and what made her so fascinating to discover.

Chapter Forty-Three

Final Destination

The view from the summit of Russian Hill is so glorious that concentrating on the tennis ball steaming toward my midsection is extremely difficult. There is the city twinkling below and the Golden Gate in the distance, making it all I can manage to get my racket on the ball and float back a return. The ball hovers for an instant against the thin, blue line where San Francisco sky meets San Francisco Bay.

Then it disappears as my opponent blasts the sitter into the far corner for an easy winner.

The Alice Marble Tennis Courts sit in a part of San Francisco that is eye-catching even by the high standards of that knockout of a city. The courts are just a block away from a tourist landmark, the fabled steep, vertical snake of Lombard Street (which is not named for Carole Lombard but is still a wild coincidence). I push past the line of people snapping Instagram-ready shots on their phones and work my way up a clandestine set of stairs on a block closed to traffic between Leavenworth and Hyde Streets. Suddenly, the half-hidden jewel of this park in the sky appears. Partially obscured by shrubbery, the words ALICE MARBLE TENNIS COURTS are stenciled into the stone that sits just past the last step before reaching this Xanadu. Otherwise, there is no mention of the eponymous star. It's a fitting blend of public bravado and guarded intimacy that perfectly captures the courts' namesake.

It is free to play on the four courts here, two designated for singles, two for doubles, appropriate given Alice's excellence in both disciplines. There is a practice wall and plenty of benches that provide exquisite views. On the day I visit, the adjacent basketball court is getting more use than the tennis courts—that's likely true on most days. I ask a few of the players if they know who Alice Marble was.

They do not.

. . .

Alice never saw the effects of her inspiring story on a new generation of fans. Her last days were not good ones. She had been dealing with pernicious anemia on top of all her other medical tribulations and then developed liver cancer late in 1990, her second bout with the dread disease. This time, she spiraled quickly, her overtaxed constitution not up for this last great challenge. Dale Leatherman talked to her on Thursday, December 6, and told *The Desert Sun*, "I could barely hear her, I had to do most of the talking. She had gotten very weak." The following day, Pearl Harbor Day, December 7, Alice was admitted to Desert Regional Medical Center in Palm Springs. She died less than a week later, at 1:35 A.M. on December 13, 1990. She was seventy-seven.

Tribute poured in from across the tennis world.

"She was my idol," said Althea Gibson.

"A pioneer," said Martina Navratilova.

"The picture of unrestrained athleticism," said Billie Jean King.

Alice's will, made out in 1975 and apparently unchanged, left her estate to her sister, Hazel, her lone surviving family member, less ten percent that she gave the United Church of the Desert in Palm Desert. After probate fees and expenses, Hazel received a little over $100,000. Alice's house was sold for $84,800, her ragged 1975 Mercury Coupe for $600. Hazel gave some mementos to the Tennis Hall of Fame, and sold off the rest. It should be noted that in Alice's will, she makes a legal declaration that "I am the widow of Joseph Norman Crowley."

There was no public memorial service, where the greats former and current could gather and tell stories of Alice. Instead, she was quietly cremated in Palm Springs. It is nice to think, however, that somewhere in a parallel universe a group got together, one including tennis stars, Hollywood glitterati, and anyone whose life she touched, from the rich and powerful to the anonymous kids to whom she taught the game, from people who bought and wore the clothes she designed to African-Americans who took up tennis because Althea Gibson got to play in the US Nationals, and of course Eleanor Tennant, busy preening and smoking and taking credit for what Alice achieved. This assemblage would surely have sat and laughed ("Wherever Alice is there's laughter," thinks Rita Mae Brown) and sipped drinks that Alice would have enjoyed mixing herself and remembered everything good that Alice brought to her world.

Her obituary in *The New York Times* mentioned her forthcoming memoir, and the espionage mission to Switzerland, the marriage to Joe Crowley, and the gunshot to her back, though only at the very end of the piece, as the book had yet to be released. It was as though the paper of record was tiptoeing up to the idea that Alice had concocted a helluva story for her final public act but out of respect for the departed wasn't going to take a stand on its veracity. Better to leave the mystery intact.

But the obit, and others in multiple publications across the country, did pay proper homage to Alice's great and groundbreaking tennis, her unique persona that captivated so many fans, including multitudes of stars from the golden age of Hollywood, her unusual successes in fashion, singing, publishing, lecturing, fundraising, and racial progress. Those feats earned Alice the courts in her name and enshrinement in the Tennis Hall of Fame and—who knows?—perhaps one day a statue at Flushing Meadows, the epicenter of tennis in the US. Her old Forest Hills stomping grounds now hosts concerts instead of tennis; if only the US Open, which supplanted the nationals, could find a fuller way to memorialize Alice and her sensational strokes that changed women's tennis.

While testimony to her life and importance is wanting at the courts that bear her name, more of her legacy is recognized at the courts where Alice got her start in the sport that changed her life. A portrait of her hangs in the clubhouse at Golden Gate Park, a black-and-white photo of her serving there during her prime. There is also a replica of her bust that hangs in the Bay Area Sports Hall of Fame, where Alice was inducted in 1985. In Palm Desert, the rec center at the development where she lived for so many years has been renamed in her honor, with framed articles and mentions of her accomplishments dotting the walls.

Yet all of it feels inadequate for such a unique and special existence. As Rita Mae Brown put it, "You only live once, and that woman lived." The fact that her career on the court has been mostly forgotten is the nature of sport; there is always another player, another event, to crowd out the achievements of yesteryear. The debate about some of her stories, and the ultimate sources and truths that they came from, likely never will be fully resolved. But the fullness of her time on the planet, whether or not you count those disputed days in Switzerland in the service of the war effort, or the ultimate choices and intimate experiences she had in private, should be better remembered—celebrated, even.

As I learned more about the questions Alice faced when she was alive, the beliefs and insinuations that inspired them, and the conflicting threads of the Alice Marble narrative as told by others and even by her, the answers came to matter less to me than other things that had been buried and nearly lost to time—especially Alice herself and the life she experienced in the world she knew. The internet ensures we all can look up her stats, or appreciate her serve, or read about her bygone matches. But the feeling I will take away from this experience was not frustration at being unable to "solve" her eternal mystery but appreciation of the good fortune I had to immerse myself in her life away from the court, to more fully understand the world of this great champion, woman, human being.

What would Alice herself have thought of all of this? Taking the court and competing at the highest level was its own reward, in her view. "The sheer joy of having played the game comes to matter more than the victories, the records, the memories," she once wrote.

So to Alice, "Angels keep." It was the phrase given to her by Jessie Marble, her mother, who used that instead of "Goodbye." Alice always bade farewell to friends and lovers with the words.

Brown, to whom Alice gifted a silver goblet inscribed with the words "Angels Keep," mentioned to me that, late in Alice's life, the two former players got out on the court to hit some balls once more.

"She had had cancer, and was in her seventies," Rita Mae said. "And the groundstrokes were still magic."

ACKNOWLEDGMENTS

The writing of this book was a long, strange journey not only into the mysteries of the past but into the enigmatic interior of Alice Marble. To find the way to my destination I required numerous guides, all of whom helped point me in the right direction and prevented me from wandering off the correct path and into the wilderness.

In particular, Anne Causey of the Albert and Shirley Small Special Collections Library at the University of Virginia, Lucas Clawson of the Hagley Museum and Library in Wilmington, Delaware, and David Hardin at the National Archives at St. Louis were particularly patient with my repeated requests. Meredith Richards, the librarian at the International Tennis Hall of Fame, was also most accommodating.

Charles Haddix and Andrew Hansborough of the Marr Sound Archive at University of Missouri–Kansas City led me through a combination audio wonderland/time machine. Jill Urquhart not only provided material for me from the Hearst San Simeon State Historical Monument but answered tons of questions as well. Jeannie Kays of the Palm Springs Library went out of her way to assist. I'd also like to thank Michelle Drobik of the Ohio State University Library and Thomas Cheeseman in the Ohio State Registrar's office, Eddie Luce at Ohio University, Susan Forbes of the Kansas Historical Society, Sarah Navins of the Franklin D. Roosevelt Presidential Library and Museum, Jennifer Barth of the Wisconsin Historical Society, Neil Hodge of the UCLA Charles Young Library Special Collections Desk, Katherine Eto-Hokin at the San Francisco Public Library, Squirrel Walsh of the Princeton University Library Department of Rare Books and Special Collection, and Dave Kibbey, realtor for the Deep Canyon Country Club.

I'd also like to thank the staffs at the Los Angeles Public Library; San Francisco City Hall; the LGBT Resource Center at the University of Southern California; the Bancroft Library at the University of California, Berkeley; the Plumas County Recorder's Office; the Beverly Hills Hotel; the Superior Court of California, County of Riverside; the National Archives and Records Administration in College Park, Maryland; and the Golden Gate Park Tennis Courts.

Ashley Brown, assistant professor in the Department of History and Department of Afro-American Studies at the University of Wisconsin–Madison, allowed me to use her publication *Swinging for the State Department,* for which I am grateful.

Rusty Brinder was a key witness to Alice's final years at the Palm Desert Country Club, and PDCC employees Dianna Todd and Patricia Moeller were also helpful.

Rita Mae Brown, while ever difficult to get hold of, was crucial in helping me understand the nuances of Alice's interior life. Thanks so very much for your invaluable help and unique spirit.

My trusty researcher across the pond, Dr. Kevin Jones, shrugged off any number of blows to his health to once again churn through the stacks for me in England. My thanks, and be well.

My good friend Liz Stubbs not only read the manuscript and gave much-appreciated advice (not to mention shot the author photo that appears on the flap), but her early guidance on the way into the story was pivotal in the final outcome. Your eye for structure is as sharp as your eye for composition, Lizzie. Many thanks for your input. Thanks as well to Rob Spears and Beth Buyert, Scott and Kirsten Nathanson, Matthew Shevin, Ted Swimmer, David Kraft, Robert Beck, and Ben Wolf for the support.

My trusty editor, John Parsley, not only brought me into his new flock but was, as he has been for three previous books, an all-star caliber shepherd. I daresay I tested his immense skill on this one more than the first three combined. Even as I twisted this way and that, he pushed and prodded and rolled with the ever-changing manuscript to help me see how the finished product should appear. Many thanks, my friend, and to Christine Ball, Cassidy Sachs, Yuki Hirose, and Emily Canders at Dutton as well.

My faithful agent and good friend Farley Chase of the Chase Literary Agency was there every step of the way, helping to wrangle this project from mere concept to finished product. Thanks as always for the even keel.

Most of all, thanks to the whole family, especially my kids, Phoebe and Marty, who rolled easily with the disruptions the writing of this book caused them. My love for you both is boundless.

The nature of Alice Marble's story is such that it would almost be easier to provide a list of source materials and archives that proved to contain no useful information. As noted in the narrative, spelunking through the huge archives at the National Personnel Records Center in St. Louis and the National Archives and Records Administration in College Park, Maryland, was a fruitless gesture. Running down information about "Joseph Crowley" at Ohio State and various institutions in Kansas came up negative. There were no records to be found at any of the New York City or State bureaucracies regarding their marriage, or Alice's car accident that resulted in her supposed miscarriage. Multiple Freedom of Information Act requests with the FBI to find any documentation of Alice's work with them, or her background check, also came up empty. Inquiries into espionage work in Switzerland, information about Swiss bankers involved with the Nazis, or archival material from trips to France in 1938 likewise were nonstarters.

Needless to say, this was a frustrating series of events.

The primary sources for much of Alice's story and inner thoughts are her two memoirs, *Courting Danger* from 1991 and *The Road to Wimbledon* from 1946. As we have seen in the narrative, these books aren't always the most reliable, so they have been augmented by a metric ton of independent research, mostly from contemporary material. That includes correspondence, archival material, and of course newspapers and periodicals, often the primary method for establishing a timeline of Alice's movements and doings that proves a corrective for what appears in her books.

There were archival sources that did prove useful, ones that made traveling the country in search of Alice's story more rewarding. The Papers of Rita Mae Brown collection at the University of Virginia in Charlottesville; the Hagley Museum in Wilmington, Delaware; the Franklin D. Roosevelt Presidential Library in Hyde Park, New York; and the Wisconsin Historical Society all contained invaluable correspondence between Alice and Brown, Will du Pont, Eleanor Roosevelt, and H. V. Kaltenborn, respectively. At the Marr Sound Archives at the University of Missouri–Kansas City were rare recordings of Alice's broadcast voice. Princeton University held material pertaining to her first memoir, published by Scribner's, whose archives were donated to the school.

In California, I retraced Alice's footsteps from the Sierra Nevada mountains to San Francisco to Los Angeles to Palm Springs. In Plumas County, the Clerk-Recorder Department held important records regarding Alice's early life, as well as those of her parents and grandparents. My time by the bay was spent visiting Alice's girlhood home on Twelfth Avenue, hauling my body up the steep hills and rappelling back down to the Golden Gate Park courts where she got her start. I also visited her namesake courts in the Russian Hill neighborhood and dove deep for records of the family at city hall and the San Francisco Public Library.

To the south, the Los Angeles Public Library held many answers to Alice's (and Eleanor Tennant's) living arrangements, and the Special Collections desk at UCLA provided tidbits on Alice's broadcast appearances. The ONE National Gay & Lesbian Archives at the University of Southern California held a rare copy of Nancy Spain's biography of Eleanor Tennant. The Beverly Hills Hotel remains much as it was in Eleanor's day, although the surrounding area is more than a bit different, and the staff there was quite helpful in fleshing out the hotel's history. Due east, the Palm Springs Public Library and the Palm Springs Historical Society were enormous aids in deciphering Alice's years in the Coachella Valley. Visiting the Palm Desert Country Club, including the club and the rec center named for her, gave a great sense for Alice's quarter century of living there.

Other overviews of Alice's life come from the International Tennis

Hall of Fame, her entries in the *Encyclopædia Britannica*, *Who's Who of 1939*, *Current Biography 1940*, and encyclopedia.com, and obituaries that ran in *The New York Times*, *Los Angeles Times*, London *Daily Telegraph*, Palm Springs *Desert Sun*, and the Associated Press. Also helpful were Charlotte Himber's *Famous in Their Twenties* and Trent Frayne's *Famous Women Tennis Players*. The collection of works in *The Fireside Book of Tennis* was greatly helpful in contextualizing tennis of various eras, along with specific information.

Most, if not all, of the writings about Alice since 1991 have included information about her WWII activity, all of which accept her story at face value and include little to no investigation of the details. Very little of these thus proved useful.

However, Alice's published works, which encompassed all manner of subjects well beyond tennis, were far more illuminating. They appeared in *The New York Times Magazine*, *Los Angeles Times*, London *Sunday Chronicle*, *Sports Illustrated*, *American Lawn Tennis*, *Guideposts*, *World Tennis*, and in newspapers in business with the Newspaper Enterprise Association, among others.

There are handfuls of videos of Alice playing tennis and meeting the press on the internet, mostly at youtube.com. These are important to get a sense of her athleticism and fluidity of movement on the court, as well as her fashion taste. They are short clips, alas, but they do bring the past to life in a way the written word cannot. And of course, the documentary/interview conducted by the Prickly Pears production company late in Alice's life proved invaluable.

Source material and narrative asides broken down by chapter are as follows.

Chapter One · High Sierra

Details about the lives of Solomon and Harry Marble, as well as Jessie Wood, the young Alice Marble, and life on the ranch come mainly from *The Road to Wimbledon* as well as the *Feather River Bulletin*, *The San Francisco Call*, and the *San Francisco Chronicle*. There are many sources illuminating the gold rush that swelled the Sierra region of Northern California in the mid-nineteenth century, including census reports, H. W. Brands's book *The Age of Gold*, and the television documentary on the subject (with accompanying print material) that aired on *American Experience* on PBS.

The Road to Wimbledon indicates Solomon Marble had two daughters, but this seems to be an error—Solomon's obituary mentions only a single daughter, and neither the 1860 or 1880 census mentions any female siblings in the Marble household.

The town of Beckwith was named for legendary mountain man James "Bloody Arm" Beckwith, who was better known as Jim Beckwourth, though the town was named "Beckwith" for his birth name, though it later changed to "Beckwourth," as that was the name given to the trail he discovered that cut through the Sierra from Reno to Portola. Got that?

Born into slavery in Virginia, the mixed-race Beckwith was given his freedom and headed west, eventually working as a fur trapper and living among the Crow Nation before pushing deep into the California/Nevada wilderness. He made a living there as a shopkeeper, a card sharp, a rancher, a hotelier, and an author, telling his story and selling the memoir *The Life and Adventures of James P. Beckwourth* to Harper & Brothers publishers in 1855. He fought in the Indian wars and was present for the massacre of Cheyenne at Sand Creek in the Colorado Territory. He died in 1866, possibly poisoned by disillusioned Crow members as revenge for the Sand Creek Massacre.

Dr. George Gere is referred to by Alice in *The Road to Wimbledon* merely as a well-known San Francisco specialist, but he was extremely accomplished. He grew up in the remote town of Pawnee, Nebraska, and practiced in several mining camps before coming to San Francisco. For five years he was chief of anatomy and chaired the surgery department at California Medical College. His specialty wasn't ailments of the throat, as Harry Marble may have thought, but surgery, in particular "correction of facial and physical deformities." He was among the first practitioners of plastic surgery—namely, nose jobs.

Yes, by marrying Harry, Jessie went from being Wood to being Marble . . .

The title of "Hathaway Ranch" for the Marble family ranch is according to documents in the Plumas County Recorder's Office.

A report in the *Feather River Bulletin* from January 27, 1916, indicates the rough terrain of the area. "Manfred Olson and C. W. Toomey [ranch hands in the Marble employ] left here this morning with 6 horses and a sled, intending to break a road as far as U. S. Bates' place today, thence to Loyalton and home to Sattley as fast as the heavy snow will let them. Errol Bates [another hand] and Mel Marble, with 10 horses, came out from their end to meet Manfred and Toomey. As they got through to Beckwith, it is fair to conclude that the others also reached the point they aimed for."

The photo of Alice at age two appeared in *The San Bernardino Sun* on October 1, 1939, as well as in *The Road to Wimbledon*. Unfortunately, its current whereabouts are unknown.

Alice's 1946 memoir claims that Harry Marble came to San Francisco on the trip where he met his wife in order, in part, to see the devastation wrought by the great earthquake of 1906. Alas, this is impossible, because the two were already married by late 1905 and were safely in the Sierra when the earth shook the big city.

A smaller reason for Harry Marble's selling of the Hathaway Ranch may have been an epic pestilence of grasshoppers that invaded the Sierra Valley in 1919 and chomped on the fertile grasses, ruining many ranchers.

Chapter Two · City Lights

Descriptions of San Francisco in the 1920s come from a variety of sources, including *The Road to Wimbledon, Travelers Guide to San Francisco*, the chamber of commerce report *Facts About the Port of San Francisco, San Francisco Almanac*, a paper about San Francisco written for the National Committee on Social Work by Robert Ritchie, the WPA publication *California in the 1930s*, and articles in the *San Francisco Examiner*. Geographical and housing information come from records stored at city hall in San Francisco, period maps and guides, as well as the author's visit to the Inner and Outer Sunset and Golden Gate Park neighborhoods.

The house at 1619 Twelfth Avenue is still there, and though it clearly has been renovated a time or two since it housed the Marble family, in the main it is recognizable from Alice's descriptions. The home remains set back from the street, and the stairs up to the front door are still in place, there to suck the last bits of energy from anyone who already walked up the steep hill to the house, which I did several times—it never got any easier.

Much more on the influenza epidemic in San Francisco can be found in an *American Experience* documentary on the subject on PBS.

Streetcars, far more than automobiles or other forms of transportation, were the scourge of San Francisco streets in the first third of the twentieth century. For example, in 1906, sixty-one of the ninety-six deaths caused by moving vehicles were the result of streetcars. They were often particularly gruesome affairs and described as such by newspapers like *The San Francisco Call* on October 3, 1906, reporting on the death of a girl named Helen Umfrid: "Mowed down by the thirty-ton juggernaut, her body was churned round the forward wheels and mangled so frightfully that it became almost welded to the [car] and could not be removed for more than an hour."

By the late 1920s, automobile deaths had supplanted those caused by streetcars in these macabre standings, as there were roughly ten times as many cars as there had been two decades earlier.

Sources differ on whether Uncle Arthur's nickname was actually "Woodie" or "Woody." It is "Woodie" in *The Road to Wimbledon*, so I used that in the narrative.

Chapter Three · The Natural

Alice's discovery by the San Francisco Seals and subsequent turn as mascot was well chronicled in the *San Francisco Examiner*. Information about the team and the experience of games at Rec Park are from the *Examiner* as well as R. Scott Mackey's book, *Barbary Baseball*, the chamber of commerce report *Facts About the Port of San Francisco*, and various contemporary accounts and histories collected by the Society for American Baseball Research. Information about Golden Gate Park and Alice's place in its history comes from the *Travelers Guide to San Francisco*, *San Francisco Almanac*, *The Making of Golden Gate Park: The Growing Years, 1906–1950*, and articles in the *San Francisco Examiner*, as well as the author's multiple visits there.

Enthusiasts of the legendary television show *M*A*S*H* will recognize Mill Valley as the hometown of Captain B. J. Hunnicutt, played by Mike Farrell.

Stinson Beach in the 1920s was apparently safe, but in recent years the area has become renowned for being the domain of the great white shark, with multiple sightings and a near-fatal attack on a surfer in 2002. The nearby Farallon Islands are the epicenter of America's white shark population.

Ping Bodie gave himself that name for (a) the sound of the ball off his bat and (b) the town where his father worked as a miner. After his Seals career he opened an auto service station down the street from Rec Park, and later moved to Hollywood and became a well-known set grip, working on many popular movies of the day.

Bodie is perhaps best known for having once been Babe Ruth's roommate while with the New York Yankees, where he uttered the immortal line, "I only roomed with the Babe's suitcase."

Lefty O'Doul, "The Man in the Green Suit," remains one of the most fabled figures in San Francisco baseball history. A native of the city, O'Doul had several excellent major league seasons, including hitting .398 in 1929 while with the Phillies. Overall he hit .349 in his career and slugged 113 home runs in an eleven-year career that took him to five teams. He then returned home to manage the Seals for seventeen years, cementing his spot as a local institution. He was also instrumental in bringing baseball to Japan, traveling there multiple times as an ambassador for the sport. In 1958 O'Doul opened a popular bar and restaurant that bore his name on Geary Street, one that remains open to this day, although it has moved to a location on Fisherman's Wharf.

One of Lefty's favorite stories, true or not, concerned a man who signed O'Doul's name to a bad check in a bar. O'Doul told the bartender, "The next time somebody comes in here and says he's me, take him out in the back and have somebody hit a few balls to him. If he catches them you know he's a phony."

Smead Jolley was indeed worthy of Alice's worship. He won the Triple Crown in 1928 and hit .397 in '27 for San Francisco. He had a brief career in the bigs, though, just four seasons between the White and Red Sox, mainly because he was a legendarily poor fielder. One of his future coaches said Jolley "fielded like a kid chasing soap bubbles."

The Seals outfield of Jolley, O'Doul, and Earl Averill (who played thirteen seasons in the bigs, mostly with Cleveland) is considered one of the finest trios in minor league history. All three are in the PCL Hall of Fame, along with the DiMaggio brothers (Joe and Dom) and more recent stars like Edgar Martinez and Sandy Alomar Jr.

In *The Road to Wimbledon* Alice states that Curley Grieve wrote the piece immortalizing the thirteen-year-old baseball fan, but the article on July 27, 1927, ran unbylined, like many pieces in that paper. A few years later, the paper began crediting the writers, and Grieve was responsible for an outsize share of not just sports stories, but stories concerning Alice.

The photos of thirteen-year-old Alice, however, were credited, to F. H. King.

The *San Francisco Examiner* offices were destroyed in the 1906 earthquake; in their wake came the Hearst Building, opened in 1909. It was expansively remodeled in the late 1930s by architect Julia Morgan, the woman in charge of designing San Simeon for Hearst.

In *Courting Danger* Alice recounts how Frank Crosetti, future longtime New York Yankee and a San Francisco favorite, "yelled encouragement" while she was shagging flies with O'Doul. But Crosetti didn't join the Seals until 1928. Alice would have gotten to know him thereafter, however.

So popular were the Seals they moved to a brand-new and far larger showcase, Seals Stadium at Sixteenth and Bryant, in 1930.

The Seals were popular in large part due to their success. The team won pennants in 1922, 1923, 1925, and 1928. The Oakland Oaks won the PCL title in 1927, the year Alice became the Seals' darling.

Other teams in the Pacific Coast League at the time included the Hollywood Stars, the Los Angeles Angels, the Seattle Indians, the Portland Beavers, and the Sacramento Senators. It has since expanded to sixteen teams and is one of two Triple-A leagues, along with the International League. The PCL today stretches from Nashville and Memphis across the nation to western cities like Fresno, Sacramento, and Tacoma.

Babe Didrikson Zaharias was one of, if not the greatest female athlete of all time. Six times she was named the Female Athlete of the Year by the Associated Press—an incredible twenty-two years separate her first such award from her last. As a golfer Babe won ten Grand Slam titles. In track she won a pair of gold medals (and a silver) at the 1932 Olympics in Los Angeles. She was a standout at basketball, diving, bowling, baseball, and virtually any sport she tried, including tennis. Babe was such a transcendent athlete that Alice rightly notes in *Courting Danger*, "If she had taken up tennis earlier in her career, the history of the sport might have been different. . . . I wouldn't have wanted to face her in her prime."

In 1941 Didrikson began to train for tennis under a new coach—Eleanor Tennant. Babe went all out, playing up to seventeen sets a day in an intense effort to become a champion in yet another sport. Soon she was beating Tennant and her celebrity clients like Paul Lukas and Peter Lorre. Didrikson teamed with Louise Brough for doubles and immediately the two were playing well enough to beat top players Margaret Osborne (later du Pont) and Pauline Betz in practice matches. Didrikson applied to play at the Pacific Southwest tournament, but she was rejected by the USLTA, as she had been and remained a professional in golf and other sports. Despite the fact she was never paid for tennis, she was barred. She never picked up a racket again.

Chapter Four · Local Hero

Information about Alice's early career in athletics, including tennis, is informed by articles in the *San Francisco Examiner* and *Call* and the *Oakland Tribune*, as well as a questionnaire Alice filled out for a Poly High School oral history project.

Poly's annual football game against archrival Lowell High was known as the "Little Big Game" and was usually played on Thanksgiving Day, forty-eight hours before Cal Berkeley and Stanford squared off in the "Big Game."

During Alice's freshman year, Poly High took on Lowell High at Kezar Stadium, drawing fifty thousand fans, still the record for a prep game in Northern California.

After Alice, Poly's most famous alumni are a pair of San Francisco 49ers—George Seifert, the coach who replaced Bill Walsh and won a Super Bowl, and Bob St. Clair, the Hall of Fame tackle nicknamed "The Geek" due to his proclivity for crazy behavior, such as devouring lightbulbs.

Like many local institutions, Poly High was destroyed in the 1906 earthquake and rebuilt in a different location. It closed in 1973.

Rudy Rintala is in the Stanford Athletics Hall of Fame and was considered equal to the legendary Ernie Nevers as a Cardinals athlete. Though just five foot nine and 170 pounds, Rintala played both offense and defense for Stanford coach Pop Warner and was good enough to be on a team selected to demonstrate football as a potential sport for the 1932 Olympic Games. He also starred in basketball, baseball, and track and field.

Chapter Five · Darkest Hour

The only source material for Alice's sexual assault is *Courting Danger*. As noted in the narrative, it is almost impossible to independently prove such an event from that time, given the circumstances of the crime and the era. Important period context is provided by Estelle Freedman's *Redefining Rape*.

Chapter Six · North by Northwest

Alice's climb to the top of the Bay Area tennis ladder and journey to Canada are informed by articles in *The Vancouver Sun*, *The Vancouver Province*, *San Francisco Examiner*, and the Associated Press.

Anyone interested in what the Berkeley Tennis Club looks like today can check it out via webcam, at www.berkeleytennisclub.org.

May Sutton Bundy was "the first hard-hitting, short-skirted American to stagger pre-war Wimbledon." Before her, "hitting a ball really hard or chasing it across court was regarded as 'unladylike,'" according to tennis historian Allison Danzig. At age eighteen she was asked to lengthen her skirts—which were one and a half inches above her ankles—and to cover her bare arms. She refused.

Bundy's nephew, John Doeg, won the 1930 US Nationals after ending Bill Tilden's quest for an eighth championship in an epic semifinal, one considered among the greatest ever played at West Side Tennis Club. Doeg, a left-handed player born in Mexico but raised in Southern California, went on to capture the final over Frank Shields, winning 16–14 in the decisive fourth set.

The respective nicknames of "Big" Bill Tilden and "Little" Bill Johnston are a clue to the overall results of their many matches. Johnston won the 1919 nationals over Tilden, then lost to Big Bill the next five times they met in the finals.

Many suspected that Johnston himself sent Alice the mysterious sixty dollars that allowed her to travel to Canada, but that was never proven.

CHAPTER SEVEN · EASTERN PROMISES

Key sources for this chapter include articles in the *San Francisco Examiner,*
*Oakland Tribune, Los Angeles Times, Brooklyn Daily Eagle, New York Daily
News, New York Sun, Calexico Chronicle,* and the AP and UP syndicates, as
well as Nancy Spain's biography of Eleanor Tennant, *"Teach" Tennant.*

At Fred Solari's well-known restaurant, the sirloin and tenderloin steaks
went for $2.25. A shrimp cocktail was seventy cents, and a wide array of
seafood, "Absolutely Fresh courtesy of Consolidated Fisheries," was on
offer, along with breakfast fare, salads, and "relishes."

The Southern Pacific Mole was also known as the Oakland Mole or the
Oakland Long Wharf. All passengers headed to San Francisco detrained
here then took a ferry to the city.

Mole is an architectural term for a massive structure, generally built from
stone, and used as a pier or breakwater. Perhaps the most famous mole in
history is the East Mole on the beach at Dunkirk, France. During the
evacuation of British troops from Dunkirk in 1940, the harbor had been
rendered unusable by German bombing, and getting to and from the
beachhead was slow. A British officer had the idea to use the mole, in
practice a long jetty made of boulders, as a place to dock ships and ferry
the men out. It was, of course, a highly successful gambit. In a historical
irony, given this book, the British officer whose brainchild it was to use
the mole was named Captain W. G. Tennant.

The American tennis calendar remains similar to that of the 1930s, in
that the summer events lead up to the (now) US Open in Queens in September. Instead of country clubs in Amtrak country, however, those tournaments are today held farther afield, in places like Atlanta, Montreal,
and Cincinnati.

Tennis tournaments at Forest Hills were played on grass surfaces until
1974, when for three years it switched to clay. Upon the move across Queens

to Flushing Meadows in 1978, it became the hard-court surface it remains today. Jimmy Connors is the only player to win on all three surfaces.

Philip Hawk was an accomplished man outside of tennis, a well-known chemist and nutritionist who wrote a popular book, *Streamline for Health*, which exposed many of the fad diets of the day as bunk. He also dabbled in botany. His wife, Gladys, was twenty years his junior.

Chapter Eight · The Fighter

The major source for the details of Eleanor Tennant's early life is Nancy Spain's biography, *"Teach" Tennant*. Eleanor's life story was also captured in far smaller scale by *Sports Illustrated*, the *Los Angeles Times*, London *Daily Mirror* and *Daily Express*, and multiple contemporary newspaper and magazine articles.

Spain was a well-known writer of several books and pal of many of England's finest, including Noël Coward and female rally driver Sheila van Damm. Many of her books were mysteries, including the popular *Death Goes on Skis* and *Death Before Wicket*. She lived openly with magazine editor Joan Werner Laurie. In 1964 she and Werner were en route to cover the Grand National horse race when the small plane they were in crashed near the racetrack, and both women were killed. Coward would write of the tragedy, "It is cruel that all that gaiety, intelligence and vitality should be snuffed out when so many bores and horrors are left living."

Despite Spain's bona fides, her biography of Tennant (really more of an extended interview put between covers) doesn't leap off the page with literary quality. The book, unsurprisingly given the times, made no mention of any romantic activity on the part of Tennant or Alice. Then again, the inside flap referred to Alice as "Marbles," so its veracity must be taken with several saltshakers.

Lytton Tennant would establish a chain of art and antique galleries in Hollywood before his suicide in his midforties.

The great quake of 1906 is among the worst natural disasters in American history, killing roughly three thousand people and devastating San Francisco. The Richter scale for measuring the magnitude of earthquakes wouldn't come into being for another thirty years, but modern estimates by historians put the range between 7.9 and 8.2 on the scale. By contrast, the 1989 quake that hit the Bay Area registered at 6.9. At least half and possibly as many as two-thirds of the city's population of 400,000 was left homeless by the disaster. The main culprit wasn't the quake itself, damaging as it was, but the enormous fires that raged out of control in its wake. A riveting account of the earthquake of '06 can be found in Simon Winchester's *A Crack in the Edge of the World*.

Chapter Nine · La La Land

Eleanor Tennant's wedding was covered by the *Los Angeles Times*, her divorce covered by the *San Francisco Examiner* and *Oakland Tribune*. Information about the Beverly Hills Hotel stems from the author's personal visit and the hotel's publication, *The Beverly Hills Hotel and Bungalows: The First 100 Years*, written by Robert Anderson, the great-grandson of Margaret Anderson, the hotel's founder. The *Los Angeles Times* also wrote multiple articles about the hotel and its guests and staff. An important source for understanding Tennant's mentality as a budding coach was Elizabeth Wilson's history of tennis, *Love Game*.

Admiral Cameron Winslow was just a lieutenant when he served aboard the gunboat *Nashville* during the Spanish-American War. On May 11, 1898, he commanded a small flotilla of boats that cut submarine cables that linked Cuba with Europe, despite intense enemy fire. Winslow took a bullet to his hand but finished the mission, for which eventually he was awarded the Medal of Honor.

Spain's biography credits the Winslow family with nine children, all in Eleanor's care, but they "only" had six.

Valerie Timken had a son, William, with George Sturgis, but she, too, would divorce. She got remarried to Winthrop Whitney, the wealthy head of the Whitney Manufacturing Company, in 1934. She remained with her son in California even as Whitney traveled the country, maintaining a residence on Benedict Canyon Drive in Beverly Hills, a home convenient to Tennant for many years. Valerie established a charity, the Timken-Sturgis Foundation, that gave millions to organizations like the Scripps Institute over the years.

Unfortunately for Eleanor, California had yet to pass a law that guaranteed divorcing partners half of their spouses' estate.

CHAPTER TEN · CANNONBALL RUN

Articles from the *San Francisco Examiner, Los Angeles Times, Brooklyn Daily Eagle, The Boston Globe, Oakland Tribune*, and the AP and UP are key sources for this chapter. The portrait of California during the Depression is informed by contemporary sources including articles in the *Examiner, Times*, and *Tribune*, plus *California in the 1930s*, Jerry Flamm's *Good Life in Hard Times*, and Michael Golay's *America 1933*.

California's suicide rate during the Depression was commensurate with that of the national rise of nearly 20 percent from pre-Depression figures.

Ellsworth Vines repeated at Forest Hills, winning the 1932 national championship over Frenchman Henri Cochet.

Joan Ridley and Elsie Pittman would both fall in the semifinals of the 1932 ladies' singles at Forest Hills, with Helen Jacobs capturing the title.

Both of Alice's memoirs state that she went from New York directly to LA for the Pacific Southwest tournament, but that is belied by local reporting from San Francisco upon her return there.

The great British player Fred Perry defeated Ellsworth Vines to win the 1932 Pacific Southwest tourney. Initially underwhelmed at the thought of playing in California, Perry had told Vines "I'm not interested unless my first date is with [the beautiful movie star] Jean Harlow." Upon his arrival, Perry's driver, having been hired by Vines, took the Englishman directly to Harlow's home. "It would be fair to say I was dumbfounded," Perry wrote in his memoir, "but I wasn't the type to stay senseless for long."

Robert Montgomery is probably best known for his roles in the thriller *Night Must Fall* and as boxer Joe Pendleton in *Here Comes Mr. Jordan* (remade with Warren Beatty as *Heaven Can Wait*), both of which earned him nominations for an Academy Award as Best Actor. Come the outbreak of war in Europe, he enlisted in the American Field Service and drove ambulances in France, and was evacuated at Dunkirk. He then came home to star in *Mr. & Mrs. Smith* with Carole Lombard before joining the US Navy after Pearl Harbor, and was a lieutenant commander on the destroyer USS *Barton*, and served during the D-Day invasion. He won Emmy and Tony Awards for directing and was a pioneer in media consultation, advising Dwight D. Eisenhower on how to look good on television while campaigning for office. One of his daughters is Elizabeth Montgomery, famous for playing Samantha on *Bewitched*.

Marlene Dietrich was nearly caught up in the rapid retreat of Allied forces during the German counteroffensive of winter 1944, known as the Battle of the Bulge. She was forced to take refuge in a series of bombed-out buildings, listening to the roar of combat just a few kilometers away. She often talked of feeling the frozen feet of rats crawl across her face while she tried (and failed) to sleep.

CHAPTER ELEVEN · TRAINING DAY

Alice's time spent under the tutelage of Harwood "Beese" White is informed in part by the *Santa Barbara Independent*.

Beese White had several accomplished brothers beyond Stewart. Gilbert White was a well-known mural painter, and Roderick White was a renowned violinist.

Chapter Twelve   ·   Duel in the Sun

Nancy Spain's Tennant biography is important for this chapter. Articles from the *San Francisco Examiner, Los Angeles Times, New York Times, Brooklyn Daily Eagle, New York Daily News,* and the AP and International News Service (INS) syndicates were also critical.

While Alice played doubles with Helen Wills Moody during her trial at Maidstone, they never faced each other in a tournament setting, in singles or in doubles. The lone time they played with any intent on besting the other was a practice set before the Wightman Cup began at Wimbledon in 1938. Alice won, though Helen was on the downslope by then. Arguing over who was better in their prime was a favorite parlor game of tennis fans and experts before the war; while Helen Jacobs thought Moody was superior, most writers felt as Mel Heimer did—"Alice would have carried far too many guns for Helen, even in Little Miss Pokerface's prime."

The US won the first Wightman Cup in 1923, capturing all seven matches. Britain took four of the next seven Cups through 1930, then wouldn't win again until 1958!

Sic semper tyrannis (Thus Always Tyrants!) was the shouted cry of John Wilkes Booth after he fired his assassin's bullet into the head of Abraham Lincoln.

Chapter Thirteen   ·   Castle in the Sky

Both Alice and Eleanor referred frequently to their visits to San Simeon throughout their lives, as understandably they made quite an impression.

An oral history Alice gave to the Hearst San Simeon State Historical Monument in 1977 was extremely informational, and a piece in *The New Yorker* from 1998, "Earthly Delights" by David Nasaw, summarized the oral history project and was particularly helpful. Also of note were the books *Hearst Castle, San Simeon* by Thomas Aidala, *Hearst Castle* by Taylor Coffman, and *Hearst Ranch: Family, Land, and Legacy* by Victoria Kastner, along with numerous newspaper and magazine articles. Notable among these is Arthur Brisbane's ode to Alice in the December 3, 1933, edition of the *San Francisco Examiner* (it also ran nationwide in Hearst's many papers).

Eleanor Tennant was close with Charlie Chaplin. On one occasion, the great comic actor bought the tennis pro an expensive polo coat and drove her back to LA, all the while regaling Eleanor with lessons in philosophy.

A stubborn myth, perhaps started by William Randolph Hearst himself, was that San Simeon cost between $30 million and $50 million (or between $500 million and $750 million today). But the truth was less exorbitant, if still pricey—records in the Julia Morgan collection at Cal Poly, San Luis Obispo, list expenditures at $4.717 million (about $70 million today), including $400,000 for the tennis courts and Roman "plunge" pool.

By the mid-1930s Hearst had become a bitterly outspoken enemy of the New Deal. What particularly incensed him were Franklin Delano Roosevelt's income taxes, which were pushing his shaky finances over the brink. Hearst had used every forum he controlled to attack the politicians who dared suggest that state and federal governments had the right to tax the wealthy more heavily than the poor. Moreover, the "Raw Deal," which was what he ordered his papers to call the new political order, was doing more than robbing him through income taxes. It was encouraging hotheads like the columnist Heywood Broun, a founder of the American Newspaper Guild, to unionize editorial offices and, in so doing, interfere with his right—as publisher—to do as he pleased with his employees.

As the Depression worsened, Hearst came to be seen as the epitome of the old robber barons: incredibly greedy, unspeakably self-indulgent. San Simeon took on a sinister cast. Increasingly, it was depicted not as a shining achievement of American vision and taste but as a symbol of the unbridled capitalism that had plunged the nation into its most prolonged economic depression.

In 1937 the gargantuan estate was placed into receivership. Many of Hearst's prized assets, including the objets d'art that infused San Simeon, were sold. The ever-proceeding construction was halted. Hearst was down and out but rebounded thanks to the war, during which time the insatiable desire for news boosted circulation in his media empire and allowed him to escape debt.

In 1947, Hearst's health began to fail, and he moved with Marion Davies from San Simeon to a mansion on eight acres in Beverly Hills. On August 13, 1951, Marion had gone to bed drunk and sedated. When she woke up the next day, Hearst's bed was empty. At the age of eighty-eight, he had died in his sleep. "I asked where he was and the nurse said he was dead," Davies told a reporter. "His body was gone, whoosh, like that. Old W. R. was gone, the boys were gone. I was alone. Do you realize what they did? They stole a possession of mine. He belonged to me. I loved him for thirty-two years and now he was gone. I couldn't even say goodbye." William Hearst Jr. later maintained that there had been no duplicity involved; Marion, he said, had been told ahead of time of the plans to deal with the magnate's corpse.

In October 1951, Davies married, at the age of fifty-four, for the first time. Her husband, Horace Brown, was a tall retired merchant marine captain with blue eyes who looked remarkably like William Randolph Hearst.

Exactly how often Alice visited San Simeon is difficult to estimate—she is vague about it in her memoirs, and remaining visitor logs from the period are scant. The best guess is that she spent several weeks, over a period of roughly half a dozen or so visits, at the estate until 1937, when Hearst's financial difficulties got the best of him. By then, Alice had become a celebrity equal to any of Hearst's usual guests, not merely a tennis-playing curiosity.

In *Courting Danger* Alice writes that it was Bebe Daniels, the silent-film star, who did her nails, not Dorothy Mackaill.

Elizabeth "Bunny" Ryan was an even greater doubles player than Alice, particularly at Wimbledon, where she won an astounding nineteen titles between women's and mixed doubles, mostly playing with the immortal Suzanne Lenglen, with whom she never lost a match in thirty-one tries at the All England Club. Her volleying style was a model for Alice's, though many fans and fellow players felt Alice was superior in the stroke thanks to her incredible athleticism. Ryan wasn't nearly as good of a singles player, never capturing a title at a Grand Slam event without a partner. She led the 1926 US Nationals final 4–0 in the third before blowing the match. Ryan lived most of her life in England and passed away the day before Billie Jean King captured her twentieth Wimbledon title, breaking Ryan's longtime record.

Thomas Ince went from being an acting failure to overwhelming success as one of the first movie tycoons. He revolutionized the way films were made, inventing the shooting script and the sound stage. He created the first studio, known as Inceville. He went on to found the studios that became MGM, where Clark Gable would later shoot *Gone with the Wind*. He then sold out and teamed with Adolph Zukor to create Paramount Pictures. By 1924 his fortunes had turned, however, and he was scraping by as an independent producer when he boarded Hearst's sumptuous yacht, the *Oneida*, on November 16 for his birthday bash. For most of the action Hearst wasn't there, but Davies was, along with Charlie Chaplin, Louella Parsons, and other Hollywood notables.

The evening is shrouded in mystery. Ince supposedly suffered from acute indigestion and was carried from the boat, treated at a hotel, then sent home, where he died shortly thereafter. According to his death certificate, the cause was a heart attack.

But immediate rumors—and even a headline in the *Los Angeles Times*—insisted Ince was shot to death, supposedly by Hearst, who came to the party late, caught Davies and Chaplin in flagrante delicto, and shot Ince by accident, the bullet meant for one of the lovers. Other rumors proliferated: Hearst stabbed Ince, Hearst hired an assassin to kill Ince, someone on board saw Ince bleeding from the head. Some evidence accumulated that Hearst bought off Ince's wife and Parsons with trust funds and lifetime contracts, ensuring their silence.

Ince's body was cremated immediately, and his wife fled to Europe. The truth of exactly what happened on board the *Oneida* will likely never be known. But Hearst was dogged with the shadow of his supposedly murderous ways for the rest of his life.

One of Arthur Brisbane's grandchildren, his namesake Arthur Brisbane, also went into journalism and was public editor for *The New York Times* from 2010 to 2013.

The sculptor referred to in Brisbane's column, Frederick MacMonnies, was a Brooklyn-born master of the Beaux-Arts school. His life-size sculpture of Nathan Hale, which stands in City Hall Park, New York, near where Hale was thought to have been executed by the British for espionage in 1776, is probably his best-known work.

Chapter Fourteen · Falling Down

Naturally, Alice's collapse in Paris was heavily documented, mainly at the time by the AP, along with the London papers—the *Daily Mail*, *Daily Express*, the *Times*, and the *Telegraph*—as well as *The New York Times* and *Los Angeles Times*.

At this stage Eleanor Tennant had moved to Gladstone, California, where according to the 1934 *City of Los Angeles and Surrounding Areas* phone book she lived at 1775 North Orange Drive.

In both of Alice's memoirs she states her fateful encounter with the psychic took place in New York on the eve of her voyage to Europe. But Tennant was rather specific about seeing the medium in action, and as stated in the narrative, psychics and various oddballs were sweeping California at the time, which likely makes it a West Coast action, transposed by time to NYC in Alice's memory.

Sylvia Henrotin would coincidentally default a match later in the day of Alice's collapse, spraining an ankle in doubles play. The London *Daily Telegraph* reported that she hopped off the court, "looking for all the world as though she were taking part in a one-leg obstacle race." The French team beat the Americans amid the carnage five matches to two.

Alice's collapse was used as evidence by certain agenda-driven folk that the Wightman Cup should not be expanded to include other countries, à la the men's Davis Cup. Travel and logistical roadblocks were many, but also, as a writer in the London *Daily Mail* pointed out, "Women cannot stand the strain of traveling as well as can men. . . . An instance of the frailty of women was offered . . . when the strongest-looking of the players, Miss Alice Marble, collapsed on the centre court, overcome by the heat."

CHAPTER FIFTEEN · THE LADY VANISHES

Information about the 1934 California gubernatorial election, and the tension surrounding it, is from contemporary accounts in the *Los Angeles Times*, *San Francisco Examiner*, *New York Times*, *Time*, and the books *California in the 1930s* and Gordon DeMarco's *A Short History of Los Angeles*. Other sources for the chapter include the *Brooklyn Daily Eagle*, and *The Literary Digest*.

Charlotte Avenue in Monrovia, California, has since been renamed Canyon Boulevard.

Pottenger's closed in 1955, when Dr. Pottenger retired at last at age eighty-six.

Dr. Pottenger's son, Francis Jr., opened an asthma hospital on the Monrovia grounds but is better known for his experiments regarding nutrition in cats. Among the theories postulated by work with "Pottenger's cats" was that raw milk is better for both cats and humans than pasteurized milk.

In 1926 the eighteen-year-old Carole Lombard was the passenger in a car driven by her friend Harry Cooper, a sixteen-year-old. The two were returning from a night on the town when their car slammed into another, shattering the windscreen. A piece of glass carved large scars into Lombard's face near her eye and left cheek. The resulting plastic surgery was performed without anesthesia, as the doctor feared damaging the surrounding nerves. Lombard was in bed for many months but came back to return to Fox and became a much bigger star—and better actress—than she had been before.

Chapter Sixteen · Triumph of the Will

Sources for the period immediately after Alice left the sanatorium include the United Press, *Los Angeles Times*, London *Daily Mail*, and the Prickly Pears documentary from 1986.

Carole Lombard was originally discovered while playing baseball in the street with the neighborhood boys, which may explain a bit of her kinship with Alice.

Other nicknames for Lombard included "the Hoosier Tornado" and "the Profane Angel."

Lombard's penchant for playing light-haired lamebrains gave rise to early derogatory slang such as "dumb blonde" and "She's so blonde."

Alice sometimes talked about the Shirley Temple incident as happening much later in her career and other times as taking place before it got started in earnest. Given Temple's age and Alice's movements, however, this period is the only plausible time for it to have taken place.

The 139 Club in Palm Springs was a decidedly unremarkable building, a private residence made of brick at 139 Broadway. While most rooms were given over to games of chance, the kitchen from the house remained in use, though there were no seats on offer. The only dish was the chili, which was good enough to earn a reputation far grander than that of the 139 Club.

Louise Macy would get married in the White House, to FDR advisor Harry Hopkins, in 1942.

CHAPTER SEVENTEEN · THE COMEBACK KID

Los Angeles battling the Great Depression is informed by *California in the 1930s* and *A Short History of Los Angeles*, as well as the *Los Angeles Times*. Alice's year on the court was covered by the likes of the *Times*, *San Diego Sun*, *Calexico Chronicle*, *The Salt Lake Tribune*, *Quad-City Times*, *The Pittsburgh Press*, *The New York Times*, *New York Daily News*, *The Baltimore Sun*, *Brooklyn Daily Eagle*, London *Daily Express*, *San Francisco Examiner*, *Time*, and *Newsweek*. Dan Marble's handball matches were covered in the *Examiner*. The Oheka Castle details are from the website oheka.com. Bobby Riggs is profiled in Tom LeCompte's biography, *The Last Sure Thing*, as well as his own autobiography, *Tennis Is My Racket*.

Charlie Farrell was best known for the silent-film classic *7th Heaven*, in which he starred with his lover, Janet Gaynor, who won an Academy Award for her role in the film. The two made no fewer than sixteen movies together. Farrell loved tennis and athletics and would become a major figure in the development of Palm Springs as a resort capital. He and Marion Davies were also rumored to have had a longtime affair, sleeping together even at San Simeon.

Ralph Bellamy is probably best known today for his role as one of the treacherous Duke brothers in the comedy classic *Trading Places*, released nearly fifty years after the founding of the Racquet Club.

When Farrell and Bellamy first bought the two hundred acres in Palm Springs, it was for a mere thirty dollars an acre, which caused Bellamy to ask, "Is it under water?" Farrell confessed later, "We hadn't a clue what we'd do with it," but the sportsman knew he wanted to make the land into some sort of athletically inclined resort. In 1934 you could play all day on the courts of the Palm Springs Racquet Club for a single dollar. Paul Lukas was the first actor to come east to join up, and luminaries such as Peter Lorre, John Barrymore, and Spencer Tracy soon followed, as did Carole Lombard and Clark Gable. Said Farrell, "The Hollywood gang flocked here when they found they didn't have to spend much money and could make their own fun."

In the Racquet Club's heyday, stars like Spencer Tracy, Marilyn Monroe, and Elizabeth Taylor lounged poolside and sipped cocktails, but it fell into decline in the latter part of the century. In 2014 a massive fire destroyed the Racquet Club for good.

Otto Kahn died in 1934, and a decade later the Oheka Castle was turned into a retirement home for state sanitation workers, of all things, then a training school for merchant marine radio operators, neither use particularly equal to the surroundings. It fell into disrepair after the war, until it was bought and redeveloped in the 1980s and turned into a wedding and party destination.

CHAPTER EIGHTEEN   ·   THE KING AND I

Articles from *The New York Times*, *New York Daily News*, *Brooklyn Daily Eagle*, London *Daily Mirror*, London *Daily Express*, *The Missoulian*, *Santa Cruz Evening News*, *San Francisco Examiner*, and Universal News Service were important for this chapter. Clark Gable's background came from many sources, chiefly Warren Harris's biography, *Clark Gable*. The Associated Press is obviously the source for its voting for Comeback Player of the Year.

Tim Marble would play pro ball only briefly. After twenty largely unimpressive games with the AA Mission Reds, he spent 1938 with Class B Bellingham, where he showed just enough (despite forty errors at shortstop) to get back to the PCL in 1939, this time with the Hollywood Stars, spending part of the season in LA and part in the far less glamorous (not to mention dusty) Oklahoma City. He switched to third base but didn't show much pop in either stop. He signed with Tacoma to play the 1940 season but got called into the service instead. All told, Marble played 205 minor league games across three seasons, hitting .240 with six home runs.

The Mission Reds were generally referred to in the press and by local baseball fans as the "Missions" rather than the "Reds." The club didn't have much history in San Francisco, having moved there from LA in 1926. The Seals already had a local rival, the Oakland Oaks, so the Missions mostly appealed to hardcore baseball fans wanting to see some action, any action, while the Seals were out of town. The Reds did win the PCL title once, in 1929, and by 1938 had moved back to LA.

Clark Gable's nickname, the "King of Hollywood," was derived from a gossip columnist overhearing Spencer Tracy calling him "King." Sensing good copy, the writer ran a poll among his readers to choose the king and queen. It caught on, and Gable was elected king (Myrna Loy was queen). He came to hate the moniker. "This 'king' stuff is pure bullshit," he said. "I eat and sleep and go to the bathroom just like everybody else. There's no special light inside me that makes me a star. I'm just a lucky slob from Ohio. I happened to be in the right place at the right time, and I had a lot of smart guys helping me—that's all."

For all his acclaim Gable only won the single Best Actor Oscar, for *It Happened One Night* in 1935, and was nominated two other times, for *Mutiny on the Bounty* (1936) and *Gone with the Wind* (released in 1939; he was nominated at the 1940 awards).

Boxer Jimmy McLarnin was third in the 1936 AP comeback poll, for "fistic wins" over tremendous fighters Tony Canzoneri and Lou Ambers. Considered by many the greatest fighter to ever come out of Ireland, McLarnin was named *The Ring* magazine's fifth-best welterweight of all time.

CHAPTER NINETEEN · BLOW-UP

Multiple newspapers and magazines were sources for this chapter, including *The New York Times, Brooklyn Daily Eagle, Calexico Chronicle, Coronado Eagle & Journal, San Francisco Examiner,* and the AP. Alice's initial trip to Wimbledon was heavily covered by the local press—the London *Daily Mirror, Daily Express, Times, Daily Mail,* and *Telegraph*. Jadwiga Jedrzejowska's foray to America as Wimbledon champ was captured by the Universal News Service. *Fred Perry: An Autobiography* helped fill in the class divisions at the All England Club, as did *Wimbledon Story* by Norah Cleather.

The RMS *Berengaria* had an eventful history. Launched as the *Imperator* five weeks after the *Titanic* sank in 1912, she was the largest ship on the high seas and the pride of the Hamburg-America Line. She was forgotten during WWI, gathering rust on the River Elbe, then gifted to the English Cunard line as reparations for the U-boat sinking of the *Lusitania* in 1915. Between 1920 and 1936 she was the gold standard for Atlantic crossings. Then Cunard launched the spanking new *Queen Mary,* and *Berengaria's* days were numbered. In 1938, while in New York Harbor, a fire severely damaged the ship, and she was withdrawn from service.

JaJa Jedrzejowska was surprisingly beaten in the 1937 Wimbledon final by Dorothy Round, the daughter of an English minister, who was the 1934 Wimbledon champ and had spent the previous two years on a semi-sabbatical (it was a small-scale version of Alice's comeback triumph at the 1936 US Nationals). Alice did capture the mixed doubles title, with Don Budge. JaJa would lose again in the 1937 US Nationals finals, with Chilean Anita Lizana winning a surprising title.

The great tennis writer Allison Danzig is credited with coining the terms *Grand Slam* and *ace*, among other contributions to the sport.

In case there is any gender confusion, Allison Danzig was a man.

Chapter Twenty · The Tailor

Key sources for this chapter include *Love Game*, Meredith Daneman's *Margot Fonteyn*, *The New York Times*, and the London *Daily Mail*, *Mirror*, *Telegraph*, and *Express*. Alice's designs and trips to check on the stores' displays were covered by the *San Francisco Examiner*, *The New York Times*, *The Californian*, *The Philadelphia Inquirer*, and the *Pittsburgh Post-Gazette*, as well as advertisements in *Life* and *Look*, plus various newspapers across the country and the Official Pro Tour program. Hazel Wightman's diatribe appeared in Herbert Warren Wind's article "Run, Helen!" in *The New Yorker* of August 30, 1952.

Elsa Schiaparelli was a designer who began operating from a small Parisian shop in the late 1920s and almost immediately conquered the globe with her taste and visionary strategies for business, including the beginning of licensee contracts to spread her clothing, jewelry, and perfume lines to select customers across the fashion world. Born in Rome, Elsa battled Coco Chanel for supremacy in fashion in the era between the wars, favoring a surrealist style influenced by the likes of artist Salvador Dalí.

Schiaparelli had previously created a scandal in the tennis fashion world by designing "divided skirts," which caused an immense stir when introduced at Wimbledon in 1931. Alice's shorts were to make those skirts look decidedly chaste in just a few years.

The Baha'i faith is a religion teaching the essential worth of all religions and the unity and equality of all people. Established by Baha'u'llah in 1863, it initially grew in Persia and parts of the Middle East, where it has faced ongoing persecution since its inception.

The partnership of ballet stars Rudolf Nureyev and Margot Fonteyn is generally considered the greatest in the history of the art. Nureyev defected from Russia at age twenty-three in 1961, finding his way to the Royal Ballet in London, where the forty-two-year-old Fonteyn became his partner and soul mate. "At the end of Swan Lake," Nureyev once said, "when she left the stage in her great white tutu I would have followed her to the end of the world." The Russian was known to be homosexual but carried on a brief affair with Fonteyn; as with Eleanor and Alice, their artistic and professional relationship was paramount. "Margot had him where it really mattered," said Fonteyn's fellow dancer Georgina Parkinson. "I think she was the dearest thing in his life without any doubt. Just knowing that she was in the world was sufficient for Rudolf."

Also on board the *Queen Mary* crossing the Atlantic with Alice and Eleanor was Alexander Kerensky, who is the answer to a trivia question: Who was premier of Russia in between the czar and the Bolsheviks?

Joe Louis's destruction of Max Schmeling on June 22, 1938, is one of the most famous fights in boxing history, both for the epic vengeance Louis wreaked on the man who defeated him in 1936 as well as for its international significance. Schmeling was German, hardly a devout Nazi but nonetheless inevitably used by the Third Reich as a propaganda tool, even though his manager was Joe Jacobs, an American Jew, and later research indicated Schmeling saved a pair of Jewish teens in Berlin from persecution. With world tensions running high, the fact an American black man was going to fight the Nazi's prized Übermensch freighted their bout with immense geopolitical weight, a sort of single combat to foreshadow the conflict to come. FDR himself had told the fighter, "Joe, we need muscles like yours to defeat the Nazis."

If only World War II were so one-sided. Louis had learned from his initial defeat, and the fight at a humid Yankee Stadium was 124 seconds of demolition. Louis floored Schmeling twice before the German's corner threw in the towel. Their man had landed but two punches against countless telling blows from Louis. The American would hold the heavyweight crown until 1949 but in later life would struggle with his finances and the limitations placed upon him by American racism. One of his benefactors was his close friend Max Schmeling.

Of Joseph Kennedy's four sons, including John, Robert, and Ted, it was the eldest, Joe Jr., who was groomed for politics (and the presidency) first. The ambassador spoke often of putting his vast fortune in place to boost his namesake's political future. But WWII changed those plans. John became a hero in August 1943 after his patrol torpedo boat, *PT-109*, was cut in half by a Japanese warship, and Lieutenant Kennedy saved the lives of his crew by leading them to a deserted island in the Solomon chain and then back to safety despite the overwhelming presence of the enemy.

Almost exactly one year later, on August 12, 1944, Joe Jr. was killed during a top secret mission that contained echoes of the death of "Joe Crowley." Kennedy was a naval aviator and had flown enough missions to be discharged. Instead he volunteered for a top secret program called Operation Anvil, which would make use of remotely flown B-17s stuffed with explosives. Kennedy was to fly the plane close to the target (believed to be German V-1 rocket sites), set the controls to autopilot, arm the explosives, and then bail out of the plane, landing by parachute. Unfortunately, the explosives detonated prematurely before Kennedy and his copilot, Wilford Willy, could exit the plane. The B-17 was destroyed, its wreckage falling across Suffolk, England. Joe Jr. was posthumously awarded the Navy Cross. His father's political plans instead turned to John, who would run for Congress as a Massachusetts representative in 1946.

Chapter Twenty-One · Brief Encounter

Alice's affair with "Hans" on the beach at Le Touquet is entirely described in *Courting Danger*. It does not garner mention in *The Road to Wimbledon*. The epic hurricane of 1938 was, of course, big news in the northeast of the country, notably covered by *The New York Times* and *The Boston Globe*, along with the AP. The US Nationals were sourced by the *Times*, *Brooklyn Daily Eagle*, *New York Daily News*, *Time*, *Newsweek*, and the AP.

Alfred Bloomingdale passed on the department store business and went into movies for a time, working at Columbia Pictures. He later became a key figure in starting the credit card industry, founding a business called Dine and Sign, which would merge with another nascent company called Diners Club, the first major credit card. He and his wife, Betsy, were extremely close with another California couple, Ronald and Nancy Reagan, and would be part of Reagan's "Kitchen Cabinet" when he won the presidency.

Bloomingdale may be best known for his long affair with a woman named Vicki Morgan during the 1970s. Bloomingdale was in his midfifties at the time, Morgan just eighteen. The affair became public when Morgan sued the estate after Alfred's death, divulging sordid details about their sexual history.

In 2017 a former singer and actress named Janis Paige wrote a first-person account in *The Hollywood Reporter* of being sexually assaulted by Alfred Bloomingdale in the mid-1940s when Bloomingdale was a film executive in Los Angeles.

The three Frenchmen called home to fight the Germans were indeed heard from again, though the war took its toll on them and their reputations. Yvon Petra's combat outfit was captured nearly intact and he was sent to a prisoner of war camp, where he spent two years before being released back to France. There, he participated in tennis tournaments, including the French Open, which the Vichy collaborators kept running at the behest of their Nazi overseers. Petra succeeded Bernard Destremau as men's champion, resulting in both of them being tarred after the war with talk of not resisting the enemy to their fullest. Such slander fell away for the most part, and both men, along with Jacques Brugnon, were inducted into the Tennis Hall of Fame.

The great hurricane of 1938 (sometimes called the "Yankee Clipper") was probably the worst cyclone to hit the New York metropolitan area, at least until Hurricane Sandy in 2012, though its truly destructive force was reserved for the New England region. It is estimated that the storm killed 682 people and destroyed nearly sixty thousand homes, with property losses over $300 million (roughly $5 billion today).

Chapter Twenty-Two · Pitch Perfect

Life, *The New Yorker*, *The New York Times*, *Brooklyn Daily Eagle*, *New York Daily News*, *Hartford Courant*, *San Francisco Examiner*, London *Daily Telegraph*, and *The Desert Sun* all were in on the extensive coverage of Alice's singing debut at the Waldorf Astoria. The *Times* and the Universal News Service covered Alice's glamour awards. The *Daily News*, *Brooklyn Daily Eagle*, and Walter Winchell's syndicated column kept tabs on her love life. Helen Wills's transparency with her travel expenses was reported by *Newsweek*.

Generally speaking, the contralto is at the lowest end of the scale for a female voice, while the soprano is at the highest end. Naturally, the mezzo (or middle) soprano is between the two.

The song "Two Sleepy People" tells of a couple so in love they can't bear to fall asleep, which would be a kind of parting. So they stay awake, even marrying while refusing to snooze. The version sung by Fats Waller was perhaps the most popular, though many artists took on the song, including Bob Hope, Sammy Kaye, and Lawrence Welk.

Gene Markey would have been a catch for Alice, as he was considered more dashing than most of the movie stars whose mouths he filled with lines of script, mostly in musical comedies. He had already been married to actresses Joan Bennett and Hedy Lamarr when the war came and later would wed Myrna Loy. One newspaper wondered of him, WHAT'S MARKEY GOT THAT WE DON'T? and wrote that legendary stud Rudolph Valentino "was no Markey." He was in the infantry in WWI, fighting at Belleau Wood, and during WWII was a highly decorated naval intelligence officer.

Kirsten Flagstad was a Norwegian opera singer whose voice is generally considered to be among the greatest of the twentieth century. Her public reputation took a hit during WWII when she returned to her then German-occupied native country, although she refrained from giving performances there during the war. Her husband was arrested after the war for profiteering in his lumber business by working with the Nazis, in an echo of Alice's "Hans," who supposedly was also in league with the Germans for monetary reasons. Flagstad returned to New York and the Metropolitan Opera in the late forties, a decision that was protested at first. Eventually the power and beauty of Flagstad's voice transcended political concerns.

Francis X. Shields was no stranger to fisticuffs and debauchery. As a tennis player he made a few Grand Slam finals without a breakthrough victory, and as an actor he had a few less-than-memorable supporting roles. He became an alcoholic, magnetic to women due to his handsome features and powerful build but anathema to domesticity. His three marriages all dissolved due to his violent temper and love of drink. His tennis friendships, such as they were, also were affected—he once drunkenly dangled the diminutive Bryan "Bitsy" Grant out of a hotel room window. One of his granddaughters is the actress Brooke Shields.

Lucius Boomer was a rare hotel management superstar, a man who started to work in hotels to raise money to pay for violin lessons and went on to manage many of New York's finest hotels, including the Waldorf Astoria. His financial partner was T. Coleman Du Pont, a relative of Will du Pont (they disagreed on whether the middle name should be capitalized). Among his many groundbreaking precepts was the idea that public relations was a vital function for hotels and should be assiduously pursued.

Chapter Twenty-Three · My Favorite Year

Alice's story of the changed hotel room in London appears in *Courting Danger*. There was heavy coverage of Alice's triumphs at Wimbledon and the US Nationals in *The New York Times, New York Daily News, Brooklyn Daily Eagle, New York Sun, New York Herald Tribune, Los Angeles Times, San Francisco Examiner, The Baltimore Sun, The San Diego Sun, Calexico Chronicle, Quad-City Times, The Salt Lake Tribune,* and *The Pittsburgh Press,* as well as the Associated Press, United Press, and Universal News Service. In England, the London *Times, Daily Mirror, Daily Telegraph, Evening News, Daily Mail,* and *Daily Express* were on top of every story line, and *Punch* added some comedy as well. *Time, Life, Look, Good Housekeeping,* and *Newsweek* added to the press blitz. Information about Bobby Riggs came from *Tennis Is My Racket* and *The Last Sure Thing.* Alice recounted the story of her prayer-filled recovery from injury before the Wimbledon final in the May 1950 issue of *Guideposts. Time* provided background on the historic ATA final match.

Bobby Riggs's victory over Elwood Cooke in the 1939 Wimbledon final was a dull affair, even by Riggs's standards. So anemic was the action that a sizable number of fans left the match during play, an action dubbed the "colossal Wimbledon walk-out." As the London *Daily Mirror* noted, "Those who like a dash of blood and sawdust with their lawn tennis went out to tea."

After his win at Wimbledon, Bobby Riggs received a champagne rubdown—a trainer poured a big bottle of bubbly on his back and kneaded it into his muscles. He laughed at the extravagance. "The boys at Forest Hills would be down on their knees, trying to catch the overflow."

Here is the third and final verse of John McCrae's "In Flanders Fields":

> Take up our quarrel with the foe:
> To you from failing hands we throw
> The torch; be yours to hold it high.
> If ye break faith with us who die
> We shall not sleep, though poppies grow
> In Flanders fields.

Gottfried von Cramm was the son of a German nobleman whose excellent game was undone by bad timing and his own proclivities. He dominated his national competitions, and won the French Open twice, but fell just short at the big tournaments, losing to Fred Perry twice in the Wimbledon final in 1935–36 and to Budge in 1937 at Wimbledon and Forest Hills. The perfect Aryan, von Cramm was blond and athletic, so the Nazis naturally turned to him for propaganda victories, but he steadfastly vetoed their cause. Unfortunately, due to his homosexuality he was left open to revenge and was thrown in jail on a morals clause due to an affair with a Jewish actor named Manasse Herbst. The tennis star's popularity shielded him somewhat from the worst; he was released after a year after claiming that his wife's own affair had driven him mad and into a perverse relationship with a Jew. But controversy and his nationality prevented his return to big-time tennis in the tense days before the war. He fought with the Wehrmacht on the eastern front during WWII, nearly dying from frostbite and earning the Iron Cross. He survived to win a shocking German national title in 1949 at forty years old.

According to legend, and Don Budge's anecdote, von Cramm received an important telephone call just before their fabled Davis Cup match. "I remember just before we took the court," Budge wrote in his memoir, "Von Cramm was called to the telephone. It was a long-distance call from Hitler himself exhorting Von Cramm to win for the Fatherland. Gottfried came out pale and serious and played as if his life depended on every point."

However, the Hitler phone call appears to be a myth. German sports historians, including Dr. Heiner Gillmeister, have refuted the tale, and von Cramm's biographer, Egon Steinkamp, explicitly shot down the story as false.

In Alice's 1991 memoir she states it was the hotel doctor who treated her injured abdominal muscle; in *Guideposts* she gives the man a name, "Dr. Dunning," but mentions he came from the outside.

All the Luce publications, including *Time* and *Life*, were unbylined except in rare circumstances. In general, reporters sent their field notes to New York, where they were rewritten and shaped by the editorial staffs to fit Luce's specific, jingoistic vision.

David Loth was the acclaimed author of *Lorenzo the Magnificent* and *The Brownings*, in addition to his Alexander Hamilton biography subtitled *Portrait of a Prodigy*. It sold for three dollars, or approximately 1/100th of an average ticket to the Broadway show about the same subject that ran some seventy-five years later.

Golfer Betty Jameson was a distant second in the AP Female Athlete of the Year voting, with only two first-place votes. Another golfer, Patty Berg, was third.

Fourth place went to the star of the World's Fair aquacade, Eleanor Holm, and Elsie Crabtree got votes for her stance as a drum majorette in Nevada who dared to show bare knees and got into a scrum with school officials. Esther Williams, a swimmer and not yet a movie star, was tenth.

CHAPTER TWENTY-FOUR · GONE WITH THE WIND

Alice's memories of the premiere in Atlanta are recounted in *Courting Danger*. The December 1938 edition of *Photoplay* detailed Hollywood's scandalous couples. Other sources for the filming of the movie and its debut included Harris's *Clark Gable*, *On the Road to Tara* by Aljean Harmetz, information held at the Margaret Mitchell House in Atlanta, contemporary articles in *Motion Picture*, the *Los Angeles Times*, and *The Atlanta Journal* and *Constitution*, and the author's visit to the Georgian Terrace hotel. Other sources include the *Minneapolis Star* and *Minneapolis Tribune*, *New York Daily News*, and *Tulare Advance-Register*.

The Encino ranch at 4525 Petit Street where Carole Lombard and Clark Gable moved came with a weather-beaten two-story house, barn, garage, and stable, and thick forests of eucalyptus, avocado, and fig trees. There was also a citrus orchard. Lombard stocked the acreage with animals— dogs and cats and birds and pigs. As wedding gifts Gable and Lombard exchanged horses, Sunny and Melody.

Hard as it may be to believe for the unfortunates who commute on the packed 101 freeway in Southern California, the area surrounding the ranch was so rural in the late thirties Lombard and Gable could saddle up and ride over the hills to Santa Monica without passing another home.

By September 1, 1939, as Selznick and director Victor Fleming rushed to complete the film before its gala opening in Atlanta, a group of technicians worked late to film the title sequence, pulling a camera on a dolly so that each word of *Gone with the Wind* could be framed separately. When they had finished, the head grip, Fred Williams, turned on the radio to hear that the invasion of Poland had begun, and the long-feared hostilities in Europe were at hand.

Cafe LaMaze, Alice's singing residence in LA, was at 9039 Sunset Boulevard on the Strip. The property would have a colorful future, changing owners and becoming Sherry's nightclub in the 1940s (infamous gangster Mickey Cohen was shot there), the Plymouth House in the fifties, Gazzarri's from the sixties through the eighties, and Billboard Live and the Key Club in the nineties. In 2013 it became 1 OAK nightclub, which it remains . . . for now.

Gone with the Wind won eight Oscars, including Best Picture. Vivien Leigh won Best Actress, Victor Fleming Best Director, and Hattie McDaniel Best Supporting Actress (becoming the first African-American to win an Academy Award). Gable, while nominated for Best Actor, was defeated by Robert Donat for his role in *Goodbye, Mr. Chips*.

Gable initially refused to attend the premiere in Atlanta after he learned McDaniel was not allowed to stay in the segregated Georgian Terrace with the other actors. McDaniel at length persuaded him to go.

Vivien Leigh's boyfriend, Laurence Olivier, also was told not to stay at the Terrace, as he wasn't married to Leigh. He stayed in the northern neighborhood of Buckhead instead.

The Loew's Grand burned down in 1978.

Chapter Twenty-Five · The Searchers

A short biography of Will du Pont appears on the website of the Hagley Museum, and of course the Hagley itself provided a great deal of information, including correspondence between Will and Alice. Alice's tour details come from the *Los Angeles Times*, *San Francisco Examiner*, *The Atlanta Constitution*, *The Shreveport Times*, and the AP, as well as the Official Pro Tour program. Other sources include *Look*, *The New York Times*, and the *Johnsonian*.

On the last day of June 1937, Ethel du Pont, Will's cousin, married the son of the president, Franklin Delano Roosevelt Jr., in a ceremony in Wilmington. That was the sort of crowd the Du Ponts ran with. A sudden

storm chased everyone indoors, which perhaps foreshadowed the couple's divorce in 1949.

In all, the borough of Wimbledon was hit by over one thousand bombs
during WWII, including the ones that fell on the All England Club. The
damage caused by that bombing wasn't fully repaired until 1949. The
1946 championships were held despite some 1,200 seats on Centre Court
being unusable due to the destruction.

The radio program *Information Please* aired on NBC from 1938 to 1951. It
derived its title from the phrase used when calling telephone operators. It
was as much a comedy forum as a quiz show, in much the same manner
as the current NPR program *Wait Wait . . . Don't Tell Me!*

CHAPTER TWENTY-SIX · THE COLOR OF MONEY

A full accounting of Alice's tour of 1941 appears on the website Tennis
Warehouse (https://tt.tennis-warehouse.com/index.php?threads/1941-h2h
-tour-marble-hardwick-budge-tilden.600809/). Stops on the tour were
covered by *The New York Times*, *New York Daily News*, *Brooklyn Daily Eagle*,
The Boston Globe, the London *Daily Telegraph*, *The Washington Post*, *Time*,
Newsweek, and the AP, UP, and INS. The Official Pro Tour program was
another key source. Also providing detail was Ashley Brown's article,
"Swinging for the State Department: American Women Tennis Players in
Diplomatic Goodwill Tours, 1941–1959" in the *Journal of Sport History*, fall
2015. The *Eagle* and *Time* covered Alice's foray into football predicting on
the radio. Rita Mae Brown's correspondence with me also provided context.

Donald Budge's Grand Slam win was unprecedented—no one had ever
won the US National, Wimbledon, French Open, and Australian Championship in the same season, mainly due to travel costs and logistical
difficulties, not to mention the competition. Budge also captured the
men's and mixed doubles titles at Forest Hills and the All England Club
and was captain of the Davis Cup–winning American side, making his
1938 about as great a season as anyone has had in any sport. His opponent

in the US final was Gene Mako, aka the "Mako Shark," the first un-seeded player ever to reach the final. The match was delayed by ten minutes due to Mako misplacing his rackets, as the West Side Tennis Club loudspeaker helpfully boomed to the massive gallery. Budge then walloped Mako and his found rackets to win his fourth singles title of the year.

The Seventh Regiment Armory was the home of the US Indoor Championships before the war, but it was restricted by the government after Pearl Harbor, along with the entirety of the nation's armories, to purely military purposes.

The match between Alice and Mary Hardwick marked the first time women played tennis at Madison Square Garden since 1936, when a player named Ethel Arnold took on fellow pro Jane Sharp. The biggest match prior to that took place in 1926, when Suzanne Lenglen played Alice's great friend Mary K. Browne there. The "World's Most Famous Arena" would host the Women's Tennis Association championships, sponsored for many years by Virginia Slims, starting in the late 1970s.

Madison Square Garden staged several famous men's pro matches, including Don Budge's debut in 1939 (he lost to Ellsworth Vines). In 1947, the Garden was stuffed despite a snowstorm to see Bobby Riggs defeat Jack Kramer in the latter's first pro match. And in 1970, Pancho Gonzales took an epic five-set match from Rod Laver in a 10,000-dollar winner-take-all match in the Garden.

The Marble-Hardwick match at MSG took in $25,614.40 in gate receipts, to be exact (about $467,000 today).

Michigan football great Tom Harmon was the winner of the 1940 Heisman Trophy as the best college football player in America. After his standout career in Ann Arbor he joined the army air force. He survived a pair of crashes—once he was the lone survivor of a crash of a bomber over South

America. Later, as the pilot of a P-38 Lightning fighter plane, he was shot down in combat with a Japanese plane over China. He played briefly in the NFL before embarking on a long career in football play-by-play broadcasting; Harmon was the longtime voice of UCLA in the sixties and seventies. Despite all his achievements, he is perhaps best known today as the father of television star Mark Harmon, whose games Tom called when his son was a star player for the Bruins.

Frankie Albert quarterbacked Stanford to an undefeated season in 1940, capped by a victory in the Rose Bowl. Unfortunately, the press voted the undefeated Big Ten champs, the University of Minnesota, as national champions. Albert went on to serve in the navy during WWII and had a stellar career in the NFL with the San Francisco 49ers. One of his three daughters, Jane, was a star tennis player at Stanford in the 1960s.

Unfortunately, no record of Alice's football-prognosticating ability was kept after that stalwart first week. She estimated her overall success at about 60 percent, which would certainly be attainable without a point spread to worry about.

When Bill Tilden was hurt in the car accident, a player named John Nogrady filled in and played with Alice in doubles, losing to Hardwick/Budge. Nogrady originally signed on to the tour to be in charge of the equipment truck and the portable canvas court. Compared to the physical exertions that duty required, a couple of sets of tennis were candy.

Tilden turned forty-eight years old on February 10.

Chapter Twenty-Seven · Pain & Gain

Articles in *The New Yorker, Time, Life, The New York Times, The New York Times Magazine,* and the AP, NEA, and Wide World Syndicate are sources for this chapter. The details of Carole Lombard's final days are from *Clark Gable,* The Vintage News, *Motion Picture, Las Vegas Review-Journal,* and the *Los Angeles Times.*

John Kelly, in addition to being a champion sculler, was a multimillionaire bricklayer and construction engineer. He had a pair of notable children; his son, Jack Jr., was a four-time Olympian rower; his daughter, Grace, was the famous movie star and beauty who married into royalty and became Princess Grace of Monaco.

Fiorello La Guardia wasn't long for the OCD, either, resigning in February 1942. He was replaced by the dean of Harvard Law School, James Landis.

There is a school of thought among Carole Lombard-ologists that Clark Gable's rumored affair with Lana Turner on the set of *Somewhere I'll Find You* actually was the cause of Lombard's death, as she was so concerned about losing her husband to the blonde bombshell she took a more dangerous flight home, rather than a safer, slower train.

Lombard's posthumous appearance in *To Be or Not to Be* was voted one of *Premiere* magazine's 100 Greatest Performances of All Time in 2006.

Gable lived on in the Encino ranch house the rest of his life. He finally did enlist in the army air force, an achievement noted in an MGM *News of the Day* newsreel in January 1943; "look out Mr. Hitler—Lt. Clark Gable is headed your way!" Ironically, Hitler had said that Gable was his favorite actor. Now the King of Hollywood was added to Germany's "most-wanted war criminals" list. Hermann Goering posted a reward, the equivalent of 5,000 US dollars, to the pilot who shot him down.

Gable's main duties were as a documentarian, out to make recruiting films to get more gunners into the planes, but he did his shooting in harm's way. He flew missions with the 351st Bomb Group based in England, living in the officers' barracks and sharing a bathroom with another officer, John Mahin. Gable was meant to be in front of the camera but often filled in for cameramen who were out of commission. He was promoted to captain and won the Distinguished Flying Cross and the Air

Medal. But his mission took so long to complete that the film was hopelessly outdated by the time he finished it, after screening some fifty thousand feet of film.

On January 15, 1944, Gable christened the Liberty ship SS *Carole Lombard*, one day shy of the second anniversary of Lombard's death. The ship would have a sterling record, rescuing hundreds of survivors in the Pacific from sunken ships. Tears slid down Gable's face as the ship made its initial voyage out of Long Beach into San Pedro Bay—it was his lone public display of sorrow.

Clark Gable died after a pair of massive heart attacks in 1960 at the age of fifty-nine and was laid to rest next to Lombard in Forest Lawn cemetery, in Glendale, California.

Chapter Twenty-Eight · Summer of '42

The portrait of WWII New York City is informed by *Helluva Town* by Richard Goldstein, *V Was for Victory* by John Morton Blum, and articles from *The New York Times, New York Daily News, New York Journal-American, Brooklyn Daily Eagle*, the AP, Newspaper Enterprise Association, and *Newsweek*. *Courting Danger* recounts Alice's affair with Margarita Madrigal, and her background comes from an article in the *Brooklyn Daily Eagle*.

The 1942 All-Star Game was delayed for an hour by rain, giving it the distinction of being the first Midsummer Classic played entirely under lights. There were actually two All-Star Games that summer; the night after the contest in Harlem, the AL team, which had won the "real" game 3–1, took the field against a team of service players in Cleveland in order to raise money for war bonds. The ALers won that game, too, 5–0.

Chapter Twenty-Nine · A Guy Named Joe

The background story of Wonder Woman's inception was told in several places—Jill Lepore's *The Secret History of Wonder Woman*; www.the marysue.com; and *The Ages of Wonder Woman: Essays on the Amazon Princess in Changing Times*, edited by Joseph J. Darowski. Detailed breakdowns of every early issue of *Wonder Woman* can be found in many places on the internet—I used mycomicshop.com. Wartime details, including background on the Stage Door Canteen, come from *Helluva Town*, *V Was for Victory*, *The American Home Front* by Alistair Cooke, "Losing the War" by Lee Sandlin, *The New York Times*, and the *New York Daily News*. Alice's time with Will du Pont is recounted in *Courting Danger* and considerably augmented by letters between the two, dated December 15, 1942; October 9, 1943; November 20, 1944; November 19, 1945; April 23, 1946; April 27, 1946; and July 1, 1946. Alice's time spent with "Joe Crowley" is taken from *Courting Danger.*

Emma Willard was an activist in women's rights and education. Evangeline Booth was a British woman who became general of the Salvation Army. Elizabeth Blackwell was the first Amercian woman to receive a medical degree.

Only one of the first twenty issues of *Wonder Woman* did not include a minibiography penned by Alice—issue #9.

Max Gaines was tragically killed in a motorboat accident in Lake Placid, New York, on August 20, 1947.

Chapter Thirty · The Road Warrior

The announcement of Alice and Mary Hardwick's WAC tour was covered in *The New York Times*, and details of the tour itself come from that paper as well as the *St. Louis Star-Times*, *St. Louis Post-Dispatch*, *Los Angeles Times*, *New York Daily News*, and the AP and UP. The US home front of 1943 is informed by "Summer of 1943" on defensemedianetwork.com, *V Was for Victory*, and "Losing the War." Alice's nighttime activities and near-death auto accident on tour are passed along in *Courting Danger*. John Burgoon recalled his wartime duty in Panama in his self-published memoir, *It All Counts on Twenty.*

The Caribbean Defense Command was in large part about protecting the vital Panama Canal. No Japanese ship had been allowed to pass since mid-1941, and the canal itself was protected by antitorpedo nets and naval mines, along with massive gun batteries and long-range radar. Occasionally hostile submarines ventured nearby but there was never any serious attack on the canal during the war.

The B-17D Flying Fortress nicknamed *The Swoose* is the oldest remaining intact plane of that type. During WWII the aircraft was in the Philippines when it narrowly avoided being destroyed on the ground, along with much of the American airpower in the area, in the infamous Clark Field raids, which took place several hours after Pearl Harbor, an event that should have warned American commanders an attack on these planes was likely. After seeing some action in the Pacific, the plane, "half swan, half goose" in the eye of one of its pilots, was flown to Australia for repairs. It was used by General George Brett, then the deputy commander of American forces in Australia, for various duties, including flying around visiting dignitaries, which is how a congressman named Lyndon Baines Johnson flew on *The Swoose*. General Brett would run afoul of his commander, General Douglas MacArthur, who had Brett transferred to the Caribbean command. He brought *The Swoose* with him.

One of the original pilots of *The Swoose* was Captain Frank Kurtz, a former diver at USC who became a record-setting pilot before the war. After the fighting he got married and had a daughter, whom he named Swoosie after the plane he flew. Swoosie Kurtz went on to become a noted actress with two Tony Awards and an Emmy Award.

CHAPTER THIRTY-ONE · BRINGING UP BABY

The Prickly Pears documentary helped this chapter considerably. Alice wrote of Joe Crowley in *Courting Danger* and also talked of him in an interview with the UP and, years later, with *The Desert Sun*. Brief mention of Joe is made in *The Road to Wimbledon*. Ernie Pyle's writings appeared in the Scripps Howard News Service. The historic match Alice played with Robert Ryland at the Cosmopolitan Club is detailed in *Charging the Net* by Cecil Harris and Larryette Kyle-DeBose.

The Captain Jack Crane who flew *The Swoose* is not to be confused with a Captain Jack Crane, this one from Texas, who was killed during a raid on German-controlled territory in Holland on May 17, 1943.

Jack Joseph Crane attended Wayne State University in Detroit, Michigan, not far from the Ohio State University, where Alice posits Joe Crowley as having earned an engineering degree. Crane likewise received a B.S. in engineering. He did get married, in 1952, to Phyllis, to whom he remained wedded until his death in 2015. For most of Crane's post-service life he was a pilot for Pan Am Airlines.

The tennis club nearest H. V. Kaltenborn's home in Setauket is called the Old Field Club and Farm, located on West Meadow Road in East Setauket. In 2015 a petition was sent to the US Department of the Interior in hopes of placing Old Field in the National Register of Historic Places. As part of the campaign it was noted that in the early 1940s "tennis star Alice Marble played there as HV Kaltenborn's guest."

Chapter Thirty-Two · The Spy Who Loved Me

Courting Danger is the only source for Alice's espionage training. Details of her spy camera can be found on the website camerapedia.fandom.com. Security around the Brooklyn Navy Yard is mentioned in *Helluva Town*.

Alice's stated travels across the East River to Brooklyn for espionage training would have taken her to a low-key WWII homosexual underground hot spot. Notable landmarks included the infamous "peg house" at 329 Pacific Street in Boerum Hill, a two-story town house where Nazi spies lured gay servicemen in order to get information via pillow talk. Later, a US senator was caught having sex there, which led to an affair known as the "Swastika Swishery" scandal. The Brooklyn Navy Yard, meanwhile, with its shadows and anonymity, was synonymous with vice and illicit sex. In the words of the writer Thomas Painter, during the war, "Millions of men . . . boys who would have stayed at home as quiet farm boys or middle-class youths in small towns, now in the Navy, will have been fellated or pedicated."

In Goethe's *Faust*, young Gretchen asks Faust, who has made his infamous deal with the devil, a question about religion, which he studiously evades. She lets him get away with the deception, leading to the term *Gretchenfrage*.

The first few months of 1945 were busy ones for Alice and can be reconstructed through articles in the AP, *Wilmington News-Journal*, Passaic *Herald-News*, *The Owensboro Messenger*, *The Montgomery Advertiser*, *Mount Carmel (PA) Item*, *Paterson News*, Minneapolis *Star Tribune*, the *Minneapolis Star*, and the *Chicago Tribune*. Her radio appearances in the Midwest were noted in the Minnesota and Chicago papers. "Losing the War" gives perspective on the clandestine nature of almost everything during the war. The Prickly Pears documentary, as noted in the narrative, led to Rita Mae Brown's involvement in the tale.

Feelers into the public relations arm of Swiss intelligence predictably went nowhere. Switzerland's reputation as a neutral that, in Winston Churchill's words of 1944, "has the greatest right to distinction" in its help to the Allied cause, has been buffeted in the last quarter century by revelations of the depths of collusion with the Nazis, especially in the banking realm. Yet another story of a Swiss national's (if indeed that was "Han's" true native land) illicit dealings with the Germans is hardly a matter eagerly pursued in Zurich or Geneva these days.

CHAPTER THIRTY-THREE · CALIFORNIA SPLIT

The Marr Sound Archives at the University of Missouri–Kansas City holds the recordings of the war bond drive on which Alice appears. The end of the war was informed by "Losing the War" and the author's previous work, *The Victory Season*. Alice's "Want to Be a Tennis Champion?" and *Courting Danger* are also source material for this chapter.

Don Dunphy is generally considered the greatest boxing announcer of all time, having called some two thousand fights. He is recognized by modern audiences as the voice calling Jake LaMotta's fights in the movie *Raging Bull*.

Red Barber was from Columbus, Mississippi, but he and fellow south- erner Mel Allen (a native of Birmingham, Alabama) transfixed New York City with their accents for several decades of baseball broadcasts.

Another Alabaman, Dixie Walker, was a five-time all-star in his pro- ductive eighteen-year career. He played for several teams, including the Yankees, but his time in Brooklyn is fabled for Dixie's popularity among the fan base in the outer borough. His reputation took a hit when the southerner tried to lead a rebellion against a new signing by the Dodgers, Jackie Robinson. Dixie's brother is Harry Walker, hero of the 1946 World Series with the Cardinals.

CHAPTER THIRTY-FOUR · AUTHOR! AUTHOR!

Alice's lost cigarette case was written about in both *The New York Times* and the *Daily News*. Information about *The Road to Wimbledon* is taken from her own writing as well as material in the Charles Scribner's Sons archive held at Princeton University, and articles in the *New York Daily News*, *Pittsburgh Sun-Telegraph*, London *Daily Mail*, *San Francisco Examiner*, *Hartford Courant*, *The Des Moines Register*, and *The Cedar Rapids Gazette*. I was put in touch with Rita Mae Brown courtesy of her editor at Ballantine Books, Anne Speyer. Alice's work as a writer appeared in *American Lawn Tennis*, UP, AP, NEA, and *The New York Times Magazine*.

The Road to Wimbledon's preface ends thusly—"I have decided to write my story. It all begins with a soldier named Joe . . ." Of course, it didn't begin with Joe Crowley in any conceivable way, though the book ends with a page about him.

Russell Birdwell achieved legendary status in 1927, when he hired a woman to dress as a widow, complete with veil, and place flowers at the tomb of Rudolph Valentino on the anniversary of his death. The "Woman in Black" garnered huge publicity, to the point that the woman Birdwell hired repeated the gimmick for many years. Birdwell's masterpiece was the three-year campaign to raise the public's desire to see *Gone with the Wind* to a fever pitch. The early stages helped push Gable to accept the role of Rhett Butler, as Birdwell made it known his fans demanded the King take the part. And of course, the endless search for the actress to play Scarlett O'Hara was created in large part by Birdwell's publicity machine. Howard Hughes used Birdwell to create an outrageous marketing campaign for *The Outlaw*, one that focused on Jane Russell's magnificent bosom in direct defiance of the era's production code. One ad Birdwell made displayed nothing but Russell's cleavage, with the copy screaming, "Here are two good reasons to see 'The Outlaw'!" He even had skywriters emblazon the Southern California skies with two huge circles—with two dots in the center. Compared to that, his barking for *The Road to Wimbledon* was rather tame.

The 1947 World Series is best remembered for Yankees pitcher Bill Bevens losing a no-hitter and the ballgame on a walk-off hit in the ninth inning in Game 4, or perhaps for Brooklyn outfielder Al Gionfriddo making a sensational catch to rob a hit from Joe DiMaggio to save Game 6. Despite the two legendary losses, the Bronx Bombers still won the Fall Classic, four games to three.

Ralph Branca, for whom Alice felt badly as he lost Game 1 of the 1947 World Series for Brooklyn, infamously gave up the home run to Bobby Thomson of the New York Giants, aka the "Shot Heard 'Round the World," in Game 3 of the 1951 playoff to decide the National League pennant.

Chapter Thirty-Five · Do the Right Thing

Alice's editorials boosting Althea Gibson for play in the USLTA appear in *American Lawn Tennis*, as do Althea's responses. An overview of the African-American experience in tennis appears in *Charging the Net*, as well as Sue Davidson's *Changing the Game* and Sundiata Djata's *Blacks at the Net Volume 1*. Gibson's background and thoughts are highlighted in her autobiography, *I Always Wanted to Be Somebody*, and in articles in *Newsweek* and *Time*. Her historic match at Forest Hills was covered in *The New York Times* and *Daily News*.

The Cosmopolitan Club began life as the Colonial Tennis Club in 1915.

Reginald Weir was one of two black players (along with Gerald Norman) to be denied membership in the USLTA in 1929, despite paying their dues up front.

Sugar Ray Robinson is generally considered one of the greatest fighters of all time. He is also a legend in Harlem, owning his eponymous nightclub there (on Seventh Avenue and 124th Street) and cruising the streets in his trademark pink Cadillac.

Chapter Thirty-Six · The Twilight Zone

Alice's letters to H. V. Kaltenborn were written on July 5 (or, as she wrote, "5 de Julio") and September 11, 1958. *Courting Danger* is the main source for Alice's health difficulties—as well as her romances with the likes of Rod Serling—along with the *New York Daily News*, *Brooklyn Daily Eagle*, and INS. Details on Serling's life come from Gordon F. Sander's *Serling: The Rise and Twilight of TV's Last Angry Man*. Notes on her trip to England and Sweden are from the London *Daily Mail* and *Daily Express*. Details of her drives around the US are from *Courting Danger*, the Minneapolis *Star Tribune*, the AP, and *The New York Times Magazine*. Notes on her speeches are mostly taken from accounts in the AP.

H. V. Kaltenborn, of CBS and later NBC, was one of the preeminent news commentators of his time. He became well-known for his brave reporting on the Spanish Civil War, then got famous during the Munich crisis of 1938, when his deep knowledge and precise diction turned him into a trusted voice as Europe tumbled into war.

Rod Serling's future writing was shaped by his time in the service, having fought in the Philippines with the 511th Parachute Infantry Regiment. The unit's bloody history in the Pacific can be summed up in its nickname, "The Death Squad," and Serling's resulting knowledge of the baseness of mankind informed his work on *The Twilight Zone* and his other material.

Turn signals were first introduced by Buick as early as 1939, but they weren't standard equipment on most American cars until the mid-1950s.

An early version of an electronic turn signal, the "auto-signaling arm," was invented by a woman with the sibilant name Florence Lawrence all the way back in 1914. The device sat on the car fender, and "[It] can be raised or lowered by electrical push buttons," as she told *The Green Book Magazine*. There was also a light that illuminated automatically whenever the brake pedal was pressed. Lawrence, who was among the nation's first film stars and was known as "The Biograph Girl," never patented the "auto-signaling arm," and it faded into history.

Chapter Thirty-Seven   ·   Valley Girl

Alice's work with Mo Connolly and rapprochement with Eleanor Tennant are from *Courting Danger*. Her work with Billie Jean King is from there and Joanne Lannin's *Billie Jean King: Tennis Trailblazer*. Her coaching of Sally Ride comes from Lynn Sherr's *Sally Ride: America's First Woman in Space*. The letter to Kaltenborn was written on September 11, 1958. The description of the Hagley Museum grounds in Wilmington, Delaware, is taken from the author's visit there. Correspondences between Alice and

Will du Pont are taken from the archives at the Hagley and are dated March 3, 1956; March 10, 1956; March 13, 1956; March 16, 1956; April 23, 1956; June 27, 1956; July 17, 1956; July 31, 1956; August 7, 1956; February 27, 1957; March 14, 1957; October 15, 1957; February 27, 1958; April 15, 1958; May 26, 1958; July 15, 1958; May 24, 1959; and June 12, 1959. Eleanor's prediction for the Riggs-King match came in *The New York Times*. More about the match is from *The Last Sure Thing*. Alice's comment about the Republican debates is from her letter to Rita Mae Brown on December 12, 1988. Tennant's obituary appeared in *The New York Times* and *Los Angeles Times*.

Margaret Osborne is one of the few women to win a major championship after childbirth. In all she captured a remarkable thirty-seven major championships, including four singles titles (one at Wimbledon, three at Forest Hills).

The San Diego Padres were still in the Pacific Coast League when Alice brought in one of their pitchers to work with Mo Connolly. The franchise began play in Major League Baseball in 1969.

Randy Moffitt had a quality career in Major League Baseball, pitching across a dozen seasons with the Giants, Astros, and Blue Jays, mainly as a reliever. He won forty-three games and saved ninety-six, with an ERA of 3.65.

Maureen Connolly's career was star-crossed after she parted ways with Eleanor Tennant. In 1953 she became the first woman to win all four major titles in the same year, winning the Grand Slam (she had won both Wimbledon and the US National to finish 1952 as well, giving her six consecutive major titles) and dropping just a single set across all four tourneys. She won the French Open and her third straight Wimbledon in the summer of 1954, then returned to California. In late July she was riding her horse, Colonel Merryboy, in San Diego when a passing concrete mixer spooked the horse. Connolly had her leg crushed between horse and truck, an injury that essentially ended her career at age nineteen. In 1969, at the tragically young age of thirty-four, she died of cancer.

Chapter Thirty-Eight · Queen of the Desert

Alice's trip east to be inducted into the International Tennis Hall of Fame is informed by *Courting Danger* and articles in *Sports Illustrated*, the *Los Angeles Times*, and on the Hall of Fame's website, tennisfame.com. Details on the 1964 World's Fair come from articles in *Mental Floss* and *The New York Times*. Her trip to Hawaii was covered in the *Honolulu Star-Bulletin* and mentioned in correspondence with Will du Pont. The business with Lake Encino Racquet Club is from the *San Francisco Examiner*, *Roto* magazine, and correspondence with Will du Pont in 1964. Will writes of his divorce from Margaret Osborne in correspondence dated February 14, 1964. The trust fund details are from correspondence dated October 2, 1963, and October 18, 1963. Alice wrote Will about Point Happy on May 7, 1965, and November 21, 1965. Jean du Pont's letter to Alice is dated December 29, 1965.

Margaret Osborne no doubt left Will du Pont for multiple reasons, but one of them apparently was his refusal to let her travel down under to play in the Australian Open. "He threatened to divorce me if I went," she said years later. "He wanted me to come to California with him. He thought I should be with him. That was that."

Osborne's partner, Margaret Varner Bloss, was a champion in many racket sports, including badminton and squash, as well as tennis. Bloss is in the Hall of Fame for both badminton and squash. Bloss and Osborne formed a partnership and were ranked among the top twenty racehorse owners in a 1996 poll.

Chapter Thirty-Nine · Defending Your Life

Alice mentioned her bartending gigs for neighbors in a profile in *The Desert Sun*, the same place she mentioned her regret at never having played on television yet not begrudging modern stars their large paychecks. *The Desert Sun* also carried details of the fire that nearly took Alice's life and the contents of her home on Indiana Avenue, and many other details of her difficulties in the 1970s, few of which are mentioned in *Courting Danger*. Her address and other details of her life in Palm Desert come from tax records and material found at the Palm Desert Country Club office. The London *Daily Mail* and *Daily Express* carried news of her appearance at the Wimbledon centennial. Other observations of Palm Desert, and the conversation with Rusty Brinder, result from the author's visit.

The centennial celebration at the All England Club saw a bit of controversy when Jimmy Connors skipped the photo with all the living champions. He gave a lame excuse—"I had a sore thumb," he told the London press. The great Björn Borg missed it, too, but he was playing on Centre Court at the time. The two Helens—Jacobs and Wills—were too old to travel and sent regrets.

In addition to her regret over not getting to ever play any televised tennis, Alice told a reporter she dearly wished she could have played in the age of the tiebreaker, thus saving some wear and tear on her legs.

Chapter Forty · Sleeping with the Enemy

Rita Mae Brown's insight into Alice comes from her correspondence with the author. All is contrasted with the story Alice told in *Courting Danger*.

Rita Mae Brown's handwriting requires close inspection in order to decipher it—in her letter to me she acknowledged her scrawl and chalked it up to fatigue and a "mare who pulled like a freight train" who had injured her hand ligaments. But Alice had mentioned it some three decades earlier; in a 1988 letter to Brown she wrote, "I loved your letter, though I think I should give you some penmanship lessons." For her part, Alice typed most of her correspondence.

William J. "Wild Bill" Donovan was a New Yorker and WWI hero who was tasked by President Roosevelt with forming and leading the intelligence campaign during WWII. The Office of Strategic Services (OSS) was his baby and became the forerunner to the CIA. Despite a mixed record during the war, the OSS has a romantic aura that gives it an outsize legend.

The Sixth Marine Division initially faced light resistance while sweeping across northern Okinawa. Then it went south to reinforce American units fighting there, and the carnage multiplied exponentially. In a single day, May 16, 1945, the Sixth suffered an incredible 576 casualties. It won a Presidential Unit Citation for heroism on that contested island and was credited with the killing or capture of nearly 25,000 Japanese soldiers.

Chapter Forty-One · It's a Wonderful Life

Laurie Pignon remembered covering Alice in the 1930s for an article in the London *Daily Mail* on June 25, 1984. Dave Kibbey provided real estate information about the Deep Canyon Tennis Club. The story about Alice's encounter with Boris Becker appeared in *The Desert Sun*, which also carried news of the various honorifics and soirees held in Alice's name. Video of the dedication of the Alice Marble Court in Palm Desert can be seen at https://www.sportspundit.com/videos/ufVT3_GaBXA. The declaration of "Alice Marble Day" was printed on a scroll that was framed and hung in the Palm Desert Country Club rec center. Alice wrote to Rita Mae Brown about her broken bones on October 7, 1987. The All England Club invited her to attend Wimbledon in correspondence dated December 9, 1987. Alice wrote to Brown about it on April 15, 1988. She wrote to Brown about Gloria Toote on March 3, 1986. Bob Prestie's background and information on the lawsuits with Taylor Caldwell's family come from articles in *People* and the *Los Angeles Times*. Taylor Caldwell's family eventually settled the lawsuit against Bob Prestie out of court. Alice wrote to Brown about Prestie on December 3, 1986, and May 2, 1988.

Gloria Toote was indeed a liberal in the 1970s; even while working for President Ford, she was aggressively pushing for funding for civil rights projects and equal-opportunity projects. Yet she shocked those who knew her when she seconded the nomination of Ronald Reagan at the

1976 Republican convention. Reagan and Toote had become somewhat surprising bedfellows, given the former California governor's race policies while in office. Toote believed the future president listened to her even though he disagreed with her, and that was the basis of their friendship and her work in his government.

CHAPTER FORTY-TWO · THE ALICE MARBLE STORY

Background on the preproduction of *The Alice Marble Story* comes from Rita Mae Brown's correspondence with the author and with Alice dated August 11, 1986. Brown's operatic breakup with Martina Navratilova was mentioned in Adrianne Blue's *Martina* and in correspondence with the author. Alice wrote Brown of her feelings for her on March 3, 1986; May 4, 1989; and September 15, 1989. Information about potential actresses to play Alice, and their salary demands, comes from *The Desert Sun*, the Prickly Pears documentary, and the correspondence between Alice and Brown of May 2, 1989. Rita Mae's correspondence with the producers behind *The Alice Marble Story* was penned on February 5, 1986; February 25, 1986; and March 12, 1986. ABC's difficulties with confirming the facts of the story are elucidated in a long letter dated April 28, 1986. A telegram frantically trying to track down Rita Mae was sent to her on February 7, 1986. The Longstreets' difficulties with the production of an Alice Marble movie were written about in the *Los Angeles Times*. Notes about the beginnings of *Courting Danger* are from *The Desert Sun* and Brown's correspondence with Alice of October 7, 1987. Dale Leatherman's entree into the project was told about in Brown's correspondence with the author and a letter she wrote to Leatherman on November 21, 1987, and Alice wrote Brown about Dale on December 12, 1988, and May 4, 1989. Leatherman's admission of mistakes in *Courting Danger* comes from correspondence with the author. Reviews of the memoir appeared in *The New York Times*, *People*, *Kirkus Reviews*, and *Publishers Weekly*.

At the time Rita Mae Brown was hired to write *The Alice Marble Story*, she was represented by the talent agency Robinson-Weintraub-Gross, which, as the reader might imagine, caught my attention.

When Rita Mae Brown says her script was for the ABC "movie-of-the-week," she most likely means just a movie appearing on ABC TV, as the branded program *Movie of the Week* had stopped airing on ABC in 1975.

Marita Lorenz also claimed to have driven to Dallas with Lee Harvey Oswald the night before John F. Kennedy was killed in the city on November 22, 1963; in her story, she and Oswald met with Jack Ruby, who would assassinate Oswald two days after he shot Kennedy, and future Watergate burglars E. Howard Hunt and Frank Sturgis, then working with the CIA. She gave testimony to that effect to the House Select Committee on Assassinations in 1977, which, according to *The New York Times*, "concluded [her story] was unreliable." Other wild details from Lorenz's life include her imprisonment as a small child in the Bergen-Belsen concentration camp, along with her mother, who worked with the French resistance. She also said she spied on United Nations diplomats in New York, was shot at and nearly killed by enemy agents in Darien, Connecticut, and had a daughter with the Venezuelan generalissimo Marcos Pérez Jiménez.

The TV movie made about Lorenz, *My Little Assassin*, starred Gabrielle Anwar as Lorenz and Joe Mantegna of *The Godfather: Part III* fame as Fidel Castro.

Chapter Forty-Three · Final Destination

The description of the Alice Marble Tennis Courts in San Francisco comes from the author's visit. Rita Mae Brown's thoughts came from her correspondence with the author. Dale Leatherman's account of her final chat with Alice was recounted in *The Desert Sun*. Obituaries of Alice ran in *The New York Times*, *Los Angeles Times*, *San Francisco Examiner*, London *Daily Telegraph*, *The Desert Sun*, and the AP.

The Alice Marble Tennis Courts are the centerpiece of the George Sterling Park, named for the California poet. According to a plaque in the park, Sterling was known as the "Last Bohemian" poet. He once wrote of San Francisco, "And great is thy tenderness, O cool, grey city of love!"

BIBLIOGRAPHY

Books

Aidala, Thomas R. *Hearst Castle, San Simeon*. New York: Harrison House, 1981.

Anderson, Robert S. *The Beverly Hills Hotel and Bungalows: The First 100 Years*. Beverly Hills, CA: The BH Collection, 2012.

Baker, Nicholson. *Human Smoke*. New York: Simon & Schuster, 2008.

Blue, Adrianne. *Martina: The Lives and Times of Martina Navratilova*. New York: Birch Lane Press, 1995.

Blum, John Morton. *V Was for Victory*. New York: Harcourt Brace Jovanovich, 1976.

Brands, H. W. *The Age of Gold*. New York: Doubleday, 2002.

Burgoon, John R. *It All Counts on Twenty*. Self-published, Lulu Press, 2014.

Clary, Raymond H. *The Making of Golden Gate Park: The Growing Years 1906–1950*. San Francisco: Don't Call It Frisco Press, 1987.

Cleather, Norah Gordon. *Wimbledon Story*. London: Sporting Handbooks, Ltd., 1947.

Coffman, Taylor. *Hearst Castle*. Santa Barbara, CA: Sequoia Communications, 1985.

Current Biography Yearbook 1940. New York: H.W. Wilson Company, 1940.

Daneman, Meredith. *Margot Fonteyn: A Life*. New York: Viking, 2004.

Danzig, Allison, and Peter Schwed, eds. *The Fireside Book of Tennis*. New York: Simon & Schuster, 1972.

Darowski, Joseph J., ed. *The Ages of Wonder Woman: Essays on the Amazon Princess in Changing Times*. Jefferson, NC: McFarland and Co., 2014.

Davidson, Sue. *Changing the Game: The Stories of Tennis Champions Alice Marble & Althea Gibson*. Seattle: Seal Press, 1997.

DeMarco, Gordon. *A Short History of Los Angeles*. San Francisco: Lexikos, 1988.

Djata, Sundiata. *Blacks at the Net: Volume 1*. Syracuse, NY: Syracuse University Press, 2006.

Federal Writers Project of the Works Progress Administration. *California in the 1930s*. Berkeley: University of California Press, 1939.

Fein, Paul. *Tennis Confidential*. Washington, DC: Potomac Books, Inc., 2002.

Flamm, Jerry. *Good Life in Hard Times*. San Francisco: Chronicle Books, 1978.

Frayne, Trent. *Famous Women Tennis Players*. New York: Dodd, Mead & Company, 1979.

459

Freedman, Estelle B. *Redefining Rape*. Cambridge, MA: Harvard University Press, 2013.

Friedrich, Otto. *City of Nets*. New York: Harper & Row, 1986.

Gelbert, Doug. *The Great Delaware Sports Book*. Montchanin, DE: Manatee Books, 1995.

Gibson, Althea. *I Always Wanted to Be Somebody*. New York: Harper and Brothers, 1958.

Golay, Michael. *America 1933*. New York: Free Press, 2013.

Goldstein, Richard. *Helluva Town*. New York: Free Press, 2010.

Hansen, Gladys C. *San Francisco Almanac*. San Francisco: Chronicle Books, 1995.

Harris, Cecil, and Larryette Kyle-DeBose. *Charging the Net*. Chicago: Ivan R. Dee, 2007.

Harris, Warren G. *Clark Gable*. New York: Harmony Books, 2002.

Hennessey, S. J. *American Catholics*. Oxford, UK: Oxford University Press, 1981.

Hickok, Ralph. *A Who's Who of Sports Champions*. New York: Houghton Mifflin, 1995.

Himber, Charlotte. *Famous in Their Twenties*. New York: Association Press, 1942.

Jacobs, Helen Hull. *Gallery of Champions*. New York: A.S. Barnes, 1949.

Kastner, Victoria. *Hearst Ranch: Family, Land, and Legacy*. New York: Harry N. Abrams, 2013.

King, Billie Jean. *We Have Come a Long Way*. New York: McGraw-Hill, 1988.

Lannin, Joanne. *Billie Jean King: Tennis Trailblazer*. New York: Lerner Publishing Group, 1999.

LeCompte, Tom. *The Last Sure Thing*. Kent, OH: Black Squirrel Publishing, 2003.

Lepore, Jill. *The Secret History of Wonder Woman*. New York: Vintage, 2014.

Mackey, R. Scott. *Barbary Baseball: The Pacific Coast League of the 1920s*. Jefferson, NC: McFarland & Co., 1995.

Marble, Alice. *The Road to Wimbledon*. New York: Charles Scribners' Sons, 1946.

Marble, Alice, and Dale Leatherman. *Courting Danger*. New York: St. Martin's Press, 1991.

Noel, Susan. *Tennis Without Tears*. London: Hutchinson & Co., 1947.

Patterson, Robert L., and Frank N. Magill, eds. *Great Lives from History*. American Women Series, vol. 4. Pasadena, CA: Salem Press, 1995.

Perlstein, Rick. *The Invisible Bridge: The Fall of Nixon and the Rise of Reagan*. New York: Simon & Schuster, 2014.

Riggs, Bobby. *Tennis Is My Racket*. New York: Simon & Schuster, 1949.

Rogers St. Johns, Adela. *Love, Laughter and Tears*. New York: Signet, 1979.

Sander, Gordon F. *Serling: The Rise and Twilight of TV's Last Angry Man*. New York: Dutton, 1992.

Sherr, Lynn. *Sally Ride: America's First Woman in Space*. New York: Simon & Schuster, 2014.

Spain, Nancy. *"Teach" Tennant: The Story of Eleanor Tennant*. London: W. Laurie, 1953.

Travelers Guide to San Francisco. San Francisco: California Guide Book Co., 1928.

United States Lawn Tennis Association. *Official Encyclopedia of Tennis*. New York: Harper & Row, 1972.

Van Natta, Don. *Wonder Girl*. New York: Little, Brown & Co., 2011.

Ware, Susan. *Game, Set, Match: Billie Jean King and the Revolution in Women's Sports*. Chapel Hill: University of North Carolina Press, 2011.

Weintraub, Robert. *The Victory Season*. New York: Little, Brown & Co., 2013.

Wiggins, David K., ed. *Out of the Shadows: A Biographical History of African American Athletes*. Little Rock: University of Arkansas Press, 2006.

Wilson, Elizabeth. *Love Game: A History of Tennis, from Victorian Pastime to Global Phenomenon*. Chicago: University of Chicago Press, 2016.

INTERNET ARTICLES

"1941 H2H Tour—Marble, Hardwick, Budge, Tilden." Tennis Warehouse. September 29, 2017. https://tt.tennis-warehouse.com/index.php?threads/1941-h2h-tour-marble -hardwick-budge-tilden.600809/.

"Alice Marble." Encyclopaedia Britannica. Accessed September 21, 2018. https://www.britannica .com/biography/Alice-Marble.

"Alice Marble." Encyclopedia.com. Updated January 18, 2020. https://www.encyclopedia.com /women/encyclopedias-almanacs-transcripts-and-maps/marble-alice-1913-1990.

"Alice Marble." International Tennis Hall of Fame. Accessed September 28, 2018. https://www .tennisfame.com/hall-of-famers/inductees/alice-marble.

"A Little Inn Sight Into Old Forest Hills." Forest Hills Blog. July 19, 2019. http:// foresthillsgardensblog.com/2019/07/19/a-little-inn-sight-into-old-forest-hills/.

"Bacterial Pneumonia Caused Most Deaths in 1918 Influenza Pandemic." National Institutes of Health. August 19, 2008. https://www.nih.gov/news-events/news-releases /bacterial-pneumonia-caused-most-deaths-1918-influenza-pandemic.

"Bill Stern Sports Newsreel." Old-Time.com. Updated July 2, 2015. https://www.old-time.com /otrlogs2/bstern2_wp.html.

Bowers, Ray. "Forgotten Victories: A History of Pro Tennis 1926–1945: Chapter XI: America, 1940–1941." The Tennis Server. Accessed May 12, 2019. http://www.tennisserver.com /lines/lines_06_10_01.html.

Bowers, Ray. "Forgotten Victories: A History of Pro Tennis 1926–1945: Chapter XIII: The High War Years 1943–1945." Accessed May 12, 2019. http://www.tennisserver.com/lines/lines _07_10_27.html.

Brun, Tanya. "Will du Pont, Jr. Papers." Hagley Museum and Library. Accessed March 3, 2019. https://findingaids.hagley.org/xtf/view?docId=ead/2317_II.xml.

Caparaz, Dean. "Jacobs: Tennis Star, Trailblazer, Golden Bear." Inside the Lair. March 7, 2018. https://calbears.com/news/2018/3/7/inside-the-lair-helen-hull-jacobs-tennis-star -trailblazer-golden-bear.aspx?.

Chen, C. Peter. "New York Navy Yard." World War II Database. Accessed October 4, 2019. https://ww2db.com/facility/New_York_Navy_Yard/.

Cronin, Brian. "Comic Book Legends Revealed." CBR.com. September 23, 2011. https://www.cbr .com/comic-book-legends-revealed-333/.

Daneman, Meredith. "The Affair of the Century." *The Telegraph*. October 11, 2004. https://www .telegraph.co.uk/culture/4730478/The-affair-of-the-century.html.

Douglass, Robert. "A Brief History of West Oakland." Sonoma State University. Accessed June 19, 2019. https://web.sonoma.edu/asc/cypress/finalreport/Chapter02.pdf.

"Dr. George Grant Gere." Find A Grave. Accessed June 9, 2019. https://fr-ca.findagrave.com
    /memorial/171507345/george-grant-gere.

Edwards, Bobb. "Russell Birdwell." Find A Grave. Accessed October 14, 2019. https://www
    .findagrave.com/memorial/11796682/russell-birdwell.

"George Leslie 'Les' Marble, 1902–1968." My Heritage. Accessed September 26, 2018. https://
    www.myheritage.com/names/george_marble.

Gunsock. "The Life and Many Loves of Clark Gable." Reel Rundown. Updated April 19, 2016.
    https://reelrundown.com/celebrities/Clark-Gable-and-the-Many-Women-in-His-Life.

Hamilton, E. L. "Clark Gable Never Recovered from the Tragic Death of His Wife, Carole
    Lombard, in a Plane Crash." The Vintage News. December 19, 2017. https://www
    .thevintagenews.com/2017/12/19/clark-gable-carole-lombard/.

Highland, Margaret. "Sea Breezes and Business as Usual: Mayor La Guardia's Summer City Hall,
    1936." Mansion Musings. June 13, 2018. https://mansionmusings.wordpress.com/2018/06
    /13/sea-breezes-and-business-as-usual-mayor-la-guardias-summer-city-hall-1936/.

Keane, Katharine. "Competition and Community: 124 Years of History at the West Side Tennis
    Club." National Trust for Historic Preservation. June 22, 2016. https://savingplaces.org
    /stories/competition-community-124-years-history-west-side-tennis-club.

"Learn About Oheka Castle: A Rich and Vibrant History." Oheka Castle Hotel & Estate. Accessed
    July 26, 2019. https://www.oheka.com/history.htm.

Lumpkin, Angela. "The Growth of National Women's Tennis, 1904–1940." Kansas University.
    Accessed March 17, 2019. https://kuscholarworks.ku.edu/bitstream/handle/1808/11477
    /Lumpkin_The%20Growth%20of%20National.pdf.

McClean, Tony. "Robert Ryland." Wayne State University Athletics. Accessed November 27, 2019.
    https://wsuathletics.com/honors/hall-of-fame/robert-ryland/94.

Morgan, Michelle. "How Carole Lombard's Career Was Almost Over Before It Began." The
    History Press. Accessed July 3, 2019. https://www.thehistorypress.co.uk/articles
    /how-carole-lombard-s-career-was-almost-over-before-it-began/.

Nowlin, Bill. "Smead Jolley." Society for American Baseball Research. Accessed March 1, 2019.
    https://sabr.org/bioproj/person/3aee5500.

"Old Field Club and Farm National Register of Historic Places Registration Form." National Park
    Service. Accessed January 24, 2020. https://www.nps.gov/nr/feature/places/pdfs
    /15001027.pdf.

Paige, Janis. "Harassment in Hollywood's Golden Age: A Survivor's Firsthand Story." The
    Hollywood Reporter. October 27, 2017. https://www.hollywoodreporter.com/news
    /harassment-hollywoods-golden-age-survivor-janis-paiges-first-hand-story-1052498.

Pastorino, Robert S. "Poly-Lowell Football San Francisco's High School Classic Game, 1912–
    1971." California Interscholastic Federation San Francisco. Accessed September 4, 2019.
    http://cifsf.org/uploads/3/0/9/7/30972031/poly-lowellfootballhistory.pdf.

Plitt, Amy. "20 Awesome Things People Saw at the 1964 World's Fair." Mental Floss. April 22,
    2014. http://mentalfloss.com/article/56322/20-awesome-things-people-saw-1964
    -worlds-fair.

Polo, Susana. "Alice Marble: Tennis Celebrity, Wonder Woman Writer, and Spy?" The Mary Sue.
    September 23, 2011. https://www.themarysue.com/alice-marble-wonder-woman/.

"RMS Berengaria." Hall Genealogy Website. Accessed November 12, 2019. https://rmhh.co.uk
    /ships/pages/berengaria.html.

Rogers, Keith. "Crash That Killed Actress Carole Lombard, 21 Others Near Las Vegas Still Echoes After 75 Years." *Las Vegas Review-Journal.* January 15, 2017. https://www.reviewjournal .com/news/politics-and-government/nevada/crash-that-killed-actress-carole-lombard-21 -others-near-las-vegas-still-echoes-after-75-years/.

"Russ Columbo." Sam Houston State University. Accessed June 4, 2019. https://www.shsu.edu /~lis_fwh/book/roots_of_rock/support/crooner/Columbo2.htm.

Sandlin, Lee. "Losing the War." Lee Sandlin. Accessed August 25, 2019. http://leesandlin.com /articles/LosingTheWar.htm.

"Spouse Surname Index." "Marble." Accessed November 21, 2018. http://freepages.rootsweb .com/~lrmarble/genealogy/spouse/SurnameH.htm.

"'The Bridge That Couldn't Be Built.' How the Golden Gate Bridge Came into Being." History Hit. January 5, 2016. https://www.historyhit.com/1933-construction-golden-gate-bridge/.

"The Flu in San Francisco." PBS. Accessed February 14, 2019. https://www.pbs.org/wgbh /americanexperience/features/influenza-san-francisco/.

"The Mysterious Death of Newport Movie Mogul Thomas Ince." New England Historical Society. Accessed Spetember 9, 2019. http://www.newenglandhistoricalsociety.com /mysterious-death-newport-movie-mogul-thomas-ince/.

"The Story of the House." Schiaparelli. Accessed October 12, 2019. https://www.schiaparelli.com /en/21-place-vendome/the-story-of-the-house/.

"Tuberculosis Symptoms." Mayo Clinic. Accessed June 21, 2019. https://www.mayoclinic.org /diseases-conditions/tuberculosis/symptoms-causes/syc-20351250.

W., Lisa. "Ping Bodie: S.F. 's Home Run Hero of the Dead-Ball Era." San Francisco History Center. Accessed June 18, 2019. http://sfhcbasc.blogspot.com/2016/08/ping-bodie-sfs -home-run-hero-of-dead.html.

Wenzell, Nicolette. "Explore Palm Springs: 139 Club." Palm Springs Life. August 20, 2014. https://www.palmspringslife.com/explore-palm-springs-139-club/.

"What Did Margarita Madrigal's Contemporaries Say about Her Teaching?" Margarita Madrigal. September 5, 2012. http://margaritamadrigal.blogspot.com/.

"Wimbledon History: 1940s." About Wimbledon. Accessed May 2, 2019. https://www .wimbledon.com/en_GB/aboutwimbledon/history_1940s.html.

"Wonder Woman 1942." My Comic Shop. Accessed July 22, 2019. https://www.mycomicshop .com/search?TID=181601.

Zimmerman, Dwight Jon. "The Home Front in 1943: Strikes, Stress, and Scandals." Defense Media Network. June 29, 2013. https://www.defensemedianetwork.com/stories /the-home-front-in-1943-strikes-stress-and-scandals/.

PERIODICALS

"13, Throop and Marbles." *Newsweek,* July 11, 1938.

"1941 Professional Tennis Tour Official Program."

"Alice Marble." *Look,* September 1939.

"Alice Marble Goes to Wimbledon." *Life,* May 24, 1937.

"Alice Marble on Football." *Newsweek,* October 21, 1940.

"Alice Marble Performs for High-Speed Camera." *Life*, August 28, 1939.

"America's Grand Slam." *Newsweek*, July 17, 1939.

"An Opportunity—and a Privilege!" *American Lawn Tennis* 17, May 15, 1923.

"Another Helen of Berkeley." *Literary Digest*, August 25, 1934.

Armstrong, O. K. "Never Again—Unless We Say So." *Good Housekeeping*, September 1937.

"At Forest Hills." *Time*, October 3, 1938.

"At Wimbledon." *Time*, July 12, 1937.

Baskette, Kirtley. "Hollywood's Unmarried Husbands and Wives." *Photoplay*, December 1938.

"Billie Jean King: 'I'll Kill Him.'" *Time*, July 6, 1962.

Blagden, Nellie. "Silenced by a Stroke, Taylor Caldwell Becomes the Focus of a Bitter Family Feud." *People*, July 21, 1980.

"Champions at Forest Hills." *Time*, July 13, 1937.

"Change in Women's Ranking." *American Lawn Tennis* 15, June 1921.

Coleman, Ronald. "Court Favorite." *Roto Magazine*, January 1964.

Danzig, Sarah Palfrey. "Me and Alice." *World Tennis*, April 1991.

Dunphy, Don. "Wartime Sports Broadcasting." *Radio Annual*, 1945.

"'Eighth Wonder' Syndicated." *Time*, September 15, 1941.

"Eleanor Tennant." *Sports Illustrated*, January 13, 1958.

"Forest Hills Finale." *Time*, September 21, 1936.

Gibson, Althea. "Dear Miss Marble." *American Lawn Tennis*, February 1951.

"Goings On About Town." *New Yorker*, January 7, 1939.

Hart, Edward. "The (Almost) Lost Gay History of Brooklyn." *New York*, March 5, 2019.

"Information, Please." *Look*, May 1940.

"Jim Crow Tennis." *Time*, August 28, 1939.

Marble, Alice. "As I See It." *American Lawn Tennis*, November 1950.

———. "A Vital Issue." *American Lawn Tennis*, July 1950.

———. "Civilian's Bit—Stay Fit." *House & Garden*, May 1942.

———. "Marble on Marble." *World Tennis*, October 1981.

"Marble's Mission." *New Yorker*, January 3, 1942.

"Marble Takes a Tennis Tumble." *Life*, August 16, 1937.

"Miss Marble Finds It All So Different—Says Her Coach." *Tennis Illustrated*, June 15, 1937.

"Modern Living." *Life*, December 5, 1938.

Nasaw, David. "Earthly Delights." *New Yorker*, March 23, 1998.

"New Net Queen." *Newsweek*, September 19, 1936.

"Not for the Pros." *Time*, September 15, 1941.

"Realsilk." *Life*, March 19, 1941.

"Reichstag Fire: Conclusion." *Time*, January 22, 1934.

Searl, Helen Hurlett. "Alice Marble: Girl of the Month." *Good Housekeeping*, September 1937.

"Soundtrack." *Sports Illustrated*, March 7, 1955.

"Sports Shorts." *Literary Digest*, May 26, 1934.

"Strokes of Genius." *Tennis*, August 1982.

Sutton, Horace. "Golden Greenwood." *Sports Illustrated*, July 20, 1959.

"Tennis Hits Beauty High at Wimbledon." *Life*, July 24, 1939.

"That Gibson Girl." *Time*, August 26, 1957.

"The New Gibson Girl." *Sports Illustrated*, July 2, 1956.

"The Old Man River of Tennis." *Newsweek*, January 13, 1941.

"The Press: Today." *Time*, August 16, 1926.

"The Pro Game." *Newsweek*, July 13, 1942.

"The Question." *Sports Illustrated*, August 28, 1955.

"The Tennis Invincibles." *Newsweek*, October 3, 1938.

"The Tennis Racket." *Newsweek*, September 5, 1938.

"Tomboy Turns Pro." *Time*, November 25, 1940.

"Top of the Tennis Heap." *Newsweek*, July 11, 1938.

"Wimbledon." *Time*, July 13, 1936.

Wind, Herbert Warren. "Run, Helen!" *New Yorker*, August 30, 1952.

Worth, Don. "Will Carole Lombard's Marriage End Her Career?" *Motion Picture*, July 1939.

Wright, Alfred. "Charlie's Seventh Heaven." *Sports Illustrated*, April 25, 1963.

HISTORICAL PAPERS

Aubry, R. F. "A House Divided: Guidance and Counseling in 20th-Century America." *Personnel and Guidance Journal*, 1982.

Brown, Ashley. "Swinging for the State Department: American Women Tennis Players in Diplomatic Goodwill Tours, 1941–1959." *Journal of Sport History*, Fall 2015.

Journal of the American Association for Health, Physical Education, and Recreation 16, no. 6 (1945).

Journal of the American Association for Health, Physical Education, and Recreation 21, no. 1 (1950).

Ritchie, Robert Welles. "San Francisco." San Francisco Committee National Conference of Social Work, San Francisco (1929).

NEWSPAPERS

"12 Women Get Style Awards." *New York Times*, March 19, 1939, page 48.

"117-Pound Girl Wins Honors at Women's Games." *Billings Gazette*, July 5, 1928, page 7.

"1,000 Watch Alice Marble." *Minneapolis Morning Tribune*, April 20, 1945, page 12.

"80,000 to Get New Medal." *London Daily Telegraph*, February 11, 1947, page 5.

Abrams, Norma. "Alice Marble Once Sandlot Ballplayer." *New York Daily News*, September 15, 1936, page 169.

Adams, Ruth. "Miss Marble to Play at Vassar." *Vassar Miscellany News*, October 1, 1938, page 2.

Adams, Susan B. "Helen Jacobs, Tennis Champion in the 1930s, Dies." *New York Times*, June 4, 1997, page 24.

"Addendum." *Hartford Courant*, December 4, 1938, page 38.

"Admiral Winslow Plays Several Sets of Tennis." *Los Angeles Times*, June 6, 1916, page 22.

"After Tennis Success the American Champion Crooned." *The Age*, July 25, 1939, page 3.

"Air Parade in Review." *Radio Daily*, May 3, 1937.

"Alice Lets a Secret out of Her Cap." London *Daily Express*, June 12, 1937, page 3.

"Alice Gets Set." *San Francisco Examiner*, April 7, 1940, page 48.

"Alice Marble." *Janesville Daily Gazette*, October 28, 1946.

"Alice Marble, 77, Top U.S. Tennis Star of 1930s." *New York Times*, December 14, 1990, page 127.

"Alice Marble: 1938." *Philadelphia Inquirer*, January 10, 1938, page 9.

"Alice Marble Appeals to Women." *New York Times*, August 27, 1942, page 12.

"Alice Marble Appointed P.D.C.C. Social Head." *Desert Sun*, August 19, 1969, page 5.

"Alice Marble Arrives." *New York Times*, July 27, 1939, page 23.

"Alice Marble at Loew's State." *New York Times*, December 27, 1940, page 23.

"Alice Marble Back in US." Associated Press, July 14, 1937.

"Alice Marble Becomes First Lady Football Announcer." *Brooklyn Daily Eagle*, October 11, 1940, page 10.

"Alice Marble Concludes Lectures for the Year on the Will to Win." *Colonnade*, May 9, 1950.

"Alice Marble Deserved Medal." Associated Press, January 10, 1940, page 8.

"Alice Marble Enters Ranks of the Big-Time." *Californian*, July 31, 1933, page 5.

"Alice Marble Eyes Air Career." *South Bend Tribune*, May 11, 1934, page 31.

"Alice Marble Fails." *Morning Call*, September 10, 1945, page 15.

"Alice Marble Faints in Play." United Press, May 24, 1934.

"Alice Marble Figures in Four Titles." *Vancouver Sun*, August 11, 1930, page 10.

"Alice Marble Gives Net Demonstration." *Richmond (IN) Palladium-Item*, January 14, 1948, page 8.

"Alice Marble Gives Secret of Keeping Trim in Figure." Associated Press, May 8, 1938.

"Alice Marble Going on Films." London *Daily Express*, July 12, 1939, page 3.

"Alice Marble Has Back Injury." United Press, June 1, 1945.

"Alice Marble Here." *Paterson Evening News*, March 7, 1945, page 13.

"Alice Marble in S.F. Net Semi-Finals." *San Pedro News Pilot*, June 30, 1933, page 19.

"Alice Marble in Spectacular Comeback in Desert Net Event." *Calexico Chronicle*, April 4, 1936, page 27.

"Alice Marble in Tennis Defeat." *San Francisco Examiner*, May 20, 1934, page 24.

"Alice Marble in Tennis Matches Against Leading Men." *News Journal*, January 24, 1945, page 11.

"Alice Marble in the Flesh." *Desert Sun*, February 20, 1976, page C3.

"Alice Marble Is Lieutenant." Associated Press, August 19, 1942.

"Alice Marble Looking for a Sixth Career." *Palm Beach Post,* January 25, 1950, page 6.

"Alice Marble May Go into Movies." Associated Press, July 11, 1939.

"Alice Marble: National Sports Figure and Fashion Inspiration." *Pittsburgh Post-Gazette,* January 27, 1938, page 9.

"Alice Marble on PD Resort Staff." *Desert Sun,* August 15, 1981.

"Alice Marble Opens Campaign." *San Pedro News Pilot,* April 25, 1938, page 8.

"Alice Marble Reaches Top After Ten Years." Associated Press, September 13, 1936.

"Alice Marble Regains $500 Cigaret Case." *New York Daily News,* December 22, 1946, page 198.

"Alice Marble Resumes Play." United Press, May 17, 1935.

"Alice Marble Reveals Qualities That Put Her on Top." *New York Daily News,* May 12, 1946, page 167.

"Alice Marble Says 'Sing to Win.'" London *Daily Express,* June 24, 1939, page 5.

"Alice Marble Secret." London *Daily Mail,* May 11, 1937, page 7.

"Alice Marble Set for Wimbledon." Associated Press, May 4, 1937.

"Alice Marble Signs for Test in Movies." *New York Daily News,* July 12, 1939, page 4.

"Alice Marble Slated to Compete Locally." *Calexico Chronicle,* April 2, 1937, page 5.

"Alice Marble's Mother Dies." *San Francisco Examiner,* January 1, 1937, page 13.

"Alice Marble Stars." *Vancouver Province,* July 19, 1930, page 7.

"Alice Marble Talks Catholic Club Plan." *New York Times,* November 16, 1941, page 104.

"Alice Marble, Tennis Champion, to Tell Experiences in Winning Crown." *State Signal* (Trenton, NJ), December 9, 1944, page 1.

"Alice Marble Thinks Tennis to Have Boom After War." *Owensboro Messenger,* February 10, 1945, page 6.

"Alice Marble Thrills Fans in Salt Lake." *Salt Lake Tribune,* May 25, 1936, page 8.

"Alice Marble to Address Huntingdon Girls." *Montgomery Advertiser,* February 11, 1945, page 11.

"Alice Marble to be Greeted by S.F. Mayor." *Santa Cruz Evening News,* October 16, 1936, page 3.

"Alice Marble to Show Styles for Women." *Tampa Tribune,* October 30, 1945, page 9.

"Alice Marble to Speak." *Philadelphia Inquirer,* November 11, 1945, page 47.

"Alice Marble to Talk at College." *Town Talk,* January 29, 1946, page 6.

"Alice Marble to Tell of Wimbledon Trek." *Desert Sun,* October 5, 1977, page A6.

"Alice Marble Triumphs at Brookline." Associated Press, July 26, 1936.

"Alice Marble Visits Barksdale." *Shreveport Times,* May 3, 1940, page 8.

"Alice Marble Wins Initial Pro Match." Associated Press, January 7, 1941.

"Alice Marble Wins Net Title." *San Francisco Examiner,* September 22, 1929, page 38.

"Alice Marble Wins State Tennis Tournament." *San Francisco Examiner,* June 15, 1931, page 20.

"Alice Marble Wins Top Sports Award." United Press, December 10, 1940.

"Alice Marble Wins Way to Maidstone Net Final." Associated Press, July 31, 1933.

"Alice Will Wear Shorts After All." London *Daily Mail,* June 5, 1939, page 5.

"Alice Win Is Not a Fluke." Associated Press, October 2, 1936.

Allen, J. P. "California Girl Loses in First Round." *New York Sun,* August 17, 1931, page 21.

———. "Marble's Loss Hits Tourney Body's Move." *Oakland Tribune,* August 18, 1931, page 34.

"American Girl Collapses." AP, May 24, 1934.

"American Tennis Stars Collapse on Court." London *Daily Telegraph,* May 25, 1934, page 19.

"American Women Lose in France." *Boston Globe,* May 25, 1934, page 26.

Arthur, Allene. "Some Stimulating Sociability." *Desert Sun,* October 9, 1981, page D7.

"Automatic Umpire." London *Daily Mail,* February 1, 1941, page 4.

Babette. "Alice Marble Shows Her New Designs Here." *San Francisco Examiner,* March 4, 1938, page 16.

Bailey, Catherine. "Recreation Roundup." *Johnsonian,* September 20, 1940.

Barrington, Jonah. "B.B.C. Sign Up Alice Marble—as a Crooner." London *Daily Express,* July 11, 1939, page 15.

Bartlett, Maxine. "Grand Opera Casts Glow on Social Scene." *Los Angeles Times,* November 5, 1939, page 63.

Baxter, Leone. "Women in News." *Piru News,* July 20, 1939, page 8.

"BC Championships Continue." *Vancouver Sun,* July 29, 1930, page 10.

Bell, Ralph. "Oswald and Marble Take State Tennis Crown." *Oakland Tribune,* June 24, 1935, page 13.

Benjamin, Burton. "Alice Marble Still Serves." NEA, May 13, 1942, page 7.

"Bill Tilden Still Winning." *Brooklyn Citizen,* May 21, 1945, page 6.

"Births." *Feather River Bulletin,* December 7, 1916, page 7.

"Births; Marriages; Deaths." *San Francisco Chronicle,* January 3, 1920, page 4.

Black, Katherine. "Her Pan-American Relations Really Are." *Brooklyn Daily Eagle,* April 11, 1941, page 10.

"Bombs on Wimbledon." *New York Times,* November 1, 1940, page 24.

Borba, Harry. "Alice Marble Conquers Miss Osborne for State Title." *San Francisco Examiner,* June 24, 1935, page 19.

———. "Alice Marble in First Net Victory." *San Francisco Examiner,* June 16, 1935, page 57.

Bradlee, Nancy. "Miss Marble Plays Sensational Tennis." *Boston Globe,* July 20, 1933, page 17.

"Bride Will Continue in California." *Los Angeles Times,* February 14, 1934, page 23.

Brisbane, Arthur. "Today." *San Francisco Examiner,* December 3, 1933, page 1.

"Britain Is Ready for War." *New York Times,* June 30, 1939, page 1.

"British Critics Change Tune." *San Francisco Examiner,* July 9, 1939, page 46.

Brodie, Ian. "Miss Evert Tops $1 Million Mark." London *Daily Telegraph,* October 25, 1976, page 25.

Bromley, Dorothy Dunbar. "Keeping Fit the Alice Marble Way." *New York Times Magazine,* October 5, 1941, page 104.

Browning, D. C. "On to Wimbledon." London *Times Literary Supplement,* June 14, 1947.

"Bundy Defeats Marble." London *Daily Express,* September 9, 1937, page 7.

Burnley, Hardin. "Coming Champions." *Brainerd Daily Dispatch,* August 19, 1931, page 5.

Burrows, Bill. "Wimbledon Is Still the Most Snobbish Sporting Institution in the World." London *Daily Telegraph,* July 4, 2015.

Burton, Lewis. "Alice Marble Sensational." *San Francisco Examiner,* August 17, 1932, page 15.

"But She Cannot Decide on Shorts." *London Daily Mail,* June 3, 1939, page 9.

"Cabbage Leaves Too Much for Mary's Curls." *London Daily Express,* June 23, 1937, page 3.

Cambridge, Caroline. "Try Miss Marble's Favorite Salad." *London Daily Express,* June 4, 1937, page 14.

Carnegie, Dale. "Girl Who Would Not Fail." *Atlantic Highlands Journal,* June 28, 1945, page 4.

Cart, Julie. "Women's Pioneer Alice Marble Dies." *Los Angeles Times,* December 14, 1990.

"Champions in New Roles." *London Daily Telegraph,* December 27, 1938, page 8.

"Choose Your Tennis Glamour Girl." *London Daily Mirror,* April 25, 1938, page 29.

"Claim Alice Marble Forced Out of Game." *Madera Tribune,* July 5, 1935, page 1.

Considine, Bob. "Lenglen, Wills, Ryan, Marble." International News Service, January 19, 1941.

"Countryman Is Married Again." *San Francisco Examiner,* July 2, 1916, page 7.

"Court Queen Courts Links Fame." *Minneapolis Morning Tribune,* November 9, 1939, page 29.

Crosby, John. "Air, Mixed with Acid, Goes Boom!" *Oakland Tribune,* January 26, 1948.

Crouse, Karen. "Bill Tilden—a Star Defeated Only by Himself." *New York Times,* August 30, 2009.

Crowther, Bosley. "Pat and Mike at the Capitol." *New York Times,* June 19, 1952, page 32.

"CRTA to Hear Marble." *Desert Sun,* January 13, 1978, page A8.

Cuddy, Jack. "Woman's Champion of Poland Over Here." Universal Press Services, July 24, 1937.

"Current Affairs at the Women's Club." *Montclair Times,* December 28, 1944, page 12.

Currie, George. "Alice Marble May Be Answer to Tennis Committee's Fervent Prayers." *Brooklyn Daily Eagle,* August 17, 1932, page 7.

———. "Alice Marble Wins." *Brooklyn Daily Eagle,* September 13, 1936, page 40.

———. "Play Begins Without Dramatic Upsets." *Brooklyn Daily Eagle,* August 18, 1931, page 21.

———. "Redraw Leaves Mrs. Moody Formidable Field to Wade Through." *Brooklyn Daily Eagle,* August 17, 1931, page 19.

———. "Seabright's Defeats and Surprises." *Brooklyn Daily Eagle,* July 27, 1933, page 18.

———. "Shorts and Poker-Face Lone Worries of Wightman Cup Team." *Brooklyn Daily Eagle,* May 9, 1934, page 21.

———. "Through the Looking Glass Tennis Conquers Miss Alice Marble." *Brooklyn Daily Eagle,* August 18, 1932, page 19.

———. "Wightman Cup Victory, Sans Star, Centers All Notice on Team Play." *Brooklyn Daily Eagle,* August 7, 1933, page 16.

Custer, James Joe. "Alice Marble to Wed After War." United Press, January 24, 1944.

Danzig, Allison. "Alice Marble Tops Miss Jacobs at Net." *New York Times,* August 11, 1940, page 61.

———. "Alice Marble Upsets Helen Jacobs." *New York Times,* September 13, 1936, page 115.

———. "Australian Player Bows in Four Sets." *New York Times,* August 29, 1950, page 33.

———. "Budge and Miss Marble Capture U.S. Tennis Title." *New York Times,* September 25, 1938, page 73.

———. "Henkel, Grant and Miss Marble Take Opening Matches in U.S. Title Tennis." *New York Times,* September 3, 1937, page 21.

———. "International Array of Stars Ready for Opening of U.S. Tennis Title Today." *New York Times,* September 7, 1939, page 37.

———. "Kovacs Eliminates Philby." *New York Times,* September 9, 1938, page 26.

———. "McNeill and Miss Marble Gain Tennis Championship at Forest Hills." *New York Times,* September 9, 1940, page 29.

———. "Miss Babcock Defeated by Miss Stammers." *New York Times,* September 10, 1936, page 31.

———. "Miss Bundy Dethrones Miss Marble." *New York Times,* September 9, 1937, page 42.

———. "Miss Gibson Bows to Louise Brough." *New York Times,* August 31, 1950, page 37.

———. "Miss Gibson Game from Victory over Louise Brough." *New York Times,* August 30, 1950, page 35.

———. "Miss Jacobs Wins from Mrs. Johnson." *New York Times,* September 9, 1936, page 35.

———. "Miss Marble Halts Miss Hardwick in Pro Tennis Debut." *New York Times,* January 7, 1941, page 26.

———. "Miss Marble Is Victor." *New York Times,* September 24, 1938, page 21.

———. "Miss Marble Moves Ahead in U.S. Tennis Play." *New York Times,* September 17, 1938, page 11.

———. "Miss Marble Signs Contract for Tour." *New York Times,* November 13, 1940, page 30.

———. "Miss Marble Takes Net Final." *New York Times,* August 2, 1936, page 118.

———. "Miss Wynne Gains Tennis Final." *New York Times,* September 18, 1938, page 79.

———. "Net Odds." *New York Times,* September 2, 1937, page 23.

———. "Perry, Budge, Miss Marble and Miss Jacobs Enter Finals in National Tennis." *New York Times,* September 12, 1936, page 11.

———. "U.S. Titles Are Annexed by Riggs, Marble." *New York Times,* September 18, 1939, page 26.

———. "U.S. Title Tennis Will Start Today." *New York Times,* September 3, 1936, page 26.

"Daring Shorts." *London Daily Mail,* May 11, 1937, page 7.

Dillman, Lisa. "Something Special on the Court." *Los Angeles Times,* July 16, 2001, page 45.

"Dog Bites Brother of Alice Marble." *San Francisco Examiner,* November 26, 1933, page 9.

"Doings." *Central New Jersey Home News,* April 11, 1941, page 22.

"Dorothy Bundy Wins over Alice Marble." *San Pedro News Pilot,* September 8, 1937, page 1.

Doust, Stanley N. "Alice Has a Game with Budge." London *Daily Mail,* June 7, 1939, page 16.

———. "Alice Marble Was Brilliant." London *Daily Mail,* July 5, 1939, page 15.

———. "Alice Was Wonderful." London *Daily Mail,* July 10, 1939, page 15.

———. "A World Trophy for Women's Tennis?" London *Daily Mail,* May 29, 1934, page 4.

———. "Best Tennis I Have Ever Seen." London *Daily Mail,* June 4, 1938, page 14.

———. "Brilliant Miss Round." London *Daily Mail,* July 2, 1937, page 15.

———. "Miss Marble—Garbo of the Tennis Courts." London *Daily Mail,* May 18, 1937, page 9.

———. "Psychology Cured Miss Marble." London *Daily Mail,* June 18, 1938, page 11.

———. "Temperature Mystery of U.S. Tennis Player." *London Daily Mail*, June 2, 1934, page 13.

———. "Weather Beats Miss Marble." *London Daily Mail*, May 20, 1937, page 20.

———. "Wimbledon Day of Shocks." *London Daily Mail*, June 30, 1937, page 15.

Duncan, Arnott. "Davis Cup Failure, Net Tactics Among Questions Asked Former Tennis Queen." *Arizona Republic*, September 4, 1955, page 48.

Dyer, Braven. "Desert Dyer-y." *Desert Sun*, March 30, 1974, page B2.

———. "Desert Dyer-y." *Desert Sun*, November 30, 1966, page 13.

"Earlham Students Get Tennis Pointers from Alice Marble." *Indianapolis News*, January 16, 1948, page 15.

Effrat, Louis. "Numerous Stars Entertain 15,000 in the Father's Day Sports Parade." *New York Times*, June 16, 1941, page 19.

"Eleanor Tennant Now Pro." *Los Angeles Times*, April 24, 1926, page 48.

"Eleanor Tennant, Who Taught Many Tennis Notables, Dead." *New York Times*, May 13, 1974, page 34.

"English Star Defeats Alice Marble." AP, August 1, 1933.

"Exhibition Tennis on Beverly Courts." *Los Angeles Times*, July 13, 1916, page 9.

"Ex-Net Great Leaves to Join Hall of Fame." *Los Angeles Times*, August 5, 1964, page 93.

"Fashion." *London Times*, June 12, 1939, page 27.

Fentress, Mary. "Glamour Crowns Are Awarded by Jury of Experts." United Press, December 29, 1938.

"First Tennis Speech by Radio to be Given by J. S. Myrick." *New York Times*, June 4, 1922, page 24.

"Forest Hills Favorites Win." *Baltimore Sun*, August 18, 1932, page 12.

Foster, Michael J. "Helen Moody Done, Alice Marble Says." International News Service, May 9, 1934.

"Freda Trounces Alice." *London Daily Mirror*, May 24, 1937, page 27.

"French Tennis Players Recalled by War Threat." *New York Times*, September 18, 1938, page 31.

Froloff, Bill. "Tennis Great Alice Marble May Write Another Book." *Desert Sun*, May 28, 1983, page E1.

"Funeral Friday for Handball Ace Dan Marble." *San Francisco Examiner*, August 28, 1963, page 54.

Gallico, Paul. "Moody by Kayo." *New York Daily News*, August 20, 1933, page 387.

Gibbs, C. M. "Gibberish." *Baltimore Sun*, July 20, 1940, page 11.

"Girl, 13, Plays with PCL Stars." *San Francisco Examiner*, July 12, 1927, page 29.

"Girl Hit by Stone Aimed at Streetcar." *Oakland Tribune*, October 2, 1917, page 5.

"Girl 'Tilden' Rocks Centre Court." *London Daily Mirror*, June 23, 1937, page 26.

"Going Places in Manhattan." *Brooklyn Daily Eagle*, December 2, 1938, page 12.

"Golf Alimony Newest Claim of Divorcees." *Shreveport Times*, November 11, 1923, page 38.

Goodman, Nathan G. "A Full-Length Portrait of Alexander Hamilton." *New York Times*, September 17, 1939, page 100.

Gould, Alan. "Tennis Title Conceded to Helen Jacobs." AP, August 28, 1933.

Gould, Filomena. "Alice Marble Pits Competitive Spirit Against Shoppers Here." *Indianapolis News,* December 3, 1946, page 28.

Goule, Alan. "Schmeling Outstanding Comeback of 1936." Associated Press, December 17, 1936.

"Gove Defeated in Vancouver Tennis." AP, July 19, 1930, page 13.

Graham, Gladys P. "Scott and Peters Winners in Nat'l Tennis Meet." *Weekly Review,* September 2, 1944, page 7.

Graves, Charles. "I See Life." *London Daily Mail,* July 4, 1939, page 8.

Grayson, Garry. "Tilden at 52." *Mount Carmel (PA) Item,* February 19, 1945, page 6.

Grieve, Curly. "Alice Marble Arrives for Net Match Today." *San Francisco Examiner,* October 18, 1936, page 57.

———. "Dan Marble Attacks Acts of Tennis Moguls." *San Francisco Examiner,* September 13, 1936, page 48.

———. "Miss Marble Is Now a Style Expert." *San Francisco Examiner,* March 2, 1938, page 22.

Gross, Jessica. "Who Made That Turn Signal?" *New York Times,* July 12, 2013.

Gundelfinger, Phil. "Alice Marble Rolling Right Along." *Pittsburgh Press,* June 24, 1936, page 27.

Guthrie, Millie. "Guests Wear Leis for Fete at Desert Spa." *Los Angeles Times,* December 8, 1935, page 65.

———."Society Sun Lights Desert." *Los Angeles Times,* November 24, 1935, page 63.

"Hail the New Champion." *Calexico Chronicle,* June 18, 1931, page 4.

Hamilton, T. J. "Alice Marble Wimbledon Victor." *New York Times,* July 7, 1939, page 61.

———. "Miss Jacobs Defeats Miss Marble to Gain Wimbledon Final." *New York Times,* July 1, 1938, page 15.

———. "Miss Marble Signs Contract." *New York Times,* July 12, 1939, page 17.

———. "Miss Marble Wins by 6–0 6–0 to Gain Wimbledon Final with Miss Stammers." *New York Times,* July 7, 1939, page 20.

———. "Miss Stammers Upsets Miss Jacobs." *New York Times,* July 5, 1939, page 23.

———. "Mrs. Moody Gains Wimbledon Semi-Finals with Miss Marble and Miss Jacobs." *New York Times,* July 29, 1938, page 22.

———. "Riggs Drops a Set but Beats Shayes." *New York Times,* July 2, 1939, page 80.

———. "Seeded Players Advance in Wimbledon." *New York Times,* July 22, 1938, page 31.

———. "U.S. Women Stars Advance in Wimbledon Tennis." *New York Times,* June 28, 1939, page 30.

Hart, Jeffrey. "When the Men of Tennis Were Gentlemen." *Wall Street Journal,* May 5, 2004.

"Have a Care, Colonel!" *Tulare Advance-Register,* November 25, 1939, page 8.

"Helen Jacobs Defeats Alice Marble." *San Pedro News Pilot,* June 30, 1938, page 6.

"Helen Stephens Is Voted Outstanding Girl Athlete." Associated Press, December 15, 1936.

"Helen Wants Miss Moody as Doubles Mate." *Oakland Tribune,* May 5, 1933, page 28.

Henry, Bill. "Alice Marble Upsets Helen Jacobs in Tennis Duel." *Los Angeles Times,* September 13, 1936, page 29.

———. "Bill Henry Says" *Los Angeles Times,* August 1, 1933, page 25.

———. "Bill Henry Says." *Los Angeles Times*, June 22, 1935, page 7.

———. "By the Way." *Los Angeles Times*, March 22, 1944, page 13.

Heyman, Evelanne. "Many Honor Tennis Star." *Desert Sun*, May 9, 1977, page A8.

———. "Trinkets, Treasures, Memories Mark Home Tour." *Desert Sun*, February 8, 1975, page 8.

Hoffman, Jeane. "Women Athletes Prove Gameness in Sports." *San Francisco Examiner*, July 22, 1945, page 20.

Holles, Everett. "Old Coach on Riggs: 'Boring.'" *New York Times*, September 18, 1973, page 50.

Hoyt, Elizabeth North. "Alice Marble's Story." *Cedar Rapids Gazette*, July 14, 1946, page 20.

Hughes, Alice. "A Woman's New York." *Star Press*, June 3, 1945, page 18.

"Items of Interest." *Feather River Bulletin*, October 2, 1905, page 3.

Jacobs, Helen. "Alice Has Game to Win—Jacobs." *New York Times*, July 26, 1938, page 63.

James, Brian. "Champions All." *London Daily Mail*, June 21, 1977, page 3.

Janssen, Robin. "Former Champ Alice Marble Visiting Here." *Honolulu Star-Bulletin*, September 22, 1964, page 29.

Kamiya, Gary. "SF Teams Have Played in Some Oddball Spots." *San Francisco Chronicle*, September 24, 2013, page C1.

Kelly, Mark. "Tennis Committee Hit for Ignoring Miss Alice Marble." United Press, July 5, 1935.

Kernodle, Margaret. "Coaches Behind the Champs." Wide World Syndicate, February 11, 1942.

Kilgallen, Dorothy. "Voice of Broadway." *New York Journal-American*, January 4, 1947, page 28.

Kinzel, Marilyn. "Alice Marble Returns Favor in Community Chest Talk." *Minneapolis Morning Tribune*, October 18, 1954, page 23.

Lardner, John. "What About It." *Boston Globe*, September 1, 1939, page 22.

"Leaders in Sports See Good Year." Associated Press, January 2, 1945.

Leavitt, Woodhugh B. "Bundy and Herd Winners." *Los Angeles Times*, September 2, 1919, page 18.

Levine, Beth. "Net Work." *New York Times*, June 9, 1991, page 111.

"Live Gallantly, Look Your Best, Alice Marble Tells Rotarians." *Democrat and Chronicle*, December 20, 1944, page 16.

"Lives Remembered—Dr. Gloria E. A. Toote." *Desert Sun*, July 21, 2017, page A12.

Lorie, Katherine. "Alice Marble Still Defying the Odds." *Press Enterprise*, February 5, 1978, page 16.

"Lovely Alice Marble Seeks Job to Keep Pantry Full." Associated Press, April 17, 1942.

"Lovers of Tennis Salute Living Legend." *Desert Sun*, April 22, 1974, page A10.

Lowry, Paul. "Alice Marble Hopes to Go On and On." *Los Angeles Times*, April 7, 1940, page 31.

Lube, Gene. "A Conversation with . . . Alice Marble." *Desert Sun*, July 27, 1981, page 1.

Lucas, Laddie. "Even in Sport Two Heads Are Better Than One." *London Daily Express*, June 25, 1939, page 31.

Lurie, Dora. "Men Have Last Word at Nets." *Philadelphia Inquirer*, June 12, 1940, page 29.

"Man Late for His Job Takes Cab, Gains $1,000." *New York Times*, December 22, 1946, page 13.

"Many Women Have Qualified to Vote." *Feather River Bulletin* April 18, 1912, page 1.

Marble, Alice. "Alice Marble Teaches You How to Play Tennis." *London Sunday Chronicle*, June 4, 1939, page 17.

———. "Alice Marble Teaches You How to Play Tennis." *London Sunday Chronicle*, June 11, 1939, page 14.

———. "Alice Marble Teaches You How to Play Tennis." *London Sunday Chronicle*, July 2, 1939, page 19.

———. "I've Won My Life Ambition." *London Sunday Chronicle*, July 2, 1939, page 19.

———. "Lost Years Were Kay's Handicap." *London Daily Mail*. July 3, 1946, page 4.

———. "Pickets Deplored." *Los Angeles Times*, August 23, 1953, page 16.

———. "Plea: Don't Be a Woman, Driver." *New York Times Magazine*, October 30, 1955, page 278.

———. "Why I Love Baseball." *New York Times Magazine*, September 28, 1955, page 223.

———. "You Can't Beat DiMag's Hours." United Press, October 1, 1947.

"Marble and Cruickshank Heading East Tonight." *San Pedro News Pilot*, May 4, 1934, page 2.

"Marble Bests Sperling." *London Daily Express*, June 30, 1937, page 5.

"Marble Home for Matches." *Oakland Tribune*, October 18, 1936, page 13.

"Marble Rolls." *London Daily Mail*, March 23, 1977, page 17.

"Marble Survives." *London Daily Express*, May 31, 1937, page 27.

"Marble Whips Jake." *New York Daily News*, September 13, 1936, page 111.

"Mayor Is Literal in Defense Steps." *New York Times*, November 15, 1941, page 13.

McAvoy, J. F. "Alice Marble Captures Third Seabright Title." Associated Press, August 1, 1938.

McCarthy, Julia. "Alice Marble Likes Singing on Her Own." *New York Daily News*, December 16, 1938, page 123.

———. "Net Queen Alice to Serve Love Songs." *New York Daily News*, November 26, 1938, page 92.

McKenzie, Douglas. "Girl Fans in Tennis 'Riot.'" *London Daily Mirror*, June 11, 1938, page 26.

McLemore, Henry. "Tilden, Budge and Vines Rated as Greatest Tennis Players." United Press, March 4, 1941.

———. "Today's Sport Parade." United Press, August 22, 1932.

Menke, Frank G. "What a Surprise Alice Gave Her Doctor." *Akron Beacon Journal*, August 20, 1939, page 49.

"Miss Bernhard Defeats Two Rivals in U.S. Girls Tennis." Associated Press, August 30, 1938.

"Miss Hardwick's Tennis Defeat." *London Daily Telegraph*, January 8, 1941, page 3.

"Miss Jacobs Defeats Miss Moody." *New York Times* August 27, 1933, page 114.

"Miss Jacobs Has No Tennis Alibi." *Brooklyn Times Union*, September 13, 1936, page 13.

"Miss Jedrzejowska Defeats Miss Marble in All-England Tennis Semi-Finals." *New York Times*, July 2, 1937, page 15.

"Miss Marble Asks U.S. Health Drills." *New York Times*, December 15, 1941, page 26.

"Miss Marble a Torch Singer." *London Daily Telegraph*, July 19, 1939, page 10.

"Miss Marble Back from Play Abroad." *New York Times*, July 14, 1937, page 28.

"Miss Marble, Back, Out of Tennis for a Year." *New York Times,* June 23, 1934, page 9.

"Miss Marble Beats Miss Miller." *Vancouver Sun,* August 28, 1930, page 11.

"Miss Marble Gains Final." *New York Times,* July 22, 1933, page 7.

"Miss Marble Impressive." *New York Times,* May 29, 1937, page 29.

"Miss Marble Out of Cup Net Series." *New York Times,* June 2, 1934, page 14.

"Miss Marble Vanquished." Associated Press, January 24, 1941.

"Miss Moody Is Definitely Lost to 1934 Tennis, Says Miss Marble." *New York Times,* May 9, 1934, page 27.

"Miss Moody Is Out of Tennis This Year, Alice Marble Says." *St. Louis Post-Dispatch,* May 9, 1934, page 14.

"Miss Nuthall's Fine Victory." *Times,* August 20, 1933, page 13.

"Miss Stammers in Wimbledon Final." *London Daily Telegraph,* July 7, 1939, page 22.

"Miss Tennant Coach Pro at Palm Springs." *San Diego Sun,* September 6, 1935.

"Mrs. Adelaide Hawley *Will* Speak Here." *Herald-News* (Passaic, NJ), February 3, 1945, page 4.

Myers, A. Wallis. "Miss Round's Great Wimbledon Win." *London Daily Telegraph,* June 30, 1937, page 21.

———. "Miss Round in Wimbledon Final." *London Daily Telegraph,* July 2, 1937, page 22.

"My Personality Parade." *London Daily Mirror,* September 23, 1936, page 9.

"National Tennis Star in Divorce Suit in Bay City." *Santa Cruz Evening News,* September 29, 1923, page 1.

Nelson, Ray. "Army Life Okay, Says Alice Marble." *St. Louis Star-Times,* August 19, 1943, page 22.

"Net Aces Out of Cup Play." AP, August 5, 1934.

"Net Finals Set for Park Today." *San Francisco Examiner,* October 22, 1926, page 32.

"Net Star Has Pleurisy." *New York Times,* June 6, 1934, page 26.

Newell, Bill. "Tennis Star's Fight." *Hartford Courant,* July 28, 1946, page 64.

"New Queen of the Courts." *New York Times,* September 14, 1936, page 26.

"No Controversy on This Aid." *Madera Tribune,* December 26, 1940, page 4.

Nolte, Carl, and Meredith May. "Shipwreck Makes Romantic Return." *San Francisco Chronicle,* May 9, 2007.

"No Pro Career for Alice Marble." Associated Press, April 29, 1940.

"Notes." *Feather River Bulletin,* May 19, 1898, page 2.

"Notes." *Feather River Bulletin,* August 4, 1904, page 2.

"Notes." *Feather River Bulletin,* January 27, 1916, page 6.

"Notes." *Feather River Bulletin,* February 5, 1920, page 4.

"Notes." *Feather River Bulletin,* June 10, 1920, page 6.

"Not Through with Tennis Yet, Says Helen Wills Moody." *San Francisco Examiner,* May 10, 1934, page 26.

O'Brien, Wilson. "Girls Net Play Starts Tomorrow." *San Francisco Examiner,* April 8, 1927, page 38.

"Once a Champ, Always a Champ." *Desert Sun,* April 18, 1977, page A7.

O'Neill, Ann W. "Playing Marbles." *Los Angeles Times,* July 2, 2000, page 41.

"One-Man Rule Hurts Tennis." *Atlanta Constitution,* April 24, 1927, page 42.

"Our Tennis Girls 'Lack Aggression.'" *London Daily Telegraph,* January 28, 1947, page 3.

"Outlines Program to Toughen Nation." *New York Times,* October 11, 1940, page 11.

"Park Net Play to Start Today." *San Francisco Examiner,* November 20, 1926, page 31.

Parrott, Harold. "Alice Marble Battles Maidstone Jinx." *Brooklyn Daily Eagle,* July 29, 1939, page 6.

———. "Alice Marble Certain of Comeback in Year." *Brooklyn Daily Eagle,* June 23, 1934, page 9.

———. "Tennis Final Gained by Nancy Wynne." *Brooklyn Daily Eagle,* September 18, 1938, page 37.

Parsons, John. "Tribute to a Pioneer." *London Daily Telegraph,* December 15, 1990, page 29.

Parsons, Louella. "Ginger Rogers Dyes Hair for Role." Universal Press Services, October 13, 1936.

Pasik, Herb. "An Ageless Wonder." *Weekend Palm Desert Post,* May 30, 1986.

"Picture Gallery." *London Daily Mail,* July 19, 1939, page 11.

Pignon, Laurie. "Court Queens." *London Daily Mail,* June 25, 1984, page 22.

"Platak Defends Crown." United Press, May 30, 1936.

"Platak Retains Handball Crown." United Press, May 31, 1936.

Plunkett, Bill. "Pioneer in Women's Tennis Dies." *Desert Sun,* December 14, 1990, page 47.

"President Hails Recreation Drive." *New York Times,* September 30, 1941, page 26.

Pyle, Ernie. "The Long Thin Line of Personal Anguish." Scripps-Howard News Service, June 17, 1944.

"Queen Alice Has Her Worries." *San Pedro News Pilot,* August 27, 1940, page 6.

"Queen Alice Plays Scribe—and Gets Single Over Third." NEA, August 16, 1942.

"Radio Highlights." *Washington Post,* July 27, 1939, page 62.

"Radio Highlights." *Washington Post,* September 12, 1939, page 61.

"Radio Highlights." *Washington Post,* August 23, 1940.

Randolph, Nancy. "Nitery." *New York Daily News,* October 6, 1938, page 49.

Reil, Frank. "Line on Liners." *Brooklyn Daily Eagle,* July 27, 1939, page 24.

Reynolds, Virginia. "Alice Marble Heeds Own Physical Fitness Advice." *Minneapolis Star Journal,* April 20, 1945, page 8.

Rice, Grantland. "Women's Singles to Alice Marble." *Baltimore Sun,* September 13, 1936, page 25.

Robb, Inez. "Alice Marble Will Sing in Warm Undies." International News Service, November 28, 1938.

Roberts, Charlie. "Marble Proud of Her Boys." *Atlanta Constitution,* May 18, 1940, page 47.

Roberts, Sam. "Marita Lorenz, 80, Whose Life Bordered on the Unbelievable, Dies." *New York Times,* September 6, 2019, page A21.

Rodriguez, Jose. "Alice Marble, Net Star, Tells Story." *San Francisco Examiner,* October 6, 1946, page 7.

Roe, Dorothy. "Alice Marble to Quit Net Game for Radio." United Press, June 27, 1934.

Rogers, Ulyss. "Alice Becomes Tennis 'Killer.'" *London Daily Express*, June 4, 1938, page 3.

———. "Alice Owes Fame to Her Coach." *London Daily Express*, July 10, 1939, page 17.

———. "American Tennis Star Faints on Court." *London Daily Express*, May 25, 1934, page 4.

———. "Glucose and 'Chops' Put Two Helens in Tennis Final." *London Daily Express*, July 1, 1938, page 11.

Romano, John J. "Uphill Fight Won by Sterling Girl of Courage." *Missoulian*, September 27, 1936, page 9.

"Ruby Bishop Defeats Alice Marble." United Press, September 13, 1931.

Ryde, Peter. "Tennis." *London Times*, November 15, 1978, page 10.

"Salute Due Alice Marble." *Desert Sun*, April 4, 1974, page A11.

"Scattering Beckwith Notes." *Feather River Bulletin*, April 26, 1906, page 1.

Schroeder, Mildred. "Alice Marble: Tennis Is Still Her Game." *San Francisco Examiner*, October 22, 1964, page 17.

"Seek to Learn if an Athletic Heart Exists." Associated Press, March 8, 1945.

"See Need for More Tennis Tournaments." *The Davenport Democrat and Leader*, May 29, 1936, page 9.

Settle, Alison. "Round the Shops." *London Observer*, June 18, 1939, page 3.

"Settle Property Division." *San Francisco Chronicle*, October 11, 1923, page 3.

"S.F. Net Ace Returns Home." *San Francisco Examiner*, August 30, 1932, page 19.

Shaw, Frank. "Kay Doesn't Even Make a Fight of It." *London Daily Express*, July 9, 1939, page 24.

Sheaffer, Lew. "Night Life." *Brooklyn Daily Eagle*, May 15, 1947, page 7.

"She Also Serves." *San Bernardino Sun*, October 1, 1939, page 29.

"Shorts Are Out of Date." *London Daily Mirror*, May 23, 1939, page 1.

Simpson, Geoffrey. "Sports Parade." *London Daily Mail*, June 2, 1939, page 16.

Singer, Jack. "Alice Marble Forced to Quit." *Los Angeles Times*, July 5, 1935, page 9.

"Sis Has Found the Good Life." *Desert Sun*, February 20, 1976, page C3.

"Social Sketches National Charity League." *Desert Sun*, November 12, 1983, page B2.

"Society Girl Seeks Divorce." *San Francisco Examiner*, September 19, 1923, page 10.

"Society Report." *New York Times*, September 12, 1937, page 88.

"Society Report." *New York Times*, September 14, 1937, page 67.

"Solomon Marble Passes Away." *Feather River Bulletin*, July 11, 1904, page 3.

"Stratford Scores Upset." *San Francisco Examiner*, June 17, 1929, page 25.

Sullivan, Ed. "Hollywood." *New York Daily News*, November 27, 1939, page 320.

———. "Little Old New York." *New York Daily News*, August 5, 1944, page 13.

———. "Little Old New York." *New York Daily News*, October 4, 1945, page 13.

———. "On Broadway." *New York Daily News*, November 15, 1943, page 22.

Swanton, E. W. "England 13 for Test." *London Daily Telegraph*, January 29, 1947, page 3.

Swart, Elizabeth Clarkson. "Alice Marble Views Her Tennis Path." *Des Moines Register*, July 21, 1946, page 51.

Talbot, Gayle. "Nuthall Puts on Rally to Enter Semis." AP, August 20, 1933.

Taylor, Craig E. "Tilden Wins from Rogers." *Baltimore Sun,* May 19, 1945, page 8.

"Tennis Champ, Screen Stars Play at Club." *Desert Sun,* April 14, 1939, page 2.

"Tennis Fans Shout for an Extra Set." *London Daily Express,* October 22, 1936, page 21.

"Tennis Glamour Girl #1." *London Daily Mirror,* June 14, 1938, page 26.

"Tennis Hit by War." United Press, August 6, 1943.

"Tennis Queen Displays New Styles." *Philadelphia Inquirer,* June 12, 1940, page 31.

"Tennis Star Carried Off." *London Daily Mirror,* May 25, 1934, page 1.

"Tennis Star Raises Ambulance Fund." *New York Times,* December 11, 1940, page 15.

"Tennis Television Succeeds." *London Daily Express,* June 23, 1937, page 19.

"The Champion Greets the Bride and Bridegroom." *New York Times,* October 2, 1940, page 33.

"The Inspiring Story of Alice Marble." *Pittsburgh Sun-Telegraph,* October 4, 1946, page 14.

"The Personal Touch." *London Daily Mirror,* May 19, 1937, page 6.

Thompson, Bob. "Alice Marble Easy Winner in Tennis Exhibition." *Coronado Eagle and Journal,* April 8, 1937, page 33.

Thompson, John. "We'll Stick to Shorts." *London Daily Mirror,* June 7, 1938, page 27.

"Tilden Blasts Skeen." *New York Daily News,* June 24, 1945, page 125.

"Tilden, Richards, Alice Marble Play at Oakmont Club Aug. 11." *Morning Call* (Allentown, PA), July 27, 1945, page 22.

Tracy, Virginia. "Alice Marble Charting a New Venture." *Baltimore Evening Sun,* May 10, 1950, page 36.

"Transparent Umbrellas Are Popular This Year." *Californian,* March 10, 1938, page 14.

"Try Putting Yourself in These Shorts." *London Daily Mirror,* July 7, 1939, page 20.

Tuthill, Harold. "Alice Learns a Rolling Marble Gathers Little Moss." *St. Louis Post-Dispatch,* March 21, 1944, page 10.

"Two Women Stars to Play For Wacs." *New York Times,* August 6, 1943, page 19.

Untitled. *Harrisburg Evening News,* April 12, 1926, page 19.

Untitled. *London Daily Mirror,* September 24, 1936, page 11.

Untitled. *London Daily Mirror,* September 26, 1936, page 10.

Untitled. *London Daily Mirror,* September 29, 1936, page 13.

Untitled. *San Francisco Examiner,* August 8, 1927, page 24.

"U.S. Names Women to Defend Net Cup." *New York Times,* August 24, 1939, page 29.

"Valerie T. Whitney." *New York Times,* February 27, 1975.

Vale, Virginia. "Star Dust." Universal Press Services, October 20, 1936.

———. "Star Dust." Universal Press Services, July 7, 1938, page 6.

"Von Cramm Denied Visa." *New York Times,* June 17, 1939, page 5.

Walker, Danton. "Broadway." *New York Daily News,* December 7, 1938, page 89.

Walsh, Davis J. "USLTA Makes Another Blunder." International News Service, August 2, 1933.

Ward, Gene. "Marble Is Marvel." *New York Daily News,* September 13, 1936, page 151.

"War Work Shoes Shown for Women." *New York Times*, February 26, 1942, page 17.

"Weddings." *San Francisco Call,* January 1, 1906, page 9.

"Well, She Lost." *Los Angeles Times*, May 13, 1933, page 5.

"W. H. Whitney Weds Mrs. Sturgis in Reno." *Hartford Courant*, February 10, 1934, page 11.

"Widely Known Two Are Brides." *Los Angeles Times*, August 31, 1921, page 21.

"Will du Pont to Divorce." *New York Times*, February 26, 1941, page 42.

Wilson, Peter. "Girl 'Alley Taw' of the Courts." *London Daily Mirror*, May 19, 1937, page 27.

"Wimbledon Final Round 4 Helen V. Helen." *London Daily Mirror*, July 1, 1938, page 30.

Winchell, Walter. "On Broadway." *Democrat and Chronicle*, October 18, 1938, page 15.

Winterbotham, Hubert. "H. W. Austin's Prospects at Wimbledon." *London Times*, June 25, 1939, page 33.

———. "Miss Alice Marble's Great Wimbledon Triumph." *London Times*, July 9, 1939, page 26.

"Women's Tennis Great Alice Marble, 77, Dies." Associated Press, December 14, 1990.

"Young Girl Killed by Streetcar." *San Francisco Call,* October 1, 1906, page 1.

Zaslawsky, David. "Alice Marble Looks Forward to Wimbledon." *Desert Sun*, June 23, 1984, page F1.

AUDIO/VIDEO

"Alice Marble and Fred Perry Win 1936 Tennis US Open." Grinberg, Paramount, Pathe Newsreels. September 12, 1936. https://www.gettyimages.ca/detail/video/tennis-alice -marble-and-helen-jacobs-walk-onto-tennis-news-footage/533077520.

"Alice Marble in Pro Tennis Debut." British Movietone News. Uploaded July 21, 2015. https:// www.youtube.com/watch?v=EZ4IcLIZHDU.

"Alice Marble Plays in England 1937." British Pathe Newsreel. YouTube. Uploaded April 13, 2014. https://www.youtube.com/watch?v=6vehUNnB71o.

"America's Wimbledon (1939)." British Pathe Newsreel. YouTube. Uploaded April 13, 2014. https://www.youtube.com/watch?v=YhLPfb3HR-k.

"Dedication of Palm Desert Resort Center Court to Alice Marble with Althea Gibson." https:// www.sportspundit.com/videos/ufVT3_GaBXA.

"Prickly Pears: vol. 48, Alice Marble, part I." YouTube. Uploaded August 20, 2019. https://www .youtube.com/watch?v=NpL6WgAeczs.

"Prickly Pears: vol. 48, Alice Marble, part II." YouTube. Uploaded August 21, 2019. https://www .youtube.com/watch?v=jk1SAaZaSGk.

"Tennis 'Greats' (1900–1952)." British Pathe Newsreel. YouTube. Uploaded April 13, 2014. https:// www.youtube.com/watch?v=t8eEfjxDeHM.

"Tennis, U.S. Open, Alice Marble, Nancy Win, Don Budge, Gene Maco, 1938." YouTube. Uploaded January 2, 2017. https://www.youtube.com/watch?v=z-2jm3Yr51Y.

"US Tennis Champion Alice Marble at Surbiton." British Pathe Newsreel. May 24, 1937. https:// www.britishpathe.com/video/news-in-a-nutshell-south-african-floods-us-tennis.

ARCHIVAL

Correspondence between Alice Marble and Eleanor Roosevelt. Eleanor Roosevelt Papers. Franklin D. Roosevelt Presidential Library.

H. V. Kaltenborn Correspondence with Alice Marble. Autograph Collection. Wisconsin Historical Society.

Rita Mae Brown Correspondence with Alice Marble. Rita Mae Brown Papers. Albert and Shirley Small Special Collections Library. University of Virginia.

Rita Mae Brown Correspondence Concerning "The Alice Marble Story." Rita Mae Brown Papers. Albert and Shirley Small Special Collections Library. University of Virginia.

Scribners Papers. Archives of Charles Scribner's Sons. Manuscripts Division. Department of Rare Books and Special Collections. Princeton University Library.

"Sports Figures—Victory Loan War Bonds Public Service Announcements." Recording held at Marr Sound Archives. University of Missouri–Kansas City.

"Tennis at the Hilltop." Alice Marble Oral History, conducted by Marie Nay. Hearst San Simeon State Historical Monument, June 4, 1977.

Will du Pont Correspondence. Will du Pont, Jr. Papers. Hagley Museum and Library. Wilmington, Delaware.

INDEX

ABOUT THE AUTHOR

ROBERT WEINTRAUB has written about sports for *The New York Times*, *Slate*, *Play*, ESPN.com, *The Guardian* (UK), *Deadspin*, and many more. He is the author of four books, including the *New York Times* bestseller *No Better Friend*. Weintraub lives in Decatur, Georgia.